ADVANCE PRAISE FOR

A Heart of Wisdom

"I begin with a question: How best to honour gifts given selflessly and without expectation of return?

I continue with a story:

I watched my dad take his last breath in the early spring of 2010. It was an expected ending. The illness slowly took over his lungs and his life until he could no longer live as he wanted. I watched with pained admiration during the last few months of his life as he faced his condition with grim courage. When the time finally came to say goodbye, I gently rested my forehead against his for the last time. I told him things that I had not said enough to him while he was healthy. I also whispered tender thoughts to him that I had not shared with anyone. I thanked him for teaching my brothers and me to be good men. In his weak condition, he acknowledged what I had said by lightly tapping my hand. Then, with much effort, he whispered, 'You guys went ahead and I just followed behind.'

My dad took his last breath soon after whispering those words to me. In that moment—as witness to an event that would mark the beginning of a new phase of my life—I recalled watching my newborn son take his first breath. It was an epiphanic moment during which I was encircled by the many stories that had comprised my life. I then realized the generosity of the gifts that my dad had given me so selflessly. His stories had become my stories. I honour the gifts by passing them on.

I chose to ask a question and share the story of my dad's death as a way to honour the many storied and poetic gifts shared so generously by the authors whose works comprise this book. Reading these powerful life-writing stories stirred within me a persistent desire to review my own life as I read along. This is the effect of all good stories, whether oral or written; we seek to tell ourselves into them. Such stories, and the curriculum insights that can be gained from them, deepen our understanding of the original meaning of the phrase *curriculum vitae*. Rather than a document pieced together in the interests of gaining employment, curriculum vitae refers to the course of our lives and the stories and experiences that characterize them. This is the source of a deeply relational curriculum for renewal and survival that lives within us and provides a means to continue on."

—*Dwayne Donald, Curriculum Studies and Indigenous Perspectives,*
Faculty of Education, University of Alberta

"This book is a timely contribution to the complicated conversation taking place within the international field of curriculum studies. The collection invites its readers to sit still and hear others speak, above and below the fray of a world inundated with suffering from the material and economic exploitations of our planetary commons.

Curriculum scholars, poets, artists, teachers, and students craft an evocative organic tapestry of life stories here that asks us to reconsider how empathetic inquiry might teach us to live life inside and outside our research and classrooms with emotion, passion, imagination, creativity, and indeed, with a heart of wisdom. As such, this groundbreaking, innovative text will be a timeless must-read for any future cosmopolitan, indigenous, migrant, or settler curriculum scholar, teacher, and student interested in trying to inquire, understand, and re-imagine the pedagogical affective and aesthetic implications of learning to live one's life empathetically with others. This book will provoke invaluable and engaging conversations with the administrators, teachers, and graduate students from other fields of study."

—*Nicholas Ng-A-Fook, PhD, Curriculum Theorist, Faculty of Education, University of Ottawa; Founder and Director of* A Canadian Curriculum Theory Project; *and Co-President of the* Canadian Association of Curriculum Studies

A Heart of Wisdom

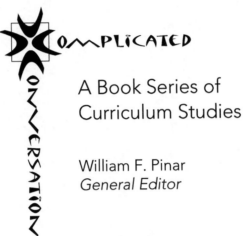

OMPLICATED

A Book Series of Curriculum Studies

William F. Pinar
General Editor

VOLUME 39

The Complicated Conversation series
is part of the Peter Lang Education list.
Every volume is peer reviewed and meets
the highest quality standards for content and production.

PETER LANG
New York • Washington, D.C./Baltimore • Bern
Frankfurt • Berlin • Brussels • Vienna • Oxford

A Heart of Wisdom

Life Writing as Empathetic Inquiry

EDITED BY
Cynthia M. Chambers, Erika Hasebe-Ludt,
Carl Leggo, Anita Sinner

PETER LANG
New York • Washington, D.C./Baltimore • Bern
Frankfurt • Berlin • Brussels • Vienna • Oxford

Library of Congress Cataloging-in-Publication Data

A heart of wisdom: life writing as empathetic inquiry /
edited by Cynthia M. Chambers ... [et al.].
p. cm. — (Complicated conversation: a book series of curriculum studies; v. 39)
Includes bibliographical references and index.
1. Education—Biographical methods.
2. Education—Curricula—Philosophy.
3. Teaching—Philosophy.
4. Holistic education. I. Chambers, Cynthia M.
LB1029.B55H43   370.72—dc23   2011036297
ISBN 978-1-4331-1530-1 (hardcover)
ISBN 978-1-4331-1529-5 (paperback)
ISBN 978-1-4539-0229-5 (e-book)
ISSN 1534-2816

Bibliographic information published by **Die Deutsche Nationalbibliothek**.
Die Deutsche Nationalbibliothek lists this publication in the "Deutsche
Nationalbibliografie"; detailed bibliographic data is available
on the Internet at http://dnb.d-nb.de/.

The paper in this book meets the guidelines for permanence and durability
of the Committee on Production Guidelines for Book Longevity
of the Council of Library Resources.

Printed in the United States of America

With deep gratitude for the teachers and curriculum theorists who came before, who took the risk to name their own lived experience as the fertile ground where their scholarly and practical inquiries often originated but rarely remained, who undertook that most revolutionary act of writing a life in the name of teaching, and theorizing, the world.

Table of Contents

Memory Work: Min(d)ing the Past, Facing the Present

Place Work: Mapping Rhizomatic Migrations

Curriculum Work: In Families, in Schools

Social Work: Vulnerable Beings, Political Worlds

Foreword

Spiritual Cardiology and the Heart of Wisdom

D r. Shelby Haque is the Islamic Chaplain at the University of Alberta, where I too live out my profession, as a 'professor' of Education. As well as being an Islamic scholar, Dr. Haque is a Western-trained medical doctor. On the university Chaplain's Association website link to him, Dr. Haque makes a remarkable suggestion:

> We have a billion-dollar healthcare system (which ought to be called a disease-care system) that treats people after they become physically sick; what we really need are spiritual cardiologists who can help humans cure the diseases of our spiritual hearts. (http://www.uofaweb.ualberta.ca/chaplains/islamic.cfm)

In terms of introduction, let me also note that according to Marcia Angell (2011), former editor of the *New England Journal of Medicine*, in North America "[m]ental illness is now the leading cause of disability in children" (para. 1). The statistics are partly the consequence in contemporary psychiatry of "diagnosis by prescription," i.e., if you feel better after taking an anti-depressant, you must have been depressed. Still, it is the very fact that so many kids are troubled that is so troubling. And not only kids. Mental illness is now the leading form of human suffering in North America.

I want to juxtapose the above notes with some words of Peter of Damaskos, an 11th–12th century sage of the Greek Orthodox tradition. These can be found in Volume III of the *Philokalia*, a compendium of Orthodox spirituality from the 4th to 15th centuries. *Philokalia* literally means "love of the beautiful, the true." Peter declares: "Distraction is the cause of the intellect's obscuration;" "forgetfulness [is] the greatest of evils;" and "stillness [marks] the beginning of the soul's purification [and is] the first form of bodily discipline" (p. 182).

These opening notes come to focus in my response to reading the present manuscript which Cynthia, Carl, Erika and Anita have invited me to reflect on by way of a *Foreword*. It is the same response I had on reading the manuscript of their 2009 book *Life Writing and Literary Métissage as an Ethos for Our Times* (Hasebe-Ludt, Chambers, & Leggo, 2009). I was overcome by an experience of stillness, of wanting to be completely and meditatively quiet, to simply allow the work to penetrate my endlessly distracted life and draw me into an understanding of Life that is deeper, truer, and indeed more hauntingly beautiful than anything my conceptually overburdened imagination could possibly imagine. In hermeneutic terms, I could say the burden of my own specificity was lifted as I bore witness to the life stories of others, and I was loved into a new kind of community, something quite beyond what any one particular story in this compendium would be capable of producing by itself. Life Writing, and its necessary sibling Life Reading, might best be described as acts of human recovery, indeed of healing. But a recovery from, and healing of what? And how so?

Life Writing implies Life Reading, or does it? Sometimes I got the sense in reading these stories that the writing alone had achieved its purpose for the writer, and that it wouldn't actually matter if the material produced was never read. The writing had allowed, indeed demanded, of the writer to slow down, to concentrate and focus (become less distracted), to remember, and to be still enough to allow for a certain purification of soul so that what might be written might also escape the tentacled entrapments of pure self-interest. You can see Peter of Damaskos's logic at work here: cut through the smoke of distraction, learn to be still, and you will start remembering what you are forgetting, forgetting by selective choice, or by fear, or by simple laziness. Through that process, you'll start to feel better, more "recollected" as they say in Benedictine spirituality, and this mainly because you are affirming the ever-elusive wholeness of your being. It's a form of soul purification and indeed bodily discipline that actually can be quite terrifying. I was going to say, "Not for the faint of heart," but then realized that it is precisely because we are fainthearted that we must do this work. Spiritual cardiology.

What happens in the act of Life Writing? Long held secrets bubble up, betrayals are noted, simple joys giggle forth like teenagers; there's an unusual attention to the details of material existence and the experience thereof, alongside a heightened awareness arising of the absolute intractability of our human inter-dependence, sabotaging the myth of autonomy. Do these sensibilities alone produce a "heart of wisdom"? Indirectly I would say yes, but the process itself needs to be carefully understood. For one thing, at the heart of wisdom lies dis-cipline, and much of the time we are reluctant to be disciplined, or at least we have to acknowledge that discipline is often painful. In Buddhist theory, disci-pline is the suffering we have to endure to put an end to our greater suffering. A friend is quitting smoking after being chained to the habit for 50 years, starting at age fifteen. The first three months were absolute hell, but at least the cough-ing has stopped, and there's a new sense of vitality and energy. Still, everyday is a struggle, since demons arrive through daily encounters with the seductive temptation filtered right into the ego itself: "I need a cigarette." Personally I find writing extremely difficult; the discipline required to stop doing 'other' things, to actually sit down and to start allowing words to work their way through me: these things are no joy. Sometimes joy comes later, for example when an insight seems to break forth from the husks of my reluctant obedience to writing's call. Anyway, the point is...*discipline.*

There's a lot of confession in these stories, and I have a confession of my own to make. The editors had asked me to write a piece for the collection, which I did and duly submitted. Then I started having nightmares about it. It was my first attempt at Life Writing and clearly I didn't know what I was doing. I'd used the piece far too much for purposes of self-vindication, vengeance even, against those I'd long held responsible for childhood traumas and hurts. So the ghosts of the dead rose up to challenge my interpretations. I decided to withdraw the piece until greater clarity has been gained into how to speak of one's relations, espe-cially relations of hurt, in a way that honours the 'other' side of the experience.

So how then does writing nourish the heart of wisdom? In my own case, the act of writing exposed me to myself in unexpected ways, and perhaps that is the first step. The exposure arrives as an invitation to consider the auspices of an unreflective sentiment. Now we are back to Peter of Damaskos, and the problem of "the intellect's obscuration."

The Greek Orthodox tradition has a lot in common with Buddhism and Taoism and the Muslim/Arabic term *waqt.* Orthodox practice emphasizes *hesy-chiastic* experience, i.e., the experience of deep silence and stillness (Gk. *hesychia*) through which the practitioner comes to real-ize a union with God, the Wholly Other. This theological language, about a reconciliation between the human and divine, simply describes the most primordial work in human experience, i.e., working out the relation between Self and Other. It is the primary work of re-ligion, which literally means "joining together again" (L. *religere*). Buddhism emphasizes the work of finding one's "Original Face," the face that is lost through actions of the delusional idea of an independent ego. Taoism speaks of the "still-point" each of us must discover for ourselves so that we can participate in life harmoniously with the Tao or Way of Life rather than always fighting against it or trying to push it in predetermined directions (e.g., through 'education'). All of these terms have a parallel or equivalent in the Arabic *waqt*.

It is important to emphasize that working towards stillness is not an act of quietism or passivity or even withdrawal of life. Instead it involves the capacity of beginning to 'see' life for what it really is, without the embellishments of culture or tradition. Buddhism speaks of this in terms of "mindfulness," clearing the garbage out of one's mind so that the mind can actually function freely to engage what is truly necessary to be done in any particular situation. Mindfulness is intimately connected to the heart, and in Chinese, heart and mind have the same word, *hsin*. In the Greek tradition too, the same connection is maintained. When Peter of Damaskos refers to the "intellect's obscuration," he uses the Greek word *nous* for intellect, rather than *dianoia*, which refers to the functioning of the intellect to formulate abstract concepts and then arguing on the basis of this to conclusions reached through deductive reasoning. The intellect, or *nous*, is the highest human faculty through which a person begins to 'know God,' i.e., the reality that transcends all concepts, and perceive the inner essences or principles of created things, and our participation in them. Even more important, *nous* also constitutes the innermost aspect of the heart and is sometimes called the "organ of contemplation," the "eye of the heart" (for further discussion, see Palmer, Sherrard, & Ware, 1995, p. 360).

"Distraction is the cause of the intellect's obscuration," says Peter. Can we, as a society, as a culture of great suffering, grasp the utter importance and relevance of this elusive saying? Obscuration literally means "darkening" (L. *obscurus*, dark). So when our minds have become darkened through "distraction," we are in deep trouble. When our highest human faculty has become subjugated and dominated by nonsensical phantasms perpetrated by intense and powerful media; when education reigns as a project of human engineering to serve only the material prospects of the market; when we invite violence into our minds and imaginations as a form of entertainment—in short, when distraction rules—we become "forgetful of Being," as Heidegger put it, and there is only one possible consequence as a long-term phenomenological reality: we start losing our minds. And when we have lost our minds, "darkness covers the earth, and gross darkness the people," as the Hebrew prophet Isaiah declared poetically some two-and-a-half millennia ago (Isaiah 60:2).

In North America, anti-psychotic drugs now outsell all other medications including those for heart disease and stroke. There is a now a psychosis at the heart of Western 'civilization,' induced by the lies and duplicities the corporate and financial elites use to protect their interests, even in universities. Most specifically this has involved demonizing a whole other civilization, Islam, through war policies based on paranoia and delusion, creating what R. Michael Fisher has called "a culture of fear" (http://www.feareducation.com). More immediately a fundamental split has evolved between the rhetoric of democracy, which holds out the promise that everybody matters in the conduct of public life, and the reality that this rhetoric now serves as a mask for material and spiritual exploitation, both at home and abroad. The point is, as commentators like David Harvey have argued (see his 2010 book *The Enigma of Capital and the Crises of Capitalism*), a global meltdown is currently taking place whereby older sureties of social, political, and economic theory are hollowing out, and once-venerated gurus are left wheezing exhausted platitudes that are no longer working and hence no longer relevant. What are we to do? Where shall we turn for personal and cultural healing? I sense that Life Writing and Life Reading hold promise, as follows.

As implied by comments above, Life Writing involves a kind of recovery of, well, Life. As the stories in this collection testify to so well, the writing process practiced in a disciplined way allows for the 'coming through' of life experiences that don't count in conventional registers of value, mainly because those registers (status ideologies of intelligence, beauty, etc.) can't allow for the true complexity and deep interdependence of all of life, to say nothing of its subtleties. Life Writing is a form of permission-giving, a granting of permission to feel and sense life-responses that have been repressed under dominant dispensations of worthiness. Paradoxically, this 'allowing' through the *heart* brings things to *mind*, so that the mind is challenged to (re)incorporate and re-evaluate things that have been forgotten and left for dead, out of fear, pride, false courage, cultural prejudice, or sheer stubbornness. In this sense then, heartwork *is* headwork, such that through the unification of their relative experience, wisdom has a chance to arise, since what comes to be *known* is known both experientially *and* reflectively. More importantly, it is the Life Reading of Life Writing that ensures my own accounts of my own experience do not drown in the pool of my own reflection, since awareness of the lives of others rescues me from myself and produces the kind of forgetfulness that is truly life-giving, claiming nothing for itself, by itself, only the wonder of 'us,' to the full extent of the ambiguity and difficulty involved in the same.

I congratulate Cynthia, Carl, Erika, and Anita on the significant achievement of this new collection. May it be fully and widely read.

David Geoffrey Smith
Professor of Education, University of Alberta

REFERENCES

Angell, M. (2011, June 23). The epidemic of mental illness: Why? *The New York Review of Books, 58*(11). Retrieved from http://www.nybooks.com/articles/archives/2011/jun/23/epidemic-mental-illness-why/

Harvey, D. (2010). *The enigma of capital and the crises of capitalism.* London, England: Profile Books.

Hasebe-Ludt, E., Chambers, C. M., & Leggo, C. (2009). *Life writing and literary métissage as an ethos for our times.* New York, NY: Peter Lang.

Palmer, G. E., Sherrard, P., & Ware, K. (1995). (Eds.). *The Philokalia: The complete text* (Vol. 3). London, England: Faber and Faber.

Acknowledgements

We thank the Social Sciences and Humanities Research Council of Canada for a research grant to support the project titled, Rewriting Literacy Curriculum in Canadian Cosmopolitan Schools.

We thank Concordia University, Office of the Vice-President, Research and Graduate Studies, for their support of this book publication with an Aid to Research Grant, and the Faculty of Fine Arts for matching funds.

We thank the Faculty of Education, University of Lethbridge for administrative and technological support.

We thank Oolichan Books, publisher of *Two O'clock Creek: Poems New and Selected*, in which Bruce Hunter's poems appeared. We thank Blue Grama Publications Corp., publisher of *Honouring Mothers* in which Bruce Hunter's essay first appeared.

We thank William F. Pinar, series editor, for his valued support and thoughtful response to an earlier draft of the manuscript. We also appreciate David G. Smith's deep attention to the spirit of inquiry at the heart of this collection, and, naming our labour "spiritual cardiology."

We thank Marlene Lacey for her professional expertise, meticulous attention to detail, and heartfelt dedication to this work during the final editing of the manuscript.

We thank photographer and artist, Fran Hurcombe (Yellowknife, Northwest Territories), for creating the cover photo. We also thank the maker of the four-braid, round sash illustrated. The braid was purchased from Northern Images, the Yellowknife gallery and sales outlet for Arctic Co-op, which promotes the work of Dene and Inuit artists. Because of its strength, beauty, and durability, people around the world make and use this kind of braided sash. In the Arctic, they fasten a "Mother Hubbard" parka at the waist, to better secure a baby being carried inside the parka and on the back. The braid on this book cover is one of these sashes. Both the colourful cotton outer layer of the Mother Hubbard and the sash were introduced to Inuit through trade with Hawaiians during the whaling era (Oakes, 1991), an east-west, north-south *métissage* of material culture still alive today.

REFERENCE

Oakes, Jillian. (1991). *Copper and Caribou Inuit skin clothing production* [Canadian Ethnology Service Mercury Series Paper No. 118]. Ottawa, Canada: Canadian Museum of Civilization.

Opening to a Heart of Wisdom

Writing is a transgression of boundaries of boundaries, an exploration of new boundaries. It involves making public the events of our lives, wriggling free of the constraints of purely private and individual experiences. From a space of modest insignificance, we enter a space in which we can take ourselves seriously.
—Frigga Haug, *Female Sexualization: A Collective Work of Memory*

This anthology explores life writing as a mode of educational inquiry, one where educators and learners may get a "heart of wisdom" as they struggle with the tensions and complexities of learning and teaching, in challenging contemporary circumstances and in a variety of pedagogical locations. The collection features teachers and learners engaging in life writing as: a theorizing approach to educational inquiry and a method for it, a curricular and pedagogical practice; an artful and literary expression, a political and personal way of being in the world; and a philosophical and spiritual attunement in relation to this world.

The individual pieces of creative nonfiction are based on the authors' first-person experiences of coming to understand what matters most to them (and others), what sustains them (and others) and the places they inhabit, and what they have given their hearts to.

Margaret Atwood (2002) suggests that "there's one characteristic that sets writing apart from most of the other arts—its apparent democracy, by which I mean its availability to almost everyone as a medium of expression" (p. 25). The democracy of writing is increasingly experienced and expressed in a diverse and ever-expanding range of possibilities. As Martin Amis (2000) reminds us, "we live in the age of mass loquacity" (p. 6). With the unprecedented proliferation of digital literacies and social networks, such as Facebook, blogging, and YouTube, many of us live in a time and place when more and more people (at least economically privileged people) are telling more and more stories about their experiences, clearly confident that their experiences deserve to be storied and shared with others, including family and friends, but also reaching out to strangers, potentially millions of unknown others. Amis is convinced that "nothing, for now, can compete with experience—so unanswerably authentic, and so liberally and democratically dispensed. Experience is the only thing we share equally, and everyone senses this" (p. 6).

Stories present possibilities for understanding the complex, mysterious, even ineffable experiences that comprise human living. We are especially interested in understanding how stories can help us live with more creative, ethical, and political conviction. Margaret Atwood (2002) wisely suggests that "writing has to do with darkness, and a desire or perhaps a compulsion to enter it, and, with luck, to illuminate it, and to bring something back out to the light" (p. xxiv).

Life writing is a way of knowing and being. Karen Armstrong (2005) provides a useful sense of myth for conceptualizing and practicing life writing in education and the social sciences. She explains that "myth is not a story told for its own sake. It shows us how we should behave" (p. 4). According to Armstrong, "a myth is essentially a guide; it tells us what we must do in order to live more richly" (p. 10). This is what we are always aiming for in our life writing. Armstrong explains that "myth is about the unknown; it is about that for which initially we have no words. Myth therefore looks into the heart of a great silence" (p. 4).

Like Italo Calvino (1995) we are seeking a "pedagogy of the imagination" (p. 92) by writing about lived and living experiences, and by ruminating on those experiences. Calvino muses:

> Who are we, who is each of us, if not a *combinatoria* of experiences, information, books we have read, things imagined? Each life is an encyclopedia, a library, an inventory of objects, a series of styles, and everything can be constantly shuffled and reordered in every way conceivable. (p. 124)

In this anthology we present a combinatoria full of glimpses into many experiences of teaching and learning, reading and writing, and being and becoming human.

As an editorial collective, we sought out exemplary creative nonfiction essays, memoirs, poems, songs, diaries, epistolary letters, photo narratives, journals, and blended genres or collaborative, interdisciplinary projects that offer unique perspectives on, and insights into, the educational interrelationships that compose lives. We particularly called for life writing that addresses questions such as: *What critical moments of learning/teaching have changed your life? What stories need to be told? What questions should be asked?*

We invited students at different levels and stages of learning, teachers both beginners and well-seasoned, university faculty and community-based educators, and artists and writers, to submit first-person writing about significant first-person learning and teaching encounters. We sought life writing that resembles the practices of wisdom traditions, where through the deep work of paying attention to particular places and events, the practitioner may be rewarded with a "heart of wisdom" (Myerhoff, as cited in Richardson & St. Pierre, 2005), a greater understanding of others, and self, in relation to others. We framed our call with our understanding of life writing as a form of truth telling and empathetic inquiry (Bly, 2001). Thus, our call became, in David G. Smith's (1994) words,

> a provocation, or "calling" (L. *provoco*, call forth)…to read and understand our own childhoods, to understand our personal and collective pasts in a truly pedagogic way, that is, in a way that contributes positively and dialogically to a new understanding of and appreciation for the world. (p. 193)

Thus we provoked writers to articulate, through both print-based texts and images of various kinds, their experiences of "wayfinding" amidst and betwixt such complicated spheres as truth and lies, eco-zone and universe, home and homeless, love and hate, courage and cowardliness, power and powerlessness, hope and despair, war and peace, relationality and genealogy, and empathy and heartlessness.

The life writing this call evoked represents a métissage of lived experiences from a rich and diverse group of authors, a mixing and mingling of lives and lines through threads of texts that are vibrant as individual compositions on their own but that, we believe, when braided together, become an inspiriting oeuvre. From our previous work with métissage and life writing, and based on Françoise Lionnet (1989) and other writers in the fields of literary and cultural studies such as Hélène Cixous (Cixous & Calle-Gruber, 1997), we claim life writing in the form of métissage to be "a counternarrative to the grand narratives of our times, a site for writing and surviving in the interval between different cultures and languages, particularly in colonial contexts; a way of merging and blurring genres, texts and identities" (Hasebe-Ludt, Chambers, & Leggo, 2009, p. 9). We heeded John Ralston Saul's (2008) claim that Canada is "a Métis civilization" and selected texts and textures of writing that weave a métissage of life writing. Collectively, these texts are grounded in a métis/sage/ing epistemology and a wisdom seeking, one that creates a new rapprochement between opposing discourses and one that renews relationships.

In *Life Writing and Literary Métissage as an Ethos for Our Times* (2009), Hasebe-Ludt, Chambers, and Leggo explored theoretical, rhetorical, and pedagogical dynamics involved in life writing and ended with a call for others to do their own life writing and to get themselves "a heart of wisdom" (p. 233). The pieces of writing we invite you to savour here form a true companion volume to the previous text. They have become our life-writing companions. The writers in this collection, who now accompany us on our life-writing sojourns, represent an organic tapestry of life-writing genres, all telling stories of lives lived/living in the eco-tones of and eco-zones of teaching and learning. With proficiency and passion, these writers delve into creative nonfiction through memoir and autobiographical fragments, poetry and lyrical prose, story and personal essay, rumination and reflection, photography and fine arts. In many cases they mix and juxtapose these genres creatively and in vibrant ways. Collectively and individually, these life-writing narratives perform the kind of literary and pedagogical memory and *currere* work that scholars such as Smith, Pinar and Grumet, along with literary writers and theorists such as Lionnet, Cixous, Morrison, and others, have called for as a way to better understand the historical and current conditions that have shaped our lives and our world. As writers and educators, life-writing challenges us to consider the obligations that come with being part of the "complicated conversation" (Pinar, 2006) in curriculum studies, the field of education, and the world. In many ways, this text is a uniquely Canadian métissage, with writers coming from, or situated in, this "Métis civilization" (Saul, 2008). However, the writers whose life writing speaks from this place are at the same time part of a larger relational network—,with multiple global connections in their public work and personal affiliations, and ancestral genealogies that are both from this land and other lands. They represent a new cosmopolitan disposition, one that is mindful of both "here" and "not here," and that does not privilege one over the other.

The organization of the book also reflects a métissage and mixing of texts. We braided the pieces of writing in, broad thematic or topical strands with a view towards mixing and juxtaposing genres, genders, and genealogies; races, ethnicities, and cultures; and professional, pedagogical, and personal affiliations. We mixed texts by experienced writers with texts by some beginning their journeys as life writers. We braided "dangerous" stories that tell difficult truths about living within compromised and compromising institutional systems with stories about personal journeys that open up to the precariousness of our lives within familial and ancestral relations. We honoured the emotional literacy of writers along with all the other multiple literacies that are part of our digital and cultural commons. We held the many stories that wove death into the fabric of life, and we grieved and rejoiced in the resiliency of the writing and the writers. We were astonished at the courage of the writers, who were not afraid to tell the difficult truths that are part of the warp and weft of their identities in relation. We braided local with global threads of witnessing and testimonial work with documentaries of becoming and being educators/educated in these precarious times and in particular places, at home and in the diaspora.

Many of the writers in this collection also bring together literary and visual expression, in particular photography, to punctuate complex relationships and interactions in a negotiation of in-between, tensioned spaces, as Stafford (2010) suggests, where the "text-image interface" is "tentative and provisional...and often highly speculative if not unfinished" (p. 31). Such spaces may be described as dynamic "assemblages" where relationships are rhizomatic, involving connections, multiplicities, and ruptures of "what we are in the process of becoming," of "our becoming other" (Deleuze & Guattari, 1994, p. 112). In this way, writers revealed their inner movements as dimensions of inquiry that blur artworks and mindful formations. Creating conversations that are retrospective and introspective with a host of social, cultural, political, and academic issues generates multiple interpretations and perspectives, offering new ways of thinking, critiquing, and being, as encounters with the stories we are.

Thus, for us editors, attending to what is here, and what is not here in these stories, by calling, collecting, editing, revising, and publishing the collection became a process of witnessing and seeking wisdom in its own right. We nurtured the writing, worked with the writers to, when needed, make their words more eloquent, more evocative, and more precise. We encouraged the kind of "writing down the bones" that Natalie Goldberg (1986) called for when she encouraged her students to "go for the jugular" (p. 10), writing that pays attention to the body, always full of energy and determination to get to the heart of the matter, with matters of the heart, often filled with pain. This kind of life writing constitutes a new reflective turn to the self—different from the egotistical, self-absorbed gaze that autobiographical writing can suffer from—one that focusses on serious introspection and close examination of one's own and others' natality, of our individual and collective embodied knowledge. This is the kind of knowing we wanted to honour: one that comes from the body, the heart, and the imagination, from having our feet planted in the humus of day-to-day, lived experience. We believe that a close examination of such visceral knowing, and of the life circumstances of being born into this world, bears the potential of becoming wise from within and through being in relation to others.

Throughout this complex process, we considered many possible ways of assessing this writing, without resorting to preconceived notions of standardized parameters. We came to see the complex sense and sensibility of living with imperfect endings; we were astonished by the beauty of the images and the words, and the stories' deep agency. This, in turn, reaffirmed our own "paradoxical commitment" (Todd, 2009) to imperfection and intimacy, love and loathing, hope and despair, and all the spaces in-between, as integral parts of our personal and public/political pedagogy of the heart (Freire, 1997/2007), one that resounds with wisdom seeking through the mixed blood of métissage work.

We also played and laboured with multiple arrangements, remixed and readjusted; we tweaked the texts more than twice. We worked with a four-strand round braid, one that traditionally has been used to make a strong, resilient working tool; an artistic, aesthetic object; or a ceremonial artifact—thus often combining the dual qualities of usefulness and beauty (Carey, 1997/2010; Grant, 1972). This type of braid has been known and used in different cultural, craft, and working contexts throughout the world: in southern and northwestern American communities for rawhide and leather horse wear and gear, such as lariats or bridles; in northern places such as Scandinavia and Canada for outerwear, for strings for mittens and boots; and in eastern cultures, such as Japan, for gear connected with warrior walks of life such as, Samurai clothing and swords or for ceremonial clothing, such as the kimono, and rituals associated with Geisha culture. In all places and contexts, they evoke both strength and beauty, making a textured material sturdier and more robust, and more complex than a flat braid with fewer strands. Four-strand round braids, because they are made with multi-coloured string, silk, or rawhide, are also often more aesthetically engaging through their intricacy of colour, texture, and materials, resulting in a highly decorative appeal. Commenting on the Japanese silk braiding technique of *kumihimo*, Catherine Martin (1991) affirms that "as with so many other disciplines, a feel for braiding cannot be taught" (p. 91). Instead what is needed is an attention to what is there—the place the materials come from, "the mysteries, philosophies, and rituals surrounding them"—and an attunement to a "deep cultural impulse which motivates the braid-maker working quietly away to produce a good piece of braid which will serve its purpose admirably" (p. 91). In the act of crafting, the spirit and the state of mind of the braid maker shine through.

In much the same way, in our braiding words and images, we put our spirits and minds into these acts, hoping our hearts would shine through, while we trusted the organization to emerge organically and rhizomatically. We aimed for a collective textual integrity and fibred texture akin to a crafted hermeneutic interpretation, one that lingers with the texts, asks questions that arise from them and interprets them critically, functionally, and aesthetically. Reciprocally, we now invite readers and viewers to engage with these lives and lines in critical and interpretive ways, to mix the texts and the topics into yet another vibrant métissage that responds to and resonates with their lived experience. We hope that this kind of selective reading, and a willingness to respond from each reader's/viewer's particular place, will create new imaginings of possible worlds.

The four strands that emerged as the fibres of this métissage—Memory Work, Place Work, Curriculum Work, and Social Work—and their various sub-strands, are reflective of a collaborative and collective working process. We grouped the texts based on the topic, issue, or "burning question" that, in our interpretive reading, sits at the heart of the narrative. We hope that these thematic groupings will be helpful for readers, students, and teachers alike, but also particularly useful for instructors with a view to assigning groups of themed readings. However, we are also aware that many pieces in each strand and sub-strand could move across strands since they often address one-or-more themes from other strands; hence we laboured to place the texts, and with meticulous, loving care, we frequently reworked and rebraided. We encourage readers to do the same.

After many months of living with these writings and their textured fibres, vicariously and viscerally, we are blessed to be able to present you with a collection of cosmopolitan life-writing tales from Canada which advocate for a better, more inclusive mixing and rapprochement of our human spirit in a non-human world. We trust that this métissage of stories of life-changing moments and times of teaching and learning will convince readers of the educational significance of this mode of inquiry and of teaching, as a form of communicative action. We see this anthology as part of the current complicated conversations in classrooms, schools, universities, communities, and homes. We fervently hope that it will be embraced as an exemplar of a new kind of literary scholarly text that is rooted in storytelling traditions which acknowledge "the truth about stories is that that's all we are" (King, 2003, p. 2), one that is not afraid to tell truths about the mixed lifeworlds present here in Canada and beyond. We believe this kind of educational rapprochement and activism, based on empathic inquiry and ethical action, is what our lands and our schools urgently need to repair the rifts between us. Finally, this collection is a call and a response to the gifts that reside in our stories and in our relations with each other, with our ancestors, with our common ground, the earth, and with our children and grandchildren.

About his books, Roland Barthes (1977) notes that "no one of them caps any other; the latter is nothing but a *further* text, the last of the series, not the ultimate in meaning: *text upon text*" (p. 120). And like Barthes, we "delight continuously, endlessly, in writing as in a perpetual production, in an unconditional dispersion, in an energy of seduction..." (p. 136). So, we called writers and their stories together, and then we composed this book. Like Hélène Cixous (1993) in *Three Steps on the Ladder of Writing*, we recognize that

> even if we think we are writing the book, it is the book that is leading us. We depend entirely on the book's goodwill. This is what makes for the writer's humbleness and the fear and hope of seeing the book come to maturation. (p. 79)

As editors we sent a call into the world, a call for words that addressed and hailed "a heart of wisdom," words that we anticipated would be fired in a heart of wisdom. Like Cixous knows, the book guided us. As the stories of our colleagues arrived, gifts of wise words offered with generous spirits filled with hope for the transformative possibilities of life writing in education, we understood how empathetic inquiry is most compellingly theorized and conceptualized in the practice of "a heart of wisdom." Above all, we were poignantly reminded of Keefer's (1998) self awareness regarding the challenges of life writing: "All the questions I need to ask; the stories I have yet to hear. The heart's two chambers—everything I most desire, everything I most fear" (p. 291).

In educational research, empathy has often been conceptualized and researched by psychologists. Much of that research has provided valuable insights and directions for the practice of teaching and learning. But we need to expand our understanding of empathy to include the insights of a diverse network of researchers, including educators, artists, writers, and poets. Noddings (2011) is cautious about placing empathy at the centre of any explanation of care ethics in education. She is concerned that "empathy has long been identified with cognitive understanding, not feeling" (p. 9), but as the authors included in *A Heart of Wisdom* clearly and compellingly demonstrate, empathetic inquiry is enthusiastically focussed on the etymology of *empathy* as rooted in emotion, passion, imagination, sympathy, and vicarious identification. By writing about our experiences, often in vulnerable, confessional, personal ways, we are creating spaces for others to join us in conversation about their vulnerable and personal stories. As Griffin (1995) reminds us, identity is "less an assertion of independence than an experience of interdependence" (p. 91).

Perhaps the most resounding and resonant question at the heart of the life writing in this book is: "Who am I?" The narratives are written from the point of view of authors who are not afraid to name their position as rooted in the first-person pronoun. But these narratives are not self-absorbed, and self-centred exercises in self-congratulation, self-mockery, or self-pity. Instead, the authors write about their experiences and understandings in stories that are aesthetically composed and ethically conscientious. These narratives of personal experience are always connected to social, political, cultural, and historical dynamics of identity, values, and transformative possibilities. Like Gates (2003), life writers hope "to see beneath the individual story to the ways of human beings—fallible, sometimes poignant, with our fears and our yearnings" (p. 149). Life writing is about seeking the heart of wisdom, as well as living with a heart of wisdom, and knowing the heart's wisdom for living in heartful relationships with others. In the hopeful way that life writing fosters, Griffin (1995) reminds us:

> If human consciousness can be rejoined not only with the human body but with the body of the earth, what seems incipient in the reunion is the recovery of meaning with existence that will infuse every kind of meeting between self and the universe, even in the most daily acts, with an eros, a palpable love, that is also sacred. (p. 9)

We agree with Hall's (2004) claim that "subjectivity itself is textual" (p. 128). We write ourselves and we are written. In his discussion of subjectivity and identity, Hall (2004) emphasizes the "tension between choice and illusion, between imposed definitions and individual interrogations of them, and between old formulae and new responsibilities" (p. 2).

He recognizes that "the text of the self offers a particularly important entry point into discussions of the textuality of culture and human social interaction" (p. 78). The educators who have responded to the call to write "a heart of wisdom" are like Heaney (1995), who describes the symbiotic relationship between words and the world as a journey full of tentative steps and abiding faithfulness:

> I had already begun a journey into the wideness of the world. This in turn became a journey into the wideness of language, a journey where each point of arrival—whether in one's poetry or one's life—turned out to be a stepping stone rather than a destination. (p. 11)

This is the kind of journey that life writing entails, a journey into language and into the world.

Our stories are always singular and plural, familiar and unfamiliar, and constituted and constituting. Therefore, the act of braiding both composes and performs startling interconnections among diverse stories while also acknowledging how we are beings with agency and responsibility. Through our writing and our willingness to share our writing with others, we perform our commitment to living with careful intent, critical interrogation, and thoughtful awareness. None of our stories are ours alone. Hall (2004) reminds us that "we are *subject* to discourse, not simply *subjects through* discourse" (p. 127). None of us has autonomy to write our stories in any ways we might like or choose. None of us is not constrained and composed by numerous social, historical, cultural, political, ideological positions, exclusions, commitments. Each of us still lives with a lively responsibility for acting creatively: "imagining that what *is* does not necessarily *have to be*" (Hall, 2004, p. 130). As the life writers who are convened in *A Heart of Wisdom* creatively testify, by attending to what *is*, we can learn together what *might be*.

Cynthia Chambers, Erika Hasebe-Ludt,
Carl Leggo, and Anita Sinner
April 2012

REFERENCES

Amis, M. (2000). *Experience*. New York, NY: Hyperion.

Armstrong, K. (2005). *A short history of myth*. Toronto: Alfred A. Knopf Canada.

Atwood, M. (2002). *Negotiating with the dead: A writer on writing*. Cambridge, MA: Cambridge University Press.

Barthes, R. (1977). *Roland Barthes*. (R. Howard, Trans.). Berkeley: University of California Press.

Bly, C. (2001). *Beyond the writers' workshop: New ways to write creative nonfiction*. New York, NY: Anchor Books.

Carey, J. (1997/2010). *Japanese braiding: The art of* kumihimo. Tunbridge Wells, England: Search Press.

Calvino, I. (1995). *Six memos for the next millennium*. Toronto: Vintage Canada.

Cixous, H. (1993). *Three steps on the ladder of writing* (S. Cornell & S. Sellers, Trans.). New York, NY: Columbia University Press.

Cixous, H., & Calle-Gruber, M. (1997). *Hélène Cixous, rootprints: Memory and life writing* (E. Prenowitz, Trans.). New York, NY: Routledge. (Original work published 1994)

Deleuze, G., & Guattari, F. (1994). *What is philosophy?* (H. Tomlinson & G. Burchell, Trans.). New York, NY: Columbia University Press.

Freire, P. (1997/2007). *Pedagogy of the heart*. New York, NY: Continuum.

Gates, B. (2003). *Already home: A topography of spirit and place*. Boston, MA: Shambhala.

Griffin, S. (1995). *The eros of everyday life: Essays on ecology, gender and society*. New York: Doubleday.

Goldberg, N. (1986). *Writing down the bones: Freeing the writer within*. Boston, MA: Shambhala.

Grant, B. (1972). *Encyclopedia of rawhide and leather braiding*. Centreville, MD: Cornell Maritime Press.

Hall, D. E. (2004). *Subjectivity*. New York, NY: Routledge.

Hasebe-Ludt, E., Chambers, C. M., & Leggo, C. (2009). *Life writing and literary métissage as an ethos for our times*. New York, NY: Peter Lang.

Haug, F. (Ed.). (1992). *Female sexualization: A collective work of memory* (E. Carter, Trans.). London, England: Verso. (Original work published 1983)

Heaney, S. (1995). *Crediting poetry: The Nobel lecture*. Loughcrew, Ireland: The Gallery Press.

Keefer, J. K. (1998). *Honey and ashes: A story of family*. Toronto, Canada: HarperCollins.

King, T. (2003). *The truth about stories: A Native narrative*. Toronto: House of Anansi Press.

Lionnet, F. (1989). *Autobiographical voices: Race, gender and self-portraiture*. Ithaca, NY: Cornell University Press.

Martin, C. (1991). *Kumihimo: Japanese silk braiding techniques*. Asheville, NC: Lark Books.

Noddings, N. (2011). Care ethics in education. In J. A. Kentel (Ed.), *Educating the young: The ethics of care* (pp. 7–19). New York, NY: Peter Lang.

Pinar, W. F. (2006). Complicated conversation: Occasions for intellectual advancement in the internationalization of curriculum studies. In *The synoptic text and other essays: Curriculum development after the reconceptualization* (pp. 163–178). New York, NY: Peter Lang.

Richardson, L., & St. Pierre, E. (2005). Writing: A method of inquiry. In N. Denzin & Y. Lincoln (Eds.), *Handbook of qualitative research* (3rd ed.) (pp. 959–978). Thousand Oaks, CA: Sage.

Saul, J. R. (2008). *A fair country: Telling truths about Canada*. Toronto: Viking Canada.

Smith, D. G. (1994). Children and the gods of war. In *Pedagon: Meditations on pedagogy and culture* (pp. 189–197). Bragg Creek, Canada: Makyo Press.

Stafford, A. (2010). *Photo-texts: Contemporary French writing of the photographic image*. Liverpool, England: Liverpool University Press.

Todd, S. (2009). *Toward an imperfect education: Facing humanity, rethinking cosmopolitanism*. Boulder, CO: Paradigm Publishers.

Memory Work

Min(d)ing the Past, Facing the Present

The attention to ambiguity, paradox, and difference—more complex and subtle renderings of experience—is libratory, in itself.
—Ursula Kelly, *Schooling Desire*

There's too much of us for us to know.
—Margaret Avison, *Concrete and Wild Carrot*

In this first strand of life-writing texts, the writers perform the kind of memory work that traditionally has been the domain of memoir, an examination of past and partial, yet significant or "sterling" moments (Goldberg, 2007) in a writer's life against the backdrop of social, political, cultural, and other conditions. The authors use various (mixed) genres of life writing (memory, poetry, poetic prose, personal essay, narrative, documentary, photography) to articulate the understandings they have come to. Through life writing they examine issues from the past that affect their own and others' present lifeworlds, thus taking up what David G. Smith (2006) defines as *hermeneutic scholarly work* based on the imagination and interest in "engaging LIFE hermeneutically, which means trying to understand ever more profoundly what makes life LIFE, what makes living a living" (p. 105). This is also the work of *currere*, defined by William F. Pinar (2004) as a conversation between self and other, a recurrent movement towards self understanding relative to historical, social, and political knowledge, one that begins with "a time past, still in the present" (p. 30).

The writing in this strand is also reminiscent of a long-standing tradition of memory work in other social sciences fields, such as women's and gender studies, cultural studies, sociology, and anthropology, as well as in the humanities, such as literary studies. In these writings, memory work performs a kind of theorizing from the ground, the *humus* we share as human beings (Aoki, 1986/1991/2005); it digs up the roots and rhizomes of past social and political conditions that have shaped the human condition and that have "woven their way into the fabric of our everyday consciousness" (Haug, 1999, p. 14). Thus the meaning, when working from this ground, comes from living and working *with* everyday personal experiences *within* a larger political context, in remembering rich details about the emotions resident in the experience and about the social/cultural background. As Frigga Haug reminds us, it is "only when we have learned to see ourselves as children of these circumstances that we are equipped to work with others as we work about ourselves" (1999, p. 7).

In the memory work these writers attempt here, they are active agents, emotionally present, and without the kind of false empathy, which remains at a sympathizing level with the other, one that is unproductive and hinders the examination of true issues at work. The writer and the text are in continuous motion, in the recurrent phases of *currere*, and in the sensory and political memory work that opens up and disturbs the "graveyard-like silence of sameness" (Haug, 1999, p. 10) and gets to "the emotional truth under the surface" (Goldberg, 2007, p. xx). As Haug insists, in this de-stabilizing and yet emancipating process, it is crucial to remember that "alone one cannot do anything" (p. 24): this is collective work that has nothing impersonal about it. At the same time, through the constructive nature of memory as articulated through life writing, writers are able to gain the ability to act and to "create a living culture of contradiction instead of a culture of inequality" (Haug, 1999, p. 28). Memory work here in this section gets to the heart of what Deleuze and Parnet (2002) claim is the aim of all writing: life.

REFERENCES

Aoki, T. T. (1986/1991/2005). Teaching as in-dwelling between two curriculum worlds. In W. F. Pinar & R. L. Irwin (Eds.), *Curriculum in a new key: The collected works of Ted T. Aoki* (pp. 159–165). Mahwah, NJ: Lawrence Erlbaum.

Avison, M. (2002). *Concrete and wild carrot*. London, Canada: Brick Books.

Deleuze, G., & Parnet, C. (1987/2002). *Dialogues II* (H. Tomlinson & B. Habberjam, Trans.). New York, NY: Columbia University Press. (Original work published in 1977)

Goldberg, N. (2007). *Old friend from far away: The practice of writing memoir*. New York, NY: Free Press.

Haug, F. (1999). *Memory-work as a method of social science research: A detailed rendering of memory-work method*. Retrieved from: http://www.friggahaug.imnkrit.de

Kelly, U. A. (1997). *Schooling desire: Literacy, cultural politics, and pedagogy*. New York, NY: Routledge.

Pinar, W. F. (2004). *What is curriculum theory?* Mahwah, NJ: Lawrence Erlbaum.

Smith, D. G. (2006). The mission of the hermeneutic scholar. In *Trying to teach in a season of great truth: Globalization, empire, and the crises of pedagogy* (pp. 105–115). Rotterdam, The Netherlands: Sense Publishers.

Bread Crumbs

Finding My Way in Poetry

Carl Leggo

Bread Crumbs: Finding My Way in Poetry

&

in busy Lisbon for the first time
I proposed taking digital photos
to find my way back
like a trail of bread crumbs,
and Ruth said,
why not use a map?

I'm not very practical

&

while I once sought the whole
I only ever found holes

because I can never tell
a whole story, I seek fragments

since I am an incomplete sentence
I seek communion with others

like the possibilities of conjunctions
ghosts are everywhere, everywhen

as they call us eagerly to connect
like bridges that lean on light

with invitations to walk in places
where we have been but never been

conjunctions invite us to know interconnections, even if our eyes are dim

&

The Encyclopedia Britannica Yearbook
for 1953, the year I was born, records how

Red Buttons told jokes on TV

Albert Einstein published
Generalization of Gravitation Theory

President Dwight D. Eisenhower
proposed an international agency
to pool atomic energy
for peaceful purposes

Mexico granted the vote to women

world tunnelling activity increased significantly

image amplification apparatus
became commercially available

a process was perfected
which turns oranges
into a powder which may be reconstituted
into highly palatable orange juice

Dylan Thomas died

the first *TV Guide* was published
with a picture of Lucy's baby
Desiderio Alberto Arnaz IV

&

    as a boy
I read that dolphins
rescue shipwrecked sailors,
and like mothers or lovers tow them
clinging to their backs to safety

    as a man
I learned that dolphins
sometimes rescue sailors, sometimes
don't, like coquettes tow them
randomly to land or sea's centre

the dolphin's purpose is play

&

long ago every Saturday morning
I waited for *The Western Star*
with the Li'l Abner comic strip because
the world was threatened by a joke
so funny everyone who read it
died laughing and I could hardly
wait to read the joke and laugh
myself to death, and week after
week Dogpatch readers died
laughing with at least a thin smile,
but the joke remained a secret
when a cow ate it and didn't die,
and Li'l Abner substituted a joke
about a chicken crossing the road,
and I didn't even chuckle, and
I'm still waiting for the joke

&

Carrie changed the pictures
in the frames in the living room
to reflect the seasons
(you could not have
summer in winter)
each season marked

with new pictures from
National Geographic
Chatelaine
The Star Weekly
cut to fit the precise frames
painted to match the changing
colours of the living room
(eager for equilibrium, even
the reality in glossy magazines)

&

one summer I worked at the mill
and dug a clean clear hole
in a single afternoon
but the foreman said my hole
made the other workers look lazy,
so I dug a second hole, slow and sloppy,
like a delinquent gopher,
in days without end

&

king of the hill my brother alone
jumped from Mugs O'Reilly's house falling
three stories up to his waist in snow,
drove a purple Raleigh one-speed straight
up Hospital Hill past the CBC to the Summit,
surfed Lynch's Lane all the way on a sled
from Old Man Downey's to Maggie Mercer's

it's about time I bragged about my brother

&

on the edge of the coulees
high above the Oldman River
I sat among the books in the library
of The University of Lethbridge
in southern Alberta in Western Canada
in North America while the earth
spun its yarn with galactic precision
and wondered if the buffalo

still remembered the way back

&

my colleague Dave was so excited
when he read his name cited
in a journal, he jumped out of
his hot tub and ran to tell his wife,
and stubbed his toe, broke it even,
and I told Dave, academics should
wear their pride in steel-toed boots

&

I thought I was in love,
wild with love,
but I was just
a chunk of knotted alder
turned on a lathe
spinning sharp, shaped
by a tungsten blade
like a kiss
till I became
a decorative spindle
without edges,
a kind of swindle

&

that February morning I missed my bus
I stood on the corner of Granville and 41st
cranky with the planet for rotating
and revolving in its own chronology,
eyes focussed on the gutter, sure only
a miscreant bugger would litter a cigarette pack
when an old woman slipped alongside me,
have you smelled the air today,
a long time ago I lived in Africa,
I still remember the smells,
we lifted our noses in the air, wide
open, smelling, remembering Africa

&

more than once Joe told me
how he buried his father
(who abandoned him as a boy
after a decade telling Joe
he was good for nothing,
would never amount to anything)
in a treeless plot with no shade,
a barren rectangle between
Polanski and Chang, writhing
in his racist stew for eternity,
and I never knew what to say to Joe

&

in Kingston at Chez Piggy,
owned by one of the Lovin' Spoonful,
I ate oven-baked duck on a bed
of purple cabbage and shitake mushrooms,
yam cream soup with coconut and whipped
peanuts, Richter's bitter, mango flan,
café au lait sipped from a bowl,
and wished only for a spoon full of love

&

if a nurse with cool hands shaved off patches of your hair,
rubbed lotion in your skin, glued electrodes to the soft raw
patches, punched switched flicked buttons on EKG
and EEG machines, would you register flat or wavy lines?

&

the world is not a trig locus
and I will not pretend because
billions of flies eat shit; it is,
therefore, tasty; I want no more
cook books: how to speak well,
live longer, pick up girls,
get picked up by girls,
take active control of your life,
pray, love, juggle; only the book
on juggling ever helped

&

while I sat in the lobby of the Eaton Centre
waiting for Bruce MacDonald's *Highway 61*
a middle-aged woman and a middle-aged man
passed by and one said, *the point is,*
just a scrap of conversation, all I heard,
but I was encouraged somebody
apparently knows the point

&

perhaps   all creation is no
more predictable than the weather:
seasons in a broken circle
Indian summer in November   snow in June
rain for weddings   sun for funerals
perhaps Pippa passes with a new message,
God is not in his heaven, all is not well with the world,
but I will still gather scraps for a patchwork quilt
to keep me warm October evenings
sitting on the verandah with cranberry tea
and geese calling the rhythms of elsewhere

&

on a plane to Vancouver I met a model
returning from a photo shoot in Germany

she was bearing a book by Primo Levi
anecdotes letters poems stories

we discussed how Primo Levi wrote hope
through decades of Holocaust survival

then hurled himself into the hole of a winding
stairwell rising stories from the ground

&

in a whirligig of wild
imaginings I breathe
raucous ramblings
with no anchor point

like a deflating balloon
that never runs out of air

&

even if life on earth is a search for the Other,
the one in five billion who can complement
you, make you whole, who can know what whole
is: a hole defined by everything not in the hole
but pressing against the (w)hole, neither black-
empty nor light-empty, since only in the (w)hole
is there known the word-created world creators call good?

&

an August morning, cool wet airsome:
I sit on the patio reading Umberto Eco's
The Search for a Perfect Language
and pull pewter grey hairs from my chest,
listening to neighbours shout at one another,
wondering what language I need to tell you
about this moment filled with growing
old amidst the Tower of Babel

&

I smile little   smiles   barbed
fish hooks buried in the lips
pulled apart   face muscles
resistant   to the heart   still
open/close/open/close/open/close
in systolic rhythm without end
but   at least   I am
smiling   (are you?)
and if he is watching
Allen Funt will know I am ready
(ready as candy) to be candid

&

at a picnic under a blind sun,
chardonnay and camembert,
sparrows and grasshoppers,

in the trees and grass
of Mt. Moriah Cemetery
near his mother's grave
Andrew told Antonia,
I want to be somebody else,
I don't know who,
his heart on fire, compelled
to go somewhere without her

&

how are you?
couldn't be better
lumbago again, often I get stomach aches,
probably indigestion though
possibly cancer, headaches, and emphysema
slow me down, prostate gave out,
I don't mind the ingrown
toenails, the rash on my back
side hurts, probably appendicitis
(nobody is cutting me open),
knees creak on damp Tuesdays, teeth
are falling out, violet varicose veins
line my legs, but I've still got my hair,
as long
as I've still
got my hair,
I am
fine, thanks, you?

&

I will not
sail in an ark with constipated animals
I will not
read the operating manual for this planet (even if I find it)
I will not
tell you I won a trophy for Outstanding Cub in 1962
I will not
gossip about what Olive did in second year of university
I will not

wear elevator shoes in order to avoid being called a stump
I will not
stare at my reflection in mirrors, store windows, still pools, your eyes
I will not
shout at God anymore because it is not easy being God

&

if we had the time
to sit on the verandah
long August afternoons,
I would tell you stories
like Dickens,
of course we don't,
now it's too late

&

never trust a speaker who says, I'll be quick

&

have you ever seen a maple leaf
after winter, filled with the sun,
cut its shape in spring ice?

&

I went to a counsellor
and she walked with me
through the tangled garden
of almost five decades
of living in the earth
to a quiet meadow
where my father and I
stood all alone
among the dandelion,
both dazed and lost

&

a man met Jesus in the mall
and said, by the way,
when are you going to return?

&

I don't want to be a soap-box evangelist
preaching damnation
or a late night show host writing
the world a bigger joke
or a car salesman promising a Land Rover
will help me wend my way
through an urban maze of rhinoceroses

what is the poet's place?

&

my dentist scrapes and grinds
my teeth and regales me
with stories of her belly dancing

&

yesterday I walked the dyke
where I have daily admired
the spring summer sartorial tastes
of cows to see autumn fields
flooded and ducks swimming
where cows once lingered

&

she told me she had lived for a time
with an older lover but the chemistry spoiled
when they disagreed about a new sofa

&

I met my friend Patrick
from Pender Island
on the bus stop
at Granville and 41st,
and he said, I'm on my way
to see my mother in England,
and I said, I don't think
this bus goes that far

&

as his prize for selling Gold Seal Cards
Jim ordered the Box of a Thousand Wonders,
one wonder was the Chinese puzzle
that tightens on the fingers
like memories and poems

&

the first birthday gift
my son gave me
was a pencil and paper
from Shopper's Drug Mart
just like I bought my father
a screw driver or a wrench
at Canadian Tire

&

with all the alphabets
spelling all the words
in all the dictionaries
of all the languages
in all the world

we still can't name
the shades of green,
the moonstruck creation
spinning out, the earth

beyond imagining, where
the story always ends in etc.

&

three sisters went to a fourth sister's funeral
and on their way home on the highway
that winds along the Great Northern Peninsula
crashed into a pick-up driven by a drunk

&

perhaps I am not as happy
as I sometimes claim

like a prospector
who reads a red outcrop
as a sign of hope

and scurries to claim
the tangled, terrible
wildness with tattered

hope like a fish hook
with a thin barb,
holding only awhile, slipping

&

memory is a winter window,
stained frost, light etched lines

&

love makes no-sense
Cupid shooting errant arrows
random like randy rabbits
will not go away
laughs at the limits of law
lives with steel in the heart
and a wanton disregard
for propriety or property
revels in the chase
litters with reckless abandon
fires the body
till the heart breaks
reminds us that grammar
the letter the law
is chimeric
love loves to laugh
with rhythms and metaphors
pneumatic and numinous

&

so I tell my stories
weaving my stories
with the stories of others,

lining a text together,
a textile sufficiently close
woven to warm reality,
to let real light through/in/out,
my writing always an SOS
sent out of fear of desertion, aloneness,
frantic for rescue, connection,
human foot prints in the sand,
wanting the search(ers) to return

&

if I went to the doctor
and the doctor said,
in six months you'll be dead

I would never again

stroll in Richmond Shopping Mall,
eat McDonald's burgers,
worry about my underarm deodorant,
growing old, going bald,
read a newspaper, watch Peter Mansbridge,
discuss the weather, my health,
God and Satan, heaven and hell,

instead I would

visit grocery stores
and eat the free samples,
ride a bus all day, round and round,
write a few notes of love,
write a few notes of regret,
sit in a rocking chair on a verandah
near the ocean, hold your hand, and

write this poem
write this poem
write this poem

until I got it right

&

the alphabet we learned
to write in school was spartan

pressed between parallel lines
eschewing swirls curls whirls

but we need to ask always, all ways,
with tireless wonder

what lies beyond the alphabet?
for the alphabet, the creation

in letters, is a letter
inviting the imagination

beyond the alphabet in lines
that do not begin, do not end

&

writing a poem
is finding my way
to the bathroom at 3 am
in an unfamiliar house
not-knowing
where my glasses are
where the lights are
where I am

&

while visiting Belfast
a city full of poets
I wondered
why poetry
can't heal Belfast

&

charge into the dark places
where lines run skew
no cursive MacLean's script
that swirls with undulating

arcs of oil in water or
July sun in a meadow

&

embrace the chaotic and scribbled lines
of light and love dazzled
within wild imagination

&

Carrie remembers
a man in Curling
who saw a baby seal
basking in the sun,
a fleck of movement
on the frozen harbour,
packed a lunch
and set out to kill it,
but returned an hour
later with no prey,
it looked so cute,
I gave him my sandwich

&

don't read the words only

read the margins where
the words begin and end

read the spaces in the words
where the unwritten is written

read beyond the words
to scribbled words
of others almost hidden
in the words

and speak in tongues
in other words
other languages
you do not know

&

jamming
jam
raspberry jam
traffic jam
enjambement
pyjamas
jam jar
jam as a noun
jam as a verb
in a jam
jam the signal
jam-packed
jamboree

&

is life a series of hurried decisions like a buffet
where you want everything but the line is pressing?

&

the stranger within
the stranger without

all connected on a string
that knows the limits
of gravity, or at least
its seductive attraction

the constant challenge
of yo-yo tangles

everything, all of us
entwined like vines

&

illegible lines scratched
in the sky like a polygraph
in vellum, tangled traces
of life almost remembered

&

what does the alphabet reveal?
I ought to ask,
what does the alphabet conceal?
a kaleidoscope of possibilities
defamiliarizing the familiar

&

in Madison's and Bellini's
we made our stories
a few more in a city
with millions of stories
that seem like one story

like a child's doodle pad
where hidden pictures
are resurrected by rubbing
a pencil over the white page
we are disclosed in storying

not unlike God's word
of creative revelation
we speak write read think
ourselves into existence
compelled to be

&

a network of lines
like arms and hands extended
out of a bog, all bony fingers
outstretched, a supplicant,
beseeching hidden gods

&

the line suggests evolution
no beginning
no ending
the path of a moving point

where, if anywhere, is the line going?

&

I write my lines across in-between through over inside on your lines,
all the lines ever written, ever to be written, a lineal writing
that defies linear measure or equation

&

the full moon remembers
the day's light amidst the shadows
and revels in the inexhaustible
particularity of a drop of moonlight

&

a poem is

the world woven in the light and shadow of words
the unmapped space beyond the alphabet
a plea for pardon from the sentence
a journey without a map
reading between the lines
the rumination of margins
living without punctuation
these words seeking their way
the way into the haunted word
finding constellations of possibilities
a word that never lets you go or lets you go
throwing lines of letters in the air, seeking shapes

&

we stand in the still place
where the end is in the beginning
and the beginning is in the end

&

this is it
this, is it?
it is this
is this it?
this it is

&

Unlearning Heartlessness, Restorative Education

Leah C. Fowler

When Pablo Casals, the cellist, was ninety-one years old, he was approached by a student who asked, "Master, why do you continue to practice? Casals replied, "Because I am making progress."
—Norman Doidge, *The Brain That Changes Itself*

Believing in *neuroplasticity* (Doidge, 2007) as I do, I must also believe in *cardioplasticity* (perhaps another enactment of epigenetics).[1] If I believe in cardioplasticity, then I can think, write, and converse about the heart that changes itself.[2] Since learning involves neuroplasticity[3] by its very definition, unlearning would involve transformational neuronal behaviour as well. Since I was a child, my changing heart, mind, and spirit have learned most through *story*,[4] *study*, and *care*.[5] What mattered most, what sustained over the arc of my life, and what I have given my heart to is implicit in these three abiding interests that have helped me unlearn heartlessness.

If a heart can "learn" through story, study, and care, then perhaps one can dwell more wisely in learning and teaching. A wise heart (Kornfield, 2008) and a mindful brain (Siegel, 2007) may increase immunity to colonization by government curricula, professional development pedagogy gurus, and business-oriented leaders obsessed with instrumentality. Education is *not* a business and *not* a machine factory. Given the "throwness" (Heideggerianly speaking) of this complex, violent, and difficult world in "an unprecedented, hybrid time" (Pinar, 2010), I am interested in how to restore education to a process where individuals conduct deep explorations of what matters to them, what sustains them, what calls their hearts. As public intellectuals, it is our responsibility to "think in front of people," to *read* what people are thinking. New brain research results (Doidge, 2007; Siegel, 2007) show that thinking *does* change us. Cognitive experiences shape our being, and shape how we come to an intellectual sense of home.

Let Bill Pinar's (2010) question reverberate for all scholars: "How does one make the field one's own?" (p. 11). Although he refers to the field of curriculum studies, the question is essential for all disciplines. To study that question, I regard my own epistemology (life-writing inquiry into the history of my intellectual and educational experience and heart) before I participate in discussions about unlearning heartlessness and becoming wise (as opposed to getting smart) as action toward what I call, inadequately, *restorative education*.

A heart of wisdom is central to restorative education. Such a heart acknowledges the specificity of an individual in five ways: 1) engagement with the process of *currere*,[6] 2) skilfull research for democratic participation, 3) non-matronizing contribution to a diverse cosmopolitan community, 4) a selfable[7] inner government, and 5) a mindful research practice that includes appropriate compassion with self and others. Here, I study heartful wisdom in education as anodyne to strategies, recipes, teaching routines. I wish to live differently and well in teaching and research, in a way that resists social engineering approaches and, instead, honours the specificity of students within larger contexts (cultural, social, political, historical) as they progress through life paths. As a curriculum scholar, I study the curriculum of heart, heartlessness, and wisdom. I have studied for decades in many disciplines; I am a slow learner, perhaps too affected by Descartes behind the early science and reason periods of my life, but I am making progress:

> While we have yet to understand exactly *how* thoughts actually change brain structure, it is now clear that they do, and the firm line that Descartes drew between mind and brain is increasingly a dotted line. (Doidge, 2007, p. 214)

My interest in wise hearts, mindful brains, understanding, and wisdom perdures, perhaps *because of* my studies in literature, biology, chemistry, genetics, and physics earlier in my life. As a result of this individual study, and of being taken seriously as a thinker early in life by teachers, I sustained confidence in my capacity to think, figure out problems and make correlative connections. Also from sustained intellectual work, I have increasing respect for human beings, sentient creatures, the foundational material world of nature, and its inorganic substrates. The sheer complexity of all that *is* invokes perennial curiosities, including the "lure of the transcendent" (Hillis, 1999). I am moved by rereading "The Problem with Curriculum and Pedagogy" where Bill Pinar (2006) writes so convincingly about study.[8] I reconsider faith for a modern scholar. What *do* I believe in? What sustains my being? What wise educational opportunities can I open for my students and me in our "co-constructed" curriculum of private and public study?

What *does* it mean to teach and to research with a wise heart (Kornfield, 2008) and a mindful brain (Siegel, 2007)? Part of my answer lies in unlearning heartlessness. *What matters* and *how I know* are essential, concomitant, epistemological studies. Auto- and allo-bio/graphical life writings honour education and being through *currere* with research of self with its privileged inner perspective, literature with its intense study of others, and long-term academic engagement and reading in philosophy, history, and all disciplines of genetics.

An autobiography of the learning heart is a multi-authored work: research notices vital statistics and registers citizens in the country of the heart, biography notes significant facts and events in a storied line from birth, emotion records the feelings, and body keeps markings of literal being. It is spirit that re/members the experienced stories of light and darkness of relationship, care, cruelty, loss, laughter, and insight. Steadily through experience, each heart works toward a charter of rights and freedoms, but actual governance of *being* a person is more difficult. Narrative has the capacity to contain all the learning: I am always in search of good research stories and especially this one about heartfulness that can encourage.

Often via this narrative life writing, movement toward restorative education in the larger world begins with each individual. Through life writing, I cultivate more attuned awareness in the humanities (literature, history, culture, politics) but also in science and art. Unlearning heartlessness means taking others' histories, narratives, work, suffering, and lives seriously, with equal value to one's own; a lifetime of reading literature changes my heartmind. Recent evidence shows that narrative activates that portion of the brain responsible for the development of empathy, so let us hear *all* the stories (Whalen, 2002).

A capacity to hear deeply can be cultivated. Mindfulness practice, for example, *Vipassana* (insight meditation), is useful to me because it is a thoughtful phenomenological study that deepens self understanding and an imaginative capacity for empathy that allows us to see more what life might be like for others. It teaches me to be quiet and open. It teaches me to imagine how others might experience me. Such reflective empathic action allows me to learn what to adjust in myself to restore me, and those around me, to more wholeness.

Baby Heart Haiku: My Grandmother's Report on Her First Sight of Me in a Hospital Nursery in 1951

First-born prairie girl.
Fifty cribbed infants that March
—Heartlet, eyes wide open.

In infancy, the specificity of heart is literal: very early infants reveal preference for one caregiver over another, notice different things as vision refines. My grand-

Arc-of-Heart Life: One

mother told me often of seeing me for the first time through the baby boomer nursery window. She saw rows of infants all tightly swaddled and sleeping in their tiny hospital cribs, except one with both arms out, looking around calmly with eyes wide open. She thought it was me. She smiled when the nurse picked me up, confirming her suspicions. I loved my grandmother from that first day until she died of a sudden heart attack in 1984 when I was 33.[9]

Preschool Heart Haiku

Value of Fords. June;
Foreground to maternal love
—Already no dress.

Awareness of what matters most begins early and lasts a lifetime, as more complex layers accumulate. Physical matter-

Arc-of-Heart Life: Two

ing begins with the body's imperatives: oxygen, water, food, vitamins, minerals, light, optimum temperature, and safety. Shelter is needed, a stable "bio/me" (for eating, sleeping, bathing, waste management). Engagement of at least five senses. Proprioception, movement, speech. Cognitive mattering may first arise from curiosity and the preschool mantra of *why?*

Fuelled by emotional needs of belonging, comfort and response, we progress toward thought and expression. The historical/cultural ocean precedes our birth, but our inchoate curiosity will develop into abiding life questions: How shall I live? What sustains? What can I do with my particular time, talent, and treasury? Where does my heart belong?

Schoolgirl Heart Haiku
> Chess playing girl—what?
> Individuates early,
> learns games, rules, control.

Arc-of-Heart Life: Three

When I began public school at age six, I became adept at reading text, school routines, and people's expectations of compliance in a "good" girl. I noticed what mattered to others, although I did not have the capacity to engage what mattered to *me*. Entitlement was inappropriate for a Christian in our house: my being existed for service to others. Because I was "born in a state of sin" as a wounded-by-the-serpent mortal, what *ego I* needed or wanted, mattered to me as an individual, was immaterial, even sinful. Expressing such hubristic preferences was tantamount to willful defiance of the creator and punishable by hell-fire, *literally.* Ironic commentary and "impertinent" questions were subdued by the spectre of a belt hanging on a nail. The question, *Why?* persisted, as my heart grew darker. I studied, everything.

By the time I was 10 years old, I wanted to be a doctor, for many reasons, so I paid attention to everything.

Doctors were smart, knew stuff, could do stuff. They healed, eased suffering; I wanted that job. Knowing how flawed I was already, hope grew in redemptive powers of work and knowledge. I learned concern for social weal, for biosphere by *reading the world*. Causality, patterns, and arcs of lives emerged from history, literature, other cultures, people, and experience itself. I began to see that the thoughtful action of an individual sometimes could edit, or shape, a direction in a happier way. I wanted personal agency, wanted to become one of the helpers in the world. I became adept at school. At home, books from school and the town library were my main teachers. I maximized time with every teacher, asked questions, and paid attention to everything. Perhaps I was already working my way toward a hope that if I could develop my mind and work on my heart, I could better navigate being *present.*

Teen Heart Haiku

> Too-early harm mars,
> teaches cruelty.
> Learning heartlessness.

In my teen years I questioned my right to be alive. I worried about differences between friends and me, especially those to whom I was attracted. My academic, literary, and scientific pursuits, my vision for adult life, interests, and

Arc-of-Heart Life: Four

abilities were at variance with a suburban prairie town. Really nowhere felt to be home. Amid these difficult years, literature, biology, physics, and chemistry became home disciplines where I could think and dwell freely with *real* questions.[10] If my mind was engaged, I felt I had dignity; I felt happy. I belonged with other scholars, saw subject disciplines as communities where I fit without someone commenting on shoes, hairstyle, or Friday dates. I could rely on my mind, be friends with it, a reliable companion throughout my life. If I persisted in study, I knew I could find sense, make connections, and contribute to wisdom that kept me alive and "mattering."

But the mind without compassion, or heart, can be a dangerous implement. The heart without intellectual understanding, reason, and contextual connection is also dangerous. In these teen years, I had not yet developed that selfable, inner government to regulate my behaviour and emotion. I was too responsive to the influence of others, too uncertain of my right to speak. I was so inured to thinking differently and feeling differently, I kept my "counsel" and learned what I could from others. It never occurred to me that others might learn from me.

This is a tendency I still have. I am even less certain about teaching as I age. Perhaps coming to selfability (not selfish, but responsible for, to, and with myself) allows me to *be* a good teacher. I am aware of potential for inner fascism, for colonizing and using my power and privilege to personal benefit, so focus more mindfully on students and what *they* need.

Young-Woman Heart Haiku

Knowledge-lust, lives hard
Refusing self, heart not yet.
Cello, art, books call.

Arc-of-Heart Life: Five

Sites of research often revolved around difficulty. Early answers were intellectual ones. Somehow I still felt separated from my "self," but reading fiction, nonfiction, poetry, and drama has sustained me. Much later in life, with the same questions, I studied curriculum studies,[11] narrative inquiry,[12] radical hermeneutics,[13] and Vipassana.[14] I began to connect heart and the mind—*my* heart *and MY* mind—together. For so long, I did not use personal pronouns with heart, mind, and indeed the body, my body. I was complicit in the erasure of my own identity. Story, study, and care taught me how to cohere and live well in learning and teaching.

Mid-Age-Woman Heart Haiku

Complicated heart
Notes, wants possibilities.

Arc-of-Heart Life: Six

Miss truth, wisdom.

Story: First one loss, then another, another....Yet she lives, because of love.

Study:

- Lessons from Loss: Not grasping, perspective, appreciation, compassion, gratitude, attentiveness to time. Language, mapping experience, and interpretive tools of my own in this place (Chambers, 1999).
- Lessons from Music: Struggling for beauty. Knitting heart-mind. Belonging. Balm.
- Lessons from Art: The way I *mark* in the world: Sight, patience, traces, horizons.
- Lessons from Science: Research. Experimentation in thought and action. DNA. Patternicity. Agency. Confidence. Meaning.
- Lessons from Literature: Empathy. Truth. Justice. Concentration. Connectedness.
- Lessons from Love: Care, vulnerability, connection, abiding, faith in Being.

Care: Care is sempiternally needed. Bodies need specific foods, play, sleep. Optimum weight. Movement. Resting heart. Stewarding emotions. Reasons to participate.

Now Heart Haiku

Restoring wholeness.
Learns. Attentive to wisdom.
Mindful being. Heart.

Arc-of-Heart Life: Seven

Imagine a large pad of art paper on a desk at Queenswood Retreat Centre in Victoria awaiting inked evidence of thought as it develops. Beginning this essay for *A Heart of Wisdom: Life Writing as Empathetic Inquiry* and "re/cording" my understanding, thinking and study of empathic inquiry toward what I call restorative education (benefitting both self and others), I consider the arc of my life, heart, and mind within the arc of my disciplines and research over a lifetime career of learning and teaching. *Currere* (Pinar, 1994) always insinuates itself: regression, progression, analysis, and synthesis. I reflect and work in deep curiosity and engagement at the edges of comfort: conceptual, experiential, professional. I scan inner videos for relevant experience, sketch a concept map.

Present perceptions on this spacious morning in the summer light over the garden outside my window let me notice the gift of solitude, rare quiet time, to *think*. On this wooden chair with this pen I consider questions posed in the invitation: What critical moments of learning and teaching have changed my life? What stories need to be told? What questions should be asked? What matters most? What sustains me and others and the places we inhabit? What have I given my heart to?

There is the-not-so-gentle insistence of a 10-day deadline. One colleague "re/traverses" toward wellness, I hope. I wonder what the editors and other writers are writing, thinking this morning. Never mind others right now: what do I do in inquiry, in living toward a heart of wisdom? First-person experiences required. My self-covenant is to write only what is true, so life writing will be difficult for me. I note not to suppress or elide insights either, troubling though they may be. Nor do I want to write obliquely, as poet Adrienne Rich (1995, p. 25) pointed to.

In the past 24 hours, I sat in a chair "with" the sun. I enjoyed a Gala apple and recycled the micro-core into the compost. I walked down to the sea, crunched arbutus leaves underfoot, felt afraid for my mortality, felt muscle-tension, and noticed my irregular, too-fast pulse. I changed direction in the woods to move toward a weak, soft bird/animal, distress call. The sound stopped before I could locate its source. I was grateful, wondering at my response to "woundedness." I smiled ruefully at my need for self-comfort and projected anodyne to my own ancient, interior, battle scars. I thought about making love: slowly, gently with kindness and patience, roughly with hunger and wanting, and heartfully with care and tenderness. No, I can't write about that; this is a research paper. Yet we do search and research loving.

I thought of multiple abuses in my life. No, not writing about that. There is no point by now, except to say that I learned some empathy at the hands of abusive people, some cautionary relational lessons, some compassion. Fiction is better for truths of the most difficult kind or stories that can hold the density of the real.

I wondered about questions about complexities of the heart. No, not that. Life writing is autobiographical, and yet, I need not be extreme in self-confession or personal revelation. But I do notice loving—mine toward others and others toward me—that sustains what I know about heartfulness and empathy. Each person we encounter teaches by being, but lovers teach us in complex dialogic matrices of intimate relationships. Through all relationships we learn about our hearts; we also learn about heartlessness.

Still reiterating questions in a research mantra, I showered, with gratitude for hot clean water and ease of bathing. Turned the shower off while biodegradable shampoo and soap lather. Thought about a heart of wisdom under the sluicing of the spigot. Cried unexpectedly, aware of my shortcomings and then thought: empathy must extend to me as well, one of many sentient beings. Supper was mango chicken, rice, and steamed vegetables; I wanted a good dinner for all beings, aware of that impossibility, given food chains. I rested in an enclosed meditative rose garden; entered and left an empty sanctuary; smiled at strangers; noticed my desire for material perfection and lines of beauty in artifact and landscape, bearing and garment, and horizon and housing. Looked at clocks perhaps 70 times. Note to self: study that! Again I lamented past wrong doings and wrong decisions. I was surprised at my inability to say even to myself what matters most and the banal comments I came up with about what sustains from literal to transcendent. Perhaps I did not really give my heart until late in life because I had not learned to possess it with wisdom.

I do believe that teachers and students through the neuroplasticity-fostering study and the cardioplasticity/empathy-fostering qualities of story will help us "get a heart of wisdom." Story, study, and care have contributed, sustained, and helped me build a wise heart and a mindful brain. If that is what students study in their time with me, I will be among the fortunate who have lived. Wisdom is not an outcome or "goal-meeting" but a quality that emerges through "uncovering a heart shrouded in needs and desires."[15] Through careful study of history (epistemologies of self, others, world disciplines), difficulty (where "we" get stuck and do not know what to do or know what we are unable to do), turning points (actions, insight, effective change), mindfulness (awareness, understanding, and knowledge), appropriate participation (noticing what is called for and acting without colonizing), and thoughtful love, the cultivation of a wise heart in research and education can inform the lives we live. We can make progress.

ENDNOTES

1 Epigenetics is "the study of how genes are expressed" or "turned on" by environmental factors. "'People say that if genetics is the alphabet of life, epigenetics is the grammar,'" says Olga Kovalchuk.…"Unlike genetic changes which are rather rare, epigenetic changes happen constantly. Knowing which external factors can trigger expressions of genes in DNA will help people make healthier decisions to lower risks of developing certain health issues." http://www.uleth.ca/unews/report/contentacademic-couple-works-toward-albertas-first -epigenetics-institute

2 We do need a change of heart and mind about education.

3 Not a new concept: Rousseau alluded to this in his book *Emile, or On Education,* where he writes about cognitive development among other things and about the organization of the brain being affected by experience. He knew the human need to exercise minds like bodies. Norman Doidge (2007) writes interestingly in his Appendix 2 about this.

4 For some of my work with story, see my website about narrative inquiry I prepared for the *In/Education* periodical: http://people.uleth.ca/~leah.fowler/Narrativefowler/Welcome. html

5 For a quick way into Nel Noddings's work, see www.infed.org/thinkers/noddings.htm.

6 See work of William F. Pinar (1994), especially his essay on "Working from Within."

7 By *selfable*, I do not mean selfish or narcissistic. I mean: possessing mature knowledge about oneself with its needs, strengths, foibles, and fit in relationship and community; having responsibility for one's thoughts, feelings, and actions without projecting onto others or requiring extra work from others to sustain existence, work, and love; exercising self-control; and becoming more sentient, aware, reflective, responsive, and willing to participate equitably in life and society.

8 I want to read what women intellectuals say about this as well; Martha Nussbaum, for example, or Jan Zwicky.

9 That story is published in *A Curriculum of Difficulty* (Fowler, 2006).

10 Irshad Manji (2005) says "home is where my dignity lives" (p. 6) and still I find that an enduring definition.

11 Especially William F. Pinar and the Reconceptualists (Pinar, Reynolds, Slattery, & Taubman, 1995).

12 Polkinghorne, Paul Kerby, Ricoeur.

13 John Caputo, after Schleiermacher, Dilthey, Heidegger.

14 Jack Kornfield, Pema Chodron, Jon Kabat-Zinn, Sylvia Boorstein in text; Heather Martin and Beth Trotter in person.

15 Heather Martin, a well-known *Vipassana* teacher on Saltspring Island, British Columbia, describes this as the work of insight meditation.

REFERENCES

Boorstein, S. (2008). *Happiness is an inside job*. New York, NY: Ballantine.

Caputo, J. (1987). *Radical hermeneutics: Repetition, deconstruction, and the hermeneutic project*. Bloomington: Indiana University Press.

Chambers, C. (1999). A topography for Canadian curriculum theory. *Canadian Journal of Education, 24*(2), 137–150.

Chodron, P. (1994). *Start where you are: A guide to compassionate living*. Boston, MA: Shambhala.

Chodron, P. (2000). *When things fall apart: Heart advice for difficult times*. Boston, MA: Shambhala.

Dilthey, W. (1976). The development of hermeneutics. In *Selected writings* (H. P. Rickman, Trans. & Ed.). Cambridge, MA: Cambridge University Press.

Doidge, N. (2007). *The brain that changes itself: Stories of personal triumph from the frontiers of brain science*. London, England: Penguin.

Fowler, L. C. (2006). *A curriculum of difficulty: Narrative research and the practice of teaching*. New York, NY: Peter Lang.

Heidegger, M. (1962). *Being and time* (J. Macquarrie & E. Robinson, Trans.). New York, NY: Harper & Row. (Original work published 1927)

Heidegger, M. (1971). *Poetry, language, thought* (A. Hofstadter, Trans.). New York, NY: Harper Colophon Books.

Hillis, V. (Ed.). (1999). *The lure of the transcendent: Collected essays by Dwayne E. Huebner* (W. F. Pinar, Collected and Introduced). Mahwah, NJ: Lawrence Erlbaum.

Kabat-Zinn, J. (2005). *Coming to our senses: Healing ourselves and the world through mindfulness*. New York, NY: Hyperion.

Kerby, P. (1991). *Narrative and the self*. Bloomington: Indiana University Press.

Kornfield, J. (2008). *The wise heart: A guide to the universal teachings of Buddhist psychology*. New York, NY: Bantam.

Manjii, I. (2005). *The trouble with Islam today: A wake-up call for honesty and change*. Toronto, Canada: Random House.

Pinar, W. F. (1994). *Autobiography, politics, sexuality*. New York, NY: Peter Lang.

Pinar, W. F. (2006). The problem with curriculum and pedagogy. In *The synoptic text today and other essays* (pp. 109–120). New York, NY: Peter Lang.

Pinar, W. F. (2010). The test our generation must pass. In *Curriculum studies in South Africa: Intellectual histories, present circumstances* (pp. 1–21). New York, NY: Palgrave Macmillan. Retrieved from http://www.csics.educ.ubc.ca/Projects/2010/Pinar_IAACS_09.pdf

Pinar, W. F., Reynolds, W. M., Slattery, P., & Taubman, P. M. (1995). *Understanding curriculum: An introduction to historical and contemporary curriculum discourses*. New York, NY: Peter Lang.

Polkinghorne, D. (1988). *Narrative knowing and the human sciences*. Albany: State University of New York Press.

Rich, A. (1995). *Dark fields of the republic: Poems 1991-1995*. New York, NY: W. W. Norton.

Ricoeur, P. (1986). *Time and narrative* (Vol. 2). Chicago, IL: University of Chicago Press.

Schleiermacher, F. (1978, Autumn). The hermeneutics: Outline of the 1819 lectures (J. Wojcik & R. Hass, Trans.). *New Literary History, X*(1), 1–16.

Siegel, D. (2007). *The mindful brain: Reflection and attunement in the cultivation of well-being*. New York, NY: W. W. Norton.

Whalen, L. (2002). The neuroscience of teaching narratives: Facilitating social and emotional development. *Brain: Broad Research in Artificial Intelligence and Neuroscience, 1*(2), 5.

Zwicky, J. (1992). *Lyric philosophy*. Toronto, Canada: University of Toronto Press.

Old Narratives Break Apart

Teresa Strong-Wilson

I have been taking my own "love medicine" (Chambers, 1998), digging deeply into the soil of slowly moving but cataclysmic shifts. These changes began one year around April 1st.

April Fool's Day is an auspicious time for troubling the lines between illusion and reality. Around this date, I stumbled across a photograph that was taken when I was five. I was in a navy-coloured dress with white apron, black patent shoes, and neatly folded-over white socks. My head was cocked characteristically to one side: pageboy haircut; sweet smile. In the background were our house's bricks, the basement windows—and tulips. I stood in front of a row of tulips coloured red, yellow, and violet. I associated this photograph with a story in which, at a young age, I was smelling flowers (*these* flowers, I thought). "Weren't you lucky," my mom always interpolated, "not to get stung?" I recently showed the photo to my mom; she laughed. I repeated the remembered childhood story about smelling the flowers and narrowly avoiding getting stung. She laughed. "No, it isn't that," she explained. The flowers were "planted" in a neighbour's garden to fool them into believing that Montréal could be like Victoria, British Columbia, garden capital of Canada, which is where my parents grew up. The photograph was also sent back home to their relatives in Victoria. My parents wanted others to believe that, despite being transplanted, they retained a Victoria "green thumb" that could perform miracles. I became enamoured of a certain interpretation that did not represent the whole picture.

More and more, I have been wondering what I really knew, and know, about my parents, especially my mom.[1]

|

We think back through our mothers, if we are women.
(Virginia Woolf, as cited in Grumet, 1988, p. 183)

Chambers (1998) uses the digging up of dandelions as a metaphor to point to the kind of writing that is necessary but frustrating: tenacious roots that run deep and are not easily brought to light. In my doctoral research, I had used probes in my memory work with teachers. More recently, I too was subjected to persistent probes and then I understood what it felt like to be pressed, however gently, to remember something I did not want to. It felt like digging up dandelions with my fingers: painful and slow. No pulling, though, was involved in unearthing the following memory of mine, which I composed in a third-person voice:

> She's 10- or 12-years old. Her hair has grown long, an orangeish hue of red. It runs in waves down the side of her head, exposing her ears. Whenever her hair gets longer, it loses its lustrous thickness and subsides, flattened smoothly against the sides of her head. Her favourite piece of jewellery is a necklace with a blue pendant of "Beautiful British Columbia." She bought it at the Royal British Columbia Museum when they visited Victoria. In the photograph, she is striding through the totems of Thunderbird Park and across the Parliament building lawns. On the pendant, lighthouse and mountains are immersed in the blue of ocean. Gold rims a circle, ponderous, weighty, magical. She can feel its power as it hangs suspended from a silver chain, long enough to pull over her head in a quick movement. It is the first in a long line of amulets.
>
> She is poised on the verge of puberty, but is as far from being womanly as could be imagined. She wears things that seem loose and comfortable but to a critical eye, stick too closely to her contours. She becomes attached to favourite things that to a finer eye, clash. She is in a dressing room and she sees herself. She is a little girl. Her mother is in the dressing room with her. It's the kind of dressing room that you would find in a cheap department store. She is in the dressing room and it's small and feels especially crowded although only the two of them are in there, isolated from the rest of the world by a door, a mere curtain. She is trying on pants. Depressing lines of clothes wait dispiritedly to be tried on, bunched uselessly on the one hook. Her period has already begun, and consequently she is "filling out," acquiring a plump mass not helped by pies and cookies and chips and cake. She loves to eat, to drink, to read, and

to imbibe. She is a chameleon who soaks up other people's energies, her pores constantly opening, shutting, like a barnacle. Impenetrable, obscure white rock developing on the outside, feelers on the inside surreptitiously pulling in. Trash and treasure. *Her mother is yelling. Not too loud of course. Yelling through clenched teeth. Loud enough to fill the space inside the cubicle right up to the empty space on top where, were she to look up, she would see another ceiling with department store lights dispassionately gazing downwards, tsk, tsk, frowning on her predicament. No help from that quarter. No, she is more likely looking down, or around, or this way, or that way. Any way but at her mother, who is as if in a crumpled heap, crying in frustration. The tears are crocodile tears and the crouch a preamble to a strike, an unmitigated rage, one that soon issues forth in a torrent of angry words and spitting eyes glaring.*

She is partially unclothed. She is trying to pull on pants, stretchy pants, and they're not budging, they're refusing to climb over the hills and valleys and troughs of her skin, which buckles and folds, as first she attempts the improbable and then cold hands intervene, painfully wrenching, tugging, bloodless tears falling on unrepentant flesh. Flesh touching flesh. Fleshes flinching. She is being corsetted and her prospects for marriage are becoming slimmer the more difficult it is to find an appropriate pair of stretchy pants to fit her.

Her mother glares, her mouth a thin line. It's no use. Disgusted, she flashes angry advice: "Stop eating!" Her daughter's tears fall heavy and wet, plop, plop, and the sobbing infuriates her. "Just get dressed."

All that year she wears ugly checkered pants, size large, or extra large, or maybe they're extra, extra, extra, extra large (she flashes back) and her mother abides their presence, eyes averted.[2]

I once thought that this was "difficult knowledge" (Pitt & Britzman, 2003). In light of memories that I *really* did not want to unearth, I wonder how this narrative slipped out so easily. My interviewer said, "Some memories come attached with spikes so that we will leave them alone." Are my memories of my mother truly of this kind?

II

I look for my mother now, and I can find her.
I look for her then, and I can't find her.
All I find is a caricature, a white goddess.

(Teresa Wilson, 2003, n.p.)

In this slow and cataclysmic shifting, old narratives break apart. One of them finds its echo in Steedman (1987), in an essay that I included in a graduate curriculum course, one that drew the attention of female students in particular. Steedman described her dream of a woman:

She wore the New Look, a coat of beige gaberdine which fell in two swaying, graceful pleats from her waist at the back....She hurried, something jerky about her movements, a nervous, agitated walk, glancing round at me....Several times she turned and came slowly back towards me, admonishing, shaking her finger.

Encouraging me to follow in this way perhaps, but moving too fast for me to believe that this was what she wanted, she entered a revolving door of dark, polished wood, mahogany and glass, and started to go round and round, looking out at me as she turned. I wish I knew what she was doing, and what she wanted me to do. (p. 28)

My mother was an elegant dresser. She often made her own clothes. I hid in her closet (during the game "hide and seek") and breathed in the odour and texture of her being.

I wonder now about my reasons for including Steedman's dream in the course syllabus. The ambiguity of the mother-daughter relation is a standard theme in feminist writing. Giorgio (2002) attests: "[T]here seems to be an endless chain of women tied ambivalently to their mothers, who replicate this relation with their daughters" (Flax, as cited in Giorgio, 2002, p. 25). Re-reading my own narratives, I hear the voice of a child angry with her mother (see Buss, 2002, who has also interpreted Steedman in this light). I do not deny my painful experiences tied to body, sexuality and gender expectations. I question, though, how such stories represent my mother, and how I carry myself in relation to her. This is a new development.

I have hesitated to even replicate the above excerpt. The narrative sounds well crafted. The unwary reader (like its unwary narrator/author) may be taken in by its verisimilitude, as representing an unyielding truth about my relationship with my mother. Is it not another trompe l'oeil? I now know that there is much more to the story that I am not telling, or even aware of.

III

The task of thinking back through our mothers...is an archaeology not of them but of our relation to them.

(Madeleine Grumet, 1988, p. 190)

In my academic writing (e.g., Strong-Wilson, 2005; Wilson, 2002), I construed, as self-deceptive, my life as a "leaving home" story (Taylor, 1989). In this story, I emerged as the only one standing: wobbly but erect; White and somewhat stained yet cleansed. My familial allegiances were given over to my First Nations relations through marriage. Key to this dynamic, I learned, was the mother-daughter relationship, which I once positioned within another narrative, a story I wrote about teaching and living in a First Nations community. I implicitly cast aspersion on the female knowledge with which I grew up. Food and the body again intruded as I contrasted the easy fluidity of tea among First Nations women with my childhood experience:

> [Tea] meant tea, coffee, cookies and cakes spread out on fluted fancy plates on top of crocheted doilies, and hot beverages served in Royal Doulton china cups with saucers. It's high English tea, or rather high Scottish tea, because most of the "relations" that we regularly visited, I now realize, were labour relations, friends who my father had met through work in the shipyards....My mother, slim and well-dressed, sat poised on the edges of chairs or couches, sipping her tea, while holding the saucer circumspectly so as to catch any wayward drops. (Don't make more work for the hostess: a legitimate form of female solidarity). I, on the other hand, inelegant, in no apparent need of dessert, luxuriated in the tasty treats then retired to a corner with a Nancy Drew mystery. (Wilson, 2000)

As with the tulips, there are things I didn't know at the time of living the (repeated) experience and at the time of writing. My father knew the men through work, but it was my mother, with her Scottish ancestry, who was the community insider and catalyst. All of the women were of Scottish ancestry; so were the men, except my father, who had British roots. He was tolerated yet teased as the outsider (as he later explained). What was missing in the narrative was my mother's life; her intentions, thoughts, experiences. Transplanted to Montréal, she was trying to replicate the same kind of *cèilidh* that was characteristic of her own growing up with her parents, her granny, siblings, and cousins. My grandfather (a fisherman from Cockenzie, Scotland) worked in the Parliament buildings as a janitor: a small wiry man who walked with rocks in his pockets to scare away the dogs in the wee hours of the morning (this in the 1930s in Victoria). His daughter played on the shore along Dallas Road while he was beachcombing. My grandmother was a domestic worker, like her mother in turn, from the romantic-sounding, Gogar Stone, in the green fields outside Edinburgh. Romance, if romance there was, quickly ended for my great-grandmother in a child born out of wedlock, a secret my grandmother bore as a source of shame.

What my mother best remembers about her family, though, is not its dark secrets but the love and laughter as they gathered around the radio listening to the hockey game, or as my grandfather shot peas at unwary guests at the dinner table. I began the work of life history with my mom antiseptically, a skilled but detached researcher. Then, I became a researcher in the field; I visited my parents who were 78 and 82 at the time. I noted my mom's lively interactions with my father over the breakfast table. Slowly, as I learned more of her story, my own life narrative began to change. The old lenses began rigid and small, providing a poor fit for what I was seeing and understanding. Metamorphosis is awkward.

Some days I truly felt out of sorts. At the time, I did not have the luxury to worry about how it felt, or looked, or whether *then* (as an untenured professor) was the right time. At 82, my mother's felt memory remained, as well as diverse means for expressing her thought, but Alzheimer's deprived her of a capacity for sustained speech. I could create a retrospective narrative from my written record, such as it was, but in comparison with the previous 3 years of life-history work that I had embarked on with my mom, I would find myself in an echo chamber: the only voice that would come back would be my own.

In my autobiographies, I constructed myself as the marginalized one, whose voice was unheard. My biggest challenge in the life-history work involved listening to what my parents said rather than what I wanted to hear. As before, I was digging, but this time, I was unearthing "precious knowledge" (Atwood, 2002) of a different sort. Margaret Atwood suggests that, as writers, we propitiate those who have come before us. We need to negotiate, Atwood says, because they can share "precious knowledge" of the utmost importance. In collaboration with my mother, I was re-vivifying a relationship that had virtually disappeared. Along with it, I was re-vivifying a sense of continuity in being a woman among women; a mother among mothers.

IV

Je voudrais saisir...la femme qui a existé en dehors de moi, la femme réelle, née dans le quartier rural d'une petite ville de Normandie et morte dans le service de gériatrie d'un hôpital de la région parisienne.
(Annie Ernaux, 1987, p. 23)

When I began life writing, I felt that by disclosing the self, I was betraying the family and behaving indecorously. And yet, no price too high, I reasoned, for choosing life (writing) over death. In my more recent work with my mother I refrained from writing. I listened and recorded our conversations. I kept a hardbound book filled with small notes, threads to be picked up in the next conversation. I helped her peel back the everyday details of her life to uncover the layers of her mother's and father's lives. Our common project became one of love. From this perspective, the openings and endings of our conversations—Hello; Goodbye—were just as, if not more, important than what transpired in the middle.

Mother-daughter relationships tend to be pursued post-mortem. This may involve pulling up dandelions and being poked by thorns, possibly with meagre results. Giorgio (2002), drawing on Chodorow's *The Reproduction of Mothering*, posits "the possibility of a female language and style located in the pre-Oedipal"

(p. 21), a thesis also explored by French feminists Cixous, Irigaray, and Kristeva. Wilkie-Stubbs (2002) distills this interest as "a submerged pre-Oedipal mythical female space in which the (assumed) early mother-daughter symbiosis can be recreated/relived" (p. 22). The daughter longs "to return to this lost realm in the language, structure, and form of women's narratives" (p. 22).

My project with my mom is not, however, an extension of my academic research and self. I understand the urgency of this research with my mother *for its own sake*, for time slips by: "This moment will not last. With every step I take, a sliver of time vanishes" (Hoffman, 1990, p. 16). Now I must write in my mother's absence, re-creating the "knowledge that one loves" (Pitt & Britzman, 2003, p. 766). In this vein, though, I may become re-imprisoned in "la femme de mon imaginaire" (Ernaux, 1987, pp. 22–23) and imprison my mother there as well. A revised narrative must root itself in an understanding of my mother as a person in her own right; this essay marks a beginning.

Who was Margaret Elizabeth Strong, née Cunningham? An embodied voice, a not-me, an individual with her own history and experiences of love and loss? This is the story that I will need to write.

ENDNOTES

1 I dedicate this chapter to my mom, who passed away on March 9, 2011, and also to my two sisters; as women and as daughters, we each have our own way of thinking back (and forward) through our mother.

2 Unpublished narratives written during 2001. Short excerpts from this writing have appeared in Wilson and Oberg (2002). Also, my published writings up to 2003 appear under the name Wilson; after 2003, under Strong-Wilson.

REFERENCES

Atwood, M. (2002). *Negotiating with the dead: A writer on writing.* Cambridge, England: Cambridge University Press.

Buss, H. (2002). *Repossessing the world: Reading memoirs by contemporary women.* Waterloo, Canada: Wilfred Laurier University Press.

Chambers, C. (1998). On taking my own (love) medicine: Memory work in writing and pedagogy. *JCT: Journal of Curriculum Theorizing, 14*(4), 14–20.

Ernaux, A. (1987). *Une femme.* Paris, France: Gallimard.

Giorgio, A. (Ed.). (2002). *Writing mothers and daughters: Renegotiating the mother in Western European narratives by women.* New York, NY: Berghahn Books.

Grumet, M. (1988). *Bitter milk.* Amherst: University of Massachusetts Press.

Hoffman, E. (1990). *Lost in translation: A life in a new language.* New York: Penguin Books.

Pitt, A., & Britzman, D. (2003). Speculations on qualities of difficult knowledge in teaching and learning: An experiment in psychoanalytic research. *Qualitative Studies in Education, 16*(6), 755–776.

Steedman, C. (1987). *Landscape for a good woman: A story of two lives.* New Brunswick, NJ: Rutgers University Press.

Strong-Wilson, T. (2005). White female teacher arrives in Native community with trunk and cat: Using self-study to investigate exile in tales of traveling White teachers. In C. Mitchell, S. Weber, & K. O'Reilly-Scanlon (Eds.), *Just who do we think we are? Methodologies for autobiography and self-study in teacher education* (pp. 218–30). London, England: RoutledgeFalmer.

Taylor, C. (1989). *Sources of the self.* Cambridge, MA: Harvard University Press.

Wilkie-Stubbs, C. (2002). *The feminine subject in children's literature.* New York, NY: Routledge.

Wilson, T. (2000). *Ravenwing.* Unpublished paper, University of Victoria, Victoria, Canada.

Wilson, T. (2002). Excavation and relocation: Landscapes of learning in a teacher's autobiography. *JCT: Journal of Curriculum Theorizing, 18*(3), 75–88.

Wilson, T. (2003, February). Remembering women through telling stories. Paper presented at The University of Victoria's Women's Conference, Victoria, Canada.

Wilson, T., & Oberg, A. (2002). Side by side: Being in research autobiographically. *Educational Insights, 7*(2). Retrieved from http://ccfi.educ.ubc.ca/publication/insights/v07n02/toc.html

Kissing Lessons

Wanda Hurren

Currere: *to run the course....The method of* currere *is a strategy devised to disclose experience so that we may see more of it and see more clearly. With such seeing can come deepened understanding of the running, and with this, can come deepened agency.*
—William Pinar and Madeleine Grumet, *Toward a Poor Curriculum*

Let the beauty we love be what we do. There are hundreds of ways to kneel and kiss the ground.
—Rumi, "Spring Giddiness"

My paternal grandmother, my father, two of my three sisters, my only brother-in-law, three of my cousins, an aunt, and an uncle—all made/ make their living by teaching. People often comment that *teaching runs in my family. Run* seems a fitting verb choice. Throughout my life I have been living in a space between *running to* and *running from* teaching. Liking it and not liking it and then liking it again. Wanting to teach and then not wanting to teach, and then again wanting to teach. And it hasn't just been me...

. . .

Growing up north of Aberdeen, Scotland, and raised by her grandparents, my grandmother received top marks in all her classes. Attending high school in Edinburgh, she was to be the recipient of a major scholarship to university. But, word leaked out that she was illegitimate and that was the end of that. As my uncle tells it, the scholarship was denied because it was determined my grandmother was "not a suitable candidate." Perhaps this was an instigating event that led to her leaving Scotland at the age of sixteen and moving to Canada to live with relatives in Southeast Saskatchewan. There, after finishing high school, Mary Barclay attended a six-week teacher-training course and started teaching in country schools. In a photograph, she is raising the Union Jack outside of a one-room school, the prairie wind whipping her long skirts and wrapping the flag around her slim body. Printed in bold letters above the door, the name of the school: *Defiance*...

. . .

Mary Barclay, Teacher, Circa 1925

The only teacher story I remember my grandmother telling us was about how small she was compared to the big, older boys who sat at the back of the classroom. In later years, these same "boys" had fun reminding my grandmother of their earlier teacher/student relationship, mimicking how she often had to tell them, in her Scottish brogue, to "si doon!"

My grandmother fell in love with a man who farmed in one of her school communities. They married and raised their family on a farm. When my dad finished high school he also chose teaching as a profession, attending normal school and taking short courses to gain certification. During one of his early assignments, teaching high-school English and history in a small Saskatchewan town, he fell in love with one of his Grade 12 students. They waited till my mom graduated that June to begin (openly) dating and were married in December. My older sister was born the following September and then me twenty-one months later, followed by two more sisters. Settling down in the prairie town to raise a family of four daughters and teach school, my dad received a scholarship from his school division to return to university. We moved to Saskatoon for 2 years and while my dad attended university, my older sister and I attended a nearby elementary school. I remember my dad sitting with a group of teacher-education students at the back of my Grade 1 classroom, observing our reading lessons. When it was my turn to read, I was doubly intent on being the good student; "See Spot Run"…

. . .

Most of the books spilling over the edges of limp cardboard boxes in the dark, damp crawl space under our bungalow belonged to my dad. My favourite

Jim Hurren, B.Ed., 1965

When my dad convocated from the University of Saskatchewan, I remember him telling my mom that he wanted a graduation gift—and not just socks. We gave him a marble-based penholder; the engraving on the plate: James O. Hurren, B.Ed.

was Scherman's (1973) oversized *The Best of Life*; the black-and-white photos appealing to my sense of aesthetics even then. Under the tent of light provided by a single 60-watt bulb, and sitting on the bare earth, I remember the beauty of the images and the excitement of the forbidden—we weren't supposed to go down into that crawl space; I only did so when my parents weren't home. As an adult, when I see Eisenstaedt's photo of the V-J Day kiss in Times Square, I can almost smell the earthy dampness of that underground hideaway...

. . .

When I decided to go into the teaching profession, I wouldn't say I was exactly *running* to teaching; it was more like a sauntering over. During my twelfth grade, my dad would ask at almost every evening meal: *So...what do you think you will do next year?*

I didn't know what I wanted to do, but I *did* know what I *didn't* want to do. I didn't want to go to school. My parents were adamant that we further our education after high school. Throughout my high-school years I was a school-yearbook photographer and I thought it would be fun to be a photographer. But I didn't think that would be enough—I'd probably have to do more than that to make a living.

I guess you could say I followed my grandmother and my dad and became a teacher. Also following my dad (and my grandmother), I fell in love with someone who lived in the town where my dad had taught school for many years, and where he met and fell in love with my mom. I saw teaching as a profession that would fit in with my plans to marry the man I loved and settle down together. I could teach and he would farm on land near the same small town where I grew up...

. . .

Wanda Hurren, First Day of School, September 1963

I spent the first week of my first grade at home, sick in bed. Remembering back, my mom says it seemed as though I didn't really want to go to school. She thought I was pretending to be sick and after a week of that I was sent off to school. It seems that my running from schooling began even before I started school...

While he was teaching school, my dad began to farm on a very small scale. He owned some land about 10 miles from town and started gathering an assortment of farm equipment, all used and most in need of repair. His summer holidays and every long weekend throughout the spring and fall were devoted to farming. We always referred to school and the farm as places to *run* to—my mom would ask us to *run up to the school* to give something to my dad, or she would gather us up in the car and we would *run out to the farm* to bring my dad a warm supper wrapped in the scratchy car blanket. From spring thaw to late November, we hardly saw my dad outside of school hours. After school he would *race* home, change his clothes and head out to the farm, returning in the early evening, often to quickly change clothes again and *run up* to the school to attend to details there, later taking a shortcut to walk home in the darkness…

. . .

During the time that I was studying to become a teacher, my dad became seriously ill. He had to stop teaching and quit farming. He spent his last years at home, on extended sick leave. When I visited I sometimes tried to talk with him about teaching strategies or issues, but he didn't seem that interested. I remember once asking him if he wanted to read a paper I was working on. He laughed and said *No*. Shortly after that he was diagnosed as legally blind, and he sold the farm…

. . .

As a "teacher in training," I completed my long-term practicum in a Grade 7/8 classroom. I remember counting the days left to complete; I did not enjoy the experience of *practice* teaching. I was just hoping I would like the *real* thing. One day in mid-March as we prepared for the Easter season (in a Christian separate school), I was working with students to create Ukrainian decorated eggs. This required heating wax on a stylus with candles. Towards the end of the class time, melting wax along with some of the flames ran down onto the newspaper that was covering the art table. Fire!

Almost before I knew what was happening, one of the boys jumped up on the table to stamp out the fire. It was 1979, and he was wearing fringed blue jeans. The fine cotton fringes caught fire and soon his pant legs were in flames. I pulled him down off the table and somehow put the fire out, without having to remove his pants. Each time I walked into the staff room that day (and for several weeks following), the principal whistled, sort of under his breath, to the tune of *There'll be a hot time in the old school tonight*. Later that afternoon, I remember thinking as I walked home along snow-packed sidewalks, that this could be a story to share with my dad; perhaps he might take some enjoyment from it.

I had only been home about five minutes when the phone rang. It was my mom, calling to tell me that my dad had passed away that afternoon. I forgot all about the story I was saving to tell him...

. . .

After his funeral, my grandmother told me a farming story about my dad. One night in early fall, just after my younger sister was born, my mom was worried because it was almost midnight and my dad hadn't yet returned from the farm. She was home with two toddlers and a newborn baby, so she telephoned to wake up my grandparents. My grandfather got dressed and drove out to the farm to check on my dad. It was a warm evening and there was a full moon. When my grandfather drove into the farmyard he caught sight of my dad in the moonlight, working on the combine that had broken down. As he switched off his vehicle motor, through his open window he could hear my dad whistling away, oblivious to the rest of the world...

. . .

After his funeral, a colleague of my dad's told me a teaching story about my dad. She remembered how on every March 15, my dad, always the English/history teacher, would issue the infamous warning in the staffroom, *Beware the Ides of March*. She said that some years, as the school principal, he would even broadcast this warning to the whole school over the intercom system.

His colleague pointed out the double tragedy of my dad's early passing: he was just fifty-two when he died—on the Ides of March...

. . .

I got married. My husband farmed, and I taught school, and for the most part I loved everything about that arrangement. Mine was the double delight of the smell of books in the fall and wet earth in the spring...

. . .

After he died, I remember several relatives commenting that my dad might have chosen farming instead of teaching if he had had the financial resources.

My mom thinks that his parents tried to convince him not to farm, because as a teenager he had been involved in a serious farming accident, almost losing his life when he was helping his dad. They were concerned for his health and safety. By the time he started teaching, my dad had already purchased land, but it was very rocky soil and difficult to farm. My mom says my dad continued to farm even though the land and his equipment were not that good because farming gave him the chance to get away from teaching...

· · ·

    I taught school for 12 years and then I left teaching, not really wanting to teach again. But, I enrolled in graduate school, loved it, and completed a master's degree and directly after that, a PhD. Throughout the years, as a teacher, and then as a teacher educator, I found ways to incorporate an attention to aesthetics in my work, whether through text or image. Photography plays an important role in my teaching and research. I have worked in the darkroom for just over eight years now, sometimes finding space in my home, other times working in studios. However, over the course of those same eight years I became increas-

Wanda Hurren, Photographer

Ever since Grade 9, when I was a photographer for the school yearbook, photography has been an important part of my life. The aesthetic of the everyday world is what I hope to communicate through many of my photographs. I also enjoy juxtaposing images that in some way thwart our desires for perfection, yet still remind us of the aesthetic of everydayness. And...I love wearing a white lab coat and working under safe lights to mix chemicals in graduated cylinders, adjust enlarger lenses, filters, and timers... a fabulous combination of science and art! (Martin Batchelor Gallery, Artist's Statement)

ingly preoccupied with concerns about my choice of profession—maybe I was doing the wrong thing; maybe I wasn't doing what I was truly meant to do; maybe because I wasn't truly "called to teach," it was a career that really wasn't for me. Maybe I better hurry up and switch to a career that *was* really meant for me. Before time ran out.

As my 52nd year approached, this worry was stronger than ever, and it seemed I was constantly running ideas around in my mind—should I continue to teach? Should I leave the teaching profession and do something else? But what else would I do? I think for several years I had been writing my dad's story as one of missed opportunities, unrequited choices. And I wanted to make sure that wasn't my story too. In retrospect, it seems that my 52nd year was a good teaching year, and not a good teaching year. It was somehow pivotal. That year I received my highest-ever teaching scores in the first term, and my lowest-ever teaching scores in the second term...

. . .

This past June I turned 53-years old. With my 52nd year behind me, it almost seems that over the summer term I breathed a long sigh of relief. For some reason I have renewed energy and appreciation for teaching. I recently ran into a friend who asked how my work was going, and I said I was just loving it. He said, "But you weren't really liking it a while back. What happened?" I could only smile and answer, "I don't know."

I am still living in a space between running to and running from teaching. Maybe I will always be in that space. It's actually not a bad space. There's lots of room in it; thankfully, plenty enough to kneel and kiss the ground...

REFERENCES

Pinar, W. F., & Grumet, M. (1976). *Toward a poor curriculum*. Dubuque, IA: Kendall/Hunt.

Rumi, J. (1995). Spring giddiness. In C. Barks, with J. Moyne (Trans.), *The essential Rumi* (p. 36). New York, NY: HarperCollins.

Scherman, D. (Ed.). (1973). *The best of life*. New York, NY: Time-Life Books.

The Gravity Garden

Rebecca Luce-Kapler

Winter

I packed the plastic IGA grocery bag in my carry-on luggage, unwilling to take a chance with my checked suitcase. My father's prized gladioli bulbs, the ones he dug up last fall, and carefully prepared for spring planting, were in that bag. The yellow corns with their dried parchment casings crackling into dust told me so much about that last season: the farmer optimism of my father finally disintegrating as continuance and death were held together by the thinnest of membranes.

Gladiolus: named for the small Roman sword and symbol for strength of character. How fitting for a man who valued ethical behaviour above all else and who drew wisdom from his wonder of the natural world. He had a remarkable sense that difficulties would come, but they would also go as life unfolded. When a hailstorm devastated part of his crop, he collected baseball-sized hailstones to store in the freezer for Environment Canada's study. When dairy regulations and

1960s Garden of Glads and Dahlias

quotas forced him to stop selling the cream from his small herd of Jerseys, he raised pigs, building one of the most progressive barns at the time. Perhaps that is why he could sustain a farming career for over fifty years.

Even when my mother was diagnosed with cancer, he insisted that we would get through this and that our family would once again prevail. All my life his pronouncements had come to fruition and so, ignoring my fearful dreams that suggested otherwise, I let myself believe this would be true.

But my mother's disease was terminal.

My first night back in Alberta after her death, I rose early in the November darkness to sit in the living room hoping for some whispers of my mother's presence. My father must have been listening too because he silently joined me. I slipped my arm about him and we gazed out across the yard to the fields that were defined in the first light.

As the edge of the winter sun appeared, Dad spoke at last. "It makes you think there has to be something, some power, doesn't it? How else could the sun come up every morning?" His tone was tentative as he searched for his familiar sense of wonder and the divine, those strengths that fed his optimism. But it was a faint attempt.

The light brightened the branches of the sugar maple that he had found during one of their visits to our home in Ontario. He had been determined to bring a real maple tree back, and I had finally located a friend of a friend who had saplings in the meadow by her house. Five years later, he had managed to save one of those trees from marauding white-tailed deer.

The garden that stretched beyond the maple was not yet covered in snow but had browned after two weeks of cold weather. The frost outlined its strong bones: rose bushes protected with straw, the collapsed corn stalks, the composting pile of pea vines. The pond Dad had built to solve a perpetually soggy section of the garden had a skiff of ice, and the muddy edge had frozen into the St. Bernard's footprints.

Once he had stopped farming, Dad spent May to September working in his garden with its adjoining pond and orchard. Every time I visited, he took me on a tour of his projects, pointing out new plants, offering samples of small apples, or identifying the goldfish that had escaped the heron. It was his way of having time alone with me and sharing what was important to him. For me, this was far different from the father who had been so busy farming during my years growing up that we barely spoke, and the times when we did were usually stubborn arguments about our always conflicting world views. Things had changed between us in the years since, as I had matured and he had softened his imperatives. This was the father who could reassure me that this loss was survivable, and yet it was he, less than two months after my mother's death, who succumbed to his sad heart, and I was called back to Alberta.

In that last trip, beside the bulbs in my carry-on bag was a photograph of my mother at twenty-six, crouched on the grass in our yard, holding two gladioli spikes. I had forgotten how beautiful she was as a young woman, smiling with her cherry-red lipstick. Her sleeveless pink dress, crisply edged in white piping, offset the cream-coloured and burgundy spikes, each with twelve full blossoms. That was probably the first year my father won a prize at the fair for his flowers. Beauty always softened him; you could see the shine in his eyes wherever he found it.

The bulbs and the photograph felt like threads I could hang onto. The family narratives that had anchored me had disappeared with my parents, leaving a schism between my old life and my new reality. I returned to Ontario in a January freeze, put the bulbs in my cold room, and went back to work, moving back to the structures of expectation that were familiar.

And yet they were not familiar. Absent were my quickness of thought, my energy for teaching, and my intellectual engagement. Early mornings I looked out at the frozen lake and wrote in my journal searching for some break, something I recognized as myself, a line of story to move forward.

Finally, one morning early in March, as the sun pinked the lake, the pen dropped from my hand, and the journal slid to the floor. I rolled into a ball as a scream gathered deep within. I let it come, my whole body wailing sorrow, echoing from the high ceiling. I became sound smashing through the window and out over the frozen lake until breathless in the cold air. A crack opened.

Spring

As March drew to a close, I wrote in my journal about my surprise at grief: "This is not a linear process nor does it suddenly disappear. It deepens and returns, sometimes its claws are sharper and pierce more deeply; the possibility always there as it skims along the surface of skin, ready to plunge the depths into our heart." There was no sense of getting over anything; rather, it was a process of understanding what had happened, sorting out what it might mean, choosing how to go forward as someone who had changed.

I bought two different Japanese maples to plant in memory of my parents, mixing some of their ashes in the roots. If one passes a young child through the branches of a maple tree, it is believed, the child will have good health and longevity of life. So the trees—maple, bone, and ash—were a kind of blessing, a hope for the health and long life of my parents' descendents. Their planting marked the edge of a garden I had been dreaming about.

In April, because I found myself unable to read much and wrote even less, sketching plans for the garden kept me from despair. I decided on where to plant the gladioli, and how to place flagstones for pathways. The garden would hold some of my father's pottery wind chimes alongside Kevin's glass sculpture. By working in Dad's media—earth and plants—I would try to learn what this grief meant, gather up the threads of our story.

All that season, I began to remember isolated narratives that took root. Like the story of the spring where we had an unexpected blizzard, and Dad came in the house, cradling a baby snowy owl. It had fallen out of its nest and before he restored it to its home, he wanted to warm the tiny bird. "Look," he told us, holding out his gloved hands, "look at how his head turns and how soft and white he is. The owls have been troubled by the weather."

Farmers read the signs; they know by the colour and the height of the clouds whether to worry about a storm; they attend to the thickness of the fox's coat in the fall to predict the severity of weather; they watch the deepening gold of the grain to determine the harvest. My father read the moon, the sky, the wind, the animals—even away from the farm. Like at my great-aunt Hilda's funeral. Because my mother was officiating at that funeral, Dad chose to sit at the back of the church, separate from the congregation. As Mom started the service, he glanced up to the skylight to see a pigeon sitting at the edge looking in. "It sat and watched the entire time," he said, "and when your mother gave the final prayer, it flew away. It makes you wonder, doesn't it?"

As late April nudged the trees to early green, I planted the maples and the ashes, but made little headway on the rest of the garden. I was amazed at how grieving spent me physically. One morning, a red house finch madly fluttered at the window, his wings suspending him at the window as he pecked the glass. Then he flew to a nearby branch chirping loudly. A few minutes later, he was back, tapping. I was puzzled by the bird's persistence in the face of obvious futility. Yet he returned several times that morning and the next day and the day after. All right, I thought, it is a sign, a message. The garden needs to begin. After that, the finch did not return to my window.

Summer

The garden began to take shape. Evenings after work, I dug up wheelbarrows of sod, shaping the beds and ordering garden soil. The physical work was satisfying because it taxed my body in creative labour. Those days I felt more at peace and was not haunted at every moment. Yet even in those times of respite, I felt an edge of worry. If I lost the sharpness of grief, it felt like the hold I had on my connection to my parents would slip further away. But it could also come back in an instant. When they mowed the ditches along our road, the smell of new cutting took me to Alberta Julys with my nose against my dad's grey denim workshirt with its sweetness of clover and its choke of dust. My father felt so present as I was overcome with longing.

The last few years when I visited the farm, I usually drove from the Edmonton airport, taking the familiar back-country shortcut past the horse and cattle farms and the fields of brilliant yellow canola. I remember thinking that the time would come when I would stop driving this route, but I am not sure I really believed that. Like the slow and meandering drives our father took us on during the Sunday afternoons of our childhood, it felt like it would go on forever. The last time I had taken a drive with Dad, we went west into the hills past the farm so he could check out neighbours' fields against his own standards of farming. He drove and pointed out landmarks that now existed only in his memory, every road of the county mapping some of his history.

I bought three roses to plant with the gladioli—roses were not my first choice of perennial, but my father had persisted in growing them the last few years. They seemed hard to grow on the prairies. Winters are too long and cold; the summers dry with wind. The story that roses bring—their secrets of confession, their moments of undying love—are not so obvious in a place where my parents' generation remembered the hard times of bare survival when feelings were kept close to the chest. But roses should grow more easily in warm and humid Ontario. And if not, my caring for them and learning about their growing would follow the processes of my father in his careful attention to where they were planted and how they grew.

The day that I planted rose bushes, we learned we were to be grandparents come spring. I brushed my hands through the new maples, imaging the baby among the leaves, blessed with an abundance of years. All life is tapped from a stream of energy, my mother told me. In birth we are dowsed like a well; in death it is to that stream we all return. Still I could not imagine losing the shape of time and narrative as the world trundled onward, our moments kept only by those who still remember.

That afternoon, I went to the greenhouse and bought an hibiscus—a flower of celebration—and planted it opposite the rose bushes. It, too, would need the tender care in the Canadian winter, but come next summer, it would spread its red blossoms wide with the joy of the birth.

Autumn

The foliage paused as the transition into another season neared. The fall light changed colour—becoming more golden as it filtered through the trees and picked up tints from the leaves. Most mornings the fog crept up the granite cliff and hid the view of the lake until the sun burned through.

I snipped the last of the dahlias in my new garden—a flower my father had grown years ago outside our old house. Somewhere in the transition between houses and landscaping, his tubers disappeared. I chose them for my garden not to replace what was lost but because I read how the Aztecs honoured them as flowers of healing. Next to the soft hue of the roses, the dahlias splashed bright colour: golden and red, tawny shades, and pinks. Their dense heads were sturdy and cheerful.

I found myself turning outward, no longer afraid to examine my thoughts through journaling in the misty mornings. But while my life started to feel familiar, the everyday things continued to undo me. I would weep in a grocery store aisle at the sight of the canned French beans my mother favoured; I would feel overcome plucking gladioli from the earth, storing them like my father. It was those day-to-day rituals where my parents had taught me to shape living where grief still came close to the surface.

As a child, fall had been my favourite season. There were new clothes for school and different teachers. September was the threshold of possibilities. But it was also a time of completion. My father would finish his combining, augering the barley and oats into granaries. My mother would can the last of the raspberries. And one weekend in September, my aunt and her family would arrive so that we could "do up" the chickens for the freezer. Beginnings and endings enfolded in a rhythm of change and continuance.

In this first autumn, as I watched the beauty of my new garden deepen into dying, I already thought about extending the border to create a collection of blue-flowering plants—my parents' favourite colour. I made a list in my journal: sea holly, baptisia, asters, and delphinium. Of the list, only delphinium had been in the Alberta garden, flourishing in the dry heat and cool nights. If your summers are long and hot, the gardening book cautioned, you may only get one season of bloom rather than lush, flower-heavy clumps. Nevertheless, I would try. I would even try planting a turquoise Himalayan blue poppy, which the book warned was a daunting challenge to grow.

This garden was acknowledging the swiftness of life but also the importance of the well lived moment. Working among the flowers, digging up weeds, and tending the soil, I felt more attuned to the rhythm of life and the inevitability of death. In Western society, we seldom speak of dying and shroud it in fearful secrecy. But the grief that accompanies death also brings gifts of understanding. It deepens our attachment to the life we still have and brightens our attention to those people and things we care for. This garden has been my learning ground; the place where I have come to know those gifts of grieving—beauty, growth, and dying—all in a season.

Interim Report to Harold: July*

Heat and rain, the maple
Growing, a surprise.
The lime green tenders
Of a life emerging, little joy

Coddled in large hands.
The new saplings slipped
Into moist loam now drink the color
Of your bones, roots firmly down.

The flutter of leaves
Wave the flag, the heart
Of absence, lonely. Prairie
And Shield we spread your legacy.

In the trees you are still here
Still a wonder of breath. The roses

Bloom, the glads spike, dahlias flower
The offspring of your garden ever coming.

*Inspired by Eiléan Ní Chuilleánain, *The Sun-Fish*

REFERENCE

Ní Chuilleánain, E. (2009). Interim report to Paul: November. In *The Sun-Fish* (p. 32). Loughcrew, Ireland: The Gallery Press.

Imagining Mothers

Re-Joyce[1]

Bruce Hunter

W hen my friend, artist and poet, Marlene Lacey asked me if I would write an introduction to a website where authors and artists celebrate their mothers, I agreed. Not because I would write a rosy tribute on the eve of Mother's Day, but because of our intensely honest conversations about our sometimes-difficult mothers. Though, I hesitated before I agreed.

Why? Partly because my mother, Joyce Hunter, is nearly ten years gone, and the anniversary of her death on 12 June 2001 marks one of the darkest and most difficult periods of my life. While she was alive, there were times when I struggled to live with her. Once she was gone, living without her powerful presence and balancing both good and difficult memories took me on a journey downward before it led upward. And ironically, the journey paralleled some of the spirals of her own life.

Not because of the "difficult," either my own, or hers, did I hesitate to write. As a writer, I peer into the abyss because it often reveals dark and beautiful truths. And I must confess, I really don't know any other way. I am sure, too, that my mother and Marlene's were as baffled by us, these spastic things that came from them and morphed into shapes unrecognizable from the frail babies they birthed. I hesitate also because I think there is no more difficult person to be and to clearly see than that behind the moniker of Mother, Mom, Mater, Madre, Ima, Mutti, or Maman, in whichever language. Literature is full of powerful writing attempting to come to terms with this person. And I am mindful and humbled reading other writers; as poet Mary di Michele (1983) says, "there's sky above my sky"—to me, a line of humility, recognizing there is greatness above, sheltering and yet inspiring, yet cautionary or even oppressive, if we let it be.

In the sky above my sky, Wallace Stegner (2000) remains luminous, in his wonderful "Letter, Much Too Late," from *When the Bluebird Sings at Lemonade Springs*. As an 80-year-old man on the eve of his own death, he takes stock of his mother, who she was and what she left him, 55 years after her death. It is an essay that is honest in its attempt to reconcile her as both her own woman and his mother. Stegner does not flinch from either the difficulty nor from the joy of their relationship, as he tells her last words, "You're a good…boy…Wallace." Her very last word was his name, but he also says, throughout his life he was anything but a good boy, and in dying she laid on him one last obligation.

I do not remember my mother's last words to me, though I remember many others she said over the years, in jest, in spite and in love. And I understood, as the eldest child, that unspoken obligation to be good. For a long time I tried to be, and my mother's death released me from that unwanted contract when I realized, I wanted just to be.

And funny though how their cruel words stay with us longest. Witness Alice Munro, a woman of the same generation as my mother. The title of Munro's (1978) book, *Who Do You Think You Are?* is as good a family "script," as psychologists say, of a mother's acid rebuke to a daughter, or a son. Once my mother turned to me as I effused at a family barbeque, happy to be back home and amongst my family.

"Did anyone ever tell you, you talk too much?"

"Many have tried, Mom. Few have succeeded," I laughed.

I recognized it for what it was, remembering Munro's words came from her mother. I thought Mom was jealous of the attention I was getting as a big brother coming home, for she loved attention. Although I turned to her and laughed, I was stung. Do I talk too much? Not surprisingly, my research shows the deaf want not so much to hear as to be heard. It's true. I probably do talk too much. I also probably eat too much, write, read, and love too much and the same could be said of her.

When the guests were gone, I asked, "Mom, why did you say that? That really hurt."

She looked truly lost for a moment.

"I don't know." She looked at her hands clasped on the table. "Maybe because that's what my mother said to me."

Someday I may write a book, *Did Anyone Ever Tell You, You Talk Too Much?* Only now do the kind words return to memory. My friend Marlene reminded me of my mother's words, which I prefer now to remember as her last. I called home to Calgary every Sunday night for the last ten-or-so years of my mother's life. Each conversation started with what we'd had for supper. For my mother, a child of the Depression and of the war-rations years, loved to cook and loved to eat. She'd tell of the blocks of fresh butter that came down from her grandparent's farm at Olds and how the brown waxed paper opened on her mother's kitchen table revealed golden treasure. And she reminded me once of how I ended each conversation.

"You always tell me you love me before I say goodbye." The script was changing. My old friend Charlie Connacher, who worked on the cracking towers and tank farms of the Imperial Oil Refinery in Calgary, a dangerous job, used to say he always told his wife, Lil, each morning before he went off to work, he loved her. "If anything ever happened to me, I want those to be the last words she'd hear."

My last words to my mother as she lay in a hospital bed 2000 miles away—I knew she would die before I could get there—were, "Mom, I love you very much, and my novel is an homage to you." I knew she was already gone to wherever they go when they leave us. She died 2 days later. It would be our last phone call, but I didn't know it at the time. I heeded Charlie's advice ever since I heard it.

Like Stegner, who admits he will leave the world more bewildered, despite his articulate stock-taking, and how he has failed to completely understand his mother, I am more uncertain now, than I ever was, of who she was—which may not be a bad thing. Despite our talks over the dining room table, which for years held her ashtray and an oversized teapot—for ours was a large family. And despite our lively fights, and arguments, and then the long periods of silence, sometimes for years, I too am bewildered. There were times I loathed her, so confused and angered I was.

Despite reconnecting through a letter, or a telephone call, and despite a novel, drafts of which I passed across that table and of which she exclaimed, "That's not what happened!"

"No, Mom, it's how I tried to imagine it happened, or might have." But I listened as she told me her story and when I returned home, I grafted her words onto mine, trying somewhere between her words and mine to find her. But not before I teased her, "You need to write your own damn book."

She never did. What's left now, a product of our shared life is my novel about a deaf son and four daughters raised by a depressed but brilliant mother. It is finished, for now, anyway. But her story is not. I often wonder about it. She loved literature, her Bible, and her own stories and puns were part of our family lore. Magic and wonder were part of those stories as much as menace and the sentimental Scottish humour of her grandmother. My mother's name was Joyce, and in a particularly religious period of her life, she signed her cards and letters, "Re-Joyce!!"

The hard numbers I know: How she dropped out of Grade 9 with the highest marks in language and literature in the province of Alberta. And how I was not the first child as I thought. There was another born before me, my brother David, put up for adoption, who was reunited with her, 4 years before her death. There were ten pregnancies, two still births and eight children total. "All of you were conceived in love," she told me once.

In my somewhat autobiographical novel, two Scottish immigrant families band together to help a young mother raise a deaf son. I am that son and my story, perhaps more so than most, is intertwined with my mother's, who was my first teacher, my translator, my protector, who took up scraps of what I could hear, for the deaf are never usually totally deaf, and from them helped me fashion a language of my own. In my novel, I try to imagine her life. She was my first advocate, telling the school nurse after my hearing was tested and after being advised that I should go to a shelter or a workshop for deaf children, "No, I want my son to be with his friends, his brothers and sisters." My mother helped me to hear and taught me to read, and today I am an English professor and a writer, against great odds. Many who are deaf are not literate in either the written or spoken word.

I look at her life now, or perhaps I should say *lives*, both the one I imagine and what little of the one I know. I shudder to think of the weight under which she lived, and often with considerable joy, I'll add. Only late in life did I learn, after teasing her that despite a long relationship with a Chinese man, she still could not use chopsticks. A brain injury after a fall from a bicycle as a child meant she could neither use chopsticks nor drive a car. And at least once she attempted suicide. She also had bipolar disorder (*manic depressive tendencies*).

What do those words mean? To her, I have no idea, nor of the heavens and hells she entered and inhabited. But I remember my mother dropped out of high school, not to have me, as she liked to say. Her mother, Ruby, said she wanted to party. Always there were two stories totally opposite to each other in nearly everything my mother did. And the truth of one didn't rule out the other. It would take nearly thirty years for someone to diagnose her condition. I'm not surprised.

That happened nearly fifteen years before she died, when I returned home for a visit. My mother was attending university then and living in my brother's basement suite. Tired from the Toronto flight, I fell into bed that night, in the spare room in my mother's apartment. About an hour later, the bedroom door opened. Haloed in light, my mother stood at the foot of the bed, with her auburn hair streaked with grey tumbling half-way down her back. Clad in a diaphanous blue nightgown, she began laying cards across the foot of my bed, one by one in a dream-like playing of a poker hand. I had woken from dream into a scene from the *Rime of the Ancient Mariner.*

"What are you doing?" I shouted, startled by the light and her appearance. I was frightened by the intensity of her focus on the laying of cards, and the spectre-woman in the door way, with her hair shrouding her face and shoulders, her voice almost a growl, and her eyes never once looked at mine.

"I want you to have these." It was not a wish, but a command. I sat up.

They were not cards. They were photographs of people I did not recognize. Strangers my mother and father had met on the only holiday they ever took, to Las Vegas in 1956. I went upstairs and learned from my brother, she had been awake for 3 days and had not eaten in 2 days. That night I slept on my brother's couch upstairs. I was terrified. I knew those moods, or episodes, were equally unpredictably benign as well as violent and self-destructive. I'd seen both for nearly thirty years. Once she'd wandered northwest Calgary in sub-zero weather because she forgot the key to her apartment. Confused and frightened, it never occurred to her to call anyone.

Once, in rage, she began pummeling my 13-year-old sister, who now has a brown belt in karate. I'm sure that's partly why. Moments of rage were followed by moments of euphoria and fantasies so real we all had rooms in them and others moved in with us too. My mother was an articulate and attractive woman who could make anything seem plausible. How she'd rented a large house with the welfare money, and convinced a music store to let her have an organ so she could start a dance studio. She'd only recently started taking interpretive dance, and as a young girl, my mother and her sister were an act, the "Wood Sisters," who tap-danced between shows at the Grand Theatre, but that was long ago.

She brought home a stranger, with his "Brylcreemed" pompadour and cowboy boots. The man looked like the pictures of Johnny Cash that adorned the insides of her kitchen cupboards. He would help with the dance studio, she said. And this was just one week in our house—the week I finally left.

But that night on my brother's couch I didn't sleep. I wondered what I could do for her, remembering how she had once stood up for me. But what? She had been in and out of hospitals all her life. I remembered one grim-faced meeting with my younger brothers and sisters, being told by a hospital director of psychiatry that we were the problem, and for a long time we believed it. My little brothers and sisters, with their white-blond hair and pink cheeks, squirmed as the doctor spoke. They were just babies.

The next morning we took Mom back to that same hospital and I waited with her as a young psychiatrist assessed her. He could have been my Doppelgänger with his beard, glasses, and Oxford-cloth shirt, and my mother, anyone's mother, smart and charming. I was nervous. Her ability to talk her way out of trouble was extraordinary and once after a manic episode and the inevitable crash, she ended up at this same hospital, in her mind not as a patient. As she told me over the phone, she was ministering to the needs of her fellow patients on the psych ward, for she was now studying theology. And she could talk her way into trouble too. As a student intern in the United Church, she stood up to give her first sermon in a posh upper-class pulpit. Seized by understandable panic, neither my mother nor the good parishioners were prepared for what followed as she began to babble in tongues like a "holy roller." If only she'd given that sermon at South Hill Baptist, she would have probably stood a chance. She was dismissed from the ministry after that. Always, there were two opposite stories that never seemed to reconcile.

When the young psychiatrist asked her, Mom gave not only her birth date, but that of her children, first in order of their birth, and then in reverse order and then of her grandchildren. I was dazzled by her memory, her precision and also how, ultimately, it went nowhere. I remembered helping her with a research paper and she couldn't understand why it was wrong to have the bibliography smack in the middle. To her that seemed logical. Quietly, the doctor concurred that she needed treatment.

Finally, I thought, help was near. Soon we were joined by the head of psychiatry, who took the clipboard, quickly flipped through it and patted my mother on the head and said, "You'll be fine. We'll be sending you home, dear."

I couldn't believe what I was hearing.

"I'm her son," I stepped forward. "If you release her, you will have a complaint on your hands."

He stared.

"I know the issues. She's not going to kill herself, or anyone else, but she cannot feed or provide for herself."

"She is in the care of an MD and they've some training in psychiatry." He dismissed my comments.

"I'm an English professor, and the operative word in that sentence is *some*, as in *not* enough. As in, she is wandering the streets with a hundred pills in her purse. Who's in charge of her care?"

He tried a different tack. "I'm sorry but there have been funding cuts in Alberta and we do not have the room."

"I have friends who are psychiatrists and others who are MDs, I'm well aware of the cutbacks. But that's not the issue. Who is going to be responsible for my mother's care?"

"I'm sorry…" he started to say, now mildly annoyed.

"I'm sure you know what malpractice is. I do." He now faced me directly.

"How far back do your records go?" I pointed to the clipboard.

"1980," he responded. The young psychiatrist, whose diagnosis had just been overruled, watched without saying anything.

It took every bit of conviction and courage I'd learned in all my years of work, and standing up for myself, to stand up to this man. I could feel my knees starting to shake, but I wasn't going to let my mother go without help.

"She has been in and out of this hospital for 20 years and if you have made your diagnosis on the basis of incomplete information, we both know what that is and I'm prepared to take this to the Alberta Medical Review Board. I want you to go back in that office and find her a bed and the name of a psychiatrist who will be responsible for her care."

He returned to his office and returned 5 minutes later. "I can't find her a bed, but I do have a psychiatrist who can see her and we are prepared to accept her as an out-patient."

"Thank you." My lower lips quivered. "That's all I ask." The young psychiatrist said nothing but shook my hand as we left.

My mother did see a psychiatrist and was assigned a wonderful psychiatric nurse who saw that the care she received was instrumental in improving her life. With medication, she was able to gain control over the episodes that took her in the slow spirals through heaven and back down through hell. For the first time since I was a child, we could talk. Before that, conversing with her was often like speaking into a human blender. My words came back at me, skewed and shredded. Now she could listen, unafraid of losing her balance on the spiral staircase linking heaven and hell. Now we could talk. When I was a boy, her grandmother, my Scottish great-grandmother, always gave us back the gifts we gave her at other Christmases and other birthdays.

What to do on Mother's Day? It's a day of painful ambiguity for some of us, like Christmas, like family holidays. For years after she died, I found myself wishing for her voice and reaching for the phone on Sunday evenings. But I think in the tradition of my family, I gave her back—or tried to anyway—the gifts she gave me, long before she died.

I sometimes felt guilty because the medication did level her moods. While I missed the manic creativity and the grand dreams, I did not miss her acid remarks or her out-of-control episodes. And as time passes, when I can separate her from her illness, I miss her greatly, the woman who went to Mexico to help build a school. The one who made us meals in her aluminum roaster, the bottom full of Chicken Paprikash, a rich Hungarian dish, a kind of chicken stroganoff made with sour cream and noodles, a recipe she learned from a neighbour. The aluminum lid full of bread pudding, feeding all nine of us, in one pot with recipes measured out in pinches and handfuls that come back to me now as I cook. A real miracle as grand as the fishes and loaves of our Sunday-school lessons. And yes, even her puns and the laughter and groans that followed telling a real stinker. She's right. Maybe it's time now to Re-Joyce.

ENDNOTE

1   Originally published 07 May 2004 and revised for this publication.

REFERENCES

Di Michele, M. (1983). *Necessary sugar: Poems*. Ottawa, Canada: Oberon Press.

Hunter, B. (2004). Foreword: Imagining mothers—Re-Joyce. Reprinted from M. Lacey (Ed.), *Honouring mothers* [on-line serial] (pp. vii-xv). Available email: publisher@bluegrama.ca.

Munro, A. (1978). *Who do you think you are?* Toronto, Canada: Macmillan.

Stegner, W. (2000). Letter, much too late. In *Where the bluebird sings to the Lemonade Springs: Living and writing in the West* (pp. 22–33). New York, NY: Random House.

Yarnnotes From a Wild Woman
Who Loves to Knit

Celeste Snowber

K nitting woos me. The steady pace of a colourful hue loops over my fingers, and the repetition of stitches dances me to stillness. No fancy patterns for me, I just want colours as variegated as paint tubes draping the shelves of the art store. When I was dating on-line I described myself in my profile as a "wild woman who loves to knit"—the juxtapositions are what always express the heart of my life. At present I am knitting a longer-term project, more satisfying and colourful than

dating-on-line. It is an oversized scarf that will be fifty-or-sixty feet long and is being knitted out of scraps to be eventually utilized in a dance/voice performance piece. The scraps consist of remnants of wool that a knitter no longer uses. It also includes a multiplicity of pieces of material, cords, or fibres from friends, colleagues, or family. There are shoelaces from friends, ribbons from boxes, lace from my Irish grandmother whom I never met, a piece from a knitted doll dress my Armenian mother made when I was a child, yarn from my children's blankets I knitted when they were young, a piece of an Austrian shirt given to me by my uncle Carney, an old towel of my partner's mother, and red yarn used as telltales from my friend Jana's boat to show which way the wind is over the sail. There is, of course, loads of yarn from the leftovers of all the beautiful sweaters, socks, and hats my friends, family and colleagues have made for others.

The leftovers are a repetition of love, material utilized from other material that was crafted, given and lived with care. The list is long, and they have become *yarnnotes*, as footnotes from the cherished people in my life. The scarf has now taken on its own existence and has become one gigantic piece of fabric; the yarn, thread, rope, scraps each have a story to tell. Interestingly enough the etymology of the word *remnant* comes from the French *remnant*, which means "to remain" or is traced back to the "end of a piece of drapery." Our stories remain far longer than anything we could imagine. Our endings break us open to our beginnings.

The one rule I gave to myself while knitting this scarf is that I did not have to follow any rules or instructions. I created new rules for this scarf and gave myself permission to integrate each new colour, skein of yarn, fibres, or ripped

material in any foreseeable way, and this would be integral to the aesthetic and its unifying element. I am not repairing knots, imperfections, or fallen stitches, so frayed pieces of material, hanging threads and loose ends erupt from all angles in the cloth. It is a scarf celebrating "the praise of randomness" and it is not going to be neat.

My life has not been neat, and this has an unforeseen kind of beauty. Now in hindsight, I see the exquisite aesthetic of randomness, how the improvisation of the years has enabled multiple imaginative ways of being and living for my children, students and myself. I am being re/knitted into the magic and mystery through honouring the patterns of my own life.

This scarf has many purposes—some I know and some are yet to be told. The project originally started as I was visiting my cousin Laura in Boston, and I was in the mood to knit, and I didn't have anything with me I was working on, so I began something from her scraps of wool. I decided I wanted to knit a very long piece that could include lots of people's scraps and memories. The scarf would be the perfect accessory or prop for a performance piece I was preparing for a

one-woman show, and integral to the one-woman show is the theme of dating-on-line in mid-life.

The piece will hang from laundry lines on stage in-between segments of the performance. I have for commited phenomenal laundry sins over the years, and this time with knitting, I would commit the sin of untidy knitting with boldness. If you need a definition of a laundry sin, here it is.

LAUNDRY SINS

it's the burgundy red
lipstick that sneaks
out of the pocket of my jeans
announces its presence
in my washing machine
and spreads red accents
all over the other clothes
clean they will be, but
anointed with shades of
crimson, strawberry smears

this isn't just a one-time event,
it's in the category of multiples
like orgasms and intelligences
they come in numbers, and
this is just the beginning
of laundry sins

they say teenagers don't do
laundry, but all one has to do
is commit a laundry sin
and the style conscious
take notice and become
initiators of laundry
and I have opened up a
space for kids doing chores
all out of default
and my red lipstick
is still hanging out in
all the places it shouldn't
but even lips have a
hankering for laundry.

Laundry has been a theme over the last 20 years of raising sons, but I have not had the luxury of hanging laundry on a line since the days of my childhood living near the sea and smelling the salt against clothes. The scarf is what I am hanging on lines of laundry, or branches. There, it can reveal its random beauty. At the time of writing this chapter, the scarf is now about forty feet long, just a toddler at 2-years old and is patiently waiting for its debut performance. I thought it was just going to be integrated in performance, but the oversized scarf has literary plans as well, for it is a multi-disciplinary artist. I'm also now hanging it from trees and rocks, integrating its textures in the natural world and letting the natural world inform its process. Site-specific performance is in the works as well for its future. Hybridity is everywhere.

The last few years have been ones of finding, decluttering, and sorting the remnants of objects within my house as well as the remnants within my heart. After many years of single-parenting my three sons, they are now living on their own, sprouting wings as they follow their individual passions. They have become a tribe of artists and are living out creative lives and launching their young adult lives. I am thrilled, but I am experiencing unexpected deep loss, missing their bright voices in our home. I put the house up for sale last week and I am flowing in a sea of emotion, more than I could have ever anticipated. The textures, colours, and shades of my life make more sense as I see the other side of the weaving, and I am initiated into a period of casting off, and it is more than yarn. I have never been good at casting off with anything I have knitted, as I wrote about years ago in my journal.

Casting off

I knit in-between my life
Like all living it happens in incremental steps.
I knit with yarn I have: indigo, turquoise, variegated purple,
blues of all shades.
It's a blanket for my son Micah. I've been knitting it for years, so many I can't
remember. I have to keep making it longer because he grows and I'm slow.
Plus, I forget how to cast off. Actually, I don't really know how to let go,
of yarn, or loved ones for that matter. At best I can let be.
I'm at the end of a cycle—one of those big shifts, after years of processing, letting
go, taking back, contracting and expanding the dreams that are not to be.
I'm also at the end of the cycle of this blanket.
My son is really too old for the blanket,
I've run out of yarn and I need to cast off.
The truth is I love knitting this blanket.

I return to it like an old shoe, an old relationship, and it keeps me warm
when I knit,
it is so long now and I've become attached to its blue-purple hues.
I can't stop thinking that it is a metaphor for my ability to hold on.
To not know, when or how to let go. I am much better at writing
or dancing about letting go
than actually doing it.
In one full sweep, I'll cast off this blanket.
One act. One action. I have woven my love into this blanket and
its finishing is an extension of that love.
Knitting from a skein of love
Casting off out of love.

I am at another stage of letting go, or more accurately, letting be; here I am beckoned to a season of savouring where knitting the long scarf and honouring a life are inextricably connected. Various pieces of cloth and yarn remind and *rebody* the difficult parts of life, whether it is through physical or emotional loss. Through each stitch, slowly over time, I embrace my own limitations and wonder as I enjoy what the cloth is becoming.

The house I have lived in for the last 21 years has been a container for many of these memories that are woven into the scarf. It too is a bearer of the beauty for many years. And beauty can be dissonant, as Rilke (2009) said, "for beauty is nothing but the beginning of terror" (p. 3).

What we hold dear most likely will change, transform into something else, and will eventually inform the fabric of our lives. As the scarf grows, shifts, changes with the textures of diverse material and vibrancy of wild, bold, and earth colours, it develops its own coherent beauty. There is something about the beauty of imperfection that attracts my attention. I've been conditioned in my scholarly and artistic endeavours to ensure that whatever I produce goes through a multitude of edits till it reaches a sense of aesthetic completion. I still adhere to my standards, in many forms, but personal lives do not always work that way. They sway, drop, fall, release to the circumstances, which can seldom be controlled or orchestrated in the fashion we might have wanted. The big events in life are never planned: death of a loved one, meeting the love of your life, illness, or deep transformation. Knitting the scarf is teaching me to bear my own beauty, one that has been woven in-between many stories.

Both the act and art of knitting teaches me to call back what has had deep wonder all along. I am asked to revisit the way I have told, or believed, the stories of my life. It is often the stories we tell ourselves that have more pain than the actual experience. I am daily beckoned to reframe my life through random stitches. I have had a long-standing conversation with a now retired colleague of mine, Stan, about the nature of perfection. His understanding of perfection is that it is perfect, as long as imperfection is understood within it. Perfection holds imperfection. I love this concept and it resonates with *wabi sabi*, which is the Japanese art of finding beauty in imperfection and honouring the natural cycle of birth, growth, decay, and death. It also resonates with the tradition of Amish and Mennonite quilters, who would intentionally leave a mistake within the quilt because no creation could be perfect unless created by the Creator. The Navajo, who are renowned for the beautiful intricate detail in their blankets, intentionally weave a mistake

so it is clear it is made by a person and not by a machine. Mistakes celebrate our humanity.

The creation of this scarf has become a contemplative practice of knitting my way to wonder embedded in the reverence for the imperfect. It is a (w)holy irreverence and I am being formed, *re*formed and *trans*formed through each stitch. It is in movement that I am slowed down enough to still the busyness of my mind. Here I am cracked open to the silent beauties and discoveries of how each turn in life is knitted into meaning. The act of knitting is a spiritual practice for me, just as writing, dancing, walking are mindful acts of connecting to the wild quiet heart. This elongated scarf is teaching me to honour the yarnnotes of beauty in my life and in others. A remnant has a new beginning, and in this swirl of colour I am a wild woman knitting.

Bodypsalm for reknitting a life[1]

You are being reknitted from the inside out
the beauty of the threads within you
are invisible yet are luminescent
to the art of a soulful life.
Honour all the textures of your years
the memories, losses, joys, forgotten secrets
which have shaped your innermost being
each colour, hue, and thread is knitted into your story

and formed the uniqueness of you
In this (w)holy place
there is an aesthetic of randomness
borne through the living place of creation
each child in the universe
is woven into the fabric of the larger story
the story whose name is
rewritten to
the place where we are known
and know.

Embrace your doubts
as you do knots in the fabric.
Caress your losses
as openings to honour the depths.

Reknit your life
to the landscape of cherishing
each fragment you live through
this is the material for sweetness
your bodyspirit made visible
in all the ways you honour
the fibres of the collective
story we knit together
into wonder.

ENDNOTE

1   This poem was previously posted on Celeste Snowber's blog, http://bodypsalms.com/

REFERENCE

Rilke, R. M. (2009). *Duino elegies and the sonnets of Orpheus* (S. Mitchell, Trans. & Ed.). New York, NY: Random House/Vintage International Edition.

Encounters with Cracked and Broken Tongues

Candace P. Lewko

Language: forest with all the roots/audible.
—Hélène Cixous, *Rootprints: Memory and Life Writing*

I arrived in the portal of the twenty-first century as a teacher with a Ukrainian last name. My accent is that of a teacher. I experience, daily, a migration of students coming in and out of the doors of the classroom. Walter Mignolo (1999) writes of "the encounters between people with different approaches to language" (p. 303), and I wonder: What is the significance of these encounters between my students and me? What is spoken? What can be heard? Hélène Cixous (1997) writes that "we hear what language says (to us) inside our own words at the very moment of enunciation" (p. 85). Eva Hoffman (1989) in turn suggests that "nothing fully exists until it is articulated" (p. 29). And so I am an utterance of ethnicity. My exigency for preserving language is one where I am able to return again, to the places in the heart, when at one time I felt exiled in the space between language and non-language. Within the space between language and non-language are storied phrases of another life. These stories are fragmented and dislocate me from the layered landscapes of being a Canadian teacher, and in returning to these landscapes, I begin one narrative in which I cultivate the experience of being in a "foreign" home.

My great-grandmother was one of my first encounters with foreignness. Her world was comprised of another language, Ukrainian, which she spoke in the home she kept. I grew up and became a part of the "language" traces of her past, manifested in food and celebrations and family. My nana opened her world to me through the country of the Ukraine. The experience of being in her language has now become central in my way of seeing, in how I understand the self in another's world, where I juxtapose my lived experiences against my teaching world. I am in the midst of otherness; otherness is immediate to my understanding about the relationship between the foreign and familiar, in relation to home. The relationship between the self and the other is a complex portrait to envisage when foreign languages and ways of living with them become locations that resemble home but are also about living in foreignness.

Narrative: Cultivating Language

He sat in a chair against the wall, knees high on the foot stool below him. He resembled a baby, his toothless grin, lips folding around the dough, passing sustenance to his soul. He stared at the wall, as small utterances of thanks emerged from him, and my great-grandmother bowed, fervently kneading her dough. There was contentment in my great-grandfather's silence.

I often felt at the centre of such familial moments, listening to the reverberating stillness—always an unexpected offering. Great-grandmother Nana spoke to herself, but seldom shared her morning conversations, setting out afternoon plans to meet acquaintances and attend to the must-visits for the day. In truth, Nana was lonely, shutting the doors to every part of her house. The home contained her. She wore her paths amongst it, ambulating in shuffles across the floor, peering down as if remembering in the moment that some task must be done. In that home, those shut doors kept me out of her rooms, except for the shrine-like room that contained the portrait of her Ukrainian wedding. I could barely make out the young bride and the handsome man with dark hair. Time had changed the appearance of the people who now lived in this house.

There were occasions when the sounds of the shutting doors were louder than Nana's silence, although the clamour of her English was equally commanding and abrupt. I turned to every sound she made, hoping that it would continue into a conversation, back and forth, but instead I would think about what I should say or how I could start the conversation. The questions persisted in my mind, waiting for an opening, and as a result, Nana remained distant. When I tried to interrupt her busyness, the possibility of a conversation became even more remote. Her routine was a pattern I could not break; it was entrenched in her everyday practice. I often had sudden urges to cry out in a strident voice that mimicked hers, to command her attention like she did mine, for this was the way she wanted to be understood. Her tone was abrasive yet filled with care and love; still there was something peculiar about the way she ignored me.

Great-grandfather, Papa, was the translator of the household. Many times when I entered this home, he would smile and acknowledge my presence. Papa knew everything. He was a craftsman. At high afternoon, he would disappear into the garage where I often followed, listening for him to guide me. I remember his soft voice; he rarely spoke, and I had to listen carefully. The shuffles and scuffs of his feet are rooted in my memory. He moved with intention, and his willingness to teach me wood crafting and gardening was a testament to his patience.

Papa's skilled hands tended the garden and in my memories food was always plentiful and abundant. The garden he tended was one of raspberries and strawberries and the odd perennial that grew in-between the berries. I witnessed the coming back of the perennials and waited for the exact moment for them to bloom. Such was the nurturing of life in their home, the silent brick house secluded in the surroundings of greenery.

My great-grandmother spoke to the garden in Ukrainian. The words were somewhat of a song and half-chant. She was at times disgusted that some plants had not grown and cursed at the weather that beat down on the fragile leaves as they peered through the earth. She often turned the heads of flowers to the sun redirecting them to the light, as if the engulfing rays were not enough in her corner of the garden. She would scream at the slugs that lived under the vegetable leaves and take my hand to show me where the potato bugs were hiding. Her garden was infested and this meant war! And yet, as quickly as spring showers would end, she was back tending her garden with gentleness, her movements light and fair-footed. And so each year, the garden grew above me, a tower of corn, peas, potatoes, carrots, beets, radishes, lettuce, and cucumbers all in a row. Her language seemed to cajole the vegetables into a growing frenzy, green and luscious. All this was ever-present in my childhood, tending the language I borrowed to begin understanding my own caring and nurturing of the things and people I loved. However harsh and abrupt on the surface, Nana's touch was ultimately delicate and her Ukrainian ways were embodied in her garden.

In my conversations with Nana, we never spoke. When she called on the phone, I would pick it up and hear the silence crackling and clicking—her tongue searching for the words.

"Nana?" I would ask. "Is that you?"

"Candace." My name was not easy for her to say. It had a variation of a pronunciation, like a multi-syllabic name.

I recall how in those moments I became frustrated with her attempts to speak English, how I hid when she called me in for supper, how I pretended not to know that she was calling me, for the way she said my name embarrassed me. I would speak over her English and correct her. Her English did not sound harmonious like the sound of her Ukrainian. Her English was broken and cracked, much like the left-over vegetables from her garden preserved in the jars in the cellar for winter. Her English remained dormant.

In Nana's imperfect English, she tried to close the silence between her language and this new foreign tongue. And just as I observed her tending her garden, now I tend my own versions of gardens—the at-times-incoherent languages of my students that circulate around the class. I have learned that to be in their languages is to know that I am with them in their own struggles to learn English. I allow myself to fall in these fractures of understanding where I am brought into translation; the meaning of the language my students use, "the English," is much like the broken, spoken version I grew up with in our Ukrainian home. Now I sit in silence, listening, and seizing meaning in the moment a language blossoms. This moment brings me to the memory of drowning Nana's English with my own. It reminds me of the guilt I feel for what might have been my impatience with her learning English. I search for reconciliation and look for a place in the language I speak. I look for my spoken "home."

Today my classroom becomes "home." I am reminded of the uniqueness of my students' stories when they speak about the places they know, where ultimately their stories, like mine, begin to heal and are transposed from the past into our shared teaching moments (Pinar, 2004). For some students, this "home" is freedom; it is a life without war and persecution, one in which people can live with a distinct voice and with choice. For me, such stories heighten the experience of being a teacher.

Being a teacher of English language learners is a place of being and living within tensioned worlds (Aoki, 1986/2005). The teaching world is dichotomous; it is split by the multiple experiences of teacher and student. In this place of being and living in dichotomies, my understandings of why I am a teacher suddenly become how I can acknowledge my students' lived stories and my own *curriculum-as-lived* within a *curriculum-as-planned* (Aoki, 1986/2005). How can I, outside the rigidity of the teaching plan for the day, display my consciousness of another's experience and my concern and care for another in my teaching? Aoki (1986/2005) provides insight into living with tension in a teaching praxis:

> [To] be alive is to live in tension; that, in fact, it is the tensionality that allows good thoughts and actions to arise when properly tensioned chords are struck, and that tensionless strings are not only unable to give voice to songs, but also unable to allow a song to be sung...that this tensionality in [my] pedagogical situation is a mode of being a teacher...marked by despair and hopelessness, and at other times, challenging and stimulating, evoking hopefulness for venturing forth. (p. 162)

In the layers of my tensioned teaching experiences and the stories that are contained within these experiences, I return to Aoki's *pedagogical watchfulness* and *thoughtfulness* (Aoki, 1992/2005), which guides me to understand my presence as a teacher in the *historical-present*. Being watchful and thoughtful points to how to be present in the dual identity of Canadian teacher as I attempt to "unfold layers of understandings" (p. 197) about my teaching praxis. My students often explain to me the relationships of teacher and student in their home countries. I often wonder if they carry these same expectations with them to Canada and if so, I contemplate how I can honour the relationship they had with their first teachers. Nana and Papa were my first teachers, and growing up in their home brings to me a deeper appreciation that begins to radiate from my heart. The complexities of growing up in a foreign language do not silence my voice, rather the silences found in my great-grandparent's home resound.

Being a Canadian teacher evolves with each new encounter of the other in the teaching situation. The teacher returns to her taken-for-granted world to live in teaching and asks: Who am I *with* this student? Past experiences influence what happens in the present moment of teaching and allow the experience of the self and the other in the educational experience to unfold. These experiences are cultivated in a shared historicity. This interaction reveals what being a Canadian teacher means in the junctures among language, home, ethnicity, and culture. Being in language opens my eyes and my heart; I wait for the next knock on the classroom door. When the door opens, I welcome the assemblage of generations of people and once again, my classroom becomes a place where "home" begins.

REFERENCES

Aoki, T. T. (1986/2005). Teaching as in-dwelling between two curriculum worlds. In W. F. Pinar & R. L. Irwin (Eds.), *Curriculum in a new key* (pp. 159–165). Mahwah, NJ: Lawrence Erlbaum.

Aoki, T. T. (1992/2005). Layered voices of teaching: The uncannily correct and the elusively true. In W. F. Pinar & R. L. Irwin (Eds.), *Curriculum in a new key* (pp. 187–197). Mahwah, NJ: Lawrence Erlbaum.

Cixous, H., & Calle-Gruber, M. (1997). *Hélène Cixous, rootprints: Memory and life writing.* (E. Prenowitz, Trans.) London, England: Routledge.

Hoffman, E. (1989). *Lost in translation: A life in a new language.* New York, NY: Penguin.

Mignolo, W. D. (1999). *Local histories/global designs: Coloniality, subaltern knowledges, and border thinking.* Princeton, NJ: Princeton University Press.

Pinar, W. F. (2004). *What is curriculum theory?* Mahwah, NJ: Lawrence Erlbaum.

After the War With Hannelore

G. Scott MacLeod

As a photographer, animator and documentary filmmaker, my research and artwork are based in life history and storytelling, and I am interested in the blending of media and cultures and my pedagogic place in them. My current collaborative life history project with Hannelore Scheiber was initiated through her family photo album and led to the making of her life history into our documentary film, *After the War with Hannelore—A Berliner War Child's Testimony from 1945 to 1989* (MacLeod, 2009). As I look back on making the film, I consider how this experience was like a form of literary métissage, what Hasebe-Ludt, Chambers and Leggo (2009) describe as braids that lead "to understanding about the self and other" and in the process, generating "insight about the world and our place in it" (p. 38).

Hannelore was born in Berlin in January 1945 and spent her earliest years coping with the city's treacherous post-war politics. She grew to adulthood on the very front lines of the Cold War. I met Hannelore in 1994 while she and her husband were living in Montréal, years after both my parents passed away. At first, we established a client-artist relationship when she became interested in my paintings. Out of this grew a personal friendship, which now has elements resembling a familial relationship. As I got to know Hannelore, I became interested in her childhood and adult years in Berlin after World War II. But thinking back, I realize my interest was something more; I was reclaiming my own loss through someone who had also overcome adversity and decided to see the future in a positive light. We both embarked on a remarkable journey that changed us forever. Hannelore was a tremendously positive influence on me and I am truly grateful for our shared experience.

Initially, Hannelore and I were intent on doing a photo-essay on her life in West Berlin during the Cold War years. While reconstructing Hannelore's life from her photo album, however, it virtually turned into a storyboard, which enabled me to see the seven key stations of Hannelore's life from her birth in 1945 to the fall of the Berlin Wall in 1989. This album helped me construct what would be the film's story, which followed a linear chronology, beginning with Hannelore's birth story in Vignette 1. *The Hospital 1945*, which began in January at the end of the war at a hospital in Reinickendorf. Here we learn about the difficult circumstances around her mother's delivery. In Vignette 2. *The Russian Occupation and Apple Cellar 1946* Hannelore describes her mother lodging a Russian officer who protected them from being raped by Russian soldiers while they hid in the family apple cellar. Vignette 3. *Home, My Father and the Railways 1947* deals specifically with her father escaping from a Russian hospital and later working in the Russian sector in the railways. Vignette 4. *The Blockade and Airlift (Die Luftbrücke) 1948–1949* is Hannelore's memoir of the Russian blockade and the Berlin airlift. Vignette 5. *School Years 1951–1967* are memoirs of Hannelore's elementary and high-school years. In Vignette 6. *The Wall 1961* Hannelore talks about the Wall suddenly going up and her student friends and family who were incarcerated and shot while trying to escape from the other side of the Wall. Vignette 7. *Checkpoint*

Figure 1. Hannelore Scheiber, Circa 1960s. Scheiber Family Photo Archive

Figure 2. Hannelore, 1951 First Day of School, Berlin. Scheiber Family Photo Archive

Charlie 1982 is a re-enactment of Hannelore and her husband crossing Checkpoint Charlie, reflecting on their courtship and the present changes since the Wall came down.

Our approach when constructing the seven-point chronology and content of the documentary embodied Michael Frisch's term "shared authority," which is "unlike the traditional authority of the historian which is based on distance" (High, 2010, p. 103). Because of our long-term relationship, Hannelore and I proceeded in a very transparent fashion. I made sure that she always had final editorial say over the film's content. Thus we began our work together. As Lillian Smith states, "there is no going alone on a journey. Whether one explores strange lands or Main Street or one's own backyard, always invisible travelling companions are close by…" (as cited in Hasebe-Ludt, et al., 2009, p. 3) Those invisible companions were the vestiges of Berlin's World War II and Cold War history, and Hannelore's family members in the pages of her photo album. What is remarkable during the post-war period when material goods were scarce to many Berliners is that her father and family had access to a camera and film processing, which was uncommon during the poverty that ensued from the post-war years. Hannelore told me that because her father was a train engineer he was a valuable asset to the reconstruction of Berlin, and therefore had certain privileges extended to him, which included access to photographic equipment and processing. It was through these personal photos that I was able to gain access to her complex life history during Cold-war Berlin and realized her story would make a compelling documentary film. In addition to her photos, I used a mix of period photography from the *Deutsches Historisches Museum* in Berlin; 16mm-stock shots from the National Film Board of Canada; pencil animations which came out of necessity when I could not afford to purchase the rights for more archival photos; and finally live-action footage, all of which enabled me to craft both a moving and personal portrait of the unforgettable Hannelore. Hannelore and I firmly believed that "our trust in this process is based on both our individual and joint intuitive insight and experiences. Trusting in these processes is an integral part of our craft and hermeneutic *Lebenswelt* as writers and researchers" (Hasebe-Ludt, et al., 2009, p. 7).

It is my hope that this documentary illustrates a woman emancipating herself from circumstantial suffering, which ensued from an incredible series of events beyond her control. From what I have learned, it was the collective effort of her communities and the Allies that helped her overcome the darkness of the Cold War, enabling her to release it as the light of compassion. "Freeing ourselves from suffering" is how Canadian filmmaker Velcrow Ripper (2007) refers to this light of compassion based on his *Tonglen* meditation practice, which is featured in the DVD extras of his National Film Board of Canada documentary film *Scared Sacred* (Ripper, 2007). In my film I have also tried to find what Ripper describes

Figure 3.
Schoolchildren in
Berlin, 1946.
Animation Cell,
G. Scott MacLeod,
2009

as the "flowers in the ashes" and looked for the positive lessons out of the atrocities of war. Ripper inspired me to also create a downloadable PDF of my production notes and an education package with the DVD, as it is my aim to offer a forum for discussion and learning, and to encourage people to tell their own stories and make their own films.

I was committed to producing the DVD as a transformative educational tool but found it difficult to find a forum for discussion and distribution, save for the festivals and cultural centres network. I believe that the single biggest problem I faced was disseminating the completed film to teachers and members of the public interested in this type of educational tool. At the Québec Provincial Association of Teachers in 2010, I presented a workshop on our film and I heard directly from teachers who stated the need for educational content via digital media. As a filmmaker and educator, I believe creating positive educational content in digital platforms is essential for people to use every day, as we are confronted with violent gaming content and war on an ongoing basis, which in my view will only engender violence and further endorse war. There is value in narrative historical documentaries that deal with the real and direct impacts of warfare on human beings. Personal testimonies such as Hannelore's offer a specific, concrete means for understanding the horrors of war, and because such stories are so personal and real, we avoid the abstraction and separation that are possible when war is discussed through the language of politics, operations, or policies. I discovered

Figure 4. Hannelore in Front of Bertha-von-Suttner High School, Holding Photographs of Her and School Friends, Berlin, 2006. Photo, G. Scott MacLeod, 2006

that documentaries of this nature offer a unique opportunity for understanding. I am hopeful that life writing through film, such as Hannelore's story, will have a place in the digital classroom, perhaps in ways as High (2010) describes the Montréal Life Stories Project:

> The National Film Board was brought into our project by a faculty member working in education technology. Its role was therefore initially conceived in pedagogical terms—an online database for interviews "tagged" for teachers, matching stories with the curriculum requirement of Quebec. (p. 105)

And in a pedagogic pivot, it became clear to me during the production and the launch of the film in Berlin that I grew up during Trudeau's policies of multiculturalism, among a culturally diverse array of families and communities in Montréal. I am deeply aware of the challenges of tracing "our mixed and multiple identities, while interrogating possibilities of identity, in a textured textualizing, both echoic and embodied" (Hasebe-Ludt, et al., 2009, p. 2). My bilingual experience in Montréal has given me a certain kind of Canadian distance and sensitivity to cultures that have been demarcated by language and politics. I grew up with a foot in both the English and the French world, which helped me deal with the charged subjects I faced in Hannelore's life story, and I am "mindful of the places we inhabit" (Hasebe-Ludt, et al., 2009, p. 2). It was from this spirit and place that I addressed Hannelore's complex life history.

Over the 3-year experience, from shooting on location in 2006 and 2007 to post-production in 2008, and finally to its release in 2009, I felt that I had posed a very similar question to the following one: "How do we create new visions of our lives within specific locations, such as a colonized one that is called Canada?" (Hasebe-Ludt, et al., 2009, p. 2). After literally being immersed in the historical vestiges of the former fascist and communist tragedies of Berlin, I looked to my bilingual experience of growing up in Montréal witnessing the October Crisis of 1970 and the two referendums that followed. When comparing these two periods of political unrest in Berlin and Montréal, I often find myself reflecting on the greater question of tolerance: How did we manage to live side by side in the multicultural métissage of Montréal, shoulder to shoulder within that "in-between space" with all of its differences politically, culturally and linguistically, without wholesale violence and mass killings? As a society, "we belong to different affiliations and relations" and therefore as people we must be "mindful of the complicated responsibilities that come with professing to be life writers in the postcolonial times and in a nation and landscape shaped by and subjected to colonization" (Hasebe-Ludt, et al., 2009, p. 1). An example would be the vestiges of the Russian occupation and siege mentality that are still present in Berlin, from bullet holes in the facades of buildings to epic war monuments throughout the city, all painful reminders of the invader/occupier history of Berlin.

In turn, Berlin is an interesting parallel to Montréal, as historically it gave birth to great minds in the sciences and arts on one hand, then paradoxically became the nationalist headquarters during the Nazi era, and then a divided city subjected to psychological terror during the Cold War. But why Berlin and not Montréal? I looked for the answers to these questions in my research, while writing the script and through Hannelore's photos, in the art of my production and finally through being a witness to her stories. I conclude that the métissage of cultures is paramount for the survival of the human race; as we see in the biodiversity of nature we need more diversity not monocultures. As history has shown us from the rise and fall of the Third Reich, the notion of a pure race is not a future for our species.

My intention with this documentary was to film Hannelore at specific locations in Berlin and document her stories and memories *in situ* through an historical context. My goal was to catch her emotions surrounding her experience of growing up in post-war Berlin. What makes these seven vignettes special is that they are so personal. Returning home in 2006 for the first time since she emigrated to Canada 20 years earlier, Hannelore revisited family homes and youthful haunts, which conjured bittersweet stories of her youth along with the often tragic history of her city. From her family's struggle through the Russian

Figure 5. Fall of the Berlin Wall, 1989. Animation Cell, G. Scott MacLeod, 2009

blockade and the Berlin airlift, through her school years in the partitioned city, to the very construction of the Berlin Wall itself, Hannelore gives us a touching first-hand testimony to the events that shaped her world and, indeed, the world at large. Far from embittered, she is a lively and insightful tour-guide, tempering wise reflection with unbridled joy at finally being home again. The outcome of this experience for Hannelore was just that, she did indeed move back to Germany. It is safe to say that the healing work has been done inside Hannelore emotionally and spiritually while living in Canada and Mexico over the last 20 years. She told me that as a result of making her film that she had overcome some of her darker memories of the Cold War and that Germany was no longer the place she left in the 1980s.

Hannelore's photo album enabled us to collectively reconstruct her experience and memory, to develop the research, collect "the data," and finally write the script for her own biography. Though Hannelore did not take the photographs in her life album, she did help create her own self-portrait with them, as well as an autobiographical life history, by collaborating and becoming a witness to her own life history—a truly remarkable gift to herself and the public.

What resulted from this methodology was that Hannelore and I stumbled into a role that was not unlike mother and son and it was in that liminal "in-between space" where I tried to be of service to her story. I worked to enable her to tell her own story by "braiding our narratives through métissage, and theorizing with and through stories" (Hasebe-Ludt, et al., 2009, p. 35). I felt a deep link to this woman from another country, perhaps because I had lost my own mother when I was 13 to cancer. This project became an opportunity for me to honour a mother figure's story from the other side of the ocean, and through The Wall that separated east and west. The seven vignettes I shot of Hannelore's life on location in Berlin were my way of reciprocating all that she's given me in our friendship. I also believe very strongly that oral histories like hers are invaluable records of the post-war period and the Cold-war years in Berlin, the epicentre of World War II in Europe.

In closing I am brought full circle to the opening scene in our film, which begins with Peter Eisenman's controversial Holocaust Memorial and my song *Freiheit* (Freedom). To me, this place, between the Brandenburg Gate and where Hitler's bunker is buried, is metaphorically a labyrinth bringing the viewer out of the dark past into the light of a promising future. I chose this location as it represents the last days of World War II and the beginning of the Cold War. What resonates with me now is the idea that Hannelore's life was a gift, and that her will to overcome the darkness of these times may inspire us to imagine and create joy in the world. Her last statement in the film as we drove through Checkpoint Charlie was an affirmation of life and living: "I believe that it is possible to be of different cultures, and live in peace, and I really hope and wish that for the world." This statement is an invitation and opportunity to see how we can construct a bridge from our tragic memories, by braiding our diverse heartfelt life histories together, all in an effort to work towards a brighter future. Drawing from Eduardo Galeano, "the storied character and the crafting of literary métissage returns the reader to the conflicted sites of home and not-home by remembering (*recordar*) through the heart" (Hasebe-Ludt, et al., 2009, p. 38). This is the truth I still carry in my heart from my collaboration with Hannelore Scheiber.

I welcome you to explore Hannelore's life map. It is my hope that stories like hers will enable us to let go of the suffering, hate, and darkness, to finally welcome the light of compassion to a city of great learning and possibility. My hope is that this film might instill hope and love as well as peace, and ultimately contribute to the democratization of our planet by helping to end fear and war. I welcome you to one woman's journey in doing this very thing.

REFERENCES

Hasebe-Ludt, E., Chambers, C., & Leggo, C. (2009). *Life writing and literary métissage as an ethos for our times*. New York, NY: Peter Lang.

High, S. (2010). Telling stories: A reflection on oral history and new media. *Oral History, 38*(1), 101–112.

MacLeod, G. S. (Director & Producer). (2009). *"After the war with Hannelore"—a Berliner war child's testimony from 1945 to 1989*. Montréal, Canada: MacLeod Nine Productions.

Ripper, V, (2007). *Scared sacred*. Toronto, Canada: Mongrel Media.

Bereaved

N. Rochelle Yamagishi

Recently, I attended a social-work workshop on bereavement. I had been drawn to the topic, since I had lost both my parents: my father 2 years previously, and my mother 26 years ago. But lately, seemingly inexplicably, I have been missing my mother. I find myself thinking about her almost daily, and in the decades since her death, the observance of Mother's Day has been particularly difficult. Each year, in the weeks before this day, wanting to honour those who had taken her place in my heart and mind—my aunt and my stepmother—I would find myself reduced to tears at the greeting card counter, and even as I write this sentence.

Common wisdom tells us that bereavement is most intense during the first year of loss. However, I now realize that my recovery from this deep loss has been impeded.

I was discussing the matter with my younger daughter, now an adult; she conjectured that having three young children at the time of my mother's death, I had been too preoccupied to grieve properly at that time. I also wondered whether my relationship with my mother had been more positive than with my father, and therefore, I missed her more. It could also have been intensified by the spiritual relationship that one has with one's mother, begun in the womb and never ending, even through death.

At the bereavement workshop, it suddenly came to me. I missed my mother because I just turned 60, her age when she died a slow and agonizing death from ulcer-related cancer. Coincidentally, I have suffered a digestive disorder since the summer after her death in the spring of 1984. Despite many varied medical investigations, my diagnosis remained vague, although I have had to severely restrict my consumption of specific kinds of foods through the years. A positive diagnosis of ulcers several years ago, and subsequent treatment, threw my digestive system into such a tailspin that my family doctor declared himself unable to assist me further. My mother had digestive problems for many years, before being diagnosed with terminal cancer.

Many people who knew my mother have commented to me that I am so much like her, in looks and manner. I take this as a tremendous compliment, since she was well-loved by people of many walks of life, evidenced by her standing-room-only funeral. Though housekeeping was not her forte, her "people skills" were second-to-none. She was gentle and unassuming, thoughtful and considerate, generous to a fault. I believe it was these qualities which took her into her marriage and kept her there.

A few years before my mother died, I had implored her to leave my father, whom we both agreed was an emotional abuser. When I asked her why she married him, she confided that her action had helped her friend, who would become her sister-in-law. When Mom married Dad, she became the woman of the house, cooking and cleaning for a household of men: my father, my grandfather, and my uncle. Thereby, my aunt, my father's younger sister, was able to leave the family home, to marry her sweetheart, my mother's brother. In later years, I came to learn that my father had bullied my aunt—likely a big part of her need to escape—and later my mother, and still later, myself and my brother.

My mother, however, was emotionally unable to leave my father, since for her generation divorce was a "dirty word." A divorcee was considered not only selfish and unaccountably individualistic, but labelled a "scarlet woman," a "tart," "used goods." The existence of divorcees questioned the sacrament of marriage, tempting otherwise good husbands to wander from their vows and duties. When I questioned Mom about having a 25th-wedding-anniversary party, she stated bluntly, "There is nothing to celebrate." At the time, I had no inkling that several years later, when the time came for my own 25th-wedding celebration, I would start to assess my own marriage. I had allowed my husband to take the lead and be the main decision-maker in our lives. I had little sense of my own autonomy, always worrying about being second-guessed and corrected by someone whom

I considered my superior in his worldly ways and social skills. My husband's learning style makes him a good decision-maker in crises, while my learning-style behaviour is seen as "wishy-washy," indecisive.

Other than helping the children with homework, my cognitive and linguistic skills were rarely recognized on a daily basis, relegated to book-learning or academics, separate from the day-to-day demands of living. My housekeeping skills—including sewing, cooking, laundry, and childcare—as for most housewives, were simple expectations for any wife and mother. The measure of cleanliness and tidiness of the house were the basis of evaluating my efforts. Since my husband did not like to return home after work to find the children and myself in any kind of mess or disarray, it was common for us to hurriedly clean up, trying to make the place presentable for their dad's homecoming. Still, we were frequently found wanting in our efforts, apologizing and making excuses. With three small children, it was an ongoing challenge.

Somehow, I found the time and space to obtain two advanced university degrees but suffered a great deal of guilt and misgivings in the process. I did not feel entitled to pursue my interests and my dreams but continually found myself rationalizing—and apologizing for—my pursuits. My in-laws had a "dollars-and-cents" mentality: My mother-in-law asked if my husband didn't make enough money for me; a brother-in-law claimed that I would never get a job, which would justify the large educational expenses incurred. I felt almost ashamed of my interests and goals. Little did I realize at the time that my yearning to "make something of myself" was a response to my mother's frequent admonishments during my formative years, and perhaps an extension of her unachieved dreams of being a teacher.

At the bereavement workshop, I learned that of the many types of bereavement, the worst was the loss of a child. I had an epiphany! I realized that my bereavement experience was quite unusual. Yes, I had lost my parents, as expected in the family life cycle, since children normally outlive their parents. However, before we were married—I was 19 and my husband was 21—I had given birth to a baby boy, whom I decided to surrender for adoption. I believed that I could not bring shame to my family, nor burden my mother with another baby. At ages 40 and 44, she had borne her last two children. My older sister had already left home for university when our youngest brother was born, while I was 18 and still living at home. Mom had understandably been very tired throughout the last pregnancy and then challenged with the care of two young sons. I believed that with a baby I would not be able to pursue my educational goals, and that I might feel resentful if I gave them up at this point.

For various reasons—one of them being the shame-based nature of our Japanese culture—I knew that I could not bring myself to tell my parents about my pregnancy. One of my aunts, who had two sons, had said once, in front of my two sisters and myself, "I would never have daughters. All they do is 'get in trouble.'" As fate would have it, I got my first menstrual period on the day we were going to visit this aunt. I was terrified that my mother would tell my aunt, but she promised that she wouldn't, and thankfully did not.

Many years later, I learned that in Japan, families celebrate a daughter's first menstruation by having rice, cooked with red beans, for the supper meal. However, in our household, like many others in Western culture, it was a well-kept secret about an embarrassing happening. There was no pride of femininity, nor celebration of womanhood. There was no sex education either. So, when I became pregnant after just one fumbling encounter, and my doctor asked if I had been "sleeping with my boyfriend," I said "no," because I didn't know what that meant. My parents had six children, but I had never heard them utter the word "pregnant," let alone "sex." Rather, when a woman was "in the family way," the time would come for her to "part company," and mysteriously a baby was born. At the age of six, I knew that I could not ask my mother how babies came out of their mothers, so I asked a friend's mother, who told me quite matter-of-factly. In retrospect, the better question would have been how they got in!

I was truly mortified when I realized that I was pregnant and when I told my now-husband, he did the gentlemanly thing and quickly offered to marry me, but I knew that I didn't want to be another statistic, someone who "had to get married." We knew many couples that had started marriage that way, and I had seen that it was a strenuous journey for all involved. I realized that there was truly no good solution to the "problem" but believed that the best scenario would be for me to go away, have the baby in secret, and try to return to my previous life. I had at that time completed one year of university, and aspired to become a child psychologist, a career planned since I was in the ninth grade. I knew that this was something that I needed to do for myself, and having a child at this age would not fit into these plans. I feared that I would become bitter, and not be a good mother, to a deserving and innocent child. Also, to make a hasty decision to marry someone was not part of my learning style!

Although my older sister and I were never very close as youngsters, as we got older, it became my habit to seek her counsel. She agreed that this predicament was something to be kept from our parents. We devised a plan for me to live with her in Montana, 350 miles away from home, where she was attending university. Luckily, my home university had a "visiting student" program, by which I could attend another university. I could have my courses transferred back for credit, thereby not interrupting my studies, and also in the process provide a believable excuse to leave town for several months. I arranged to take summer, fall, and winter quarters at the University of Montana. In another fortunate circumstance, my sister arranged for us to live upstairs from a law office, situated in an old, two-storey house not far from campus. For cleaning the law offices at night, we earned our room upstairs, along with kitchen privileges. The arrangement was logistically ideal. My sister supported me emotionally in every way possible, and we enjoyed living on our own and working together. This was a new experience for both of us. We tried new recipes and enjoyed the summer and fall together in the Bitterroot Valley. We lugged our laundry to a nearby laundromat and ferried our groceries home by bicycle.

My sister was able to obtain babysitting jobs for me, to earn a little extra cash. Her friend also recommended a sympathetic gynecologist, who suggested that I arrange the adoption through Lutheran Social Services. The agency required me to attend weekly counselling sessions with their social worker, an older woman. I could not develop a rapport with this wife of a well-to-do lawyer. Most perplexing was her repetition that I should remember that my baby was "a person." Now I realize that with my prefrontal cortex not yet fully developed, I could not grasp the significance of her statement. However, I did have the presence of mind to request that the adoptive family should already have at least one child, thinking that their parental skills would be developed. Beyond that, I had no conception of what would happen to our son. For the next 39 years, in my mind, he remained my "long-lost baby."

Our son was born on October 1st, exactly nine months from our intimacy on New Year's Eve. Ironically, it was that year that oral contraceptives became legal in Canada, a fact which I learned many years later.

Later that fall, my sister started getting serious about her boyfriend, and guessing that our living arrangement might soon change, I decided that I should return to Canada at the Christmas break, rather than staying in Montana for the whole year. I returned to my home city, feeling emotionally fragile, disoriented, and depressed. I felt like there was a palpable wall between myself and everyone else. It was almost as if I were playing out my life from a distance. An integral part of myself had been taken from me, and had to be hidden and denied. Not only did I feel estranged from others, but I felt like a part of me had died. I went through the motions and assumed some outward normalcy. Since the majority of our friends were getting married, I pushed to get married too, partly to gain a sense of rightness. After all, I knew that my husband and I would be forever linked, due to our son, and I yearned for at least the semblance of typicality. We were married less than two years after our son was born.

It was difficult keeping up appearances. When our friends would talk about their babies, of course, I had to feign ignorance and lack of experience with pregnancy and childbirth. I longed for a child but persevered with my career path, to make my decision worthwhile. When it came time to start a family, our first experience was a miscarriage, which was more devastating than people could fathom, since I hoped against hope that I had not given away my chance to have a family at all. Once our older daughter was born, I tried to become the perfect mother. During the first 2 years of her life, she most certainly could sense my anxiety and would cry unceasingly if I left, even for a few hours, during her first two years of life, even though my husband tried his best to care for her in my absence.

Although I adored my daughter, girls were not the preferred gender for my traditional Japanese mother-in-law. When seeing me in the hospital room after our daughter's birth, her first words to me were clear: "Next time, boy." I was overjoyed when I did deliver a boy "next time." That joy turned to inexplicable sadness as our son grew. Periodically, I would be overcome with sorrow when he would excel, or when I would think that I could lose him. The sight of him as a young man dressed in a tuxedo reduced me to tears, for no apparent reason.

Sandwiched between an older and a younger sister, our son would sometimes wonder out loud why he didn't have a brother, and why he looked so different from his sisters. I ached to be able to tell him, but it wasn't the right time, and what would I say that a child could understand?

My husband and I worked hard on our careers and within a few decades, we both became high-profile personalities within the local school district. As time wore on, I periodically asked my husband if we weren't going to try to find our older son. He preferred not to talk about him, even between us, for fear that someone might find out. He was, apparently, trying to protect me from the public humiliation of our secret being exposed. Once we both retired, and not incidentally while my father was dying, he agreed that now was the time to begin the search. I was even more motivated to find him since meeting our daughter's boyfriend, who also had been adopted. When I first met him, I was overcome with the newfound realization that our son could also be a grown-up: a handsome, talented, physically fit, caring young man.

Since Lutheran Social Services was still operating, it was relatively simple to locate our son, after being instructed to write a non-identifying "letter of intent." Fortuitously, he had contacted the agency just 5 years previously, for medical information; and the agency still had his address. When he received our letter, he was instructed to write a letter of response, either accepting or declining our offer to reunite. After an agonizing month of waiting, we finally received a beautifully composed letter, with a hint of restraint, stating that his life was quite satisfactory as it was. He wrote that he owned his own business and lived on the U.S. west coast, enjoyed a supportive group of friends, and was all but estranged from his adoptive family, except for his mother, with whom he remained close, since she had always been loving and supportive.

However, our son agreed to a meeting, although we found out later that he had been leery, due to his adopted sister's meeting with her birth mother, which had been disappointing. After completing legal papers on both sides of the border, we began email correspondence, and then phone conversations. These went well, and once we met him in his home city, we had definite leanings in the "nature-nurture" controversy. The physical resemblance to his brother was remarkable: the same height, weight, facial features, mannerisms, and left-handedness. Growing up in Montana and Idaho, with few Asians around, he had often looked in the mirror and wondered why he looked so different from everyone around him, but he now had an abundance of relatives who all bore some resemblance to him.

While planning the reunion, my husband and I discussed how we would tell our three children, now adults and living away from home. We conjectured about possible responses but did not anticipate that their reactions would be unequivocal, and across-the-board, excitement and delight. Similarities and connections were almost instantaneous. Happily, we had circumvented the bereavement process for them.

However, to this day I continue to burst into tears at the slightest provocation, never having been allowed to grieve my loss properly through the decades. Our son, wise beyond his 40 years, perhaps due to the stresses and strains of growing up "different," has reassured me that I should not feel guilty, since he has turned out so well. "It was obviously the right decision at the time. Let's just move forward from here." I marvel at his positive attitude, his generosity of spirit, his willingness to forgive and forget. And I am grateful that he has tried to understand the heart and mind of a young woman 40 long years ago, his mother…

Tears…
Salty, hot,
Whether grief or joy…
I know not.

On the Esoterics of Thread

Nané Ariadne Jordan

I have just overturned three large plastic storage tubs from the closets of our apartment. I am looking for a small, sealed Ziploc bag containing two colourful cotton outfits from my childhood—matching tops and shorts that my mother sewed for me during the 1970s. I am in a frenzy looking for these things, upturning fabric and art supplies, the stored children's clothes. Where are these outfits—and where are the 1970s? A lost decade and now lost outfits. I want to grasp this past and all of its intricate affects upon me, paradoxically halcyon and chaotic days of my childhood spent travelling between divorced parents in Toronto.

My artist mother sewed much of our clothing back then. We often browsed fabric shops on College Street, which I loved to do, a calm oasis in our lives—feeling the focus of textures and imaginings of cloth from which my mom stitched a variety of funky coats, bags, skirts, pants and matching tops. We lived within her stitching—just as we lived within her moods of euphoria, pain, and rage. My mother's clothes and feelings stretched out and spun around to claim me, a whirlwind language of colour, its texture a physical and emotional path of making. I began to hand-stitch cloth dolls at this time, satisfying my own creative urges with fabric and thread, as my mother worked on her many projects. I found ways to engage the time and space around me.

Now I am looking for these two outfits that my mom recently mailed to me in Vancouver from the depths of her home storage in Toronto—something special for me to see again. I know one of them has a checkerboard pattern, soft turquoise-and-white colours. Just now, my search for this Ziploc bag was inspired by a local Vancouver designer and artist[1] who has committed herself to wearing only self-made clothes for one year. She is inquiring into the time and effort it takes to clothe the body, and the human energy, excess and waste that go into the global clothing industry. And I think, "but that is what we did in the 1970s!"

It was a way of life back then—*all* about hand making. My artist mother drew from the sewing traditions of the women in our family before her. She continued this way of being and making in the world, enacting the skill and ability to create one's clothing for oneself. Yet she sewed from the vantage point of the 1970s with its counter-culture and hippie sensibility that heralded a second wave of the 1870s Arts and Crafts Movement. This movement was rooted in a protest of modernity and a philosophical return to pre-industrial roots of providing for one's basic needs by making beautiful, functional things (Spretnak, 1999).

In a way, aspects of these counterculture movements have morphed into the new culture of "sustainability" with its necessary focus on the environment and reduction of the ill effects of overconsumption of Earth's resources by industrialized countries, and the pollution of this Earth, our home. Though mainstream discourses of sustainability focus on how to "re-duce, re-use and re-cycle," there seems to be less emphasis on learning basic skills with our hands, on re-claiming lost arts of making needed things, on understanding and teaching the reasons for and satisfaction gained from such making.

With this in mind, I wanted to see and look at my colourful childhood outfits, and re-use them as artful life-writing examples, artifacts, for a studio textiles class I teach in art education. I have been teaching this class to pre-service and art-diploma teachers, an introduction to the making and meanings of textile art. What I love to dwell on within my own art practice is the esoterics of thread, the deep spirituality of thread itself. My mother named me for Ariadne, the Minoan priestess, who in Greek mythology leads Theseus out of the Cretan labyrinth and away from death by the Minotaur, with her ball of thread. I have always thought of her thread as red, the colour of life's blood and renewal. Thus, in making thread and cloth, entire cosmologies can unfold, both intimate and world-forming. I am fascinated by long ago and still present *ways of thread*, rooted as they are across cultures and traditions to what ties, binds, unwinds, weaves, tears, and mends people to themselves and each other, to the places and ecologies they inhabit and call *home*.

There is a deeply relational call of thread in its hand making, into the forms that cover and hold our bodies and spirits. In the wisdom tradition of Hindu Tantra, the meaning of Tantra is *fabric*—denoting "connectivity" (Chopra, 2006, p. 103), an energy that weaves self/other and world together, undergirding existence. "Weaving" is forever also a linguistic metaphor, a way of describing how things come together in the world as we weave stories and spin tales. In Greek mythology the three Fates, a triad of women, are said to spin, weave and cut the duration of our lives within their very hands, reflecting the fact that we do not control the measure and span of our lives. The anthropologist, Barbara Tedlock, in her text on the feminine shamanic path,[2] discusses how spinning and weaving are synonymous with the growth of the fetus and the birth of a child. The rhythmic, life-giving pulsations of each activity have passed through women's hands and bodies for millennia, as ongoing, relational forces that remake the world against the "reality of change, destruction and death" (Tedlock, 2006, p. 223).

There is an intimate feeling in wearing something made from ones' own hands, or from the hands of a loved one. There is comfort sleeping under such quilts of love and self-formation. I felt the play of my paternal grandmother's knitted sweaters on my small bodily form over so many years of growing up, the gift of texture and the sweet smell of each sweater as it emerged from her hands and needles. Modern practices of industrial production, and our dependence on the often impoverished working conditions of others, contribute to a diminishing relationship to these relational cosmologies of "care-full" making. Teaching textiles in the context of busy, "over-full" lives with multiple deadlines in the teacher education program, my students often comment on how much time it takes to do this kind of art work, how they "lack the time" in their lives for such activity. Yet we take the time in each class to discover together how such processes are inherently grounding, slowing the body and mind to a meditative focus where contentment and relaxation can emerge within a shared community of makers.

Some students find their knitting and stitching spill over into other areas of their lives, as knitted or woven forms emerge while they listen to lectures, sit on the bus, or teach such practices in their classrooms with children and youth. One student spent the semester knitting purple wool into small woven forms with little buttons, until she was able to attach and cover her entire bicycle with purple wool. The knitted covered bike is ride-able, and brings delight and curiosity to all who behold its magic travelling form. Thus, I think of thread as a kind of inner and outer writing, a language in the text of textiles, a secret code of contemplative knowing if we will take the time to work with it once again, spinning its care-full mysteries through our hands and through our communities.

Yet despite this deep desire to teach from my life and these threads of know-ing, I can't find the childhood outfits made by my mother as I search my apart-ment home. I am troubled by the thought that I might actually have given them away in one of my recent purges while re-cycling our old clothing and no-lon-ger-in-use items. Though our co-op housing unit off of Commercial Drive has three bedrooms and an open kitchen/living area, it is relatively small. My two daughters seem to crowd the apartment more and more. Lately I am always try-ing to make more room for something within all their growth and its energy that so fills our space.

I can't believe I would let the hand-sewn outfits go, though I know I might have. What I remember in this search is that my streak of letting go has not, and cannot, extend to my grandmother's wool suit still hanging in my closet. My mom handed me this suit from Grandma's closet after her death in Toronto, thinking I might alter and even wear it—a stern warning *never* to give it away. I loved to have it straight from Grandma's cupboards, which still had the smell and feel of her. My mom and I could just imagine Grandma's incisive commen-tary on the outfit itself.

Grandma was a proud seamstress, with a discerning, critical eye on the overall look of any outfit you wore, especially the quality of its making. She had sewed much of her family's clothing with well-honed skills in the economy of her day. My mother's own art-full designs, and the freedom she accorded me as a child in clothing choices and combinations, did not always meet Grandma's approval. Nor would Grandma ever enter the lived realities of my mother's chosen artful academic-cum-bohemian life of the times. We visited Grandma—in the comfort of the east-end Toronto home she would live in for over forty years. As a child, I would sit in her sun-lit sewing room, with its partial view of Danforth Avenue, watching her stitch and mend. She would carefully show me the details of what she was working on.

The suit that now hangs in my closet is an elegant, simply cut 1950s style I have always admired but really wouldn't wear. My mother informed me it was the very suit Grandma wore on their first family visit home to Ireland after immigrating to Canada in 1948. At that time, they still took the boat to Ireland, as they would 8 years later for the second visit home when my mom was 16. *Home*—that word was always applied to Ireland by my grandparents in Canada. Their continuous stories of family, people and villages there formed many after-dinner tales. Yet I have never been to Ireland, nor has my mother been since.

I have always felt bereft from this motherland, feeling close in many ways but not really knowing it for myself. I know many immigrant families who keep up their physical ties to other "homes" through more than one generation. My mother never found a way to return to Ireland within the strains of creating her own life and my grandmother's firm hold on this place of origin. Nor did my grandparents take me with them on their later, infrequent visits.

Thus *home* is a word I now trace through textual and textile passages of styles, feelings and things stitched, kept, lost and found in our familial closets, passed from mother to daughter through the challenges, and love, of our relations. Such threads are always working to mend and bind once again. One day, I might take myself to Ireland, my own daughters in tow. Who knows what I will wear for the occasion?

And my inspired pedagogical textile moment—the hand-sewn children's outfit from the 1970s, seems lost.

All I can find are the threads of this story.

ENDNOTES

1 Natalie Purschwitz—*makeshiftproject.blogspot.com/*

2 *Shamanism* is a term coined by Western anthropologists to describe aspects of the healing and medicine systems of traditional and Indigenous peoples. Depending on their practice and context, the shaman incorporates practical knowledge of local plants, herbal medicines, massage and other such techniques, as well as ceremony, dance and song in communication with spirits, ancestors and other worldly beings in order to affect cures for the patient.

REFERENCES

Chopra, L. S. (2006). *Yogini: Unfolding the goddess within*. New Delhi, India: Wisdom Tree.

Spretnak, C. (1999). *The resurgence of the real: Body, nature, place in a hypermodern world*. New York, NY: Routledge.

Tedlock, B. (2005). *The woman in the shaman's body: Reclaiming the feminine in religion and medicine*. New York, NY: Bantam Books.

Place Work

Mapping Rhizomatic Migrations

There are places that cannot be paraphrased. The sky curved behind wind-shield glass, muffled pines, the scarred pelt of a mountain range, reason in all its convex forms.

—Méira Cook, Slovenly Love

Homesteading an emotional territory as I have takes a lot of simple hard work.

—Jane Rule, A Hot-Eyed Moderate

Movements of the second strand begin in relation to, with and in-between place. Like a Deleuzian subterranean web of rhizomatic roots and radicles, bulbs and tubers, these tentacles map migrations, routes travelled elsewhere, as well as returning home and returning to that which is no longer home, rooting into place, growing roots in new places, and attending to old roots, only to begin again (Deleuze & Guattari, 2005). Such rhizomes are "the best and the worst," the stories of joy and hopefulness, and actualization and strength; stories of struggles and hurt, continuously connecting as lines (not points with other points) in a heterogeneity of place that brings our attention to the spaces between sites of contact, to the liminality of place, a demarcation of self *as* movement (Deleuze & Guattari, 1988/2005, p. 7).

We witness in these stories how lines can rupture for life writers, and how the breaking of the rhizome makes possible new directions. Sometimes this signifies a new beginning from an existing place that brings forward "transformational multiplicity" in social and cultural formations, memories and historical ruminations, and concepts of un/belonging in different lifeworlds (Deleuze & Guattari, 1988/2005, p. 11). We linger with writers in their experiences of uncertain relations in complex and precarious living places, where lines become entangled, and insights through stories, infinite. Such organic openings are reminiscent of Bhabha's (1994) intervention of "The Third Space." They constitute intensive fragments of whole beings that invite our meditative attention to the educative task of critically engaging in these storied experiences as ways of coming to know. The rhizomes of place work to generate new maps with each reading. They make life writing a relational, interrogative, and generative outspreading that is not defined as past, present, or future but as a simultaneous mixing, or weaving of all time dimensions. Upon entering these transitional places we discover how this second strand of narratives mixes creativity with consciousness as a tentative, paradoxical, and often incomplete condition of self, one that dwells in the interiority and exteriority of multiple locations. It is along these storied lines of place that learning begins and where, as Keith Basso (1996) noted, "wisdom sits in places."

These writers predominantly do their work from various mixed-identity (racial, ethnic, cultural, linguistic…to name only a few) situations across Canada and bridge other post/colonial home/not-home contexts. Their life writing relates and responds to one of the challenges facing curriculum theory internationally: to write and theorize from particular curricular locations, but in a way that speaks to educators beyond that place (Chambers, 1999). Historically, mainstream curricular discourses have been notorious for their imperialist intentions and effects, written and theorized within particular national locations but in a language and a manner that assumes universal significance and application (Pinar, 2003; Pinar, et al., 1995). Freire (1997) encourages educators to consider the implications of this in their own lives and work. "The more rooted I am in my location, the more I extend myself to other places so as to become a citizen of the world. No one becomes local from a universal location" (p. 39).

In this strand on place work, we revisit this challenge at a time of new migration and heightened sensitivity to what goes on in the minute, rhizomatic movements between local and global transnational experiences and relationships (Alerby & Brown, 2008). We trace the writers' movements as they are redefining what "writing from this place" means at a point of unprecedented global and local migrations that, as Zygmunt Bauman (2007) tells us, are both generative and precarious, and a signifier of our "liquid times."

REFERENCES

Alerby, E., & Brown, J. (Eds.). (2008). *Voices from the margins: School experiences of Indigenous, refugee, and migrant children.* Rotterdam, The Netherlands: Sense Publishers.

Basso, K. (1996). *Wisdom sits in places: Landscape and language among the Western Apache.* Albuquerque: University of New Mexico Press.

Bauman, Z. (2007). *Liquid times: Living in an age of uncertainty.* Cambridge, England: Polity Press.

Bhabha, H. (1994). *The location of culture.* London, England: Routledge.

Chambers, C. (1999). A topography for Canadian curriculum theory. *Canadian Journal of Education, 24*(2), 137–150.

Cook, M. (2003). *Slovenly Love.* London, Canada: Brick Books.

Deleuze, G., & Guattari, F. (1988/2005). *A thousand plateaus: Capitalism and schizophrenia* (B. Massumi, Trans.). Minneapolis: University of Minnesota Press. (Original work published 1987)

Freire, P. (1997). *Pedagogy of the heart* (D. Macedo & A. Oliveira, Trans.). New York, NY: Continuum.

Pinar, W. F. (Ed.). (2003). *International handbook of curriculum research.* Mahwah, NJ: Lawrence Erlbaum.

Pinar, W. F., Reynolds, W. M., Slattery, P., & Taubman, P. M. (1995). *Understanding curriculum.* New York, NY: Peter Lang.

Rule, J. (2002). *Hot-eyed moderate.* Richmond Hill, Canada: Firefly Books. (Originally published 1985)

Triumph Street Pedestrians

Erika Hasebe-Ludt & Anne Scholefield

W̶e invite you to accompany the two authors on their walk of contemplating *place*. Here, they *braid* three writing strands into a conversation with each other. They intertwine the insights of those mentors, poets, and scholars who have influenced them and walked this *topos* before them.

Strand I

> *Almost no one sees*
> *the blossoming chestnut*
> *under the eaves*
> —Matsuo Basho, *Narrow Road to the Interior*

Erika: Earlier this year, with my friend Anne, and with blessings from Ted Tetsuo Aoki, I walked the "tensioned textured spaces" (Aoki, 1997/2000) of this beloved scholar's life, along Triumph Street in Vancouver, British Columbia. As a teenager during World War II, Ted had lived on this east-side street with his family.

Anne and I walked in the mixed, transnational landscape where this *sensei* dwelled, hoping to learn more about his *life world*, and work. I also walked to reconfigure my own *lived curriculum* as a shifting topos inspired by Aokian-curriculum theorizing. I walked across this urban streetscape as an immigrant, a sojourner born-and-raised across the Atlantic in post-Holocaust Germany. Into this Canadian *terroir* I carried with me an ambivalent legacy of European education from the German-French, Alsace-Lorraine contact zone I grew up in, a place deeply scarred by centuries of political and linguistic ruptures in the course of the European colonial enterprise. Walking, reading, and writing about Vancouver was my attempt to interpret my small, personal narrative in relation to the worldly *grand narrative* that still remain present in this *postcolony* (Mbembe, 2001; Pinar, 2006). My other purpose was to honour the memories of the people who have put their mark on this Canadian topography and those who have influenced me (Chambers, 1999; Coupland, 2009; Stanley, 2009).

> The city is layered, splayed, even unrepresentable in categories where lawns are trimmed and grammars snooze in the late colonial sun. The rim is one horizonal sign—looking to the pacific through the crevices of discourse blocks…(Miki, 1998, n.p.)

Anne: Shortly after Erika was born, in post-Holocaust Germany, I was born in post-World War II British Columbia. Erika and I met when we were appointed to work together in a 1996 teacher-education program in Vancouver. My father was a veteran of the Royal Canadian Air Force. My mother was a witness to the forced incarceration of neighbours of Japanese ancestry from Vancouver Island where she and some of Dr. Aoki's family were born.

In 2000, I moved two blocks from Dr. Aoki's home on Triumph Street. A new century. A new millennium. But an old, tired, multi-layered street with a sloppy warp and weft of lifelines, coming and going.

Blocks and blocks of civil legacies worn thin by the lyric in one's i. The seams in the social and linguistic folds disclose formations of some interest here. In the practice of writing, for example, who's there—out there listening. (Miki, 1998, n.p.)

Erika: During a recent visit with Ted and his wife, June, at the extended care facility where they now live, we read together from the writings of Basho, Japan's luminary 17th-century poet, who chronicled his walking sojourns through his homeland in notebooks, travelogues, and through haiku (Basho, 2000). Reading this historical poetic text, compelling in its reverent attention to stepping lightly and lovingly in an insular, rural landscape steeped in spiritual richness and torn by feudal strife, created a tensioned counterpoint to Ted's and June's stories of growing up Japanese Canadian in the small-island towns of Cumberland and Fanny Bay in coastal British Columbia. Listening to their narratives, walking and tracing their footsteps along just one street between transnational movements of migration and expulsion, illuminated the harshness of exile, the perseverance in the face of it, and the hope of rapprochement in the volatile post-colonial terrains of our precarious times. I walked among the mixed artifacts of migration on this wet, spring morning. With every step, I felt the effects of relentless resettlement of the inhabitants of this place pound into my body.

> how precarious
> rusty eaves heavy raindrops
> livelihood *sonzai*

Anne: Erika and I have stayed in touch, personally and professionally, and I have had several visits with Dr. Aoki since our first meeting. So I was interested to learn that he had lived on Triumph Street. Erika was also surprised. When Erika invited me to join her to on a walk to explore the present state of "Ted's block," I put on my rainy-day clothes and accompanied her. We enacted an Aokian curriculum, akin to my orientation to the neighbourhood: As a pedestrian without a car, I had become educated about the community through encounters with other people, on the sidewalks, in the shops, and at the bus stops near my home.

My meditating that day, and my reflecting afterward, evokes layered impressions of a mostly down-and-out neighbourhood. My actual address was on Templeton Drive, facing Triumph. Templeton felt like "the happy address." Triumph, despite its name, was derelict, discouraged, and transient. The street breathed poverty, and frequently, violence.

It was by the brutal but indifferent letter of the law that [Japanese Canadians] were absorbed into the many to become strangers in their own place, scapegoats forced to incorporate and hence disguise the relentless power of an underlying violence (here) towards otherness in all its forms. (Miki, 1998, p. 31)

Strand II

Beyond our understanding is the changing form of that tree; we do not know its beginning, or its ending, or its roots.
—Ursula Le Guin, *Blue Moon Over Thurman Street*

Erika: When Ted Aoki told me that in his youth he had lived on the same street in Vancouver that I live on now, just a few blocks west, I decided to more closely explore the neighbourhood in which we have a common history. There is irony in the address: 1934 Triumph Street in East Vancouver, just off North Salisbury Drive, between Victoria and Templeton. In 1934, Ted's father, a teacher by training, had moved his K-12 school for Japanese Canadians from Cumberland, where Ted was born, to this more-prosperous, urban location and larger premises: a solid concrete and brick building that housed classrooms on the main floor and the family's living space upstairs. The Triumph Street school flourished for 8 years, until 1942. When the War Measures Act declared all Japanese Canadians "enemy aliens," the Aokis were stripped of their livelihood (Ayukawa, 2009). Ted and his family, along with 8,000 other Issei, Nisei, and Sansei Canadians were evicted from their homes, put into livestock corrals at nearby Hastings Park, pushed onto a train across the Rockies to Lethbridge, Alberta, to work on sugar beet farms in the unrelenting wind and dust of that prairie landscape (Aoki, 1997/2000; Roy, 2007).

Almost seventy years later, Ted remembers this painful episode vividly.

So does June: As a young girl she overheard someone—a white, older, English person—declare what a good thing it was to rally all the "Japs" into Hastings Park. That way it would be easier to kill them all at once (June Aoki, personal communication, April 2010). Hastings Park still exists today: a race track of a different kind, transformed into a horse-gambling venue—an artifact that reminds casino visitors and neighbourhood residents alike of the persistence of the banality of the colonial, economic enterprise (Stanley, 2009) and its enduring effects.

Anne: My partner, Madeline, and I bought our little apartment at Triumph and Templeton from a colleague, Violet, who worked in the same program as Erika and me, after Erika had moved on. Violet's father came to Vancouver from China in the 30s, prevented by Canadian law from bringing his wife. When that law was repealed following WW II, Violet's mother and father reunited in Vancouver. Violet was born on the corner of Triumph and Templeton, two weeks before Erika was born in Germany. Ten years later, a block north of Triumph, Violet's father was killed by a car while crossing the street.

The Triumph neighbourhood of the 50s and 60s was diverse: A Greek family lived on the adjacent corner, a Chinese family to the north, and a Japanese couple owned a home half a block away, also on Triumph. Many of the families maintained large gardens. Violet remembers swapping vegetables with the neighbours.

In 1996, Violet and her husband replaced the family home where her mother raised Violet, her brother and sister. They built a pretty apartment block on the corner of Templeton and Triumph. There, Violet's mother lived to the end of her life.

> i had meant to write about a pear tree i knew as a child when i lived over the mountains in a small prairie town but the language of that pear tree belonged to my mother tongue. it bespeaks a lost childhood language one which the pear tree in our backyard in chinatown has a nodding acquaintance with.
>
> how many languages does a pear tree speak? (Kiyooka, as cited in Miki, 1997, p. 208)

Strand III

I do not know...if we belong to the place where we are born, or the place where we are buried.
                                              —Anne Michaels, *The Winter Vault*

Erika: When the Aoki family lived and worked on Triumph Street in the 30s, their neighbourhood was a vibrant cosmopolitan mix of middle- and working-class European and Asian immigrant families, many employed by the harbour, the lumber mill, Rogers' sugar plant, the Wheat Pool, and the Burrard Inlet canneries (Coupland, 2009; Sandercock, 2003). Centuries before that time, this waterfront ecosystem, with its abundance of salmon and other native food sources, was home to the flourishing communities of the Coast Salish peoples. In 2010, this streetscape bears the scars of unrelenting waves of  expulsion, economic exploitation, and racial discrimination that continue to affect the most vulnerable citizens of this country: the First Nations population was driven into the urban core of the Downtown Eastside, and immigrants moved in, desperate to make a living from the industries that spawned along the waterfront (Demers, 2009). They laboured in the warehouses and docks of the industrial complex, their lives on the shore a stark contrast to those of the offshore "rich people" which gave Vancouver its label as a desirable "Shangri La" destination (Ross, 2010).

I have lived on Triumph Street on the other side of Hastings Park for almost thirty years, with my Japanese Canadian husband Ken, whose family was among those evicted from their homes in Steveston in 1942. Ken's family moved to the mountains via Hastings Park. Ken and I raised our daughter on Triumph Street. The small, elementary community school that Charlotte attended bears the name of a British Arctic explorer, Sir John Franklin. The school was her home as a young mixed-race, *hapa* student among many other children from races that mixed and mingled on this soil. Here, I began my teaching career; here, my learning from the multiple threads of racial, linguistic, and ethnic diversity deepened. Charlotte followed in her mother's footsteps. She became a teacher, currently teaching a short distance from where she was raised.

Anne: Madeline is a migrant to Vancouver—her roots are deep in Nova Scotia. Some of her ancestors came to Canada as cargo, left by a slave ship on the south shore, expected but not destined to float out to sea. Other ancestors immigrated from the US to escape slavery. In the 1700s, they arrived as United Empire Loyalists, and later came from the West Indies for employment.

She has an Irish great-grandmother, and *Mi'Kmaq* First Nations ancestors on both sides of her family. She is the only one of her five siblings to make a home on the west coast.

My family history goes back to Great Britain: My paternal grandparents are from England; Mum's father's clan came from Scotland, in the 1800s. They arrived in Canada, like Madeline's family, as United Empire Loyalists. I was born on Vancouver Island. I lived in various communities across Canada, before living in Japan for a year and a half. For 9 years, I made a home on Triumph Street.

Discovering our new neighbourhood was a matter of sustained rediscovery. A transient population revealed comings and goings from everywhere. Our own building, with just nine suites, represented Indigenous, Asian, Southeast Asian, European and African heritages. And although Violet's entrepreneurial husband liked to tell us we were in an "up and coming" place, we witnessed police stake-outs, domestic violence, drug transactions, prostitution, and homelessness, all on our Triumph and Templeton corner. We found needles in our hedge, a bag of marijuana on our walk, and witnessed "johns" and sex-trade workers negotiate and litter outside our windows. To our west, on Triumph, a social housing complex provided home for needy residents. Across the street, we witnessed the renovation of a "leaky condo," transformed into a home for tenants with mental health issues. Madeline and I would discuss over dinner which of us had had a chat with "the guy with the oxygen tank," the woman who talks to dogs, the mother with developing dementia and her son who walked the local park above Burrard Inlet. Recently, a year after we moved east and south of Triumph, a young man was shot in the alley behind our former home.

Our sense has always been that this neighbourhood, from Nanaimo Street to the east, and Victoria on the west—Ted's block—is populated with people in transition, either pausing to regroup and move "up," as we have, or arrested by loss; of health, of jobs, of prestige, of confidence. There are many who have succumbed to the unrelenting rigidity of systemic inequalities, or just have not recovered from bad choices or bad luck.

> ...ideological processes are not merely superstructural...They are embodied in people's daily practices as the normal ways of doing things; in other words, ideology, including racist and sexist ideology, is taken for granted and normalized...and continues to be an integral part of the way things are done in Canadian society, which in turn illuminates the connectedness of race, gender and class relations in organizing social life. (Ng, 1993, p. 57)

Erika: And so the geo/topographic rhizomes spread, and the history lessons continue in this small neighbourhood, crossing continents and streetscapes and burrowing in concrete structures that have shaped the destinies of Ted's family and mine along with that of many other migrants within Canada. These rhizomes and roots unearth tangled questions of belonging and birthplace, and home and not-home that are difficult to answer, all arising from the colonial terrain of Vancouver, British Columbia. This topos we walked on this spring constitutes the Indigenous *terroir* that generated the nourishment and livelihood of the Coast Salish peoples for centuries—until three centuries of colonization evicted them from their native soil, and the economic greed that motivated it turned into ecological ruin.

I want to believe that there is hope and strength in the métissage of Canadian identities, native and otherwise. However, pervasive racism is still visible and surfaces on our streets, in our schools, and our society over and over again. It goes hand in hand with the relentless ecological devastation of this place as a vital part of the biocultural diversity of the Pacific rain forest Indigenous ecosphere (Suzuki, 2006).

I wish I could read Basho's haiku in their original language with Ted and June. But I do not know their and my husband's family's mother tongue. So I listen to June's translation from English back into Japanese, am grateful for the gift of her still-strong, beautiful voice in her childhood language—a fleeting moment, a partial glimpse of ancient poetry from another place taking on new meanings right here, right now.

William Pinar (2006) has paid homage to Ted Aoki as one of the few curriculum scholars who has modelled with grace and humility the complexity of a genuine *East-West* dialogue though his own life. Ted's and June's vibrant métissage of identities as both Japanese and English Canadians is a true testimony to the resiliency of the new life that they forged and the conversations that can come out of living through injustice and discrimination. Their memories and their experiences, steeped in the places they lived, were precious "things they carried with them" (Chambers, 2003), things which shaped their *dharma*—meaning "that which carries and sustains us," as David Smith (2009, p. 94) reminds me. Reading and writing and walking relationally, in this way, helped me remember what carries and sustains my family in this mixed Asian-European-Aboriginal topos far from the ancestral places from where we have migrated. In my ever-evolving humus of longing and belonging, it is these kindred relations and residents of Triumph Street, then and now, that sustain me while learning to walk in this landscape and honour the rhizomes and roots of this place, the old shoots and the new ones, the buried and the blossoming ones.

REFERENCES

Aoki, T. T. (1997/2000). On being and becoming a teacher in Alberta. In J. M. Iseke-Barnes & N. Nathani Wane (Eds.), *Equity in schools and society* (pp. 61–71). Toronto: Canadian Scholars' Press.

Ayukawa, M. M. (2009). *Hiroshima immigrants in Canada 1891–1941.* Vancouver, Canada. UBC Press.

Basho, M. (2000). *Narrow road to the interior and other writings* (S. Hamill, Trans.). Boston, MA: Shambhala.

Chambers, C. (1999). A topography for Canadian curriculum theory. *Canadian Journal of Education, 24*(2), 137–150.

Chambers, C. (2003, December). Things I carried with me....*Educational Insights, 8*(2). Retrieved from http://www.ccfi.educ.ubc.ca/publication/insights/v08n02/contextualexplorations/curriculum/chambers.html

Coupland, D. (2009). *City of glass: Douglas Coupland's Vancouver* (rev. ed.). Vancouver, Canada: Douglas & McIntyre.

Demers, C. (2009). *Vancouver special.* Vancouver, Canada: Arsenal Pulp Press.

Kiyooka, R. (1997). Excerpt from: "Pear tree pomes." In R. Miki (Ed.), *Pacific windows: Collected poems of Roy K. Kiyooka* (p. 208). Burnaby, Canada: Talon Press.

Le Guin, U. (1993). *Blue moon over Thurman Street*. Portland, OR: NewSage Press.

Mbembe, A. (2001). *On the postcolony*. Los Angeles: University of California Press.

Michaels, A. (2009). *The winter vault*. Toronto, Canada: Emblem/McClelland & Stewart.

Miki, R. (1998). *Broken entries: Race, subjectivity, writing*. Toronto, Canada: Mercury Press.

Ng, R. (1993). Racism, sexism, and nation building in Canada. In W. Crichlow, & C. McCarthy (Eds.), *Race, identity, and representation in education* (pp. 50–59). New York, NY: Routledge.

Pinar, W. F. (2006). Complicated conversation: Occasions for intellectual advancement in the internationalization of curriculum studies. In *The synoptic text today and other essays: Curriculum development after the reconceptualization* (pp. 163–178; 194–195). New York, NY: Peter Lang.

Ross, G. S. (2010, March). A tale of two cities: The Vancouver you see, and the one you don't. *The Walrus, 7*(2), 22–32.

Roy, P. E. (2007). *The triumph of citizenship: The Japanese and Chinese in Canada, 1941–67*. Vancouver, Canada: UBC Press.

Sandercock, L. (2003). *Cosmopolis II: Mongrel cities of the 21st century*. New York, NY: Continuum.

Smith, D. G. (2009). Critical notice: Engaging Peter McLaren and the new Marxism in education. *Interchange, 40*(1), 93–117.

Stanley, T. (2009). The banality of colonialism: Encountering artifacts of genocide and White supremacy in Vancouver today. In S. Steinberg (Ed.), *Diversity and multiculturalism: A reader* (pp. 143–159). New York, NY: Peter Lang.

Suzuki, D. (2006). *The autobiography*. Vancouver, Canada: Greystone Books.

A Season for Less

Veronica Gaylie

Every day do something
that won't compute....
Love the world. Work for nothing.
Take all that you have and be poor.
Love someone who does not deserve it.
—Wendell Berry, *Manifesto*

It is late August and I have been writing this piece all summer in my mind. These words came to me while climbing mountain paths and walking in forests that I know well. It is the end of August and I have come down from the mountain; I still feel the fresh air, still hear the crunch of dry arbutus leaves. It is time to share.

During the past academic year I found hope in the earth, at ground-level.

(This is a piece best read outside).

1.

> People interfere with nature, and, try as they may, they cannot heal the resulting wounds. (Fukuoka, 1978, p. 34)

In *The One-Straw Revolution*, farmer philosopher Masanobu Fukuoka (1978) describes his journey of discovering *do-nothing farming*, a technique he introduced to Japan around the middle of the last century, where rice is grown without pesticide, or even removal of weeds. The technique both conserves water and helps retain the integrity of the soil.

Decades earlier, during the 1930s, Fukuoka abruptly left his job as a scientist working in an agricultural lab in Japan. Upon Fukuoka's departure, colleagues and friends begged him to return to work and to his old life. Fukuoka describes this time as a transformational turning point in his life where he left his job and began wandering the countryside to consider new farming methods. For a time he returned to his father's farm where he began cultivating ideas around organic farming methods and gentle ways of working with the earth.

Eventually Fukuoka began his own farm on the side of a mountain where, over the decades, students and other visitors would follow him to learn his revolutionary techniques around *do-nothing gardening*, which ultimately transformed farming techniques in Japan. Fukuoka writes that "the seven herbs of Spring" bring peace and contentment to the human spirit, yet:

> Modern people have lost their clear instinct and consequently have become unableot gather and enjoy the seven herbs of Spring. They go out seeking a variety of flavors. Their diet becomes disordered, the gap between likes and dislikes widens, and their instinct becomes more and more bewildered. (p. 15)

Fukuoka's subject is farming, and in particular, rice cultivation. He also writes about care for the soil and for the world based on integrity, trust and inner instinct. In a modern world that constantly demands more, Fukuoka is a call to less, as a model for both farming and life. Through reading his work I discovered that *less* is not only a solution to the problem of *more* but a response to nature that is very close to the ground-level rhythms of nature. Being a human, doing nothing, we are free to listen and learn.

> I often tell the young people in the huts on the mountain who come here...anybody can see the trees up on the mountain. (p. 25)

2.

> My paw is Sacred,
> the herbs are everywhere.

> My paw is Sacred,
> all things are Sacred.
>
> (Song of the Lakhóta Bear Doctors)

At the place of less there is a wisdom so clear. Such wisdom arrives at the ground level, a place and perspective I have learned to deeply trust.

I also know that place as poetry.

There, words rise from silence. If you wait, quietly, in open observation, words arrive.

In the world of running around, it's easy to forget this place, this deep, this place of less. The place of poetry belongs to silence, trust, care, love, and it is at once powerful and gentle. The place of poetry is also a place of vulnerability. For many people, a difficult place.

Nature brings a change of heart. A gentle approach to the planet. A way of listening. A hand held out for a bird with a few seeds until the wild gently settles there. A way of finding the story in the mountain.

3.

Directions to the Farm:

Drive to Kettle Falls.
From Kettle Falls take Highway 25 south.
Look for the barn.
(Bring:
journal
head lamp
long sleeves).

4.

First Day: The Linden Tree

Under the Linden Tree I feel
like I am
falling in love, I feel
someone should strum a song
or I should just stand here and look
up in wonder
taking in the flower's light scent
the pale flowers

the branches slightly waving in the wind
in a way   .
that settles me deeply
down, brings me back to being
a child of the planet
just looking
up in wonder
not-knowing
why
I am in love
I just am.

5.

This summer I was invited to speak at a workshop for teacher educators on a working farm in Washington State. The workshop was called *Education That Sustains: Sparking a Love for Learning*, and at the time I was invited, I wondered how I could spark a love of learning when I was feeling anything but sparky, or sustainable.

The farm. Where wisdom finds a place large enough. The place and the people are so gentle and true I can see myself in the world, and in my work, again.

Learning to milk goats, make cheese, feed chickens, repair a chicken tractor, and weed vegetable beds in the hot sun, I learned again. I learned to trust community. I recalled that I have never really been comfortable with fitting seamlessly into mainstream ways of working, thinking, or being. I am not comfortable with politics, or air, thickened with self-importance. I am not comfortable ignoring what is real.

I am not comfortable with the fear of being left behind in a world that is often looking backwards. I also now know that feeling comfortable and at ease within the corridors of academia is probably not a place I will ever be.

And I am at peace with that.

The farm reminds me: out here, I have company. With others who care about peace and community. Who care about the ground, the weeds, the goats, who are not afraid to say *what is real*. The farm reminds me of my priorities. It reminds me, like Fukuoka, to taste the seven herbs of spring.

What have I learned? What is my wisdom story? How did I return to this place?

In being outside. In hearing new words. Amongst others, being human beings. In vulnerability. In silence. In waiting. In peace. In the wild.

6.

Farm Table

The first morning
in the white-walled kitchen
not-knowing
anyone and surrounded
by American voices
I feel shy
and suddenly Canadian
or something
so the only thing to do
is eat

and from
the heavy wooden table in the kitchen
called an island
filled with goat cheese, cherries, boiled eggs
with sunny yellow centres
a little dill dusted on top
I take a slice of zucchini bread
put butter on it
then rhubarb jam

then find the place assigned to me
and sit
and meet new friends (good ones)
and no longer scared

I eat the cheese, the cherries, the cheery
eggs with sun-dappled centres
the entire world here
on the plate,
a chicken
a goat
a fruit, the whole place
where they live
the ground they walk on
the well water
the well worn path between farm house

chicken coop
and barnyard,
it is the place itself I taste:
the zucchini bread with rhubarb
the milk
the land
and just a second I fly to heaven

before gently floating down
to the farm house
between the barn and the garden
where the conversation continues
and everything lives.

7.

I am here to "spark" others and instead I am sparked.

It starts with an electric fence. I am standing in the chicken pen and want to cross over into the next pen with Liz, Katie and the goats. All that stands between me and them is an electric fence. Liz has crossed, telling me that her legs are short too. Katie, who is shorter than Liz, crosses just fine. It seems an easy shortcut.

I look at the fence and know: I will never get over this. I will need to go around the long way. I think: Taking shortcuts is not for me, even as I lift my leg over the wire...

Inside the goat pen one of the taller goats is, somehow, drinking water from a gushing tap. The goat is intent on getting the water. My last words are: Hey isn't nature cool? I even hear someone say: Yeah.

When I come to, I am lying on the ground in the goat pen with a small, brown goat trotting quickly towards me. She rubs her head on my arm and scratched leg, then stares fondly into my mud-streaked face with abject love. Liz says: "She is saying: 'Oh. I so get it.'"

I wonder if I am alive, and I laugh. Liz is right. The goat has *been there*. Has been too close to the fence, too near the boundary. And yet, the goat lives.

I remember how, after being zapped once, I planted my hand on a grounded fence pole and vaulted myself into the goat yard in what someone called "an amazing somersault and safety roll." Seeing the blood on my leg, Liz says: "Hey! War wounds! Lu-cky!"

I landed a perfect safety roll in a goat yard in Washington State.

Wow! Where did I learn such moves? Have I always had this in me?

I am bruised, my leg is bloody. The goat sniffs my face, begins eating my sleeve.

That evening I take out my knitting needles on the front porch. I find my story.

8.

Three on a Log

I go swimming with Americans in Lake Roosevelt
and one girl and I climb on a log
meant to keep the waves out
and the calm in
and heaving myself up onto the log
it starts to roll and I laugh
and laugh
like I am with my sister
when we were little
and I remember I have not laughed like this
for a while.

We balance ourselves.
Someone else swims over
and sure enough
the log rolls again.
(We laugh again,
we balance again).

9.

This place is healing. I meet new friends. I swim, I milk, I laugh, I spark. I learn to roll, I learn to fly.

During the week I hear and live good words: sustainability, respect, care, healing.

I find myself in a garden weeding herbs. I am a teacher, learning.

I try a little of this and that. I pull weeds, like it. I milk goats, love it. I feed goats weeds. We make cheese from the milk and later that same day we eat the same cheese from the same goats. I rise at dawn. I pull a portable chicken tractor between grape vines. I learn a hundred good uses for weeds.

When I leave, the smell of the goats are still on my hands, on my clothes. I am filled.

The moment that has made the most sense to me in a while is that little brown goat running towards me. It was as if it knew, and understood, I had just been zapped out of the blue. It knew what to do. That little goat nudged me, just enough.

10.

Goat Milking

Dear goat:
I don't know what I'm doing.
It is five a.m.
The farmer told me to grab hold
with authority and I do
but soon lose
my grip and slowly
the milking ends and I am just standing there listening
to you chew barley.
The smell here is good,
the milk, warm and fresh.
The border collie, Jet, is outside the door,
banished from the room, hurt.
The cats on the barn floor wait.
The farmers bring the goats up the ramp
the sound of their hooves on the barn floor,
the rest peak around the corner
curious of the new voices
like kids at school (oh no,
a new teacher).
Then they stand and wait
for me
to do something besides think,
trusting I will.
They have more faith in me
than me but then it is the way
the goat turns around
encouragingly, warm breath
on my shoulder and cheek
and begins eating my sleeve
that helps me try again,
learn to grab hold,
return to rhythm.

11.

On the last day a beekeeper tells us that in ancient Egypt people kept bees on a boat on the Nile River that floated back and forth to follow the flowers as they bloomed.

Humans and bees have lived in balance together for centuries. They don't know what is happening now, or why bee colonies are collapsing around the world. In some cases, beekeepers arrive to find their hives suddenly empty.

One reason may be that toxic chemicals in the environment have altered the bee's ability to navigate home.

12.

When I leave the farm it is like the final scene from *The Wizard of Oz* where Dorothy tells her new friends just how much they have helped her on her journey.

I really don't want to leave.

Melissa, a word I think means *honey*, gives me a hug.

The beekeeper says: Hey, I've never hugged a Canadian before!

I'm warm from food and friendship. From goats, milk and cheese.

The farm itself is like a hug. Here you are hugged by fences. Rubbed up against by animals all day long. They look for you coming. They jostle to get a glimpse. When you leave them, they watch you til you are all gone. And when you arrive they crowd around again. To them, you are food and relief. To us, they are food and relief. Here, we co-exist.

13.

Goat Cheese

We don't need to talk in the cheese room
just look at the white cheese on the counter
such a serene scene
from the goats waiting
at dawn in the barnyard
looking over the fence
wondering who I was
then trooping in
standing in full trust
I knew what I was doing
(warm breath

on my cheek).
How I owe this moment to them.
White cheese, the whitest I have ever seen
white sheets
white clouds
white fences on white beaches
the white walls of the farm
built by the farmer
the purest moment I have known
in months that weren't the whitest
or the nicest
but all is new
like dawn:
cold air, warm barn, warm breath.

14.

Epilogue

Nature, left alone, is in perfect balance. (Fukuoka, 1978, p. 34)

After a season of less, I return with better sense, trusting instinct. I am in touch with myself, my body, my head. I learn just how far away I have travelled from this place, from writing things down, from touching and being touched by the ground.

This season, nature taught me:

I am an earth citizen. (Where my loyalty lies.)
I need to be outside. (Easier to breathe.)
I prefer to live with less. (Less to worry me.)
The forest is my place. (I will return to you.)

15.

State Park

Fearless deer leap below the dry arbutus trees,
crackling leaves. She is going the same way
as me. On a long path up the mountain I know
I could live on the scent of bay leaf
and the site of live oak
on tall yellow grass.

Another steep path.
And another.
A black fly chases me the whole way.
For it to stop chasing me
all I have to do is not breathe.
It is not a swarm, just one fly.
Nothing to fear.
It finally leaves me.
(I never stopped breathing.)

A long downhill stretch on a path of
dried
pink
bay
leaf.
(Wild. The word in my mind the whole way: Wild.)

Deer
on the Planetary Trail
Deer
on the Meadow Trail.
Rustles in the underbrush.

Still.
Clear as blue sky.

REFERENCES

Berry, W. (1973/1991, Fall/Winter). Manifesto: The mad farmer liberation front. *In Context: A Quarterly of Humane Sustainable Culture, 30*, 62.

Fukuoka, M. (1978). *The one-straw revolution*. New York: New York Review Books.

Song of the Lakhóta Bear Doctors. Retrieved from http://www.indigenouspeople.net/sioux.htm.

Tutelaries of a Place We Came Into

Christi Kramer

It is that this hand, reaching back, reaching forward, extends 200 years.
My grandma was my first-grade teacher. She taught generations. In her classroom, one could crawl up and sleep on the fire escape in the sun. Light there, more gentle than these determined knuckles backed into my mother's palm; both hands, concentric, pressing into wood and lead and word: our effort heats the pencil: this is what I smell. Some rhyme chiseled, burned into dream of waking, writ, or stitched, in this skin of my making. If I am to know the *Word*, I must know world, I've heard. In the valley where I was raised: in the lap of my grandmother, I learned to read. In Grandma's garden, field, and kitchen: the world. Tradition may be rooted, tough and learned. Wisdom may be light and hover; certainly, it's near the smell of skin and extends beyond where our counting can.

Barefoot

Witchcraft (it must be) that
what holds her to him

waterfall splash and dazzle
somebody saw their shadow, embrace at falls

*

What drives her there, through blackberry rip and thistle;
that walks her straight (must be, how she wishes)

unnamed bush, hanging sweet clusters and white petal; could be God.
Not overlooking foxglove, to pick bouquet for mother

It is the wound—she knows she wounded—that moves.
Anything born wounds.

*

What was it left her there?
Meadow large: lupine, huckleberry, spider, rose.

*

Foot crunch dry weed, grasshopper scatter
what blessing, this too hot sun; creek far

It is another that runs faster, cooler; another weighted step.

She checks; she's still.

Bio

Excerpts from her biography say "any regular day, she rode an elk through gardens of delphinium and snapdragon to her grandmother's house for gingersnaps; swam in their bottomless crater lake and took baths with a bear." Could it be she remembered the story wrong? Were there regular days, or was each day full of the smell of earth, the summer heat on skin, or the burn from pulling honeysuckle with the tongue? She remembers the gingersnaps were store bought (she doesn't even hint at this in the telling). Why, in the world, would she speak in past tense when describing the generations of geese that she watches as they come and go? How can the spirit be separate from the body/the senses, if it is embodied and known from the heart? All members are present here in that beat and in each breath. How about the stories of "miss-spellings": her name and *Christ* with an *I*. Since all the repeated searching, over-and-over, the *I* is lost, again.

Blotched, betrothed, botched

A good woman spills none of the rice
Laughs only when her hearts a-fire
Looks you in the eyes

> My grandmother,
> in the fifth grade was expelled
> for having crossed her legs, her mother,

A good woman is beautiful, loves well
Tells those secrets to no one
Sits quietly in the moon's swell

> Great-grandmother Robinson,
> with legs like heaven, or fate, died young.

A good woman is a fine mother, rises early, works late
Is not dizzy, does not tire. Wears blue
Makes one sweet smelling, scrumptious cake

> They say she had the flu,
> heard something like coughing from her bed
> A good woman can fly if she wants to

Is careful when she stitches with red thread
Or zips, or buttons, or holds, like potato in her palm,
The pulsing glob from beneath her rib.

> Great-great-grandmother Rivers was made to pay alms
> jailed for hanging wash on Sunday, sin
> another time for carrying a pot to a friend, ill. Stew and bagbalm.

A good woman might dance, might drink a bit, or not; loves wind
a good woman, a good girl,
knows where to find the best in him

> My mother says don't ask; don't mention it again—
> Her mother's mother
> The grass around her grave grows long,

Red, maroon, crimson.
Says something else went on, gone wrong.
Bachelor button, lily, iris, rose and pearl.

In a corner the half-moon burns

—Octavio Paz, *Natural Being*

Today we burn the fields. It is best to drag the rake through dry winter grass; hold briefly, pull up, allow air to pass through. Light from the farthest corner; water the ditch. Notice where the wind is, where the moon is. The moon has nothing to do with our burning. Move steady and quick.

Enheduanna carried the fire in her voice because her hands were full of baskets, harps, necklaces and a crown. She, first author, noted where the moon was. This had nothing to do with us. Burn the fields. It is Easter and when Christ was hung he was naked. It is Easter and this year there is one white swan on the lake. It is spring and time.

"When Loren and I were courting or when we were just married and young, it was spring, or it was goose season and he, a strapping buck, came holding this white goose, high so all could see." Shooting swan is illegal. Growing the wrong poppies. Awareness of certain things is frowned upon, or is it that indifference is wrong?

The mountains where the fields touch are the long black hair. Head hung prostrate. Ash Wednesday: a cross on the brow. Mourning a criminal is illegal. Sunday, they said, Mary did: who was, or was not, a whore, went to where the burning was done. Soot after feet washing. A year's wages poured; poppies smell as sweet.

Gasoline was dumped on Grandma's field. Helicopters flew out back. Smoke swirled in a dirge, rose. The moon is behind, somewhere. Grandma leaned her rake to hide the flowers she picked. Water in a jar. Seeds in the yeast can. We had nothing to do with the burning.

The moon is breast and metal, wails and sucks in our song. After rain it will be again. New and waning. Seeds moved by the wind. She liked them best because the blowing petals looked like lips, red and bitten. Mourning is forbidden.

Grandma hung black cloth on the windows, plucked the feathers. She could have made a pillow from all that wasn't down. Enheduanna clenched a chisel. Burned her passion into stone. Nothing to do with us. Drag the rake along the moon.

No matter what earth

She took the fallen chickadee, took the walnut boat, interred the two,
patted smooth mysterious dirt. (her logic that the bird might float)

The roots dug here: once cedar, the baobab elsewhere, cavity in granite;
What kept us here, once decomposing fir and fig; what about this place?
My mother's hands fold little boats from foil, hats from newsprint.
I can't do this. Lost at sea, I navigate not by stars, which govern and burn out

but by her voice and lull, a pull as constant as tide and depth. In dream
the word returns to meaning; the face turns to itself in sunlight, to mirror
or crowd.

Bread dipped in soup, milk poured into the ground, absorb. Logic that the
bird might float.
Wren on lily pad, flutter. Underneath depth; underneath snake.

Make sure you say she was a loving woman.
Honey, sometimes good is just good.

The colour of her silk blockquilt is hyacinth, straw daisy, impatient. Is myrtle,
sage and cradlewort. Is crocus, lily, onion. Is mustard, bear grass, iris in the
fall. Is marigold. Is hyssop. Is wild faithful rose.—Jesus, when he came to
Mary Magdalene, fresh from death and not quite yet returned, looked to be a
gardener, smelled of lily and of myrrh.—Her loom is made of fruitwood. Her
shuttle is cherry and pine. Same as her cross in the garden: moss, grapevine,
wisteria, hemmed. Her stitch: exact and fine. Make sure you say about harvest,
about bringing in fruit, especially the cherries. Sour and wild. That branch of
the plum outback is stained hibiscus, where she hung the cloth to dry.

Do we miss these things in heaven?

Everything remembers. Wood remembers heat once it has been burned. Charcoal keeps a glow, secret. Trees remember water, call the rain down again, reach branches up and call.

Earth remembers herself, remembers herself. Opens up, rumbles, shakes and pulls us all back in again.

I remember in half-light and fever how her hair coiled around her head in a great
    grey braid, forever.
What I knew as sacred fell, fell, fell in waves. Aunt Mable let her hair down; no
    ordinary visit.

We talked like nothing was going on about beading, fishing and cabbage, about swimming in the dark part of the lake, late, when everyone else thinks you're weeding the garden.

Aunt Mable stitched silk blocks; Grandma Gurt knitted purses. They said they had come to take me to heaven. Oh, I told them, I decided awhile ago I'd never go to heaven.

It was when I was peeling the label off a sauerkraut jar; ran the water over it, over my fingers enjoyed it all too much. It was then I thought aloud I was done believing in heaven.

Gurt told the story of when we were huckleberry picking and how there was a baby, alone, crying in the back of a pick-up; about how everyone heard and no one did anything

until the dad came back. I remember she chased him, beat him on the head with her iron wood cane all the way to the bottom of the hill.

At noon, the sky remembers the stars, the place they hold at night. If we ever feel sorry in our longing, we must remember the moon was once part of the sun, once part of the earth.

Have you ever stood looking at something you love but cannot touch forever? I said, I was done believing in heaven.

Aunt Mable reached up inside me; took out the baby already dead; wrapped her in a silk blockquilt; paid me with three pieces of licorice from Gurt's purse; carried the baby and closed the door behind them.

Remember how rain feels on the skin, or how it is to float just under the surface; how water holds us; how we hear what is beneath us only? Or how fire burns if we touch?

A note at the time of revisions:

Significantly, the tutelage, my grandma's home—where these poems are located—burned and today what is left is being bulldozed back into the ground. When we receive this anthology in print, by then I am sure it will be at least spring…and the snow, gone, may leave a brighter green patch where the tutelage, my grandma's house, would have been. In the meantime, today I make a cake: another kind of life writing that proves itself when egg whites peak, when frosting is licked from finger and you know just how much you have yet to understand. Every year for the past 60 years my grandma has made my mom a German chocolate birthday cake. Today it is my turn. Every single egg I broke had two yokes. Grandma, does this equal two eggs or one?

AND ENHEDUANNA'S CHILDREN SAID (REFERENCES):

Bachelard, G. (1964). *The poetics of space, the classic look at how we experience intimate places* (M. Jolas, Trans.). Boston, MA: Beacon Press. (Original work published 1958)

> The title of this article is in direct reference to this passage from William Goyen's novel, *House of Breath*, cited by Bachelard:

>> That people could come into the world in a place they could not even at first name and had never known before; and that out of a nameless and unknown place they could grow and move around in it until its name they knew and called with love, and call it HOME, and put roots there and love others there; so that whenever they left this place they would sing homesick songs about it and write poems of yearning for it, like a lover….The soil in which chance had sown the human plant was of no importance. And against this background of nothingness our human values grow! Inversely, if beyond memories, we pursue our dreams to their very end, in this pre-memory it is though nothingness caressed and penetrated being, as though it gently unbound the ties of being. (p. 58)

> Other notions recognized in these poems: The poetic image as direct ontology, as phenomenology of the soul. The imagining consciousness as origin; our house, or home, may be made of [our] breath, wind, voice; *the corners*: intimate spaces of dream/home.

Freire, P., & Macedo, D. (1987). *Literacy: Reading the word and the world*. Westport, CT: Bergin & Garvey.

> [If I am to know the Word, I must know world, I've heard.] There is an interview I enjoy, posted on Youtube http://www.youtube.com/watch?v=pSyaZAWIrlI where Freire speaks of his movement in the [his] world: "to the streams of Recife; to the mounts of Recife" and

of movement from and to Christ-as-comrade and Karl Marx, movement within *transcendentiality* and in *worldliness.*

Lederach, J. P. (2005). *The moral imagination: The art and soul of building peace.* New York, NY: Oxford University Press.

Also from his work in the world, as a peacebuilder in places of violent conflict, Lederach, within his argument for the power of art—its ability to move within complexity and in the creative act, transform—asserts that the moral imagination requires that we imagine ourselves in a web of relationships.

Like Hannah Arendt speaking of the story and the hero and the action and the reasons for telling story, where "the disclosure of the 'who' through speech, and the setting of a new beginning through action, always fall into an already existing web where their immediate consequences can be felt," says, "...Somebody began [the hero's story] and is its subject in the twofold sense of the word, namely, its actor and sufferer, but nobody is its author" (Arendt, 1958, p. 184).

Arendt, H. (1958). *The human condition.* Chicago, IL: University of Chicago Press.

If there were a spider in these poems, we could invoke the image of a web: the academy, my grandmothers' lap, the poem each—in full complexity—elegant strands in the world brought into being by (and bringing into being) the spinner. The poems here consider this temporal world in which the relationships and learning take place. [It is that this hand, reaching back, reaching forward, extends 200 years]. Lederach's arguments build on the idea of *The 200 Year Present,* offered by Boulding (1990).

Boulding, E. (1990). *Building a global civic culture: Education for an interdependent world.* Syracuse, NY: Syracuse University Press.

Considering poetic inquiry—poetry in research, in teaching, in peacebuilding, in life writing—I note that it is from a web of intricate and intimate complexity (more than the position of dichotomy, either art, or the academy) that these poems emerge.

The academic community, unlike the artistic community, often begins its interaction with and journey into the world by stating a problem that defines both the journey and the interaction. The artistic community, it seems to me, starts with experience in the world and then creates a journey toward expressing something that captures the wholeness of that feeling in a succinct moment in time, they both rely on intuition. (Lederach, 2005, p. 5)

Paz, O. (1976). *Eagle or sun? Aguila o sol? Natural being* (E. Weinberger, Trans.). New York, NY: New Directions.

(Homage to the Painter Rufino Tamayo). The half moon burns in a corner. It is not yet a jewel, but a fruit that ripens by its own interior sun. The half moon is radiation, womb of the mother of all, womb of each ones wife, pink shell...

Liminal Lessons
From Two Islands and One Son

Tasha Henry

A s I stare at the world map, thumbtacks, and strings marking the trajectories of experience, identities lost and found, I see my life's collage. There are bands that intersect and collide and there are tacks that stand alone. Each pinpoint punctuates a significance, a subjective signpost. I find I am drawn to the

complex of crossings and the brightly woven macramé of movement indicating distances traversed, departures, and beginnings. I am not focussing on the destination points; rather I am trying to make sense of the gestalt of life's occurrences and the junctures where teacher, traveller, and mother merge. I want to speak about the crisscross of cultures, and the palpable disorientation that comes from living in two countries. Underneath the desire to speak from both within and outside culture's language is the hope that by describing the places I live I can learn to be both here and there with others, better. Donna Haraway wrote, "we are all in chiasmatic borderland, liminal areas where new shapes, new kinds of action and responsibility, are gestating in the world" (Haraway, as cited in Gregoriou, 1995, p. 311). This notion of liminality (Heydon, 2001), or threshold, in relation to pedagogy, leaves me asking, what can be learned from teaching, mothering, and moving in and between disparate cultures?

My son sleeps on my chest.
How is it possible that something so small, so dependent
could transform my every cell?
His weight is teaching me
about an answerability to all things.
It seems the weight of childhood
has rendered me its worthy student.

Tobago: Sitting in the humid morning sun, watching my son play with sticks under the shade of banana leaves, I am finding it challenging to capture how the taste of mango can change a worldview. It is as if this place is teaching me through the layers of its taste. This mango, on this particular morning, is helping me understand Canada through everything that it is, through everything that I am not. It feels incomprehensible: how a place can alter every aspect of your life, and leave you bewildered, grateful, lost. If I were a translator of these worlds I would speak precisely about mangoes so squarely opposite. But as I claim the words I move farther from the living sensation. I am beginning to think that my relationship to place is tacit, understood only in the measure of its inarticulateness. By describing cultural spaces do I render them comparable? Are they reduced to judgements coded in language, islands competing? It feels to me that it is the incomparability of sensations, of being in two places at once, that allows me to live the textures of this two-fold life. More importantly it is clear that this mango, and the fragrance of everything here, is what calls into question the degree of my receptivity to it. Is that lemon I taste folded between layers of mango? Is there a trace of something familiar? Somehow my place in the world begins to move through me when I struggle to listen to its elements. I feel as if I am living on the edge of frayed borders and blurred cultures. And now, this sweet juice running from the corners of my mouth, sticking to my chin, is telling me the experience is already fleeting; a disintegrating description of home.

In this fray,

amidst the stickiness of extraordinary juices—
unravelling
subjectivity's macramé,
a receptivity emerges
to places
both familiar
and foreign.

By living in two countries and raising a son who spans both, I am beginning to see how my life's movement is teaching me about receptivity. Just as I continue to discover the layers of living in community, I see my receptivity to my students as an endless practice that can only be described as a deepening practice. Learning about and through receptivity is an infinite lesson. In the same way that the birth of my own child has opened me, and continues to open me, so does my work with children. My son initiates me into the layers of parenthood just as my students establish me as their teacher. Being with children and witnessing childhood has humbled me, cast me into baffling and heart warming waters. Could it be that the depth of my "engagement with the world" (Pinar, 2009, p. 143) is measured by the quality of my work with children? Is my place in the world revealing itself through a life touched by children? It seems clear that the purpose of my work with children is to receive and exchange a multitude of worlds *through* them. It is a reflexive structure indeed, where subjectivity is defined by this receptivity to, and a responsibility for, the other (Levinas, 1998). Could it be that a teaching subjectivity is self-constituted through appropriate responses to children? Could it be that we must lose ourselves in the culture of childhood in order to teach children? And by becoming lost, responding to the call of the child, we stumble back, disoriented, to a self now initiated and substantiated through the act of the response?

Listening to Childhood

My son grows like a rapid spring river after a heavy rain. He is a conduit for two cultures. He somehow knows how to *be*, how to move in each country. His father and I are islands cast in our fixed ways, stuck in the earth, rooted in the places that raised us. But our son has rendered these places fluid and has disintegrated our perceived borders. Where I am stranded, he finds ways of moving between, through and over cultural and national boundaries. When we are in Tobago his skin turns from cinnamon to deep caramel. His muscles visibly take on the history of his ancestors as he learns to swim in the waves and trudge through wet sand. He narrates stories he has never heard through the unconscious cadence of his gestures. He tells me about the ocean and its brightly scaled creatures. He eats cassava and kingfish. He moves like his very limbs are an extension of the ecosystem. I see his physicality change before my eyes. He is at home here, naked, feet planted in the hot sand—sand as soft as whole-wheat flour. He tells me about the phenomenology of this place through his movements. He whispers in his pre-verbal babble, small hands pressed against my face, the secret to being here, now.

By witnessing him grow between cultures, I am learning about the opening between them. Through him, I am discovering new crevasses and areas of over-lap. His exigency through this world is my benevolent teacher. I can *live* in the Caribbean but my son *belongs* here, like his father. I know they taste breadfruit, roasted on the open fire, differently than me. I nibble, compare it to potato and then I look at them, breathing in the salt spattered air, butter dripping onto chests, and they seem to be listening to the secrets of the sea. I suddenly feel so alone. I know I must learn to listen differently. Luce Irigaray's (2002) question returns to me: "how to listen to the other, to open oneself horizontally, to the other's sense, without preventing the return to oneself" (p. 58). Is it the candour of childhood that allows my son to listen, to receive these worlds? Or is it his genealogy that instructs him? I recognize culture's elusiveness through him (Yon, 2000). Like estuaries where salt water meets fresh, running seamlessly into each other, he lives the fluidity of culture animated. He knows these places and the space that resides between them. I long to swim as he does.

You swim,
little turtle,
easy in her gentle wake
adept in sea,
seamless on sand
thick-skinned tortoise,
shelled by love
lulled by two-tongued sea songs
'the chile have joy in he eyes'
they say,
from the shore.
You are both ship and storm
salt and fresh water
borderless estuary.
Bronzed, half-webbed feet
carry you between
two extremes,

extremely met
bound by the ever surprising bounty of impossibility
and the caress
of a warm lapping tide.

Looking at the faces of my students, I am thinking about my son on the beach. My students wait for me to start, but I am lost in questions. How do I begin to describe whole worlds and the spaces between them?

Vancouver Island: He loves the rocks on this beach. They fit into his small hands perfectly. Layers of fleece and thick socks break the northern wind. The crisp air attacks my lungs. My body likes the cold. I feel alive here. The sensations of home, distant like a childhood memory, envelop me. I inhale the cavernous smell of evergreen, fern, and kelp. But on the heels of familiar scents is the feeling that I still live on the periphery. It appears I carry the feeling of outsideness with me no matter where I dwell. Immune to familiarity and recipes of home, my life is homeless despite its various habitats. But this outsideness is not without gifts. It has taught me that being in the world is a practice defined by boundlessness and the quality of my responses to others and other places. I am beginning to understand my life teaching as a teaching life—something that can only operate on the edge of what it can know. It is a life full of lessons, of deepening, but not necessarily of attaining knowledge. Teaching, for me, is a curious practice that must remain defined by its ability to be poised on and between multiple thresholds (Heilbrun, 1999). And only by continuing to question this boundlessness do I stay perched, rooted in the manifold of place, responding to life's call. To be perched on multiple thresholds has allowed me to continue asking questions about teaching and learning. It has taught me how to be in, and learn from, the world.

I have found myself deliciously lost,
  practicing on the edge
  a conduit of worlds still unknown to me,
beleaguered by the invitation of expansiveness
childhood's
    ever captive
student.

REFERENCES

Gregoriou, Z. (1995). Derrida's responsibility: Autobiography, the teaching of the vulnerable, diary fragments. *Educational Theory, 45*(3), 311–336.

Heilbrun, C. G. (1999). *Women's lives: The view from the threshold.* Toronto, Canada: University of Toronto Press.

Heydon, R. (2001). *Which way to insight? A special educator's search for an ethical praxis in an area of liminality* (Unpublished doctoral dissertation). Ontario Institute for Studies in Education, University of Toronto, Toronto, Canada.

Irigaray, L. (2002). *The way of love* (H. Bostic & S. Pluhacek, Trans.). London, England: Continuum.

Levinas, E. (1998). *Entre nous: Thinking of the other* (M. Smith & B. Harshav, Trans.). New York, NY: Columbia University Press.

Pinar, W. F. (2009). *The worldliness of a cosmopolitan education: Passionate lives in public service.* New York, NY: Routledge.

Yon, D. (2000). *Elusive culture.* Albany: State University of New York Press.

The Gates of Butterstone Farm

Ahava Shira

The motion of the heart to wonder, to investigate, to offer ourselves full-out to whatever is most true.
— Bonnie Myotai Treace, Foreword to *The Eight Gates of Zen*

This thought of the heart returns us to an animal intimacy.
—James Hillman, *The Thought of the Heart and the Soul of the World*

I am a poet, arts-based researcher and healthy-relationships educator. In the fall of 2007, after many years of teaching about healthy relationships in the classroom, and writing poetry and essays about my experience of relationships with people (Shira, 1998, 2005, 2007, 2008, 2009), I moved to Butterstone Farm and discovered a new place of learning.

As I walk through the farm, I am surrounded in every direction by fences. Arranged around the perimeter of the forests, gardens and pastures, these fences protect the gardens and orchards from the appetites, and deceptively far reach,

of the white-tailed deer that wildly inhabit the island. Each fence has its own particular gate.

Walking through the gates of the farm is a journey of encounter, marked with a tone of sacred possibility. Attending to the ongoing sensual, visual experience of opening and closing the gates, I attend to the relationship between self and other. Through the arts-based research practice of *Loving Inquiry*,[1] I learn to pause, attend, breathe in, and open my heart. Sounds, smells, visual cues, sensations as well as images, metaphors and linguistic resonances all invite me into connection.

Gate of Presence

In entering the domain of the heart, I yearn for a language.
(Denton, 1998, p. 33)

*What takes place here is not ordinary or commonplace unless my precon-
ceptions make it so. What takes place here is extraordinary.*
(Meyer, 2006, p. 5)

It begins as it always begins, somewhere in the middle of the daily chores of living, a pause, a moment of deep listening, looking closely at, paying attention. Sun sits in sky above, warms my arms and legs. A belly full of scrumptious lunch, hand-picked from the garden. Maple dances in the breezes from the valley, leaves touch, shuffle like the crowds of browsers at the Saturday market in Ganges. Raven makes itself known, above wings thrush past, chitters of smaller birds rearranging themselves in trees around the farm.

Over in the south pasture, barn swallows new to this world are learning to fly, diving and climbing over the parched summer grass. Suddenly a raven swoops down, catches one in its beak, lifts it off and away. I walk over to the nest to check on the other nestlings, their burgeoning tail feathers all I can see of them.

Cultural anthropologist and educator Arrien (2005) suggests:

> Gates are often considered places of initiation or entryways into holy places, sacred grounds, or spiritually significant transitions. Deep archetypal feelings may surface when we are "at the gate." Instinctively we recognize that we are required to let go of what is familiar, and prepare to enter and open ourselves to the unknown. (p. 9)

Butterfind

My lover brings me a butterfly
perfectly intact

must have hit a car on our road, he says

I smoothe its soft wing
imagine its last flight

a western tiger swallowtail

place it inside one of the nests
I have collected on my windowsill

Lay it beside an opal stone egg
and an eagle feather

It is the present I seek. Not to deny the past and not to ignore the future, but to have them live where they must, in memory and imagination

(Lane, 2004, p. 20)

The Horses

lived here for a while
boarded in our pasture

just yesterday
I stroked their necks
let them smell my hand
fed them apples from our trees

Farley tried to climb
onto Trisha

a game of dominance

Java nodded her head
Maggie stamped her foot
on the ground

this afternoon
I looked for them
in the field
and in the forest—

they like it there
especially when it
is hot

I found three of them
bowed in the grass,
nuzzling the green blades like nipples

watched their tails flick flies
from their neighbour's eyes.

Gate of Listening

There is poetic knowing. It can't be explained, only encountered.
(Friesen, 1995, pp. 121–122)

What is the nature of a loving relationship? How do I engage in loving relationship with nature?

In *The Way of Love*, feminist philosopher and writer Luce Irigaray (2002) says, "Silencing what we already know is often more useful in order to let the other appear" (p. 165). In order to enter and embrace the reality of another, I have to let go of my ideas of who that other is, and/or who I want them to be. Irigaray suggests we find "gestures or words" that "touch the other in his, or her alterity" (p. 151). She adds:

> Attraction is often awakened by the difference between two worlds, by the mystery that the one represents for the other....Such an approaching can exist in the respect of two familiarities which wed without cancelling each other out. (p. 151)

Language as a bodily phenomenon accrues to all expressive bodies, not just to the human. Our own speaking, then, does not set us outside of the animate landscape but...inscribes us more fully in its chattering, whispering, soundful depths.

(Abram, 1996, p. 80)

Thresholds

1.

Here on Butterstone Farm

the moon at night
is a kerosene lamp

I hike across a
frozen field in
Tibetan Sherpa boots

consider bright
stars of garlic
growing beneath
snow and straw

secure the latches
of wooden gates

wonder at hands
deft with
corralling branches
into thresholds

2.

Each day I light fire
after fire
and sip tea

rituals I never tire of
instead I regard them as
sacred, textured

When the fire doesn't light
at first match
I try smaller logs, more paper

3.

Being alone here
with words

without needing them to mean
anything

to say anything important
without needing to be anybody
important

*This is what I seek to do in
my poetry—to be attentive,
listening with care, seeking
to learn by heart.*

(Leggo, 2004, p. 31)

Riot

I step outside
our loft

blue sign
says SLOW

careful
not to slip on
the deck where ice
remains for days

I'm greeted by a
rush of sound

a riot of birds

whistles

chirps

CAWS

tweets

I have never heard
so many birds
outside this house
before

how I adore
the calm velocity
they bring

Gate of Interconnection

Where you are is who you are. The further inside you the place moves, the more your identity is intertwined with it. Never casual, the choice of place is the choice of something you crave.

(Mayes, 1996, p. 86)

At its best, the poems are those of offering and love. We need a background that will let us find ourselves and our poems, let us move in discovery.

(Rukeyser, 1949, p. 211)

A tiny fly lands on my skin. A moth with light brown wings alights onto the wooden planks of the deck, zips its body around this way and that, shows me its beautiful pattern before it retreats to the edge between two boards and disappears.

How to Pick Cherries

(The birds will give it away)
    Take the ladder folded up by the barn
    Carry it over to the cherry tree
        Shopping bag slung across your chest to keep your hands free
          One holds onto the ladder as fingers ply stems gently
            From their branches
              Look for those that blush
                Rosy cheeks on a yellow face
                  Do not to disturb those still turning
              When your basket is full
            Birds still nibble those
(out of reach)

Gate of Generosity

Generosity to the stranger acknowledges that community exists beyond one's own family, social group, species.

(Hirshfield, 1997, p. 210)

Poets write in and with the facts and frameworks of what they see in themselves in relation to Others, in particular landscapes, emotional and social situations.

(Brady, 2009, p. xvi)

Linger

You wonder
how the birds feel during sunrise

which gate is yours to
open this morning

how many years you have left
to practise this singing

you have never been a solo player
have always loved this accompaniment

robin's saxophone
rooster's trumpet blare
sparrow's throaty oboe

you belong to this orchestra

though it's not what you thought life would be
you have both nothing and everything to do with it

Meetings at the crossroads
between dragonfly and rose bush,
fence post and grape vine,
fig leaf and horizon.

Once these too were only words   concepts
Now you linger with their bodies,   grateful

Inside doesn't mean anything here

A Loud Thud

Out of sleep
another stunned
young robin

they are having a good year
she said, that's why so many are
down

its beak bowed in the ground
you lift it out gently
have become accustomed to
this holding

its legs grip your bare palm
strongly a good sign

it is warm
heart pumps hard
beak open wide
tongue a sliver
like golden rice paper
big brown black eyes

with pupils like yours
only darker

you sit back on the deck chair
smooth the top of its head
wind blows you both
relaxes

loose feathers drift around its
face, rusted belly

Curious, it looks at you
mouth starts to close
you wish for a song but
nothing comes

another wind shuffles
it rises onto its legs
talons secured to this
low perch

continues to stare
you smile, laugh

recall this week's earlier casualty—
how you rushed it to the wildlife centre
your best friend from high school
didn't know what to do when she found it.

you went on habit, grabbed
the new balance shoe box the keys
and were off—

down the mountain
through town and up
the now familiar driveway

placed the bird in healing hands
perhaps this one would live

witnessed a harbour seal
smile, almost enter her pool.

A sudden shift.
first attempt at reentry
you stay put watch it prepare
for departure

charcoal and white feathers
catch air, the maple its first landing.

You promise to change that line
in your poem *fear of falling*

"I've never saved anything besides myself."

It's no longer true

Gate of Intimacy

*Everyone is nourished and augmented by the other. Just as one is not with-
out the other, so Writing and Loving are lovers and unfold only in each
other's embrace, in seeking, in writing, in loving each other.*
(Cixous, 1991, p. 42)

Relationship is not just about caring for people, although that certainly is important, but the ability to relate to everything, to be open, to learn and grow through every situation and circumstance.

(Smith, 1998, p. 78)

Through my practice of Loving Inquiry, I search for those gestures or words that touch the other in their alterity, or difference, to approach the other in what Irigaray refers to as a "poetic way of dwelling" (p. 152). Ecologist Stephan Harding (2006) offers a similar understanding with regards to our relations with the natural world:

> We need to allow ourselves to be open to the subjective agency at the heart of every "thing" in the world so that we can speak and act appropriately in their presence and on their behalf. We must keep alive and nurture a sense of "otherness" of whatever phenomenon we might be considering, allowing a strange kind of intimacy to develop in which the urge to control is replaced by a quickening awe at the astonishing intelligence that lies at the heart of all things. (p. 37)

Through poetry, narrative, and photography, I seek to enter into relationship with an openness and intimacy that keeps alive this sense of "otherness."

Three

1.

Here in the garden—beneath cherry and plum, and walnut and maple—we sit like two school children reading our study books   Your head perches on my knees; my hands rub your neck; a mist hovers like bullies in the hallway, but nobody can touch us We are invisible indivisible Raven Raven overhead startles, you look at me with your green green eyes, turquoise stones like waters that curl around Polynesian islands Every now and then I get up and move, trail my fingers along limbs of true cedars, stretch my hand toward cheeks of roses, caress soft crimson ovals, whisper to those still unfolded Steady, steady.

2.

Here I come home with you beside me like vines climb cedar boughs Mist has ears and beads of rain pearl my waistline This dark becoming land opens vistas and voices I wake up bearded and boastful, look at where the children have left their backpacks, footprints We are alike—you and I—nomadic, rooted, and winged We meet in this middle place when no one watches, rub up against each others' wishes, run over leaves veined and copper, rinse in questions, and savour the silent.

3.

Here is the time when my heart rests with splendour Ripple of cloud light encroaches, teal confetti grazes air, branches are bear hugs and moss lunches on mushrooms and slivers of ant hill Here is no wanting when surrounded by this many robes of green.

Gate of Joy

Often the tug is direct and contemplative—the impulse to awe pulls me immediately to stillness; draws me, with no intermediary, to centre and adore.

(Lee, 1995, p. 39)

What if we stopped assuming that to be powerful means to require worship and obedience? What if we imagined that it might mean the ability to participate in pain and joy?

(Ostriker, 2000, p. 15)

In *The Gateless Gate* (Shibayama, 2000), Zen master Wu-men used koans—short phrases or sentences—to awaken his students to the path of spiritual freedom and enlightenment. He called it the "gateless gate" because he taught that those who recognize that they are free, perceive no gate, whereas those who are not free, have to pass through the gate in order to learn that there is none (p. xiv).

What does it mean to be free? In the Buddhist tradition, it means to have relief from suffering through recognizing the non-existence of the self. When we don't cling to our experience as a separate self, we become free to experience life as a vast and vivid array of interconnections.

Horizon

The way I forget, each time, how the end
is there, already, in the beginning of things

(Joseph, 2004, p. 13)

Dawn scribbles wind

wayward leaves guess
at heaven

hope atoms into brown

we lift off, feathers curl

ENDNOTE

1 My doctoral thesis, *Through the Gates of Loving Inquiry: Where the Heart Opens Into Relationship* (Shira, 2010) documented this creative and contemplative practice. Poems and photos in this chapter are excerpted from the thesis.

REFERENCES

Abram, D. (1996). *The spell of the sensuous: Perception and language in a more-than-human world*. New York, NY: Vintage Books.

Arrien, A. (2005). *The second half of life: Opening the eight gates of wisdom*. Boulder, CO: Sounds True.

Brady, I. (2009). Foreword. In M. Prendergast, C. Leggo, & P. Sameshima (Eds.), *Poetic inquiry: Vibrant voices in the social sciences* (pp. xi–xvi). Rotterdam, The Netherlands: Sense Publishers.

Cixous, H. (1991). *"Coming to writing" and other essays*. Cambridge, MA: Harvard University Press.

Denton, D. (1998). *In the tenderness of stone: Liberating consciousness through the awakening of the heart*. Pittsburgh, PA: Sterling House Publisher.

Friesen, P. (1995). Gathering bones. In T. Lilburn (Ed.), *Poetry and knowing: Speculative essays & interviews*, (pp. 118–122). Kingston, Canada: Quarry Press.

Harding, S. (2006). *Animate earth: Science, intuition and Gaia*. Tortnes Devon, England: Green Books.

Hillman, J. (1992). *The thought of the heart and the soul of the world*. Putnam, CT: Spring Publications.

Hirshfield, J. (1997). *Nine gates: Entering the mind of poetry*. New York, NY: HarperCollins.

Irigaray, L. (2002). *The way of love*. London, England: Continuum.

Joseph, E. (2004). *The startled heart*. Lantzville, Canada: Oolichan Press.

Lane, P. (2004). *There is a season: A memoir*. Toronto, Canada: McClelland & Stewart.

Lee, D. (1995). Poetry and unknowing. In T. Lilburn (Ed.), *Poetry and knowing: Speculative essays & interviews* (pp. 29–44). Kingston, Canada: Quarry Press.

Leggo, C. (2004). The curriculum of joy: Six poetic ruminations. *Journal of the Canadian Association for Curriculum Studies, 2*(2), 27–42.

Mayes, F. (1996). *Under the Tuscan sun: At home in Italy*. New York, NY: Broadway Books.

Meyer, K. (2006). Living inquiry: A gateless gate and a beach. In W. Ashton & D. Denton (Eds.), *Spirituality, ethnography, and teaching: Stories from within* (pp. 155–166). New York, NY: Peter Lang.

Ostriker, A. S. (2000). *Dancing at the devil's party: Essays on poetry, politics, and the erotic*. Ann Arbor: University of Michigan Press.

Rukeyser, M. (1949). *The life of poetry*. Ashfield, MA: Paris Press.

Shibayama, Z. (2000). *The gateless barrier: Zen comments on the mumonkan*. Boston, MA: Shambhala.

Shira, A. (1998). *Womb: Weaving of my being*. Vancouver, Canada: Butterfly Press.

Shira, A. (2005). Tahiti. *Arts-Informed: The Journal of the Centre for Arts-Informed Research, 4*(2 & 3), 3.

Shira, A. (2007a, June). Inside SWOVA's respectful relationships program. *Canadian Women's Foundation Newsletter, 2*. Original work retrieved from http://canadianwomen.org/

Shira, A. (2007b). Re/considering writing—a journal writer's response. *Educational Insights, 11*(1). Retrieved from http://ccfi.educ.ubc.ca/publication/insights/v11n01/readersresponse/shira.html

Shira, A. (2008). i.e. *Educational Insights, 12*(1). Retrieved from http://ccfi.educ.ubc.ca/publication/insights/v12n01/poeticmoment/shira/index.html

Shira, A. (2009). Writing the Number 4 bus: A poetic inquiry. *Educational Insights,13*(3). Retrieved from http://www.ccfi.educ.ubc.ca/publication/insights/v13n03/articles/shira/index.html

Shira, A. (2010). *Through the gates of loving inquiry: Where the heart opens into relationship* (Unpublished doctoral dissertation). University of British Columbia, Vancouver, Canada.

Smith, R. (1998). *Lessons from the dying*. Somerville, MA: Wisdom Publications.

Treace, B. M. (1992). Foreword. In J. D. Loori, *The eight gates of Zen: Spiritual training in an American Zen monastery* (pp. ix–xv). Mt. Tremper, NY: Dharma Communications.

Confessions of an English Teacher in Francophone Québec

Lynn Thomas

In my 15 years as a teacher educator, in a variety of contexts and institutions across Canada I have come to an awareness of the subtle and slightly subversive nature of what I do. Being a teacher educator means that I teach my students how to become a teacher. Whenever a person in authority directs another to become a "something," there is a direct effect on that person's sense of self, their identity and their relationship with others. Being a teacher educator of francophone pre-service teachers of English as an Additional Language (EAL) in Québec has also made me acutely aware of the political nature of what I do in terms of teaching and learning languages in this province. My professional role is to help pre-service teachers understand what it means to learn a second language, and how we as teachers can be inspiring, motivating, informative, and empowering when teaching the English language to our students. My goal is to nurture in my students a passion for the language so that they themselves will be able to inspire that passion in their own students. In order to do this, I need to be able to establish good communication and a good working relationship with my students because I am English, the voice of the colonizer, while they are French, the colonized people. Not only do I hold all the power of the professor, the capacity to pass or fail, praise or humiliate, encourage or denigrate; I also hold the power of the colonizing language and I am the one to sanction, or dismiss their ability to use it, and with that, their access to a future profession.

In French language schools in Québec, English is a compulsory subject for all students from the first year of primary school until the last year of high school. It is one of three required academic courses, along with French and math, which determine a student's academic average for promotion into the next grade. For many adolescents, English class is one more arbitrary school subject as they do not use it during their daily lives, particularly if they live outside of the metropolitan region of Montréal. For English teachers, it is a class where they struggle to convince students of the advantages of learning a second language, despite the complex cognitive challenges it also poses.

While I chose to learn French as an adult and live in a French-speaking part of the country, I also believe that there are many excellent reasons for francophones in Canada to learn English. It is the language of economics, of global popular culture, of tourism and travel and it is the international language of communication between people everywhere. At the same time, in Québec, English is the language of the oppressor; the colonial power that in the past has prevented (and some say still continues to prevent) Québeckers from realising their full potential through preventing them from taking leadership roles in business, politics and the arts in their own language. The media constantly remind us of how, despite 40 years of laws and legislation, English encroaches, slips in, takes hold, and sometimes takes over.

As many of my students have not had opportunities to practise using the language they intend to teach, their level of knowledge of the language and skills in using English as a means of communication varies a great deal. Despite the advantages that it would bring them, the great majority of them, like most people in similar situations, prefer not to take advantage of the opportunity to practise using their second language with their colleagues, preferring instead to favour real communication in everyone's first language. I am often faced with the temptation to establish rules governing the use of language, with imaginary mental black marks going to students who consistently speak in their mother tongue in my classroom. *Make the most of your opportunities to practise and become fluent*, I think. *You need to improve your language skills in order to be able to use the language to teach it; teaching will be easier if you are not also struggling with what to say and how to say it; our pupils deserve the best English teachers we can be.* I don't say these things out loud. Once, I commented to a student teacher on the fact that he spoke a lot of French with his students while on practicum, as well as with his associate teacher and fellow pre-service teachers.

"I knew you were going to say something about that," he told me. "But you can't stop me from speaking French. French is my language; it's my identity: who I am and how I interact with the world." He is right, I cannot stop him, and nor do I want to be the person who prevents people from using their native language to express themselves. Yet, how else can I encourage high levels of language skills among the future teachers in my care? Can I simply step back and allow them to choose not to become fluent speakers of a language they intend to teach? How far does my responsibility to their future students go?

My reaction to these types of situations has been to work on building personal relationships with my students, to will them to want to improve because of our mutual respect for each other. But that in itself is problematic when I think about my goal for wanting my students to be inspired by and passionate about the language itself, and not because they want to please me. Yet, it is only realistic to think that our relationships with language develop as a result of our relationships with the people who speak that language, and who come to represent a language and culture for us. How can I move beyond the simplistic "do this to please me" to a profound mutual regard that is grounded in the common goal of striving for excellence for the benefit of future pupils? Is it possible to imagine that type of relationship between a teacher educator and a pre-service teacher, or between a professor and student for that matter? If not, why not?

Where does this leave me in terms of being a teacher educator, wanting to encourage and inspire excellence in my students? Where do I find the comfortable place to begin a deep dialogue about learning to teach when I feel I must tiptoe around these issues of language? How do I communicate my concerns about student teachers' lack of fluency and how this will impact on their ability to teach without implying a criticism of their identities as minority-language speakers? How do we create a balanced relationship that permits us to work together as a team with similar goals?

Sometimes students are insecure and apologetic about their language skills in class. They are reluctant to participate, yet they bring many strengths to the classroom, not the least of which is a clear understanding of what it is to be an English language learner. In many ways, they fit into their apprenticeship classrooms in French language schools better than I do. They are well-equipped to discuss discipline problems with the vice-principal, praise individual student efforts to parents, and discuss the latest episode of a popular TV show in the staffroom. In my university courses they may feel inadequate, but they are often right at home in schools where everyone is a non-native speaker of English. A recent posting on the TESOL (Teaching English to Speakers of Other Languages) website is an article by a young Thai graduate student in the United States about his experiences as a non-native English-speaking tutor of English. In his article, Chamcharatsri (2010) describes how he came to hear of the native/non-native dichotomy only after arriving in the United States. He recounts how a personal experience helped him to understand how complex and multi-layered this issue is in terms of authority and identity. He concludes the article by imploring scholars to create awareness of the dichotomy in order to help break down stereotypes about non-native speakers. I agree with the author that we do carry many assumptions about native speakers of a language being the best teachers, when in fact non-native speakers have many important skills, such as better meta-linguistic awareness than their native-speaking counterparts. I truly believe that my students have the potential to become excellent teachers of English because they will augment their superior meta-linguistic awareness of the language with a vivid knowledge of what it is like to be a student of English in Québec. At the same time, I want my students to aspire to native-like fluency, an aspiration that scholars such as Chamcharatsri question and even denounce. I see the irony, but I must admit that a part of me wants them to be able to take on a persona that is English-speaking, English-thinking and "at home" with the English-language culture because I truly believe that that will make them better teachers of English. But is that realistic, or even healthy?

Perhaps this says more about my own need to fit seamlessly into my adopted community, as I strive to speak French without an accent, and to laugh at jokes in the right places. In my professional position, I have resisted taking on roles that require me to speak my second language, French, in front of large groups, despite the fact that I am quite fluent. It is only now, after 6 years of working in a French-language institution, that I have agreed to coordinate the internship, a role that will require me to work closely with large groups of students and colleagues in the French language. Yet I expect my students to take on teaching and stepping into roles in their second language within weeks of enrolling in the university.

I must learn to work within the paradigm in which I find myself, and that begins with exploring it fully. I need to have a clear sense of who I am and what I stand for in relation to the curriculum I enact, despite the many paradoxes that this may include. I need to be able to communicate *this* honestly with my students. My experiences have shown me the importance of continuing this quest to clarify my beliefs about learning to teach a second language and my expectations for my students, while still seeking to connect with them at a basic human level. I need to believe in the person I am, and not in someone else's construction of me based on a historical legacy. I can project my real self through what I say, and the stance I take on what gets included in my classes. With all of the historical and political legacies that my students and I bring to our professional relationship, it is crucial that I negotiate with them to establish a respectful space in which we can hold the important conversations about language-and-learning and learning to teach.

REFERENCE

Chamcharatsri, P. B. (2010, August). To be proud or not to be proud: That is the question. *TESOL Connections*. Retrieved from http://www.tesol.org/s_tesol/tc/index.asp

Mzungu

Marguerite Leahy

❝ *Mzungu*, Mzungu, Mzungu."

I heard the rustle of shaking cassava leaves and soft thuds on the red earth long before I heard the repetitive, high-pitched chant of young male voices.

"Mzungu, *una fanya nini*?" (European, you are doing what?)

To me it was obvious. I was running along the quiet dirt paths in the fresh car-free air in the heat and dust of the Kapsengere evening. A leap here, a dodge there, my feet would avoid an eroded dip in the earth, or pellets of goat droppings.

Can't I ever be alone? Can't I ever blend in? I despaired.

One young dusty boy about five-years old veered in at the elbow, touching my forearm, then raced forward, stopping to laugh, his thin face beaming with bright white teeth.

To my left, a light-footed streak in green shorts, a torn, pink, school shirt and dusty, tough feet mimicked my loping gait as I jogged along in my pricey Nike running shoes.

A man, using a *jembe* (African shovel), stopped his laboured, squatted digging way in the centre of a maize field to stare at the commotion and entertainment of our moving crowd. Thin, sinewy arms clutched the short handle of the jembe, but the bloodshot brown eyes stared over.

An old mama (granny) in torn, brown, slip-on runners stopped with a huge, heavy twig bundle on her head. One hand balanced the load while she said, "*Chum gai?*" (Hello).

"*Ah chum gai missing,*" I replied. (The hello response).

"*Eh!*" (Yes)

"*Eh.*" (My yes response between gasps.)

"*Moi ainay?*" (How are you?)

"*Mumming n'ala.*" (I'm fine.) This really wasn't true. I would be branded *rude* for continuing to run and not stopping to shake the work-worn, thin hand of the elder. But then I would never be able to exercise if I stopped and formally greeted every elderly person. I glanced at her rheumy eyes and long earlobes which touched her shoulders from years of stretching with bone plugs. Yes, I knew she had stopped to talk before. I remembered her lower front teeth had been removed in her youth as a sign of adulthood in the Kalenjin tribe.

Meanwhile the sure-footed shadows of the 5- and 6-year olds closed in as they cut in front of me zigzagging in laughter and fast-spoken Kalenjin. I'm sure they were saying, "Look at her! She does not know how to run. Ha, ha she moves like an old mama."

Why can't they speak in Kiswahili? At least I can figure out what they're saying. But with Kalenjin, I'm really at a disadvantage.

The *duka,* or *Kona* shop comes into view. I don't stop to look long as about nine cows are coming down the path; a serious, 10-year-old, herder boy shakes a thin bamboo stick at his charges.

I try to think that I'll ignore them. I will keep on running as sprinting never works; and maybe, they will give up. The green fields of thick sugar cane stand close and tall above the dark shadows where black mambas hide. The ringed, lime-coloured stalks peek out under the mottled emerald leaves.

"Mzungu, mzungu, mzungu, mzungu." The chant is loud and continuous, so an old *muzee* stops and looks. His thick-soled feet are wide, calloused, and dusty. "Madame, help me with a shilling?" he mutters.

No, I think, *I gave that guy two bob before. What am I, either an amusement, or a bank?*

"*Mayai iko?*" (Eggs there?) I yell to the duka man.

"*Hapana,*" ("No.") he replies.

Too bad, I think that means a shopping trip to Kiboswa on market day tomorrow.

"*Malimu, haberi yako?*" (Teacher, how are you?) A voice yells in the distance from another path by a barbed-wire fence.

"*Nzuri sana,*" I smile.

"*Eh? Maji-moto.*" (Yes, hot water).

I hate the name "Maji-moto," and love it at the same time. I've been given this name by the people of Kapsengere because it implies restlessness, movement, boiling.

"Madame, give me sweets," another ragged dusty-headed boy joins in the pack from another *shamba* (small farm). Kenya has so many needs and they all seem to be following me today.

Why bother saying, "I'm not a rich mzungu, just a teacher. If I was a rich mzungu, I'd be lying on a beach in Mombasa, not hanging out in Kapsengere."

"Madame, your hair is too long. Too much food is going to your hair." This too I have heard enough times so I don't respond, but keep jogging. Maybe I can lose them by the next town called Gambogi, but no, they persist. It must be the highlight of their day to harass the foreigner.

This is the tropics, sunrise at six o'clock and sunset at six o'clock. We are 3 miles from the equator. I look at the *paupau* (papaya) trees framing the red, hazy ball as it slouches rapidly down. If I don't turn around now, I won't make it back before darkness. There is no twilight here.

Turning around leads to more laughter and one boy says in slow, deep, nasal English, "Hello, how are you?" then he bursts into more laughter. He thinks my English sounds like this.

"That mzungu, is she normal?" the patients have asked the Ugandan *Daktari* (doctor) at the Kiboswa clinic.

"Yes, in her place they do this running all the time," replied Daktari over the last few months.

"But she's always moving up and down, up and down like a mad person."

"I've seen. But that is the habit in that place," the doctor reassures.

Yet, Kenyans have produced some of the most gifted runners in the world and still they find it odd that people, other than schoolchildren, run.

I don't care about the dust, mosquitoes, and other bugs. The choking green of maize, beans, cassava, and paupau is a symphony of colour and texture...truly a rare, quiet, rural place which can never be enjoyed alone because I am different.

"Madame, give me your shoes."

Finally I respond between gasps. "If I give them to you, what will I use?"

We pass the strains of Lingala music coming from a round, mud house on a shamba, "See you, you get another from your place."

"True," I reply, "but I can't get any now and this is my only pair." I breathe a sigh of relief as I run through the gates of my secondary school.

Benjamin, our watchman, scowls. Thomas, the school "stores man," clicks in disgust; Benjamin yells, "*Wey! Enda! Enda haraka!*" (You! Go! Go quickly!) Click!

The click sound is made using the back of the tongue. These deep sounds are clicks of disgust directed at the boys who are not even breathing hard as they scatter in several directions and look refreshingly afraid.

Thomas shakes his *rungu*, the 40-centimetre knobbed stick he and all circumcised men carry to show their status. The boys know he means business.

I walk back, relieved of my small shadows, to my teacher's bungalow on the edge of the compound avoiding the students in the outdoor dining hall. I can be alone at last as I pass by my corrugated-iron water tank with a lock on it to stop people from stealing my water. Finally, the cool red-painted concrete floors welcome me in their silence and there is no offensive chanting. I swear that somehow those small guys spy and watch me every day from outside the school compound. I seriously consider the possibility of bringing a rowing machine to Kapsengere so I can exercise in peace. From behind the chemistry lab, I can see Mr. Kagodo tilling the soil near his bungalow preparing to plant his groundnuts. "Leahy, you are not married, you'll miss your market," he always warns. I don't want to hear those words today.

Wendy, the British VSO (Voluntary Service Overseas) volunteer, waves to remind me to eat dinner with her. I change my shirt and go into the coolness of her teacher's house.

She speaks in bursts. I am in a fog; I hear, but don't want to understand what she tells me in her crisp, British English.

"You mean that small one? The one with the big tummy who lives just outside the gate? He's the one who died?" I croak the words out remembering the mournful wailing and drumming from two nights ago.

Oh that kid annoyed me, but now he's dead; yes, he too used to be one of those bothersome runners. He died from a worm infection? He was 5-years old. HE WAS JUST 5-YEARS OLD!! I ignored and brushed him away from my life because he interfered with my run. I never even learned his name, but he knew mine. Mzungu.

Travels Through Global Indigenity

Priscilla Settee

I am a First Nations woman and university professor at a major Canadian university. I have worked with Indigenous[1] students since the mid-1970s as a university sessional instructor for a First Nations-operated college in remote communities, a secondary classroom instructor, a post-secondary counsellor and academic advisor. I have worked with Indigenous peoples throughout the globe, including recently as developer and manager of a program at one of Peru's major public universities. I am a parent to a daughter who now works in the public school system as a high-school teacher and who benefitted from a teacher-training program established by Métis education activists many decades ago. I have volunteered as a board member on Indigenous-education training programs such as the Saskatchewan Urban Native Teacher Program, Children of the Earth High School (Winnipeg) and have chaired and currently co-chair Saskatoon's Aboriginal high school, Oskayak, for the past 15 years.

I have a vast network of internationally, nationally and locally valued colleagues and friends who share my passion for Indigenous-educational liberatory matters and who are on the leading edge of the Indigenization of education. Our view is that if education serves Indigenous students, who far too often are marginalized, then all students will benefit. My informal and formal education experiences have provided a framework for my life work. While I have worked within my extended communities on other activities that provided services for Aboriginal women, much of my work came back to the important role of education and how it can serve to create social change.

Educational Framework

During the early 1970s, my studies at Trent University in southern Ontario afforded me an opportunity to hear first hand about political, cultural struggles and how the James Bay Cree were being displaced, both geographically and culturally. The construction of large dams in the Cree territory of northern Québec became a rallying point for the many young James Bay Cree colleagues attending Trent University. In my undergraduate classes, I was developing a critical consciousness of the oppression of Indigenous peoples in other parts of the world. During my early undergraduate work I became *conscientized*. The concept of *conscientization*, or critical awareness, is foundational to the work of Paulo Freire (1970). Freire's critical awareness made possible through praxis, which Freire defined as "...reflection and action upon the world in order to transform it" (p. 33), spoke deeply to me. He connected reflection and action together as part of the process in the recognition and transformation of social, economic, and political contradictions. The readings of Paulo Freire, while international in scope, resonated with the critical rereading of my people in Saskatchewan, whose quality of life and living was substandard and for many today remains substandard. In those early days of Western schooling, I became aware that as Indigenous peoples, we inherited a colonial system that did not critique our circumstances, pose solutions to community problems, or consider our organic Indigenous experience. I learned that critical consciousness encouraged us to question the nature of our historical and social situation and to read the world with the goal of acting as subjects in the creation of our own democratic society. I became a voracious reader of Paulo Freire; his methodologies irrevocably changed my life. I was intrigued by the educational transformation he described in places like Guinea Bissau and Brazil. Later I would read works by Henry Giroux (1983), a disciple of Freire, who used the terminology *radical pedagogy*: "Its spirit is rooted in an aversion to all forms of domination, and its challenge centers around the need to develop modes of critique fashioned in a theoretical discourse that mediates the possibility for social action and emancipatory transformation" (Giroux, 1983, p. 2). I read Antonio Gramsci (1971), whose writings contextualized my situation and that of my community within a broader analysis, one that introduced me to the concepts of *hegemony* and *cultural domination*. John Porter's (1965) *The Vertical Mosaic: An Analysis of Social Class and Power* explained social stratification that transformed my understanding of inequality and power and privilege.

It was also during the 1970s that I became familiar with the writings of Franz Fanon (1963), Eldridge Cleaver (1968), Angela Davis (1974), and Albert Memmi (1974). Advocates for equality and basic human rights like freedom, their writings stress that intellectuals must always remain connected with the struggles on the land and home communities. These writers helped me understand the impact of racism, cultural and political hegemony, and the domination of peoples of colour and women. Later, I would read bell hooks (1984), Howard Adams (1975), Gloria Anzaldúa (1999), and many others whose work were either influenced by or had similar experiences to Gramsci. Gramsci (1971) wrote extensively from his prison cell about the deep layers of state domination over oppressed groups. This domination was so entrenched in all levels of society—including education, literature, church, government, and the legal system—that it impacted every aspect of humanity. He wrote prolifically during a time when he faced personal persecution, which included being jailed for challenging oppressive regimes. Many of the writers Gramsci influenced made links among class, race, and gender; and they described the deep impact of colonialism, racism, and hegemony. As an Indigenous scholar and a follower of Gramsci, Freire, Giroux, and others, I feel the importance of challenging the hegemony of Western knowledge. It is my goal to ensure that Indigenous knowledge systems take their rightful place within the academy as legitimate knowledge. As Indigenous scholars, we have an important role that we inherit from our culture. It is also an intellectual role in defining, challenging, and working to eradicate oppression. This is the role of intellectual sovereignty:

> Indigenous intellectuals in the United States and Canada are living at the center of the global empire, and we are the best-placed people in the world to counter the ongoing production of imperial attitudes and to defy its pretensions. It is our responsibility to reorient our own values and our ways of being away from cooptation into the imperial system. (Alfred, 2004, p. 97)

After my introduction to higher learning and with one university degree to my name, in the late 1970s as a young woman I had the unique experience of teaching in northern Saskatchewan and travelling with some of our early Indigenous mentors and political leaders—John B. Tootoosis, Smith Atimoyoo, and Cy Standing—all important leaders in Saskatchewan First Nations communities. The impact of underdevelopment in some northern communities sent me looking for answers. While teaching was a magnificent experience for someone so young, I didn't understand much of the poverty and despair that I witnessed in many northern First Nations and Métis communities where I taught and lived. The topic of colonialism and decolonization were never introduced. Inspired by the book *Fanshen* (Hinten, 1966), I decided to find some answers travelling and working in the international realm in Indigenous communities in Latin America. I took my life savings and followed a life dream to travel to unknown parts of the world. I booked a return flight from Saskatoon to Rio de Janeiro. Working at Canada's first Indigenous college at that time, Saskatchewan Indian Federated College, gave me a vantage point. I was able to make contacts with Indigenous organizations through the World Council of Indigenous Peoples and the ground-breaking work of George Manuel from the Secwepemc First Nations in British Columbia. I set up meetings over a six-month period from Mexico to Ecuador. At that time I admired the work of George Manuel in the international sphere and his human-rights work. In 1970 Manuel become leader of the National Indian Brotherhood, which later became the Assembly of First Nations, Canada's first major Aboriginal organization. Manuel worked on treaty rights, land claims, economic independence and education.

In 1975 George organized a large delegation of nineteen Indigenous nationals from all over the world and founded the World Council of Indigenous Nations (WCIP). For his work Manuel received the Order of Canada and in the 1970s he was nominated for the Nobel Peace Prize for the work of the WCIP. Those of us who work in the international Indigenous sphere owe him a great deal of gratitude as Manuel's early work continues to inspire us. Manuel was the first leader of the WCIP. What I was about to learn during my six months of solo travel was at the core of Manuel's work and has been an organizational and foundational experience that set me on a journey of self and socio-political discovery. These early experiences have been a framework for my life work.

During the 1990s I worked as Program Director for the Engineering Access Program at the University of Manitoba. I found that none of the curriculum applied to the forty-five, or so, First Nations and Aboriginal men and women who were studying engineering. During that time I put together a course called *The Impact of Western Development on Indigenous Lands*. Most First Nations and Aboriginal communities have been negatively impacted by development such as mega dams, mines and deforestation. I also completed a Master's of Education degree which leaned heavily on the engineering course elective that I had developed. My Master's degree was called *Honouring Indigenous Science Knowledge as a Means of Ensuring Western Scientific Responsibility* (Settee, 1999). This thesis made the case for Indigenous science. It explored the work of Pam Colorado, Oscar Kawagley, Greg Cajete, David Bohm and others who considered Indigenous peoples' knowledge as scientific and knowledge which modern science borrows from. This thesis described some of the nightmares that Indigenous communities have been forced to live with as a result of irresponsible science: the nuclear-bombed islands of the South Pacific, the location of nuclear dumpsites that many Indigenous communities are forced to fight. The thesis also included the impact of such development on biodiversity, land, animals, local food sources, and the many plants and medicines that kept communities healthy, and that fed and supported a way of life.

My participation in the work of the United Nations Convention on Biological Diversity broadened my understanding of the ways that the world's biodiversity was under threat. I met Indigenous groups who were fighting against genocide and biopiracy, theft of intellectual property rights and plants. Indigenous lands are highly sought after as neocolonial greed for money and resources intensifies. Some have called this lust for earth's last precious resources the new conquistador, a reference to the gold seekers who first colonized and pillaged the "New World." Feeling a great need to document some of the stories of the communities I visited, I decided to do a Ph.D. This was not my initial intention but I felt paralyzed by the information from my colleagues in the so-called least-developed nations, as it reflected the stories from my own community. The Indigenous leaders at the Permanent Forum on Indigenous Peoples at the United Nations were a great source of inspiration. Since Indigenous leaders first stepped into the international arena at the United Nations in the early 1970s, solidarity networks developed and continue to grow stronger to this day. Indigenous peoples have clearly articulated the impact of Western development on their lands and have called for respectful development. Indigenous peoples have been very clear in their analysis and understanding of global forces that impact their daily lives. The Declaration on the Rights of Indigenous Peoples that was passed 2007 at the UN General Assembly outlines the minimal standards of development that Indigenous peoples have requested. Self-determination; land and resources environment; and sustainable, culturally sensitive development are focus areas of the Declaration. Free, prior and informed consent as it relates to development on Indigenous lands has been a central feature of the Declaration. Indigenous communities are demanding equal and transparent partnership processes and a halt to destructive economic development processes in their communities. In addition they are asking that full environmental and long-term impacts on traditional lands be fully understood. Indigenous peoples want to be equal beneficiaries and desire democratic decision making processes in development issues.

Why an Internationalist
Perspective Drives My Life

My extensive travels throughout the world not as a tourist but as a learner taught me that Indigenous people worldwide share common beliefs, practices, and similarities of knowledge including the experience of the tension of Western development. In many cases, the issues of land, power, disenfranchisement, and even genocide of Indigenous peoples keep surfacing. My first experience with genocide in Central America was in Guatemala. A commission concluded that army massacres had destroyed 626 villages; more than 200,000 people were killed, or disappeared; 1.5 million were displaced by the violence; and more than 150,000 were driven to seek refuge in Mexico.

In El Salvador, the situation was chillingly similar. I travelled to El Salvador at the invitation of the National Association of Indigenous Salvadoreños (ANIS) and visited the village of Santa Anna, the site of the *matanza*, or massacre which took place in 1932 against El Salvador's Indigenous peoples. Following an armed uprising of *campesinos* in January 1932, most of whom were Indigenous, the Salvadoran armed forces massacred as many as 30,000 in reprisal. I travelled with the president of ANIS, Adrian Lisco, a Nahuatl Pipil Indian, and several of the ANIS members. I saw first-hand the machete slashes on the doors of village buildings, a grim reminder of the massacre that had taken place. After this massacre, the Indian community was greatly reduced in the country; many of them changed their habits, i.e., clothing and cultural practices went underground for people's fear of being killed. From El Salvador, I travelled to Panama and caught a smuggler ship to Colombia.

I had only been in Colombia for a few days when I reached the Sierra Nevada mountain region and made contacts with the Indigenous Council (Consejo Regional Indigena del Cauca, or CRIC), a day-or-two prior to my arrival, several members of CRIC had been murdered for their political role with CRIC. We clandestinely travelled to some of the areas where the Colombian army had control and whose presence served as intimidation. Several community meetings were disrupted by gun-wielding members of the Army. I sensed that soldiers were not able to differentiate my appearance as an Indigenous Cree woman from the local Indigenous culture. It both frightened and politicized me. During that time I was caught twice in gunfire: once in the Sierra Nevada and once in Bogota. I made my way by bus to the south, fearing for my life. In 2003, after I had visited, more than 100 Indigenous people and leaders were murdered and the Indigenous community in Sierra Nevada, de Santa Maria was forcibly displaced. Recently and in the last 15 years, as political violence has escalated, more than 2,660 cases of human-rights violations have been reported. Reports confirm that Indigenous peoples have been the victims of several massacres perpetrated by paramilitaries, the guerrillas and other armed groups. State-sponsored military activities have included aerial bombing of rural and Indigenous communities. Thousands of Indigenous peoples have been displaced, resulting in increasing populations of refugees in the neighbouring countries of Brazil, Ecuador, Panama, Peru and Venezuela. Throughout the country, forced disappearances of Indigenous leaders and representatives have been documented, as have reports of mass arbitrary detentions carried out by the military. My own friend and colleague, Ingrid Washinawatak, a Menominee from northern Wisconsin, was captured and murdered along with two of her colleagues in 1999. The three were working with the U'wa Indians, helping to build a school.

After leaving Colombia I entered Ecuador and my situation "normalized." I did not encounter genocide but instead was deeply moved by the culture of Indigenous peoples whose history and culture was omnipresent in their arts, language and cultural expressions. Ecuador was an embodiment of beauty and was a welcome respite from some of the state-induced poverty and human-rights abuses that mired much of my 6-month journey. In May, only 6 months after I began, I boarded a plane from Guayaquil, Ecuador and flew to Miami en route to my home community of Saskatoon. I believe I was experiencing culture shock as I sat in an airport restaurant, my plastic fork chasing my eggs around on my plate and unable to stomach the tasteless mass-produced American airport food. It was a metaphor for the hollow, empty sensations I could not shake. The stories of massacres, the actual massacres I had witnessed, the hepatitis that lay dormant and that would soon ravage my body left me with a sense of loss. I knew my life could never be the same and indeed it never was. I wept inside for the people I had shared 6 short, but intensive months with, confused about how I would carry on my life. The bright lights and sterile airport food intensified the contradictions I experienced.

Today as a senior academic at a mainstream Canadian university, I am constantly reminded of the human-rights abuses that continue to plague Indigenous peoples. My forays into the United Nations Permanent Forum and the stories of human-rights abuses shrouded by mainstream media have continued to inspire and direct my teaching, curriculum development, and educational relationships with students and colleagues. The difference from that lonely, desperate-to-tell-my-story, disenfranchised individual sitting in the Miami airport is that many years later, I have established intellectual, political, and personal relationships that create a sense of solidarity and community, one that inspires, supports and ensures that we collectively carry on and move forward. I believe the many experiences that have spanned the thirty-plus years since I left the Indigenous jungle communities of Latin America and the many other regions of the world have enriched my perspective and approach. Seeking out communities and individuals of support has made the journey not only possible but deeply empowering. I have learned, and teach, that while one is imprisoned by poverty and suffering from human-rights abuses, none of us is free.

ENDNOTE

1 Throughout this paper, I use the terminology *Indigenous peoples, Aboriginal peoples,* as well as *First Nations, Métis,* and *Inuit peoples* sometimes interchangeably. The latter are legal terminologies that have been given by the Government of Canada.

REFERENCES

Adams, H. (1975). *Prison of grass: Canada from a native point of view.* Toronto, Canada: New Press.

Alfred, T. (2004). Warrior scholarship: Seeing the university as a ground of contention. In D. Mihesuah & A. Cavender Wilson (Eds.), *Indigenizing the academy: Transforming scholarship and empowering communities* (pp. 88–99). Lincoln: University of Nebraska Press.

Anzaldúa, G. (1999). *Borderlands/La Frontera: The new mestiza.* San Francisco, CA: Aunt Lute Books.

Cleaver, E. (1968). *Soul on ice.* New York, NY: Dell.

Davis, A. Y. (1974). *Angela Davis: An autobiography.* New York, NY: Random House.

Fanon, F. (1963). *The wretched of the earth.* New York, NY: Grove Press.

Freire, P. (1970). *Pedagogy of the oppressed.* New York, NY: Herder and Herder.

Giroux, H. (1983). *Theory and resistance in education: A pedagogy for the opposition.* New York, NY: Bergin & Garvey Publishers.

Gramsci, A. (1971). *Selections from the prison notebooks.* London, England: Lawrence and Wishart.

Hinten, W. (1966). *Fanshen: A documentary of revolution in a Chinese village.* Berkeley: University of California Press.

hooks, b. (1984). *Feminist theory: From margin to center.* Cambridge, MA: South End Press.

Memmi, A. (1974). *The colonizer and the colonized* (H. Greenfeld, Trans.). London, England: Condor/Souvenir. (Original work published 1957)

Porter, J. (1965). *The vertical mosaic: An analysis of social class and power.* Toronto, Canada: University of Toronto Press.

Settee, P. (1999). *Honouring Indigenous science knowledge as a means of ensuring Western scientific responsibility* (Unpublished master's thesis). University of Manitoba, Winnipeg, Canada.

Nigglings From Kurdistan

Sheila Simpkins

Swimming lessons

It is hot...hot and dry and arid...unbelievably hot...the thermometer reads 50°C and it's only the beginning of June.

The heat is...*relentless*
> *lung searing*
>> *body scorching*
>> *lip parching*
>> *moisture sapping*

As I walk along the path beside the pool in my complex...it seems idyllic... azure sky, shimmering water, the promise of a cool escape.

I can smell the water...I can almost feel the blanket of wet that it invites.

I hear pool sounds...laughter, squeals of delight, giggles of glee, splashing, the smack of bodies hitting water.

I see the pool...surrounded by the wrought iron fence, the gap in the bars allowing a peek inside.

I see men…young men, old men, and boys…at play, wrestling, jumping, diving, immersed in the moment, immersed in the cool wet of water in the midst of the blistering dry heat.

I see girls…young girls…as young as nine-or-ten-years old…peeking through the gap in the fence. They watch silently, look longingly. I wonder what they are thinking…I wonder what thoughts go through their head as they watch the boys splashing and playing in the pool…I wonder who told them and how they were told and what reasons were given as to why they are not allowed in the pool…I wonder if they cried, were sad, angry, questioned…I wonder what it's like for them.

I don't know the etiquette. I don't know at what age girls can't go into the pool anymore. I have seen young girls around 6- or 7-years old in the pool, but exactly when the cut-off age is and how it is determined…I don't know. Seeing those little girls, their faces peeking through the fence…makes me angry. I want to yell and scream and tell those men how cruel, stupid, and idiotic they are. I want to berate the women for their seeming acquiescence. I want to tell them how backwards and archaic their culture is…I want to tell them…I am disgusted…

and then I remind myself that I see through my eyes and because that is so I cannot see through theirs. I remind myself that I experience the world through the lens of my culture and so I cannot experience their world in the way that they do. I remind myself that our cultures are different…very different…in many ways incommensurable. I tell myself I must/can not judge, for who am I to even think that I should judge what is right or wrong?

and then I think to myself…this is cultural relativism. Is this some poor excuse for lack of action? Is this some poor excuse to assuage my feelings of helplessness? Does this kind of thinking lead any/no where?

I am in a bind…on the one hand…I want to rail at/take action against what I think is injustice…

> *on the other hand…I understand that to rail against what I think is injustice is to universalize…it is to set my biography as the measuring point for all others…*
> *it is cultural arrogance.*

I share this memory of Kurdistan, of young girls standing on the outside looking in through the gaps of the wrought iron fence, because it is symbolic of many moments of cross-cultural mis/not understanding of my time spent teaching and living abroad in Kurdistan. While I lectured at the University of Kurdistan, in Erbil, Northern Iraq in 2007–2008, my mind was preoccupied trying to understand a traditional tribal society, where gender roles and boundaries are severely drawn and strictly reinforced. For me, a woman and a Canadian-born WASP, witnessing the everyday lives of Kurdish women was soul-wrenching, crazy-making.

Homi Bhabha (1994) explains that in the midst of what seems to be incommensurable differences between cultures there is the possibility of change, that positions of polarity can be budged, and that cultural binarism can be avoided. In other words it is possible for me, amidst feelings that range the gamut of slight bewilderment to all-out repugnance, to reconcile cultural differences, but it requires some work. It requires me to be willing to open myself to living in/ passing through what Homi Bhabha calls "The Third Space." Let me introduce you to Bhabha's idea of social change and transformation.

At the heart of Bhabha's theory is his idea that cultures are indeed different. If we understand that cultures are different, then we can understand that these differences "very often set up among themselves an incommensurability…it is difficult even counterproductive, to try and fit together different forms of culture and to pretend that they can easily coexist" (Rutherford, 1990, p. 209). So, how does Bhabha imagine we can work through the impasse of these cultural differences? He introduces the ideas of cultural translation, hybridity and The Third Space.

To open the discussion on cultural change and transformation Bhabha introduces the linguistic turn, "The Third Space of Enunciation." Language is never for *ourselves*, it is always for the *other*. In an utterance, the *I* needs the *You* in order for there to be communication. The production of meaning requires that the You interpret what the I has said. The act of interpretation, or of meaning-making, is "mobilized in the passage through a Third Space" (Bhabha, 1994, p. 53). This creates ambivalence in the act of interpretation, "[t]he meaning of the utterance is quite literally neither the one nor the other" (Bhabha, 1994, p. 53). He then extrapolates the Third Space of Enunciation of language to cultural analysis.

Bhabha argues that all cultural systems and statements are done through the Third Space of Enunciation. He believes that there is no essence to culture and that claims to the inherent purity and originality of cultures are "untenable" (Bhabha, 1994). Culture is always being interpellated; he describes this interpellation as translation. When translation happens, there is a notion of "imitating an original in such a way that the priority of the original is not reinforced and because it can be simulated the original is never finished and complete in itself" (Rutherford, 1990, p. 210). Because the act of cultural translation denies the essentialist conception of a prior original, or originary culture, we can conclude that cultures are continually in a process of hybridity. For Bhabha, "the importance of hybridity is not to trace two original moments from which the third emerges, rather hybridity is 'the third space' which enables other positions to emerge"

(Rutherford 1990, p. 211). Cultural transformation occurs through The Third Space where the outcome is neither one culture nor the other culture, "but something else besides, which contests the terms of both" (Rutherford, 1990, p. 211).

I am drawn to Bhabha's analysis of culture because I recognize myself and my life experience in his theorizing. I understand that we are continually living in The Third Space, but in the everyday rhythms of our lives we may not be conscious of our passing through/living in that space. It is a generative site; however, it can be a problematic, uncomfortable site to inhabit.

Language Lessons

Lesson #1

We are contemplating language as a purveyor of culture. I ask the students, "What can we learn about a culture by looking at its language?" What I learn is that, in both Arabic and Kurdish, terms used to express family relations are more explicit than in English. In Arabic and Kurdi there are four words to describe the English words *aunt* and *uncle*; *father's sister* or *mother's sister* and *father's brother* or *mother's brother*.

There is no single word for the word *cousin*; there are eight terms to describe *cousin*…you say *son* or *daughter* and follow it up with the specific *uncle* or *aunt*— *son of my father's sister*. That way you know exactly how a *cousin* is related to the person speaking. This certainly reflects the importance of family, which is very evident in Kurdish and Arabic cultures; however, it really emphasizes the importance of relations and relationships in the society. I learn that with/in each of the family positions there are certain roles and duties and expectations that must be lived and carried out. I begin to understand how the family/tribal system works, how each of the members is intricately intertwined with/to each other, and the daily workings of the tribal society. I begin to see how/why the survival of the tribe is dependent on each of the members carrying out their duties.

As I gain this insight…

> *the niggling of an understanding stealthily creeps into my conscious…*
> *and while it nestles in and takes*
hold…

> *my biography is*
screaming…NOOOOO!
> *It is clinging to everything it holds near and dear…*

kicking and scratching and clawing...

but to no avail...

a part of me understands...understands...is not quite the right word...I will say...
...a part of me can acknowledge
why the strict gender roles
why the oppression...

I'm not sure what I think about that niggling of an understanding...

Lesson #2

I had been dancing around the issue for weeks, wanting to establish a relationship with the students before I told them. It was around six weeks into the first semester when I finally decided that they knew me well enough; I could share the news with my poor unsuspecting students. Their teacher is an *atheist...*new word...new concept. For Kurdish students religion and belief in God defines them and their society. Their world-view tells them non-belief means immorality, iniquity, sinfulness. *How could this be?* The teacher they had come to care for and respect...*was someone who did not believe in God!*

I wonder if their biographies...
were *screaming...NOOOOO!*
clinging to everything they held near and dear...
kicking and scratching and clawing...

as the niggling of an understanding stealthily crept in...

I was back in Canada when Balien wrote,

I always used to tell myself that it is very difficult to compound two things, such as believing in God and not believing in God. The condition with Sheila is really different than my imagination. You are making a very unique behaviour. (personal communication, October, 2008)

I'm not sure Balien knows what to think about that niggling of an understanding...

To dwell in The Third Space requires relationship. It requires care and concern and a willingness to listen with new ears, to see with new eyes and the courage to open your heart to the newness.

REFERENCES

Bhabha, H. (1994). *The location of culture*. New York, NY: Routledge.

Rutherford, J. (1990). The third space: Interview with Homi Bhabha. In *Identity: Community, culture, difference* (pp. 207–221). London, England: Lawrence and Wishart.

Ókonokiistsi

Hali Heavy Shield

It was last summer when my daughter and I pulled up to the house. The same house that my grandmother *Issitakii* had lived in for much of her life was now home to her daughter, my mother. Inside, my mom, my brother and his girlfriend, Colinda, visit around the kitchen table. They've been waiting for us. I get teased for being late; *kipitakii* (old lady) is the word I hear. We laugh and visit awhile. A light breeze enters through the open window and is a relief from the sweltering heat.

We went berry picking in the middle of the afternoon, even though we had planned to pick berries in the morning to avoid working under the sun. To the east, *mokowansiistsi* (the Belly Buttes) still cradle a handful of tipis that remain from the Sundance, a reminder that summer, too, will be ending soon. It is about a fifteen-minute walk behind the house and down a small ravine to reach the berries. As we set out, each carrying an empty pail, there is no trail to guide us, so we make our own path.

My mom uses a walking stick to help her hike through the tall grass and I am reminded of *old grandma* by the way she wears her flower-patterned scarf to wrap her hair back. My daughter Marley follows close behind. We are careful to avoid the hidden burrows in the prairie floor that may be home to gophers, badgers, or rattlesnakes. Anyone who has ever walked to their vehicle in the evening after a powwow, knows just how quickly you can go from sauntering along one minute, to laying in the grass the next.

When we reach the top of the hill, I take a moment to rest and observe the valley of trees and listen to the river that flows through it. A deer appears in the thicket below and leaps into the forested area, its white tail waving good-bye. On the other side of the river is the neighbouring Hutterite colony—a place my uncle sometimes goes to buy eggs and homemade banana bread for bargain prices.

Once we get to the bottom of the hill, I find a good spot and start picking. I try grabbing at clusters of berries (to fill my bucket faster), but the most I can pick are a few at a time. At first, I taste as I go, and it is not long before my fingers are stained deep purple.

Lowering one of the branches hanging overhead, I am reminded of a *Napi* story that an elder once told me...

As the story goes, one day, Napi was very hungry (knowing Napi, he was probably *starving*). Looking for something to eat, he came upon a riverbank and noticed a bulberry bush, there at the bottom of the river. Right away, he dove into the water and tried to swim to the bottom. But before long, he returned to the surface without any berries. After several attempts, Napi became frustrated and was now more determined than ever. Just then, an idea came to him. If he tied two large boulders to his waist, surely he would get to the bottom, where at last he could reach the berries. And so, with two large boulders tied to his waist, Napi jumped in the river and sank straight to the bottom. Searching for the bulberry bush, Napi found nothing but pebbles and weed. Frantically, he worked to free himself and swam to the top, choking and gasping for air. Tired and out of breath, Napi crawled onto the riverbank and lay on his back to rest (still hungry). When Napi opened his eyes, there was the bulberry bush hanging over him.

"How do you say Saskatoon berries in Blackfoot?" Henry's voice yanked me from my storied thoughts.

"Ókonokiistsi," my mom replies.

"Ókonokiistsi...ókonokiistsi," I say the word a few times, knowing that if I don't, I will soon forget.

That is when I notice that growing out of the bleached grass around me are tall ribbons of sage. I heed the warning, *careful not to pull the root*, knowing the plant would then cease to grow. I put down my bucket and gather a small bundle (to use for the times I like to smudge).

When we decide to go back up the hill, a couple of hours have passed. Our ice-cream pails are full and I have a new appreciation for the grandmothers who gathered here before me. I stop and crouch down to bury a fresh cigarette in the dirt—an offering to *Á'pistotooki* (the Creator) and I realize home will always be my greatest teacher.

Curriculum Work

In Families, in Schools

And now I am drawn into the fold of a discursive imaginary that can entertain "both this and that," "neither this nor that"—a space of paradox, ambiguity and ambivalence.

—Ted Aoki, *Five Curriculum Memos*

Tears for the lost language,
The geography of the heart.
—Robin McGrath, *Covenant of Salt*

The notion of curriculum as taken up by the life writers in this section can be seen as profound relational work. The writing coming forth from various institutional, pedagogical, and familial contexts is richly layered both within the narratives and between them. We hear the voices of teachers, students, kin, and other relations (grandmothers, grandfathers, mothers, fathers, daughters, sons, and more) resonating within the "layered voices of teaching" (Aoki, 1992/2005). Curriculum, understood as *currere*, constitutes a living text that attends to the daily experiences of students and teachers in relation with each other and with events and people from past times. These are what Aoki calls "metonymic moments of living pedagogy" between the "curriculum-as-plan" and the "curriculum-as-lived" (Aoki, 2003).

Attending to the relational and dialogical nature of curriculum work features large in Aoki's life work and in his dialogues with scholars across disciplines, epistemologies, and geo-cultural locations (Aoki, 1991/2005). Many other hermeneutic scholars' work attests to the centrality of documenting and interpreting what goes on in the fertile dialogues that are part of the process of evolving relationships between students, teachers, family networks, and the larger commons (Jardine, Clifford, & Friesen, 2003).

In this strand, life writers are paying attention to these processes within their own *currere* and curricular worlds in ways that are organic, original, and aboriginal. These writings remind us that, both for the Canadian context they are familiar with and for curriculum beyond this geo-cultural contact zone: "We are all related." The writings in this section remind us that it is the deep rapprochement between different epistemological, political, racial, and pedagogical frameworks and lifeworlds that remains our biggest challenge, in the North and in the South (Chambers & Balanoff, 2009; Donald, 2009; Meyer, 2000).

REFERENCES

Aoki, T. T. (2003). Locating living pedagogy in teacher research: Five metonymic moments. In E. Hasebe-Ludt & W. Hurren (Eds.), *Curriculum intertext: Place/language/pedagogy* (pp. 1–9). New York, NY: Peter Lang.

Aoki, T. T. (1991/2005). Five curriculum memos and a note for the next half-century. In W. F. Pinar & R. L. Irwin (Eds.), *Curriculum in a new key: The collected works of Ted T. Aoki* (pp. 247–261). Mahwah, NJ: Lawrence Erlbaum.

Aoki, T. T. (1992/2005). Layered voices of teaching. In W. F. Pinar, & R. L. Irwin (Eds.). (2005). *Curriculum in a new key: The collected works of Ted T. Aoki* (pp. 167–197). Mahwah, NJ: Lawrence Erlbaum.

Chambers, C. M., & Balanoff, H. (2009). Translating "participation" from North to South: A case against intellectual imperialism in social science research. In D. Kapoor & S. Jordan, (Eds.), *International perspectives on education, PAR and social change* (pp. 73–88). New York, NY: Palgrave MacMillan.

Donald, D. (2009). The curricular problem of Indigenousness: Colonial frontier logics, teacher resistances, and the acknowledgment of ethical space. In J. Nahachewsky & I. Johnston (Eds.), *Re-imagining the historical, personal, and social places of curriculum* (pp. 23–41). Rotterdam, The Netherlands: Sense Publishers.

Jardine, D., Clifford, P., & Friesen, S. (2003). *Back to the basics of teaching and learning: Thinking the world together.* New York, NY: Routledge.

McGrath, R. (2005). *Covenant of salt.* St. John's, Canada: Killick Press.

Meyer, M. (2000, Spring). Aloha is the intelligence with which we meet life: Five points on Hawaiian epistemology. *The Journal of Maori Studies, 6*(1), 31–34.

Spelling and Other Illiteracies

Cynthia Chambers

I never wanted to be a teacher. Not because I hated school. I felt more at home in school than in most other places. Not the case for most of my schoolmates. Like many students, I had my favourite teachers and schools; unlike many students, I had twenty-one schools, from Grade 1 to Grade 12, to choose from. I dropped out of Grade 12 at Easter in 1968 and it took me 2 years, three towns (Victoria, British Columbia; Hay River and Yellowknife, Northwest Territories), and three high schools to graduate.

Even by today's standards, with family mobility and student transience on the rise, twenty-one is still a large sample; every twenty-one locations had its own literacy that I had to master before I felt I belonged.

While that number is not statistically significant, there were differences among the schools. For example, provincial and state curricula varied. I moved from the Northwest Territories to British Columbia at the end of Grade 10, just as "new math" was introduced, so I got "no math" instead. Without "new" math, I had to rely on "ancient" trigonometry to meet university requirements. In Aldergrove, British Columbia I studied *Lord of the Flies*, and in Bellingham, Washington, *The Grapes of Wrath*.

Schools had different smells. In the North, schools reeked of Misto-Van, a chemical deodorant that promised to overpower bacteria in the chemical toilets or "honey buckets." In the South, schools smelled of floor wax and cigarette smoke from the teachers' lounge. In modern southern schools, I held freshly minted worksheets to my nose and inhaled the sweet fumes of the Gestetner spirit duplicator.

Schools looked different, as well. A portrait of the Queen hung above the blackboard of the one-room school in Aklavik, Northwest Territories; a crucifix hung in the two-room Federal Indian Day School in Fort Good Hope, Northwest Territories. At John A. McDougall Junior High in Edmonton, Alberta, there were marble staircases, concave from decades of students' steps; and separate entrances for boys and girls at opposite ends of the school.

In spite of the differences, each school was more familiar than strange. The rituals of bells, line-ups, and assemblies were similar; the little ceremonies of classroom life were recognizable. There were always reading groups; I was always the "bluebird," never the "crow." There was always the blackboard, filled with notes to be copied; there was always the yellow chalk dust. There was always the alphabet with the same twenty-six letters above the blackboard, the same red-white-and-blue-striped brushes below. There was always the pull-down *Map of the Dominion of Canada*, with the Neilson's logo at the top and bottom, and pictures of Neilson's chocolate bars in each corner.

Each *new* school was recognizable; each first encounter was an intimate affair. The smells, sounds, and textures of the school and classroom were deeply familial and familiar.

Even examinations were well known foes. In the fifties and sixties, intelligence quotient (IQ) tests served as standardized assessment and placements tools. Since I often arrived at yet-another-*new* school well ahead of the cumulative file sent from the *old* school, I took the same IQ test several times.

The colourful ways that teachers marked student progress was intimately familiar: there was red ink and there were gold stars. Any good student learned to avoid the former and seek the latter. My academic career began in Grade 1 when I received my first gold star. Not for arithmetic, new or old. Not likely for hygiene. Each pupil's personal cleanliness was tracked publicly on a chart: stars for those days when inspected hands were scrubbed and fingernails were cleaned fastidiously, blank spaces for those inspections that deemed digits dirty. In this particular star search, pupils that came from homes with indoor plumbing had a distinct advantage over those of us with honey buckets. No, I probably did not earn my first gold star for hygiene. Probably the gold stars were in my Dick and Jane workbook, *Work and Do*. Work hard and do well. Gold stars for "word recognition" and "phonics," the jigsaw pieces of early literacy, then and now. Enough gold stars that by Christmas break of Grade 1, I "skipped" into Grade 2.

Actually, like any addiction—which is what gold stars became for me, and for many, particularly female, teachers—the drug doesn't really matter. What matters is the intensive quest for a particular feeling: the thrill of excellence, the kick of recognition, the buzz of achievement, the rush of success, and the self-satisfaction of being right.

I loved to learn with, or without, the gold stars. Whenever the trajectory of my young life careened wildly, I ran away—headed for some known or unknown destination, as long as it was away—curiosity, love of reading, interest in ideas, or perhaps "sheer buzzard luck," as the Powder Blues Band called it, swung me back on course, away from the streets toward a high-school diploma.

My first attempt to run was in Grade 2, my last in Grade 10. Although I knew what I was running from, I only recently understood where I was running to. What I craved, even at the age of seven, was a place where I belonged, a place that recognized me: *Cindy*. Because each northern village—with its dishevelled shacks, its secret trails and languages, its frozen creeks and hiding places—was foreign territory. I was the foreigner. Because each southern town—with streets paved on a grid, with manicured public playgrounds, and with fenced and well tended baseball fields—was strange. I was the stranger.

In school, seated in a small, wooden desk with a drawer and an inkwell, a straight nib pen and a jar of India ink, somewhere near the back row, I belonged. I belonged even if I was the new girl in town. With each new school, I learned more about how to be a *pupil*. As an itinerant and constant immigrant, I may not have known how to be a neighbour or a friend, a cousin or an older sister, a Girl Guide or a candy striper; as a foreigner, I may not have known how to snare rabbits, play tennis, or send thank-you cards, but I knew how to be a pupil. Luckily, whatever I needed to do to earn gold stars, in school, at least I could do. I could read, I could write, and I could speak, in English. I had the literacies that mattered, in that cloistered, colonial world.

What was this literacy I had acquired? What was it for? What were the gaps?

Two of my great-aunts earned their living as artists. Both my mother and grandmother painted and drew as well. I never learned to do either. My mother was an accomplished athlete: swimmer, diver, figure skater, and tap dancer. She was a good enough softball player to catch the eye of her coach. The newly engaged couple moved from Whitehorse to Vancouver where they were married in 1949. I was born 2 years later. My father played semi-pro Senior AAA fastball and hockey. The last time I played softball, I caught a black eye. I had missed a simple throw to first base; I never did play hockey. In 1934 when my mother was only 2-years old, she was coached by Percy Norman, mastering Vancouver's Crystal Pool high-dive board. My only attempt at the high-metre board, I retreated backwards down the stairs.

In spite of my DNA, walking and Hatha yoga are as close to athletic as I get.

Although I lived in the North and on the Prairies for much of my life, I never learned to two-step, jig, foxtrot, tango, rumba, or dance at a powwow. If I relax and feel the beat but don't think too hard, I can round dance. But the truth is: I rarely do.

Though I joined the choir in Grade 6, the training didn't stick. I still can't sing "Happy Birthday" on key, or in tune. While my mother could play piano by ear—a talent my daughter inherited—I have never learned to play any instrument, even the humble recorder. I can't read music, not a note.

What kind of literate person is that? What are the gaps?

So…what is literacy for? What are its aims and purposes in the world?

In the Western European and English-speaking tradition, if you were literate, you were cultured, knowledgeable and competent: you *read* and *knew* letters, that is, fine literature; and you *wrote* letters, epistles that is, as well as, poetry, essays and other forms. Literature was the source of your knowledge; *to be literate* was to know the literary canon and to be able to navigate within that world. To be literate meant you read inter-textually and inter-referentially; you carried meanings from one piece of literature to the next, from *real* worlds to *imaginary* ones and back again. What you learned from literature, and the accompanying grammar and rhetoric, fitted you for public life: be it as a politician, a teacher, or a writer.

Gabriel García Marquez's (2003) memoir *Living to Tell the Tale* is an unapologetic confession of his early indulgence in what he called the "vice of reading everything" (p. 194) and his relentless compulsion to discuss all that he'd read with friends. Eventually, Marquez began to read not only for pleasure, but like a novelist, with what he described as "an insatiable curiosity to discover how books by wise people were written" (p. 367). An apprenticeship in letters may sometimes leads to a life of letters, and in Marquez's case, a Nobel Prize for literature. Gabriel García Marquez exemplifies the literate person who is both knowledgeable and competent.

This vital link between knowledge and competence still holds in specialties such as ecoliteracy, spiritual literacy, and technological literacy. In these hybrid literacies, to be literate means to be competent in a set of discrete practical activities. These competencies enable you to learn and use a particular body of knowledge. In such literacies, there is an almost immutable relationship between knowledge, say of the environment, and the competency necessary to use that knowledge, say to read animal tracks and weather formations, or to recognize plants and their uses.

The words *relation* and *relationship*, that is, something related to something else, are etymologically "carried back" from the Latin *relatus,* the past participle of *referre* "carry back, refer to" (Ayto, 1990/2001, p. 438). So in ecoliteracy, the text to be read is the ecology which refers back to competencies necessary to read that place. *To read the place* means you are able to dwell within it, to inhabit it, to gather from it the knowledge that makes life there possible, as well as intelligible and meaningful.

More important, in these hybrid literacies, your knowledge and your competency bear certain responsibilities; they compel you to act in particular ways. Being ecoliterate means you can and will engage sanely and carefully with that place and the other beings who live there with you. To be ecoliterate is to act in the world as if you were literate, rather than illiterate. Thus, these competencies, or *literacy skills*, and the *texts* they enable you to read, are inextricably bound together. In turn, they are bound to an ethics of reading. That is what you are called to do once you have the knowledge and the skills. Enmeshed in these kinds of literacy are texts, skills, and ethics. On their own, these texts, skills, and ethics are rendered indecipherable, insignificant, impotent, perhaps even dangerous.

For the socially and politically conscious, *literacy* is still necessary for citizenship; it is what enables you to participate more fully in public life. As Eduardo Galeano (1983) asks, "what literary piece is not political and social?" He claims *all* literary pieces are social, because each piece of literature belongs to human society. All are political as well, to the extent that "political" implies participation in public life, whether the author of a book, an article, or a short story wants it or not; knows it or not (p. 121).

That is one kind of literacy, a very important kind. But the most common use of *literacy* equates it with the ability to read and write alphabetic text. In education, literacy is a *process* through which you achieve certain goals and outcomes, if you are competent. Enough.

Gold stars.

The metaphor of *process* is particularly plastic and can mean just about anything. But when you divorce *process* from content and product, the *relationship* between knowledge and competency is severed. So nowadays, it seems as if you don't have to know anything in particular to be literate. You are literate if you read and write well enough to learn what you need to know, just in time to use it. This idea of literacy is oriented to the future rather than the present or past. Literacy divorced from a body of knowledge has become a necessary competency for managing the future. This assumes that literacy is ethically neutral, culturally neutral, and politically neutral. But it is not.

As public participation loses ground to private consumption—some months going to the mall or a movie theatre is as close to public participation as I get—so social and political literacy loses ground to literacy for individual economic gain. Rarely does public discourse about education refer to literacy as necessary for people to participate actively and authentically in public life (Chambers & Balanoff, 2009; Young, 1990), to engage in collective decision-making about what little remains in the public common, or the "common bowl" as the Nishga call it.

No, literacy is equated with equal opportunity for economic prosperity.

Literacy for gold stars.

Divorced from knowledge and tradition and imagination, literacy becomes a technology instead of a practised craft (Ingold, 2000), the kind of technology that industry claims the economy needs, the kind of literacy in which governments are willing to invest public money, the kind of literacy that earned me gold stars: tenure, a full professorship, and a defined-benefits pension plan. *Illiteracy* is a disease to be diagnosed, tracked, and remediated. Like Eduardo Galeano, I believe schools need to teach a kind of literacy and a body of literature that commits children to engaging in life and to the places that they live, to the social and political change necessary to heal the gaps. Curriculum needs to be dedicated to literacy and literature that nourishes collective identity, "rescues the memory of communities" (Galeano, 1983, p. 122), and nourishes the places we live and expands the human spirit (Chamberlin, 2003; Galeano, 1983). What is needed is a kind of literacy and a body of literature that helps adults and children find their way home, no matter how far they have run, no matter how long they have been running.

Reading and writing linear text on the page—paper or electronic, alphabetic or binary code—seems unequal to the task of ensuring societies remember, ensuring that they embrace the young, ensuring they give children and young people an education that matters. Literacy skills, when divorced from knowledge and responsibility, are thin and malnourished and end up to be incomplete or partial literacies, in other words, *illiteracy* skills.

So What Is Literacy For?

In Ulukhaktok, and in many Indigenous communities, literacy could be described as that which makes it possible to dwell in the land that nurtures them, to belong to and with each other, human and other-than-human, in that place.

These relational knowledge and highly contextualized literacies are phenomenological; they are acquired in the activities of dwelling in landscapes with others (Ingold, 2000), with kin, with "bone people," those to whom you are related through naming as well as through blood. Relational knowledge and literacies are learned through your kinship with other beings on whom you depend and with whom you live in social and spiritual contract. And they are continually renewed through lived experiences of being together, through ceremony, language, and song: the feeding of the sun when it returns in Ulukhaktok, and the opening of the long-time, medicine-pipe bundles after the return of thunder each spring in Blackfoot territory. Relational knowledge and literacies are what makes you Inuk or Inuinnait; they are what make you *Kainai* (Blood), *Piikaanii* (Peigan), or *Nehíyaw* (Cree).

I live in the gaps between what counts as literacy in school, and what counts as literacy outside school. I navigated those gaps as I migrated in and out of those northern communities. As a vagabond, there were gaps I couldn't see, gaping holes I didn't anticipate, and portages I couldn't cross until much later in life. Learning to mind the gaps and navigate them has been long and slow and hard. And I still live those gaps, handicapped by the very literacy that brought me success in school.

I never wanted to be a teacher. But I became one. And with being a teacher came responsibilities to the word and to the world, to myself and to others, to the stories told and to those not told.

As a teacher and a Canadian curriculum scholar, I needed to give up my gold stars and correct Canadian spelling. I needed to fall *out* of love with knowing and being right and fall *in* love with learning and living. I hope I never forget this because to forget can be fatal. For me, it almost was.

REFERENCES

Ayto, J. (1990). *Bloomsbury dictionary of word origins.* London, England: A & C Black Publishing.

Chamberlin, J. E. (2003). *If this is your land, where are your stories? Finding common ground.* Toronto: Alfred A. Knopf Canada.

Chambers, C. M., & Balanoff, H. (2009). Translating "participation" from North to South: A case against intellectual imperialism in social science research. In D. Kapoor & S. Jordan, (Eds.). *International perspectives on education, PAR and social change* (pp. 73–88). New York, NY: Palgrave MacMillan.

Galeano, E. (1983). The imagination and the will to change (M. Valvere, Trans.). In The Toronto Arts Group for Human Rights (Eds.), *The writer and human rights* (pp. 121–123). Garden City, NY: Anchor Press/Doubleday.

Ingold, T. (2000). *The perception of the environment: Essays on livelihood, dwelling and skill.* New York, NY: Routledge.

Márquez, G. G. (2003). *Living to tell the tale* (E. Grossman, Trans.). Toronto: Alfred A. Knopf Canada. (Originally published in 2002)

Young, I. M. (1990). *Justice and the politics of difference.* Princeton, NJ: Princeton University Press.

Pedagogy of Papa

Phong Kuoch

This piece was originally a speech I wrote and delivered at a commencement ceremony to the graduating class of 2010. The graduating students reflected the diversity of the school they attended. Many of their parents were new or recent immigrants from many parts of the world who left their homeland, family, friends and respectable careers in search of greater educational and life opportunities for their sons and daughters. Although life in a foreign land was full of daily challenges as these new immigrants tried to weave themselves into the dominant Canadian cultural and social fabric, their resolve was unbreakable. To witness their child crossing the stage in their cap and gown was testimony that the sacrifices they had made for their children's future were indeed well worth it.

My father was a high-school dropout. He dropped out when he was only 14-years old. He traded in his education for an ice cream cart. My father chose to drop out because his father (my grandfather) passed away unexpectedly. And because he was the eldest of nine children, he felt the duty to sacrifice his formal education so that he could help support his mother (my grandmother) and his sisters and brothers. For 12 hours a day, every day, my father pedaled his ice cream cart around the streets of Saigon, selling cold treats at about five Canadian cents a piece.

Although my father did not acquire a formal education, he did, however, possess a will for hard work. He applied his impeccable work ethics into amassing quite a successful shampoo-and-hair product business with his brothers. With each passing year, he enjoyed the luxuries that wealth brought, giving his young family a very comfortable life amidst the poverty surrounding him. He told me how he would invite the neighbours over to our house because we were the only family who had a TV. But surrounded by the opulence, my father was not satisfied. He looked at his children and realized that although he could give them all the basic necessities and even more required to live a productive and happy life in Saigon, he knew that there was something missing. Because my father never received a formal education, he desperately craved one for his children. But not just a basic education; rather, he dreamt of an education that he believed only a *Western World* could offer.

So he relinquished his business, got rid of all his assets, and left the world and the people he had known all his life for the unknown destination ahead. With wife and three young children in tow, he embarked on the harrowing journey to a refugee camp in Indonesia. He had unwavering faith that his ultimate sacrifice would reap greater rewards for his children. Although life in a refugee camp was difficult, his gamble paid off, for our family was offered citizenship in Canada.

But life for a new immigrant who did not speak the dominant language and who did not understand the culture was a life of challenges. My father, who worked his way up from an ice-cream vendor to a successful business man found himself right at the bottom again, washing dishes in a foreign land. He slaved for Canadian employers who exploited his immigrant status by overworking him, underpaying him and sometimes not paying him at all. While he shuffled between his two low-paying and hard-labour jobs, he would make time to remind me how important getting a good education in Canada was. To this day, I still remember his saying, "Son, I use my hands so you can use your head."

Needless to say, my father has taught and continues to teach me many conventional life lessons. But by no means is my father a conventional teacher.

My mother told me that my father had a very unconventional way of toilet training his children. He wanted us all out of diapers as soon as possible as he believed that the quicker one is able to control one's bladder, the sooner one can control one's destiny in life. Whenever I soiled my diaper, my father would remove the contaminated diaper and press it against my nose as I writhed with discomfort and disgust at the odour of my excrement. He would hold the dirty diaper against my face until I was wailing uncontrollably. He would do this over and over again until I learned that if I didn't want my own poo shoved in my face, I had better poo in the toilet.

Like all children, my sisters and I enjoyed eating candy. Although my father did not approve of the many Western candies we were consuming, he was wise enough to know that banning sweets altogether would only make us crave them even more. Our favourite Western candy was Smarties because the colours were so intoxicating. Although my father could not read the names of the chemicals found in Smarties, he knew they were not good for us. Rather than forbidding us to eat them, my father would pour a handful into a sifter and run cold water over them to rinse off the rainbow of colours. I remember still the first time my father handed over wet, sticky and greyish-coloured Smarties to my sisters and me. Needless to say, we lost our sweet tooth at a very young age.

It's normal for siblings to fight. My eldest sister and I were no different. We fought over the most ridiculous and minute things. My father became so sick of it that he decided to teach us how to get along. After one particular quarrel with my sister, my father wanted to teach us the meaning of sibling bonding. No, he didn't read us a picture book about how a brother and sister became the best of friends. No, he didn't sit us down for a heart-to-heart conversation about how we are family and that family means we love each other. Rather, he grabbed my younger sister's Strawberry Shortcake skipping rope and gave us each a good whip on our toilet-trained bottoms. Then with the same skipping rope, he tied our wrists together. He told us that we would remain tied together until we could prove to him that we could resolve our differences. I protested and demanded to know how my father expected us to use the washroom when we were tied together. His response was simple—"Figure it out yourselves." Well let me tell you, it requires a lot of coordination, team work, and collaborative effort to be able to pee while your sister is tied to your hand.

One afternoon in my fifth grade, I stumbled upon a half-full bottle of apple cider left on the kitchen table. All I was taught is that apple cider is for adults. Predictably, I took a sip. And then I took another sip. And another. Of course, I was oblivious to the fact that my father was watching me the whole time. I remember hearing him slowly walking over to the fridge and taking out four full bottles of apple cider. He sat down beside me at the kitchen table. He opened each bottle and lined up all four in front of me. My father told me not to leave the table until I finished all the bottles, including the initial one I was so curious about. My mother, who overheard my father's orders, protested bitterly, calling my father *crazy* for making a child consume alcohol. My father responded by saying, "The boy is curious. Let him drink his curiosity." By "drinking my curiosity" as he put it, I was no longer curious about alcohol but rather learned to be curious about other things that are more important in life.

Perhaps if a social worker were to parachute into our home, my father probably would not be seen favourably. "What kind of a family is this?" Certainly we do not fit into the normal concept of family in Canada. But then again, is there such a thing as a normal family, whether it be in Canada, Vietnam, or anywhere else for that matter?

During my recent teaching of *Hamlet* with my high-school students, we paused to discuss when we arrived at Act I, Scene 2, where we learned that Hamlet's mother has married his uncle, only a few months after Hamlet's father's death. The general consensus, which was so eloquently expressed by one of my students, was that "This is one messed-up family." I remember thinking the exact same thing about my family after I was exposed to Western popular media's portrayal of families. How come my parents never told me "I love you" like the moms and dads on *Family Ties* and *Growing Pains*? I foolishly equated their silence with their lack of love for me until I realized that my parents' "I love you" were manifested in many non-verbal ways. This prompted me to ask the students about their "messed-up families" and challenge the notion that a normal family can even exist. As student after student shared countless examples about how their family was "strange," "weird," and even "crazy," we came to the epiphany that what makes families normal is how abnormal they are. Family dynamics—shaped by family history, cultural practices, generational beliefs, economic situations, hegemonic forces—all contribute to the fluid, contradictory, and multi-dimensional nature of families and the members within, even the fathers who intoxicate you with alcohol and excrement.

My father, the high-school dropout, is not Dewey, Piaget, or Freire. He is neither Mr. Cleaver nor Mr. Cosby. For what he *isn't* is what Papa's pedagogy is all about.

Dezi Was a Drummer

Christy Audet

Dezi was a drummer. I didn't know it for a long time and I didn't realize just how good he was until he played at our school talent show. The first time I saw Dezi, he was wearing canary yellow skinny jeans and a big black hoodie that barely covered the brightly patterned underwear showing above his apparently useless belt. He had long jet-black hair and a big smile, and immediately asked to borrow a pen. I indicated where I kept my supply of extra "stuff" at the side of the room. He borrowed a pen and some paper that first day and almost every day for the next year-and-a-half as we journeyed through social studies, English, health, and creative writing.

Dezi was good-natured enough, but he rarely completed assignments and his attendance was sporadic. Group assignments were definitely a challenge—for him and for his group—unless there was music involved. Like most ninth-grade boys, Dezi always had earplugs in, even when he wasn't supposed to, and was usually tapping along to some tune, either real or remembered. He talked about forming a band in his basement and was one of the strongest advocates for our students' union to put on a school talent show. The night before our show he made arrangements to meet me at the school to set up his drums. No problem with commitment and organization when music was involved! He and another older student with a guitar even had an impromptu jam session that evening. She later said to me, "It was really fun playing with Dezi. I always thought he was a bit weird but he's nice. We've even made plans to play together again."

Dezi's group won the talent show. As I watched him perform that afternoon, I thought about how joyful he was in that moment and how important it is for every student to have the opportunity to lose themselves in the moment, enjoy what they love, even if it is not officially part of the curriculum.

When Dezi came back to school the next September he was quieter, he tapped faster, and his attendance was even worse. Because his parents were getting a divorce, I shared my concerns with them at separate parent-teacher interviews. They said he didn't see the point in school. We agreed all we could do was just keep trying to encourage him; hopefully he would work through this hoop he called high school.

Our school had a late policy that required students to attend detention if they had been given three late slips. Not attending detention was considered an act of disrespect, punishable by an in-school suspension. By the end of the first semester of his tenth grade, Dezi was missing as many school days in detention as he was skipping. A week into the second semester and my social studies class, I saw Dezi sitting in detention yet again. So, I appealed to administration to allow him to come to my classes because I couldn't catch him up with notes alone. Reluctantly an agreement was made. For a time, Dezi and I were happy, but relations between the administration and Dezi continued to deteriorate. Dezi didn't come to school for over a week. I was getting worried. His sister told me he was running away to the big city to find a job and play in a band.

The week crept on and there was no sign of Dezi until late on Friday. The crowded hallway was just thinning out in anticipation of a glorious sunny weekend when I saw him. We walked to my room and talked about what was happening in his world. He told me he was coming to say good-bye because he was determined to quit school and move on. Yet, Dezi offered a parting present because, as he said, "I will be famous one day and you'll be glad you have it." It was a broken drumstick with the words, "'til the last breath I take," and his signature. I wished him luck and told him he was always welcome back. And tried not to cry.

Shortly after Dezi's departure a teacher observed that if we didn't consistently waste so much time on kids like Dezi we could spend the time attending to specific Grade 12s, under-achieving on the government diploma exams.

Do we really have to pick who we "save"? And, how do we judge failure/success? Dezi was bright, creative, articulate and we, as a school, clearly failed to engage him. Why?

Last week Dezi's sister brought me back a novel she found in his bedroom. She shared that he had read and really enjoyed *Men of Stone* by Gayle Friesen, a novel dealing with the issue of a boy finding creative acceptance within his school environment. She was looking forward to reading it in my class as well. Already I have heard comments about how the sister is breaking the dress code policy by wearing tank tops with straps far too thin. Men of stone, indeed.

Curricular Fixations
and Poetic Tactics

Sean Wiebe

In *The Invention of Solitude*, a memoir of fatherhood, Auster (1982) notes that every story begins with the father. This piece begins by looking back to how a father's use of tools lends wisdom to notions of *fixing and unfixing*. I look back to a time when I was doing graduate studies at the University of British Columbia; writing autobiographically about my relationship with my father, I was learning that much like life curriculum is replete with mystery and ambiguity. I was learning to shift, that is "unfix," my mistaken assumptions about what was permanent and fixed in life and curriculum. Using a combination of narrative and poetry in the two movements which follow, I set out to disrupt, question, and create greater gaps in the processes used to investigate and represent knowledge in our lives.

Movement 1

In curriculum class last night, one of the students leapt up and wrote his definition of curriculum on the white board. I'd been sitting for a long time, and I hoped, like me, he had risen simply to rest his bum and by shifting his weight redistribute the wealth of blood to other parts of his body. But hopes are short-lived. Apparently, he felt that by fixing his definition to the wall an important step in understanding would be served, our task made clear, *right* thinking separated from *wrong* thinking. With definition came purpose and a reason to exist. Now the real business of ordering things, developing schema, and organizing structures could begin. We had a centre from which all lines of thought could flow.

I, too, come from a long line of "fixers" though I've never been much of one myself. It is my father who can fix everything. He built our house, then renovated the basement, then built a garage, then a deck, and then started again with a new house. He could fix anything from cars to toilets, and the surest gift at Christmas was a tool purchased at Canadian Tire. There is a deep connection between this man and his tools. My brothers are just like him, so when we get together the talk is always of what's wrong and what needs to be fixed, always, forever fixing.

So when the definition of curriculum was fixed right there in front of me, I felt I was somehow on familiar ground. That what was broken was now whole, that what was once an empty white board now had some purpose and value. Like the pouring of concrete, we now had a foundation on which we could build.

But I also knew the illusion of fixation. Being too fixated on a world where everything works. There was not a single day of growing up where my dad sat down on the couch to watch the *The Red Green Show* and said, "I've got nothing to do tomorrow. It's all been fixed." A man's work was never done. In class that night, I wondered if I should say something. Perhaps share Doll's (2005) insight that vigour and possibility come from seeing anew, from seeing beside oneself (p. 37). Perhaps even a little witticism, that something fixed on a wall is not fixed at all. Because after all, we live in a temporal world. Ideas wear out as fast as, and even faster, than our bodies. In *Everyman*, Phillip Roth (2006) structures his story around operations the narrator has undergone. Perhaps that which we collect and canonize, our body of knowledge, should wear out like our bodies. Each generation, then, would need to discover its own body for its own time. We couldn't simply inherit our father's house perfectly fixed up anymore than we could inherit our father's body.

Like Jardine (2003), I've come to see the danger of fixing. "[Fixing] seeks to eradicate difference; but it also eliminates openings and possibilities" (p. 43), but I am not a proponent of cutting family ties. My father was a fixer. He was acting with his tools the same way early curriculum scholars like Tyler, Bruner, and Schwab were acting with their empirical, and overly reductionist pens. And still, one of my favourite activities when I return home (and my father's home is still also home), is to hold his tools, to gaze and admire what he has fixed and fixed again. There is incredible order there, his tools in gigantic, red tool boxes.

Jardine (2003) says that "children can bring about the transformation and renewal of the center" (p. 43). So I take a second look at my father's tools, each with its place, its purpose, and function. The sheer volume of it all. I am in this place of generosity, somehow feeling my technical inheritance to tools, to technique, to problems and solutions but simultaneously knowing that I can discover tools for myself, that I can even add to my inheritance, contribute to my father's world which is not dead, but ever alive in me and others who look back with a willingness to understand anew. This new life of my father in me is new blood to me and new blood to my father. "Bereft of new blood," says Jardine (2003) "the senatorial becomes merely senile" (p. 57). In other words, I will not be prostrate to the past, though I will share its prostate.

A brief hermeneutical example might illustrate such a relationship. In texts, a *lacuna* is a gap, a missing piece, or a silence. For those who take up the task of translation, like the son who translates his father's world, often there is no direct, one-to-one corresponding lexical unit. In such cases, a descriptive phrase is usually used instead. Sometimes in these old manuscripts, when there are blemishes and weathering, the missing words are inserted from the context. This troubling slip of language creates possibilities for rethinking what is sometimes previously taken for granted. Going back to consider the many layers of meaning should be more than fitting an appropriate link for the lacuna but should be a genuine receiving of difference such that multiple understandings can be held at once. When I think of my father's fixing, that means holding his tools in my hand again. Re-thinking what it meant for him to be always fixing. With so many tools in my father's house, I wonder why I didn't see it before: I'd always thought he was an idealist, that he was Kantian, and wanted to nail it all down, once and for all with some kind of pure hammer, some smooth unbiased swing.

But looking again, choosing to add to my inheritance, to actively construct the context of my past, I have this new sense that my father's many tools were like many voices, many possibilities, many nuances. That he did believe in the need for continual fixing. Often my father bought a tool just in case, in wise anticipation that he would need a tool like this someday, that he could be confident again, and again, and again, that there would be work to be done.

The hope is that by daring to make commentary on what has become stratified and fixed, that to explore the boundaries of text and subjectivity, that to question the sacred is not sacrilege, or a sacrifice, but a process of freedom, a process which makes a text a living thing. Lewis Hyde (1983) suggests that "the way we treat a thing can change its nature" (p. xiii). Such an approach parallels the hermeneutic tradition, which both respects the sacred but offers translation and interpretation of it. Genuine inquiry shares a hermeneutical inheritance in that research defined as inquiry tends to be open, meditative, and circuitous (Douglas-Klotz, 1998). I've come to believe the rich possibilities in blurring prose and poetry.

Salves From St. Jude

Drink up, imagine that you are caught
inside a delirium, churning chaos.

Dive down to reedy edge of those candles,
listen. Tilt your gaze. I will play

that recognizable melody rocking you,
catch it for later. Shun the same sad

stare gnawing, and take your
whimpering swamped body to the soft

mud floor, rolling onto your side,
play Xs and Os as a welcome distraction.

Save confession for after breakfast,
back to the sink, history will vomit

worse than you have, a slack jawed
capacity for cruelty. Tree bark boiled

in oil is the only remedy for desperate
cases and lost causes. Ingest every

syllable, persevere, bound by nothing,
tumble away, depression is never

about just one thing, but a slippery
balance of passions. Skip across

inconsequential voodoo, twirls
and throbs of booga booga.

We are in life, squeeze it, cherish
the difficult way. Use a soft sponge

if you are helpless, a goner, the only
one, enjoy gravity, be swept away.

The dangerous river, with its curves
and bends, always flows to the big
upstairs room, where an injection
of grace is a flame for your head.

Poetry is more than commentary; there is reply, excess, new growth; it is palimpsest. Poetic writing as a form of wisdom treats texts and lives with respect, but rejects the dust on them. And so, in shaking off the dust of my memories of my father, I see that already some words are falling through the cracks. In such an erasure, these words still leave their traces, thus the spaces are openings to the new and the old, a portal for going back and forth.

Movement 2

Ralph Angel (2006) in *Exceptions and Melancholies* hints at some of the reasons why we experience disenchantment in learning: "Never before/had we been so thin and so clear/and arranged always/and in the same way" (p. 4). Here is a caveat to our "arrangements" of courses, our confidence in our own clarity. Perhaps our striving for what is a best practice, what information is of most worth, or what is the best way to say *this* or *that*, is "thin" like chicken noodle soup without the chicken, or the noodles. Aoki (2000), in "The Thing Never Speaks for Itself," is also suspicious of a rationality and kind of enlightenment clarity. He explains that *clarity* produces and reinforces power and exclusion.

What? I'm a writing teaching who is suspicious of clarity. Don't print that in the newspapers.

Fortunately, Angel, in that mischievous way that poets can put us into a bind, also kindly offers a way of escape on the question of clarity. For me, it is a moment of enchantment in learning: He says (2008), "I assure you that we have only one pleasure: learning what one does not know, and one happiness, loving the exceptions" (p. 151).

Walker (2003) says that our task as scholars is to make theories explicit, to clarify them, work out their consequences for curriculum practice, compare them to other ideals, and justify or criticize them (p. 60). To read Walker's claim poetically is to find a harmony, to add into the mix an experimentation, a possibility for new blends and bends. In this way, heartful poetic writing can have a restoring influence on structures which tend to reduce possibilities with justifications. Poetry encourages the discursive journey, and opens additional spaces for personal histories and identities, for those places of pedagogy intimately connected to time and place.

Poetic Tactics

I'm a poet who can whine in metre.

Seized in the wing, poets have ways

of doing things, moving their hands around
wildly, between the aesthetic and great cynicism.
Their eyes are their ears low to ground

open to every sensory encounter.
They constitute from constitutionals
the borders between shopping, reading,
cooking, knowing how to get away from

things with things, and imagination,
polymorphic simulations and so on.
They find the time to wander aimlessly,
the strategy of meticulous attention,

sensation and reflection, their mouths
stretched into crisp, white breath pushed out
clear and distinct, like toxins from their skin.
Fragmentary and fragile, their hope lies

with seduction, clever tricks, joyful discoveries
with slipping out of checkmate and under
covers, the trouble being too many lovers,
terrain introduced into their lives like a foreign

power. Eventually, barking, they depend on
timing and repartee, whine of what is possible,
in the realm of metre and rhyme, and in very specific
historical moments, they improvise.

After Walker, I turn to Greene (1995) because it is her insistence on cultivating the imagination which provides fertile ground for poetic experimentation. Greene (1995) says,

> It is understandable that… boredom and a sense of futility are among the worst enemies of education. At a time of diminishing opportunity in so many lives, at a time when upward mobility cannot be guaranteed, feelings of futility are widespread. (p. 141)

My hope, like Greene's, is that imagination will lead students to the confidence to live outside of the structures which restrict them. As a father, a son, a teacher, and a poet, I practise poetry as a means to understand how teachers understand themselves in relation to a human and living curriculum. Poetry can be a kind of translation of experience, particularly the inner, often unseen experience. To approach the translation of my life poetically means to utilize artful and poetic means to inquire and theorize, to form and reform, to question and trouble, and to make merry in the meaning and process of living. I believe a heartful, poetic mode of writing and living is particularly needed for disrupting the overly reductive forces of the rationalist discourses, such as privileging linear thought over intuition, teaching as if thinking is aggressive and confrontational rather than collegial and collaborative, or neglecting and downplaying emotions (Bailin, 1995, p. 190).

Red Delicious, Extra Fancy

We don't just watch things happen.
Watching automatically makes the watcher
part of the happening.

At the great Canadian poetry store
I search alcoves for some ripe plum
or a paltry pear nestled under there
with the grocer's choice recommendation
(16-years old at ½ that wage)
of lush red Birneys or Brants.

Sure he's young, but selective, having
already learned that righteous scorn
of the unknown apple, not worthy
of his finger grime to place
upon display. Subtle spy, I scheme
to misdirect attention, slide my own

so zesty apple there, and slink away,
born identity, covering a blushing ego
of the regal poet, the south-side shelter's
poet laureate, saviour of strays, discards,
other deletions and indiscretions.
We have our reasons, to stare

each other down to the shoes, he and I
entangled in a larger chorus
of Cohens or Croziers, as if
this is all there is to Christmas shopping,
finding the greatest poet of our generation
as compliment to Hallmark, unwrapped.

In a world which distrusts emotion, poetic writing is a kind of reminder, a re/membering to return to my personal stories. For poets who are researchers and teachers, it becomes necessary, as those who live in/ with/ by/ and through language, to write poetry so that a poet's understanding of the world can celebrate its difference rather than fixedness, can offer ongoing hope for change, which is ongoing difference, and can thus face society's collective fear of intimacy (hooks, 2000, p. 91), that "extreme isolation" of love's discourse that Barthes speaks of (1978, p. x). hooks (2000) believes that "fear is the primary force upholding structures of domination [because] it promotes the desire for separation, the desire not to be known" (p. 93). Thus, "[t]he choice to love is a choice to connect—to find ourselves in the other" (p. 93).

To engage in meaningful dialogue in our lives and in our classrooms, the conversation which is our curriculum ought not be simply a set of fixed learning outcomes, resources, or teachers' plans which occur ahead of time. To not welcome student voices changes the nature of knowledge: primarily, it suggests that knowledge exists beyond us, away from us, somewhere out there that only a few have access to—the few who were invited into the backroom planning session. Clifford and Friesen (1993/2003) describe a classroom practice which welcomes their students' rich experiences as important community knowledge. They argue that "[o]ur curriculum work demands mindful, deliberate improvisation" (p. 21). Thinking on how my writing narratives and poetry is like my father's ongoing fixing, this chapter shows the multiple ways that pre-planned knowledge is a dominant and privileged knowledge which shuts the door on the rich voices of our lives that should bring ongoing life to curriculum. Understanding this will help us, as educators, to question our easily held custom and set in motion a kind of poetic imagination for the creation of a better world. The hope is that our varied voices, bodies, and ways of being can more honestly and equitably unfold in our lives and classrooms. A process of freedom makes curriculum a living thing. The hope is that this process will evolve when we dare to comment and break through fixed, stratified boundaries of teaching, when we can question "the sacred" as neither sacrilege nor sacrifice.

REFERENCES

Angel, R. (2006). *Exceptions and melancholies*. Louisville, KY: Sarabande Books. Retrieved from http://www.versedaily.org/2006/exceptions.shtml

Angel, R. (2008). Author's bio. In C. Wright (Ed.), *The best American poetry* (p. 151). New York, NY: Scribner Poetry.

Aoki, D. (2000). The thing never speaks for itself: Lacan and the pedagogical politics of clarity. *Harvard Educational Review, 70*(3), 347–370.

Auster, P. (1982). *The invention of solitude*. New York, NY: Penguin.

Bailin, S. (1995). Is critical thinking biased? Clarifications and implications. *Educational Theory,* *45*(2), 191–197.

Barthes, R. (1978). *A lover's discourse: Fragments* (R. Howard, Trans.). New York, NY: The Noonday Press.

Clifford, P., & Friesen, S. (1993/2003). A curious plan: Managing on the twelfth. In D. Jardine, P. Clifford, & S. Friesen (Eds.), *Back to the basics of teaching and learning: Thinking the world together* (pp. 16–28). Mahwah, NJ: Lawrence Erlbaum.

Doll, M. (2005). The body of knowledge. *Journal of the Canadian Association for Curriculum Studies, 3*(1), 33–40.

Douglas-Klotz, N. (1998, July). Midrash and postmodern inquiry: Suggestions toward a hermeneutics of indeterminacy. Paper presented at the *16th International Meeting of the Society of Biblical Literature,* Krakow, Poland.

Greene, M. (1995). *Releasing the imagination.* San Francisco, CA: Jossey-Bass.

hooks, b. (2000). *All about love: New visions.* New York, NY: Harper.

Hyde, L. (1983). *The gift: Imagination and the erotic life of property.* New York, NY: Vintage Books.

Jardine, D. (2003). The profession needs new blood. In D. Jardine, P. Clifford, & S. Friesen (Eds.), *Back to the basics of teaching and learning: Thinking the world together* (pp. 56–69). Mahwah, NJ: Lawrence Erlbaum.

Roth, P. (2006). *Everyman.* New York, NY: Vintage Books.

Walker, D. F. (2003). *Fundamentals of curriculum: Passion and professionalism* (2nd ed.). Mahwah, NJ: Lawrence Erlbaum.

A Pedagogy of Hearing

Janet Pletz

In the midst of a recent move from one dwelling to another in the city where I now live, I picked up a box from a closet, and at arm's reach hesitated under the storied weight of it. Knowing I had hours of work ahead of me, I grappled with impulse, but in the end I couldn't thwart curiosity. I knew what was in the box, as I had put it there, taped and marked, just eleven months ago. The box contained decade-old collections of a teaching life. A collection of day plans, jot journals, a few coil notebooks, marked and folded pieces of paper, and even Post-it Notes in rows inside file folders—a teaching life exposed in the form of life-writing narratives and reflections of a primary teacher in a large cosmopolitan city in western Canada. These artifacts were distilled from various distances, times, and places by way of a geographic and pedagogic movement: from one province to the next, from one cosmopolitan setting to another, within juxtaposed identities of my Self: classroom teacher, middle-aged woman, and full-time doctoral student. Now this collection of memories and early accounts of a teaching life were spread on the floor, and I embarked on a journey that would prove beguiling, challenging, and provoking.

I entered into a deliberate process of reflecting back in order to see again, of learning the pedagogic relevance and understanding of what matters most in my practice, of re-reading perceptions of Self, and perhaps understanding differently my lived experience of teaching (Hasebe-Ludt, Chambers, & Leggo, 2009). I was curious about how, or in what ways, these past narratives and reflections of a teaching life have informed and/or shaped my pedagogic practice. In particular, I am drawn to paying attention to one aspect of my pedagogic life as its full impact unfolded in a story of Self always in relation with "Other;" in this case, my Other is severe hearing loss. Teaching young children in the midst of struggling with the complexities of hearing loss has always been challenging. I have always welcomed this challenge as a responsibility, and as a learning event, one which Pauline Sameshima (2007), prompts me, as a researcher and teacher, to re-create as a new way of understanding embodied wholeness, as an active state for renegotiating perceptions of Self in context. Situated consciousness turned toward re-reading found narratives of life writing also provoked complicated spheres of paradox and truth telling.

I feel grounded in knowing that writing "in ways that foster the heart of education...truthfully, requires practice" (Hasebe-Ludt, et al., 2009, p. 179). Likewise, as Maxine Greene (1995) offers, reflecting back on the narratives of lived experience not only shapes "meaning-making," it also allows us to see our lives as quests, seeing them in "terms of process and possibilities, in terms of experience which gradually clarifies itself, rectifies itself, and proceeds with itself and with others" (Merleau-Ponty, as cited in Greene, 1995, p. 21). It is this seeing for possibilities, the clarification of which prompts the quest to re-read my life-writing narratives in the form of found poems (Leggo, 2010), poetic transcriptions (Glesne, 2006) of research journal entries, and creative non-fiction accounts of teaching and learning. In conscious light of heartful living, as Sameshima (2007) suggests, I am listening for wisdom in the audible and in/audible of a teaching life.

Paradox Betwixt: Connectedness in the Middle

"Don't give in to your fears," said the alchemist, in a strangely gentle voice. "If you do, you won't be able to talk to your heart."
—Paulo Coelho, *The Alchemist*

Sitting on the floor, with anecdotes and captions of my teaching life spread in front of me, I noticed another collection of material leaning against the inside of the box, bound and secured by two elastic bands. Now released, and viewed with a hesitant gaze, I held a decade-long running record, a time-line of narrative fragments and documents of hearing and loss.

Run-on-paradoxes

audiograms—able hearing/deaf
    yes—no
        coping strategies—useful/ineffective
           either—or
               life events—capable/unconfident
               this—that
                    hearing mistakes—humour/embarrassment
                    right—wrong

Interpretations of these long-ago personal and institutional artifacts hinted at paradoxes, at a mind-body split. I saw this bundle of creative snippets and records as stand-alone and impenetrable opposites. A sense of tension rose again as I looked at five audiograms over ten years and all I could see were the changes in the steepness of the ski-slope line defining my hearing profile, above the line (hearing) and below the line (not hearing). My mind held court, my eyes riding that line like it was all or nothing, this or that, either/or. I stood up from my place on the floor and paced the room recognizing that my "critical sensor was whispering," and in this "unguarded moment," I was startled (Fowler, 2007, p. 42). Back in the midst of this tension, a tumble into opposing dualisms, I broke the niggling in my mind by inviting my body into the story. This return to wakefulness, soothed by the co-mingling of heart and mind working as one, served to remind me that teaching and learning are inextricably linked to these same sensations. In teaching, opening and yielding to the lessons of discovery and difficulty is also the lens opened by creative synthesis and learning.

Poststructuralist Jacques Daignault (as cited in Sameshima, 2007) theorizes that this disruption of dualisms involves attempts to portray thinking as "between," to articulate the space as liberation. By disrupting dualisms, the journey of reflecting back through a decade of classroom practice is a means of nurturing alternate ways of knowing, as Sameshima (2007) suggests, inviting an articulation and disruption of the between spaces. In his work on the significance of paradox in a pedagogical paradigm, William Doll discusses the reintegration of mind-body, teacher-learner, noting the paradox that neither is the other, yet "neither is without the other" (Doll, as cited in Pinar, et al., 1995, p. 502). By embracing this work of an embodied wholeness I develop new understanding of how to hold the paradoxical poles of my identity together, and welcome the truths that reveal the possibility of "and" instead of my mind's fall into "or/but" dualisms.

Reflecting Back: Consciously Forward

Be patient toward all that is unsolved in your heart and try to love the
questions themselves....Do not now seek the answers, which cannot be
given you because you would not be able to live them.
                                    —Rainer Maria Rilke, *Letters to a Young Poet*

Taking up this educational inquiry of reflecting back on life writing in order to learn and know differently in the present, also led me to wonder how pre-conceptual consciousness enters again over time, and to ask what meaning the original writing holds. And likewise, what is the nature of reading the self in the past subjectively in order to transform teaching and learning in the present, capturing the imagination for possibilities? In these curricular queries, safety in risking the transformative, pedagogic pose is realized through the dynamic process of *currere*. William Pinar and Madeleine Grumet (1976) provide a pedagogy for locating self in context, in relation to tracing the path to seeing the pre-conceptual experience with freshness (Pinar, 2004), a conceptual frame in which I find an intent towards understanding lived experience in teaching with hearing loss. Situating myself this way will always allow me to look back, re-read and re-present the personal with a reflexive stance for self-study and imaginative re-discovery. Biding the difficulty and dance in-between the audible and the inaudible supports the quest to take this "biographic situation" (Pinar & Grumet, 1976, p. 51) expressed through my autobiographical voice (Pinar, 2004) and to see it as a data source. Through this process of looking back, I am attuned to the imaginative possibilities of a pedagogy of hearing.

Bracketed in a Single Breath

Bracketed by your sentence that
erupts in a single breath
I experience a (dis) connect.
A flurry of unvoiced consonants pour
from you as merry escapees-in-taunt,
their secret assembly into waves
a mirage-of-untouchables.

I hear the shape of your voice,
the lilting of now unintelligible sounds,
the tone of your emoted speech,
But I cannot ascribe meaning to your diction.

In this moment-place,
where sound comprehension fails
and time compresses,
where entry into a familiar abyss chimes
between the next phonemes and
the words that spill over and around them, here
I dwell in a different sense of hearing you
(several times a day).

All-at-once
I follow the largest shapes your lips are making,
affixing to your cheeks and mouth as they emit their subtle,
    breathed clues
I gather the true story that your eyes unwittingly narrate
while absorbing the stature that your verbal body tells
I ride the moving waves of intonations and denunciations
I sense what is held in-between the spaces
of silence—

In the absence of hearing.

Engaging with this reflective writing now, in the present, is preceded by memory of the original journal entry 4 years ago; writing the poem was a re-representation of the journal entry. I was particularly sensitive to, and aware of, my frustration, the pedagogic "kick" at my inner being of the challenges in teaching with hearing impairment. In an effort to articulate the experience of my daily struggle to hear the tiny, precious voices of 6-year-old students in the shared curricular space of our classroom, I attempted to describe the minute calculations and hope-for-best guesses of "what happens" in the absence of hearing, especially when my students' voices drift in and out, always teasing, between audible and in/audible ground.

As an alternate reading 4 years later, re-visiting this life writing calls to me as an imagined sojourner engaged in a "pilgrimage of seeking and searching... researching the past, present, future...attending to where I am...at the junctures and ruptures of pedagogic progress" (Hasebe-Ludt, et al., 2009, p. 98). Reflectively, I interpret the poem in the present as an expression of my relationship of being-in-the-world, the experience of embodied (un)hearing as the awareness that my ears are merely one tool in my ability to perceive. By themselves, they are, according to Merleau-Ponty (1945), "an instrument of bodily excitation only, and not of perception itself" (p. 247). The notion that Merleau-Ponty offers in this statement is the lived knowing that our senses do not arrive "at the thing" without our thinking, and perceive consciousness to create meaning from our experiences. In order to know what my body perceives, I do not enlist my eyes to know what I see, or my ears to know what I hear; thus, the caution inherent is revealed in not defining my senses, specifically hearing. Instead, my experience is that my senses distribute through my body all the perceptions to which I assign a cognitive and bodily power, thereby, "putting perception into the thing perceived" (Merleau-Ponty, 1945, p. 247).

Lacings

My students' thoughts
stream together as words,
through vocal chords that inscribe vibrations,
launched as undulating sequences of sound,
fused into chorused, audible meanings
of textured proportions—
for me to hear.

Simultaneously
the words that are thoughts
arrive in their usual way—
twined with the blessing while on their
wave-journey of in-between
A cache of hope released onto them—
lacing the words and meanings together.
Imagination, chaos and potential meet as I begin my
ritual of gathering and interpreting
sound
into meanings.

Many reflections documented in my writing expose the strategies I employ in order to relate with my students during acts of speaking/listening/dialogue. Greene (1995) provides a springboard through her discussion on imaginative capacity. In my relating with Other, the call for imaginative capacity is to perceive and interpret experience as if it could be otherwise. Imagination as a "gateway," through which meaning is derived, frees me to see "new order in experience," possibly supporting an opening for interpreting in/audible experiences (Greene, 1995, p. 20). In hearing, imagination may well refer to an ability to know beyond what is fixed while remaining in touch, in presence. Sartre simply states: "I visualize… in the world, and my power of imagination is nothing but the persistence of my world around me" (as cited in Merleau-Ponty, 1945, p. 210). True, the persistence of the world, and relating with Other, demands the hard work of diligence, of embodied hearing, recognition that the gateways through which meanings are derived, arouse empathetic understanding.

Listening With the Inner Ear

Wisdom's teachings come from many sources—written and spoken—as well as from archaic sources found in depths. Reading with the third eye, listening with the inner ear, we can perhaps, at last, come to regard wisdom, not knowledge, as education's only real concern.
—Mary Aswell Doll, *Like Letters in Running Water*

The significance of reflecting on decade-old writing and discovering something new about teaching and living offers a poignant example of the relevance of writing as a way of learning to live. The challenge is to engage consciously, with the courage to let the mind and heart lead in wholeness for what might be waiting to be heard. Objectively and subjectively, the paradox of choosing an embodied way of knowing "Self in the world" is to embrace the possibilities without being torn apart by the tensions. Indeed, the paradox of hearing and not hearing, being perceptive to the audible and in/audible, is to be patient that this embodied knowing evolves out of engaging with this difficulty so that it can re-educate and inform pedagogy.

To be rewarded with "a heart of wisdom" is to live awake, perceptively attuned to hear what is yet to be known in the world. I imagine the silence that accompanies the quiet intake of breath, and the space that is filled just before the body exhales, as the space where pre-conceptual consciousness occurs. In breathing, the paradox that neither is the other, yet neither is without the other (Doll, cited in Pinar, 2004) defines the embrace of embodied wholeness (Sameshima, 2007) in this educational inquiry project. To be a teacher and a learner is to recognize that each needs the other for its own sense of being. Life writing is the method— at the heart of wisdom.

> Embodied hearing perceives all language
> all the meanings my students show
> all-at-once.
> I sense their excitement
> their questions, and their hesitations.
> The way their eyes move between the pages of the story and

their faces also let me
hear their pauses in imagination
as they negotiate new possibilities.
I perceive with my body
the questions that will surface as the last page turns
and the discovery of life meanings
that they bring into their own light for erudition.
It is impossible to name all that
I hear with my body.

REFERENCES

Coelho, P. (1993). *The alchemist*. New York, NY: Harper Collins.

Doll, M. A. (2000). *Like letters in running water: A mythopoetics of curriculum*. Mahwah, NJ: Lawrence Erlbaum.

Fowler, L. (2007). *A curriculum of difficulty: Narrative research in education and the practice of teaching*. New York, NY: Peter Lang.

Greene, M. (1995). *Releasing the imagination: Essays on education, the arts, and social change*. San Francisco, CA: Jossey-Bass.

Glesne, C. (2006). *Becoming qualitative researchers: An introduction* (3rd ed.). Boston, MA: Pearson Education.

Hasebe-Ludt, E., Chambers, C. M., & Leggo, C. (2009*). Life writing and literary métissage as an ethos for our times*. New York, NY: Peter Lang.

Leggo, C. (2010). *Tangled lines: Nurturing writers and writing*. Unpublished manuscript, Department of Language & Literacy, University of British Columbia, Vancouver, Canada.

Merleau-Ponty, M. (1945). *Phenomenology of perception* (C. Smith, Trans.). New York, NY: Routledge.

Pinar, W. F., Reynolds, W., Slattery, P., & Taubman, P. (1995). *Understanding curriculum: An introduction to the study of historical and contemporary curriculum discourses*. New York, NY: Peter Lang.

Pinar, W. F. (2004). *What is curriculum theory?* Mahwah, NJ: Lawrence Erlbaum.

Pinar, W. F., & Grumet, M. (1976). *Toward a poor curriculum*. Dubuque, IA: Kendall/Hunt.

Rilke, R. M. (1993). *Letters to a young poet* (M. D. Herter Norton, Trans.). New York, NY: W. W. Norton.

Sameshima, P. (2007). *Seeing red: A pedagogy of parallax. An epistolary* Bildungsroman *on artful scholarly inquiry*. Youngstown, NY: Cambria Press.

So Far From Shore

Daniel Scott

10 AM, I am in my office. A phone call: my son, in trouble. "The psychiatrist says I should go the hospital. What do you think?" I'm suddenly disoriented. Other voices in the background. "The psychiatrist is here." "In your room?" Then a man's voice on Skype asking me to convince my son to go to the clinic. "He wants to come home but is too sick to travel." We talk back and forth. My son agrees to go.

I head off to teach. A knock at the door. "You have to call the hospital. Your son thinks you are dead. He is in a panic." So am I. I race home. It is the middle of the night in Europe. We call the clinic. A male nurse answers. He assures me: "I have comforted your son. He has taken a sedative and is sleeping." The evening is long as we discuss options. We finally sleep.

1:30 AM the phone ringing. Another voice almost incomprehensible. "Your son, he has tried to escape, thrown a chair through the window. He is now an involuntary patient." She was sorry to have to tell me. "Should I come?" I asked as if she could tell me. As soon as I asked I knew I had to go.

Michel Serres (1997) suggests that learning always involves leaving and does not really start until you make the choice not to turn back. It's swimming a channel and only after you are more than halfway across does learning begin, when you leave the familiar shore behind and forget about returning to the already known.

I have been wrenched out of what I know and am more than halfway across. The continent, the Atlantic, the space between me and my son. What will I learn?

> I slept most of the flight to Amsterdam. I was entangled in passages, crossing over. I had only had about 5 hours sleep in total over the last 2 nights.

> > between the edges of where
> > the abyss squeezes up against
> > the day's routine to devour
> > the ordinary, erasing
> > any illusions of ease.

Now I wonder if beginning to write about something is to call it into being, to summon it up to presence in my life. I had been writing poems about depression, about madness. And suddenly I am in the middle, caught.

out of the ordinary

> on the crumbling edge
> of his mental landscape
> his footing slips away:
> he tumbles into
> interior chasms of symbols,
> words, innuendo
> crushed by the weight
> of possible meanings,
> lost in thoughts, doubts
> and falling
> disconnected
> from ground.

> in attempts at return
> to ordinary day,
> ordinary time, he lunges
> for earth, trampling
> the present moment

startling those around him
with his awkward re-entry
trailing intensity and concerns
of too much significance
for a kite flying picnic
or a crying baby
at the back of the bus.

the loneliness
of bottomless interpretation
sits askew on his clumsy
posture as he
tries to be part of
the daily world he longs
to be comfortable in:
the familiar is awry
his mind swallows the day
gnawing on the moment.
his soul vomits the excess,
embarrassing everyone.

My son is confined involuntarily after a psychotic break. More than clumsiness, more than I can imagine.

> I could not turn back. I had to go to Holland—it was necessary—
> to accompany my son on his journey away. When he began to
> be able to explain, he described the moment when he snapped.
> He heard a snap. He was worried that I was dead. I had to look
> up a word: crazy. "Dad" he said in a covered whisper, "You have
> to get me out of here, it's filled with crazy people." People like
> him, I thought. "Wounded" I said. "Some much worse than you
> and they are trying to heal, just like you."

He had lost his soul in a card game in his mind and thought I would die to save him and so thought he should die, kill himself, to save me from having to die. He was worried I was dead.

> **Craze**: *v.t.* to shatter, to crack, to cover with fine cracks (as pot-
> tery), to weaken, to impair, to derange (of the intellect),— *v.i.* to
> develop fine cracks: to become mad,— *n.* a finely cracked condi-
> tion: insanity: fashion, fad. (Geddie, 1968, p. 247)

and **crazy**, frail: cracked: insane: demented: fantastically composed of irregular pieces.

Fine cracks, breakages, impairment, disorder: it is his world now and mine. I feel fragile, close to breaking. I hold the tears. My cracks and fragility, his cracks and fragility: son and father, father and son. Parallel voyages in the domain of fine cracks.

> I am at school, being forced to learn in passing, about passages, about madness. I did what I could being with him, listening, holding, telling, waiting and walking precarious miles on the cobblestone streets and paved bike paths along the canals slippery underfoot with ice and snow. A long winter that would not go away they said.

I wrote. About me, and him, and others around him. Trying to learn so far from shore. On another shore immersed in a language I did not know in terrain I did not know, in a condition I did not understand.

> **along the edge**
>
> travelling
> along the edge of
>   tears
> between
> shadows and light
> in the mind storm
>   of fears
> where unknowns
> take shape, speak
> command
>   where
> what is, is not
> and twisted shades
>   become
> what are.
>
> and then
> the watching eyes
>   assessing
> sanity

making choices
judgements, diagnoses
    injecting
pacifiers, doses
to do battle with
his unsettled weather.
    claiming
management of his storm
and control of his
    journey
back to ground.

living for a time
as companion of
no certainty; like him
no ground, like him
no control
    hoping,
hoping yet afraid
of shadows
of power in the hands
    of others
of power that reshapes
reality,
    borders
and classifies with
titles
afraid of losing
    a son.

Cracks: where the light gets in says Leonard Cohen (1992), or leaks out I reply. Is light getting in for him? Into his nightmare and darkness with its haunting voices and temptations to death: a call from a siren of bleakness. He is so far away. Will he come back? What will return be? Bringing him home?

it feels like i have been poured out. my feet hurt but i cannot stop walking back and forth beside the canals. over the bridges and down the long driveway. usually alone, usually unsure. trying to understand, to see where he has been, where he might go next and whether he will come back to me, to us, to himself.

i'm trying to empty myself,
abandoning the chaos
but it clings to me
its roots tapped down
into his soul beyond
where he can reach.
arms and branches
shadowing my life holding me
in a tenacious grip.

i gasp for air
leaking fragility
from my eyes
moving along
the edge of loss
and sanity labouring
to stay his companion
along his journey
through wastelands
and watery places.

i am not sleeping well—not helpful under the circumstances of
fragility—brittleness. so now out into this world (an unknown
place of people and language) to see what can be done. oh help.
i keep calling out like praying. i haven't prayed for a long time.
but this journey crashes me into the impossibility of prayer. oh
help. oh help. i am grateful for support but help—what must i do?

What does coming back mean? What is a self in madness? His eyes changed when
he was spinning in the winds of his mind. His eyes were vacant so it was a relief
when he came back to himself, became present. He was in his eyes differently.
And voice. He is closer in his voice.

trying to figure out what to say to him. how will i know? seeing him slip away or get lost, realizing how close danger is for
him, the patterns he has established that now have to be altered.
the journey back from the wasteland. "crazy people" wounded,
broken, lost: his dark whispers and the flood of questions about
time, healing, recovery, mind, triggers, pathways…no ends in
sight, nor answers. what does compassion look like?

He is slowly returning to himself, fighting the side effects of his meds. We walk and talk. Trying to make sense of how he got here, of what is next, of what accumulated to create his break. He tries to play a guitar but his muscles won't relax. He wants to walk miles but my feet are so sore and he wants to go so quickly. We visit the gym, the computer room. He is checking email. Another man enters, trailing energy. I want to leave: he makes me nervous.

mindstorm

his chair spins past us.
he flicks the door shut
    slam.
he faces us, electric hair and beard
framing his face.
his hands flicker in
graceful dances around
the pocket size
New Testament and Psalms:
a potent totem presented
charged with power.
he babbles a stream of thoughts
in several languages
swiveling between us on his wheeled
computer chair;
intense disconnected convictions
sacred insight
poured out in a torrent
of discontinuity, oblivious to our
incomprehension
in the blur of tongues, the storm
of possibilities

        he follows his own traces
        at speeds faster than his tongue
        can shape, riding a crest
        of energy welling up,
        overwhelming
        to his captive audience.

we rise in mid flow.
we have to go i say.

the man hesitates, we leave
unconverted to his causes.

behind us
the door slams.

> and one of us
> knows much more
> of storms and journeys
> is sure he understands
> refuses medication
> prefers meditation
> to heal himself
> worries about worrying
> and works to manage
> another rising wind.

the weather remains bleak—cold, snow, grey—
the grey lingers in my memory more than the sunshine:

the poetics of it—seeing links, images.
a mind in full extension: the excess of some other place.
perhaps is it only a matter of degree? poets and madmen
the nightmare being the excess
where control is lost
to what is arising unbidden.
reality not so far away—

is that the fear of madness and the mad: a glimpse of recognition in
an only slightly twisted familiarity, an echo in my own soul? revul-
sion of the crazy.

Or the danger of the attractive
seduction of heightened experience.
voices taking hold, high calling, vocation.
then the crash.

on the café radio Sting is singing "I'm an alien, I'm a legal alien"
(Sting, 1987). me a present outsider having breakfast, a stone in the
river washed by a language i do not know flowing over me.

What am I learning in this Dutch school this cold February? How life can also
give gifts, grace in the midst of difficulty. Human kindness is astonishing—small

gestures across language and place. Affection, care, accompaniment of my passage across unknown terrain. How did these angels find me? Or I them? Gifts. Grace. I know no other way to name them.

> i am getting anxious about going and losing my hand so directly
> in things and daily readings of him. it will be hard. just writing
> this much has me trembling. another leaving: return and leav-
> ing all tangled up.

> > i drift into signs: the symbolic.
> > the layers of meaning in language,
> > gesture, signs and how the weight of words
> > alters meanings—
> > the small becomes monstrous,
> > light blinding, heavy,
> > the weak feeble, heroic, grand.

> > (is my journey parallel to his?)

Oh the borders we have to maintain sanity, their porosity under pressure. How leaks occur, cracks, breaks, amplification, acceleration, diminishment. I feel so close to him, so near. So far away.

his mind has always been magnificent
sailing across concepts, seas of theory,
vocabulary, languages, formulae. now
            unleashed
signs, words, meanings
woven
            together
turning, turning
            doing, undoing
his mind, his mind taking him
away from us, from himself
on long polar journeys arcing
across ice and tundra
words spill out, he breathes
and whistles arguing
logics of control.

i surrender in hopelessness
sinking under the weight
of the apparent lightness
of his knowing, i sink into
my heart's sorrow in silence
beneath the floe ice
wondering if he can survive
if he will crack again
if i can bear the sorrow
the hope all entangled
and the coolness
of waiting in the unknown

i am leaving this phase of accompaniment shattered by meeting him in a manic state, mind racing, disconnected sentences, refusing medication, wanting to heal his own way, using his mind, unaware of deception or that it was his mind and all that thinking that sent him into this spin. i cried myself to sleep. so afraid.

on the train swaying—tears on the brim, sun shining. some help to see the sun. i wonder if i can manage all that lies ahead. i hope his brother can now that he is there, taking my place.

in flight heading north and west. another arc of departure, a leaving that is not leaving but a messy separation where threads entangle and awful adhesions remain. having been touched by mindstorms and heart wounds, having clung together: his descent, my following soul. leaving is not entirely possible. i have left some piece of me strung thin and taut across the polar flight path, high cold, a molecular chain that perhaps will signal his next descent, his next break, his return across the border.

What have I learned: one thing that has focussed me, altered my way of reading the world: all that matters is compassion. Small gestures of care, words or silence, touch or stillness: the form is not so important as the care. "Dad, you have to be in good shape to be compassionate." "No son, we can't wait for that in one another. We have to be compassionate from wherever we are."

Watching him, seeing the birth of compassion in him as he returns to himself, to being with others. Grateful for the compassion I have received.

> i suddenly don't want to be anywhere, have an urge to say nothing, to disappear into silence, tell no stories, afraid of telling a tale that will come true, having it come alive because it is told. i cannot speak of his healing. i am afraid to speak of his illness. i don't know what to believe about the future.

I love him. I have wandered to an edge with him, peeked over, stumbled. I am returning: accompanying now from farther away. It is what I must do. Take up life again. But it is not the same. I have been changed. I have new questions: about how he came back to being himself, returned to his eyes and voice. Some odd core of being present in himself—his body and mind. I have no idea what it means. But I have been taught some small lessons about being human, being somebody—not easy learning about cracks and fragility and wounded souls—about being humane in the midst of difficulty. In the foreground: compassion, but all is tinged with the closeness of madness and the array of cracks in me, in us all.

How close is fragility. How near, how awfully near. How thin the borders between the sane and the not sane in us, in all of us.

And how all that matters is compassion.

TEXTS OF INFLUENCE

Cohen, L. (1992). Anthem. From *The future* [CD]. New York, NY: Sony Music.

Geddie, W. (Ed.) (1968). *Chambers's twentieth century dictionary*. Edinburgh, Scotland: W. & R. Chambers.

Gergen, K. J. (2009) *Relational being: Beyond self and community*. Oxford, England: Oxford University Press.

Podvoll, E.M. (2003) *Recovering sanity: A compassionate approach to understanding and treating psychosis* (2nd ed.). Boston, MA: Shambhala Publications.

Serres, M. (1997). *The troubador of knowledge* (S. Faria Glaser & W. Paulson, Trans.) Ann Arbor: The University of Michigan Press. (Original work published 1991)

Sting. (1987). Englishman in New York. On *Nothing like the sun* [record]. Montserrat: Air Studios.

The Shape of Questions

Daniela Elza

> *Teacher: What are you drawing?*
> *Child: I am drawing god.*
> *Teacher: But, no one knows what god looks like.*
> *Child: They will, in a minute.*
> —Sir Ken Robinson, *Schools Kill Creativity*

. . .

we have to   (talk

my toddler   two   needs to talk
all the time   I am more concerned
with someone   listening.

lonelier   than we appear
driftwood of the mind   seeks
the company of streams

the tentative encouragement
of the banks
                    that bear us.

I go around   the water clock
explaining   to her
the possibility of tributaries.

         in their flow
our streams   of mind
wrap around   each other
for a sense of   permanence.

so   when my daughter   talks
I listen.   because
I don't know   when

she will   need   me   to.
or when   her words   will
flood my banks
        to seek
          new depths.

. . .

we walk through   the neighbourhood
art studio.   she is drawn to the walls
where the paintings   are still.
she sits and   listens.
each one— a seashell   to her ear.

. . .

we eat kiwis.   she explains
how they taste   like something else.
how   when you close   your eyes
and you sink your teeth into   the fruit,
"it is like a dream   coming to your mouth."

. . .

self-portrait

her face was green   and blue
like earth
no ears   no eyes   no mouth.

she knows   she is a child
protected only by   the paper skin

of light.

. . .

burning trees

she drew a picture of...
I could not tell what.
I thought: *seashell?*

she corrects:
tree stumps   mama.
see the trees have burned.

indeed two red glowing dots
the eyes of tree   or root
underneath   a mouth
as if the earth was hurt.

the third stump had wispy lines
coming up from it   faint
like the memory of something gone

look
and this is   the spirit of the tree
that has burned.

. . .

Journal:[1] (age 5)

D[2]: Guess which hand the little world is in?

Mama: The left hand. [She shows the right one.] I said the left, not the right. [Then she shows an empty left.] But that isn't fair. You moved it. You are not playing by the rules. You do not know the rules of the game.

D: Yes, I do.

Mama: What are they?

D: The rules are that you never guess which hand the world is in.

can we not imagine?

it took us seven songs to get there.
we drove in rain
I do not remember   traffic.

the bookmark   she made on the trip
is a scribble drawing.
mommy, doesn't all this make sense
she said   looking at the outcome.

there could be a ghost		*there*
there could be a girl	*there*	*right?*
there could be a truck	*here*	
and there could be a fish	*over here*	

she points to the bottom of the bookmark.

there could be a crow in the tree
her finger moves upward.
there could be a sun under the tree
and can we not see a spiral in the sun?

Can we not imagine things?

.   .   .

D (age 5): Mama, don't you get scared when you see pretty things?

Mama: No, I get excited.

D: I get scared when I see pretty things that it makes me so surprised, I get scared out of my eyes.

.   .   .

Journal: (age 4)

Mama: How come when you were two you got up to go to the potty by yourself, but now at four you are scared to get up?

D: Because small don't know. Then you get bigger, you know, and you are scared. Then you get even bigger and you are not scared again. So it's like that change.

. . .

Journal: (age 5)

There is no six

She made a paper fortune teller. Wrote numbers on the inside. Decorated it with mosquitoes and ticks (the blood sucking insects) and the other one with good insects (tarantulas and spiders). Then she decorated one with dinosaurs. When we got to the numbers on the inside, she wanted to write the little fortunes hidden under the numbers. She opened the flap under six and said: *Papa, how do you spell: There is no six.*

. . .

Meeting the tooth fairy (age 6)

After the excitement of losing her first tooth I heard the following exchange at bath time:

D: Papa, will you tell mama something? When I put the tooth tonight under my pillow, promise you will not take anything out, or put anything under it. It's a science experiment. I have to find out if the tooth fairy exists. [pause] I *have* to know.

Dad: And what happens if she doesn't? What if she isn't real and you don't get a quarter?

D: [big sigh] Then I will let you help her [pause] tomorrow night.

. . .

O.pening the Parent.hesis

My son, almost one, puts his head between the covers of a cardboard book. His body—an instrument which fearlessly exp.lore.s his f.our degrees of freedom, tests my body—an instrument for measuring what fear hides in k.nowing.

The difference between soul (dushá) and suffocate (dúsha) in Bulgarian is only a matter of emphasis. A fine line to walk. A tight rope. Balancing on a gesture, a face, a pitch, a phrase, the close knitting of words.

In the midst of washing dishes, or cooking, I am bombarded with *questions* from my 4-year-old daughter. "And how did life begin anyways?" she asks. I misunderstand, and explain the seed. "I mean the first person on earth?" she corrects. On her brother's first birthday she says: "The earth went once around the sun for him." And then assures him: "The first birthday is the longest. Then they come faster."

Her answers and observations arc like rainbows through sometimes very grey days.

She tells me: "The spider turned into a living spiral and lived in space forever."

That, "Bread has two heels, just like us." Or that: "*Continents* are *islands* too, you know."

How to claim my answers are more real than hers? More true? There are so many degrees of separation in these "truths" that are not mine. These hand-me-downs, worn thin, I have to clothe my children in. Rags she sees through, doesn't feel the duty to pretend.

Opening the parenthesis, she invites the world into the equation. My eyes turn, not to say too much, too soon. Ellipses left hanging…footsteps walking…a.way.

"Look, Mom, he has his head in the mouth of a crocodile," she comments on her brother's struggle to fit his head between the covers of a book. We laugh and she twirls in her dress.

"Mom, what do you think?"

I say, "very pretty."

She corrects, "not very, *fairy* pretty."

Much later she concludes: "Maybe the reason there's no such thing as fairies is that no one cared to take care of fairy eggs."

Note: *Faërie comes from* feral, ferocious, *and* fierce. *"Faërie is, or was once, not a playground filled with diminutive amusements for young minds but the mythworld itself, which is everything outside of our control."*

—Robert Bringhurst (2007, p. 248)

in the child footsteps of light

through regular windows   on regular days
this century-   old house   stands
perfecting the art   of light.

still invites   the day into itself
as if it were   sustenance.

beveled glass edges   turn playground
for even a little bit   of sun.
draw music out of   the language of
                                        shadows.

in this house   rainbows are born.

she captures them in an old straw basket
plucks blooms   off white walls
transfers them   onto pieces of paper.

the light disguised in the blue furniture is
still   a mystery to   her.   child eyes
capture.   refine.   distill.

a rare brew   I drink   from.

she will later learn   light gives
colour   and light takes   colour away.
that   rainbows are   light's willingness
                    to be known.

that each day   there comes a slant—
the moment when light   reveals
the flaws   in a house

those   even the builders   gave up on.

intimacy   begins with this revelation—
with the smell   of burnt milk
over   spilled rainbows.

the big snow of the year

we stomp up the hill to daycare.
in his third winter
face the colour of   sunrise
maroon hat   turning white
shoulders   easy under snow.

he makes the sound of someone crying.
"who's crying?" I ask.
snow crying.

"why?"
because we step on snow's face.
snow   has so many faces.

. . .

after his bath   he ate
mandarins.   naked
just him   and the fruit
separated by his 3-year-old
curious skin.

he sits on his heels   gracefully
peels   orange skin with
fingernails   a whole fist.

separating   himself from
shadow.

his eyes—   a mirror
entering light.

I try   to trap this moment
with a butterfly net.
like a kid   I believe I can.

. . .

at four he said:
mama, do you know   why dandelions will never die?

why?
because   they are in my head.

. . .

Are children poets?   Are they philosophers?
                    As a parent,   educator,   philosopher   and poet,
                        I think of the child's world as   a natural place,
                            where   "[n]ature is not merely the collection
                    of undomesticated biomass. Nature is the tendency
                in things to be what they are,   and in that tendency
            to present themselves as both distinct   and connected,"
            (Zwicky, 2008, p. 90).   A place resonant, and coherent.

            I cannot help but notice the qualities that come naturally
        to them. I cherish these same qualities in myself as a poet.
                I have to jealously guard them.   Both in myself
                and my children.   Even more so, as they get older.

            "When we become truly ourselves, we just become
            a swinging door, and we are purely independent of,
        and at the same time dependent upon, everything else."
                            —Shunryn Suzuki (1992, p. 31)

. . .

Journal: (Son 5, Daughter 9)

D and S are playing an adventure game where they are exploring The Pits of Doom.

Dad: Why are they always the pits of doom and despair? Why not the pits of joy and happiness?

D: Really, it's happy and fun, but if we call it that, it will be boring.

the flower girl

While I wait for my *latte*, the girl at the flower shop on Granville Island fills a whole garbage can with flowers. Rubber gloves on, an expression of tedium on her face. Stuffs them in a grey cracked bin and when it appears full, puts her foot in, steps hard.

A stubborn pink flower keeps rearing its blossom out. My daughter next to me restrains the urge to run and pick up the rest of the blooms scattered on the ground.

An elderly woman catches my eye, her eyes wide moons of disbelief. When the bin is full, a muscular young man carries it off to the *organics* dumpster. My daughter follows.

He dumps it. Walks away without a second look and, perhaps, thought. Without a second thought, or look, my daughter climbs on the bench next to the dark green dumpster, reaches in and pulls out two yellow edged with orange and one wine red.

She holds them so tenderly, I am embarrassed. She brings them close to her chest. I am embarrassed for feeling embarrassed. She holds them so lovingly. I look around, uncomfortable.

She shows me, still standing on the bench, how the big bud looks like it has little teeth. I am pulled into her world so quickly I forget to care what others think. I join her on the bench. Her urgent excitement growing light in my belly. While the "flower girl" keeps her hourly job filling the bin.

. . .

"Poetry forms the dreamer and his world at the same time."
—Gaston Bachelard (1969, p. 16)

My children's thought is fuelled by curiosity, wonder, the virtue of naïveté, and a fresh way of bringing the *world* into the *word*. Like a good poem, they pierce me with their observations. Perhaps, any true and honest inquiry into the world begins with poetry. Can we sustain this state of mind throughout life?

For Bachelard (1969) *childhood is a state of mind.* "A potential
childhood is within us" (p. 101). Linda Barry encourages us
to think of childhood as a place, not a time. "A place that
already exists like an unplayed-with play set, needing only
one thing to set all things in motion (put your name here)."
(Barry, 2008, p. 159)

"Furthermore, this childhood continues to be receptive to any opening
upon life and makes it possible for us to understand and love children
as if we were their equals in original life." (Bachelard, 1969, p. 101)

Are we open to the discovery of this place? Are we willing to step into
the wild meadow a child can offer us? Are we ready to explore it?

"The poet can call us back to that place. Poets will help us
find this living childhood within us, this permanent durable
immobile world." (Bachelard, 1969, p. 20)

I take my apprenticeship seriously.

of jewels

I pluck dandelions   show
my daughter   how to make

a wreath)

                    (underground   the mine
                    works overtime digging up
                    diamonds

she dances   in the grass
dreaming of
                    (the earth   is nursing
                    to perfection.
what she will   become.

a ring)

my son
already   learning to be tough
with tiny daisies in his hands

a bracelet)

the rooms in which we dream

I remember childhood— clean sheets
flapping in the wind.   snapping a tune.

we laughed vertically   through ourselves.
thought ourselves tangential to everything dying.

(being with you makes me   remember.
makes me   again known   to myself).

most days the mind is a sharp blade that cuts
through my morning.   squeaks rusty.
some days it is   still   a bird flying north.

the rooms in which we dream have fragile walls.

words become slippery fish   in the hands of
ghosts   as they argue over their lost names

as they sit over my shoulder   so many
eyes fastened to the night.

on days   when the shadows creep up
our forgetting   I squeeze out the backyard

through a loose slat in the fence (which partitions
the meadow into strips of light).

I am swallowed whole by the tall yellow grass.
remember   through my hands   and knees.

my body—   a flock of starlings   rising up
into the sky as if they are one.

hoping   I will not   be found yet.
hoping   I will be   missed.

We have been at the beach for hours.
As we get in the car my son (seven) begins:

it feels like life is a system
                    [I pull pen and paper out and begin to write]
when god is dreaming he dreams about all this
then he tries to make it when he is awake

and this time the finish of the dream would be
the sun does a supernova
and it will be dark

and when god's up
he tries to make things   and he fails.
                    [I am puzzled by where all this god talk comes from.
                    We do not talk much about god.]

                    Why does he fail? I ask.

because it is pure dark for a long long time

                    Does he succeed when there is light?
well   there is light all around him
but when he dreams...
or   it could be the other way around
his dreams are all dark and nothing
and when he is awake he invents different things
and they become real

                    What made you think of god dreaming?
I don't know,   [shrugs his shoulders]
maybe I dreamt of it.   [pause]
mommy   why aren't you starting the car?

                        . . .

            Two years later I find a quote by Li-Young Lee (2008, p. 20):
                        "Maybe this isn't the news.
                    Maybe this is a dream God is having
                        and somebody should wake him."

. . .

"Poetry is within the original wilderness of the world."
—Mary Oliver (1994, p. 106)

Bringhurst (2007) says   it is not the versification
       that makes poetry out of language,   but the texture
and shapeliness   of the thought.   "When you think
       intensely   and beautifully,   something happens.
That something is called poetry" (Bringhurst, 2008, p. 143).

In this sense   poetry rolls off the tongues of children
with the certainty of a dewdrop rolling off a blade of grass.
When it has reached   a fullness,   that is too much
for a grass blade to bear,   it spills forth into the world.

"In his reverie the child realizes the unity of poetry,"
       (Bachelard, 1969, p. 125).   This condensation
of observations, imagination, and memory   seems
       to come out of thin air,   but when reverie settles
       on the cool blade of the world   this condensation
is inevitable. What drives it is a state of wonder, a willful
seeking, an unconditional curiosity,   an active hunger.

"We need lessons so badly   from a life which is
       beginning,   from a soul which is blossoming,
from a mind which is opening!" (Bachelard, 1958/1969, p. 132).

It is up to us to listen.

. . .

"The natural world is the old river that runs through everything
and I think poets will forever fish along its shores."
—Mary Oliver (1994, p. 106)

the weight of dew

can I fill these words with what is not

intended?   with what the river keeps
hidden   under her tongue.

with the maps birds carve in my marrow
fill my bones   with air
my eye   with their dying.

to wait on the river bank   long enough

to know what knowing   looks like
before   it is disturbed.

stepped on.   sanitized.
poked with   a stick.
put   in a vial.   anesthetized.

to know the shape of   me

nameless— my given names left out
like shoes   I was meant to fill.

they gather dew now
it slides down their tongues. I watch them
through this open door   where

even the clock   wipes its face clean.

the shape of questions

- *daughter*

trees	sleep quietly	on my chest.
the years	grow deep.	distracting.
their branches	search for	the turn of veins.
questions hang	(like moss)	
on the limbs of	my child.	I keep her
small (y)ears	all	to myself
sometimes	even	

| pressed | between | the pages of books. |

- *son*

| the debris | on the beach | lies |
| like questions | that have never been | |

| asked. | (we get closer | the crunch |
| of pebbles) | they fill | the palms of |

| my now | 3-year-old son. | |

| his eyes | filled with | blue wonder |

| | his footprints | full of |
| ocean. | his warm | hands |

| already | altering | the questions. |

ENDNOTES

1 Entries from a journal I kept of my children.

2 D stands for daughter, S stands for son.

REFERENCES

Bachelard, G. (1969). *The poetics of reverie: Childhood, language, and the cosmos* (M. Jolas, Trans.). Boston, MA: Beacon Press. (Original work published 1958)

Barry, L. (2008). *What it is: The formless thing which gives things form*. Montréal, Canada: Drawn and Quarterly.

Bringhurst, R. (2007). *Everywhere being is dancing: Twenty pieces of thinking*. Kentville, NS: Gaspereau Press.

Bringhurst, R. (2008). *The tree of meaning: Language, mind and ecology*. Berkeley, CA: Counterpoint.

Lee, L. (2008). *Behind my eyes*. New York, NY: W. W. Norton.

Oliver, M. (1994). *A poetry handbook: A prose guide to understanding and writing poetry*. Orlando, FL: Harcourt.

Robinson, K. (2006). *Schools kill creativity: TED talk*. Retrieved from *TED: Ideas worth spreading* http://www.ted.com/talks/lang/eng/ken_robinson_says_schools_kill_creativity.html

Suzuki, S. (1992). *Zen mind, beginner's mind: Informal talks on Zen meditation and practice*. New York, NY: Weatherhill.

Zwicky, J. (2008). Lyric realism: Nature poetry, silence, and ontology. *Malahat Review, 165*, 85–91.

Professions of a Stay-at-Home Father and Writer

GW Rasberry

An Abstract/ion (a.k.a. Stories Don't Keep Good Time)

*Days up and down they come like rain on a conga drum....Forget most
remember some but don't turn none away.*

—Townes Van Zandt

*Some days you feel as if you've lived too long, days drip slowly on the page
and you catch yourself pacing the cage.*

—Bruce Cockburn

Stories don't keep good time. They arrive late, if at all. Or early, in a language
that strangles the tongue. Early or late, the best ones unsettle. "Forget most
remember some but don't turn none away." Expect a narrative to fragment, shred,
tear, and resist any and all attempts to tame or tell it.

I've climbed high enough to glimpse innocence lost. Climbed high enough to fall from grace. The stories I choose to tell (about) myself sway and shift. They take on a weight and gravity that pull me off course, drag me into the ditch. My stories re-story themselves with and without my help (usually when I turn to look the other way). "Half-full" of empty. "Sometimes you feel you've lived too long. Days drip slowly on the page."

The story I'm going to tell is over and ongoing. It happened but it's still happening. Time has dragged my story off the road and in many ways made a predictable mockery of it. (My story: "As-if.") This story is a story about a "newborn parent." Eyes wide open. Thrilled and "shit-scared." Full of wonder. Eventually, the parent becomes a "toddler-parent." Lots of drooling and stumbling and laughing. More wonder. Several chapters later and the protagonist is an "adolescent-parent": subject to hormonal tides, judgemental, courageous, uncertain, confident, forgetful, insecure, and raging. "Days up and down they come. Like rain on a conga drum." Before the story is even close to an end the teller pulls up lame. Disoriented, dispirited, he looks for some way to find closure and cut his losses. Despite his best attempts to bring "dys" and "functional" together, this parental unit still finds himself steering his life with a dumb, unaccounted-for optimism.

This story is fuelled by music and love, caffeine and loss. It's about writing as a means of finding out what the story might be/come.

Writing the Parenting Life/Parenting the Writing Life

Here's one way to begin writing the parenting life: Gather up words and place them on the page, carefully. Or in a rush, on the fly. Borrow words, lovingly. Or without thought. Look for words that will act in place
of the lived life—as if they were real, as if
writing them down confirms
that life is happening
to you, affirms the life that is   your own.

You might also look
for words that seem to live
inside of you: They are also real.

Collect and sort them—these words—shuffle them occasionally. Act with conviction, tentatively. Examine closely. Look further. Invent. Re-invent. Turn toward the act of "word-making" with introspection and outward abandon. Learn, "how to care," as Joni Mitchell (1982) puzzles, "and yet not to care (since love has two faces, hope and despair)."

Be existential: Do words help express the experience of a life unfolding or do they simply help construct it? Savour ambiguity: Maybe it's both of these, none of these, somewhere in-between. Learn to live well with not-knowing. Embrace contradiction. Change your mind, often.

Love words: Your own, others: Follow words to discover the ways they help give thought form. Follow words to find out what you are thinking, doing. Polish words, hold them up to the light. Bury words: See what the damp dark earth will do to them over time.

Journal: Keep one. Be fastidious. Bear the weight of history: all that has gone before, all that is still to come. Know your words might make a difference: Somewhere, sometime.

Journal: Keep one. Throw it away afterwards. Know that words burn well, make excellent kindling; trust them to give off great light in their burning. Watch in quiet amazement as the flames heat up the hyphenated space of "dis-comfort." Rest in this "un-easy" place where waking and memory and dream flicker together, falter and flash.

   Writing the parenting life, I am beginning to discover and believe, as these words fall out, involves parenting the writing life. There is the watching, the waiting, the worrying over lines and lives. Lines *and* lives are not separate as we might like to believe. There is: Intentionality. Understanding. Disbelief. Beauty. Hurt. Confusion. Cruelty. Faith, hope, love. There is also compromise. Humour. Dysfunction. Exhaustion. Darkness. Uncertainty. Playfulness. Contradiction. Juxtaposition.

.   .   .

If your husband can
arrange his   schedule so
that he can be
with you both for the first
week or so, he is probably
your best
baby   helper...

He is probably your best baby helper: This seems as good a place as any for a fledgling father to begin talking about mothering: with a healthy offering of self-effacement, committed to a life of self-reflexivity.

Baby helper: Know, as these words unfold and something resembling a narrative emerges, that I try to entertain the possibility of humour in this label in the same breath that I reject it, make fun of it, find it insulting in its insinuation. How is it that the father continues to be trivialized and written into the childbirth/parenting books as a cartoon caricature? (Likely because the weight of history confirms such a caricature.) Yes, I was certainly a *baby helper*. But after "the first week or so," I did, in fact, "change my schedule": I became a full-time, card-carrying, stay-at-home father but I'm getting ahead of myself.

As a father who writes (and/or as a writer who fathers), I look to writing as one means for speaking to the experience of fathering. Following my writing then, to a place where labels fall away or become something else, I am a writer and a father who sometimes mothers. (To be sure, a much-needed qualifier regarding what might be rightfully considered my irreverent co-opting of "mother" will follow.)

I was once a newborn parent. Then I became a toddler-parent who did his best to learn how to toddle. Toddler time: Is it slow or is it fast? What words might we invoke to talk about toddling? In what ways might we speak to the experience of one who grasps and grapples with the world in the most joyous and impossible of ways? In what ways do we learn how to listen? To speak? How do we gather the necessary fortitude to take that "First Step," knowing that the trip most often involves a fall? What courage it must take to toddle.

My story wanders with the familiar (as well as the familial) with any number of touchstones available to those who have chosen to grow themselves into a family. As I began to become somewhat accustomed to toddling, I returned to the world of newborn parenting. Again, there is nothing truly new in this story, save for the particulars of our own daily exigencies, dilemmas, and dramas. We had another baby and I continued to be "The Father" who tended the home fires.

I am not a mother, no. Getting even this close to birth/ing makes it clear that it is my privilege to simply bear witness to the women of the world, fierce and loving, who seem to move to sounds men can't hear. Yet neither does my story seem to belong to the historically noisy and often cluttered conversation about fathering. (Who will listen when we are all busy talking at the same time?) I am a father. (So I can self-efface.) Laugh at the stereotypical father jokes. Put on my smoking jacket and exchange knowing and articulate ruminations on parenting with other fathers (while the children are put to bed by their mothers).

I can also be hurt by fathering stories and the way they have played out through my short time on this planet. I am part of a cultural landscape still rife with land mines left by my father, his father, someone else's father. By "Every Father." I am one of them. I am not one of them. There are not enough fathers to go around. Many that do stick around are, in my opinion, sadly lacking in their capacities for fathering. This is their fault. This is not their fault. Many are plentiful in their capacity for cruelty. Some are absent even in their presence. And, still, others are quiet and generous and loving. But these are not my stories to tell, though they remain as whispered stories of a legacy that still lives in and through me.

Fathering: such an interesting looking—and sounding—word. Not used all that often. At the same time, if one dwells with it long enough, "fathering" seems to hold the capacity to take on a certain quality of lightness, a characteristic not often associated with the role of "father." The father has long been storied as "the heavy." (Wait until your father gets home.) *Father*, at least for me, still holds a memory that is weight itself, although paradoxically it is often a weight most present in its absence, an authority that took on a certain gravity through the long arc of days when father was at work, or off on a business trip, or golfing, or...

Yet, the act of fathering that I desire to know, wish to manifest in my own stumblings as father, has a softer, more rounded shape; it longs to listen more, become more malleable in its form. One might even imagine, eyes closed, listening, as fathering learns to float and flutter in new and fatherly ways.

So why am I here, spilling words in this particular way? I believe it may be because I am a father who is discovering that the role of father seems too restricting. I am a father who finds myself playing a role that our culture, in a paint-by-number fashion, has traditionally and stereotypically painted as "mother." That is, the current structure of my life, the ongoing living out of days and nights, centres around being—in contemporary "parentspeak"—the "primary caregiver." This designation says very little of course. What might I offer to the ongoing conversation that speaks of parenting—speaks in particular of fathers who mother? Am I here so that I can politely but firmly educate people in check-out lines at supermarkets who make comments like, "Oh, it's so nice that you're taking your children out for the afternoon. It must be nice to give their mother a break." Or is it so that I can learn to talk to other mothers and fathers about the ways that we feel we can and can never be parents?

When our son was three weeks old, Rena, his mother, my wife and partner, by our mutual choice, drove out of the driveway and off to work. I was not ready. Of course I was not ready. I would have preferred one more day, one more week, one more year before "This Happened." Yet this was the "Gift" offered me. Our son, Hayden, had passed the initial litmus test with flying colours. He was happy enough taking his Mother's milk expressed from breast
to bottle. From her to me to him. Simple   enough.

I guess this is where the story ends

and begins. Begins and
ends. Begins and
begins.

. . .

We named both our children, Hayden and Zinta, while they were still in the
womb (a womb of their own). When they arrived, we recognized them. We kept
a journal for each of them from conception onward. So we learned to write

both Hayden and Zinta into the world
just as we continue to learn
how Zinta and Hayden write our world.
We don't know   how it's going
to go but the sentences are marked
by punctuation, filled with
exclamation...

I recently re-discovered a poem I'd written for Hayden (before he was born) on
a beautiful old Underwood typewriter.

Writing a forest poem with an old typewriter, waiting for a new baby

I put moss under the old
typewriter to get the angles just
right—so the keys might sing
your name in notes
not yet named.

Very tiny frogs catapult their greenness over
"lilypaddreams," no space greener
than this day.

Hard to slow the bluesky swirl and no need to
with your breezycloud intentions
dotting the horizon.

Impossible? No!
Worthy of exclamation that points

my eyes off the page that catches
a piece of light dancing the forest
dance and many birds chatting the day late.

So many leaves wishing you here
with us. Our nakedness so much
clothing next to your original skin.

Caterpillar dreaming a life
to unfold, greenest stories
in brown earth and blackrock sketches

making the belief true.

Pinetree'd fables of water and stone,
fire and old summer Spirit.

A dog napping on the open/ing page,
gentle, lazy reminder of poetspeed oversight and a sampler
of simpler ways to love love while you're   waiting.

So, this is how it tends to go in our lives. The words—and our living of them—fall out in bits and pieces, often as *poems that refuse to become prose*. My stories of becoming a father and watching Rena becoming a mother are a gathering of straight and crooked lines that remind us that our lives could never be otherwise. This leads me, then, to speculate in a wildly inconclusive fashion that writing and living are inexorably linked to one another. That is, our living and our writing of that living—as well as our writing and our living of that writing—serve to inform and deepen one another. To grasp for yet another connection in this lovely and complex nest of interrelations, I would like to suggest that parenting, embedded as it is in our living, is a form of writing. Parenting and Writing. Writing and Parenting.

· · ·

Waiting to be born (for Hayden)

Of course I haven't
read enough

books on birthing and becoming
a parent. Like You
I will emerge not so much headfirst
as by the seat of my pants.

No machines hooked up to monitor my heart
rate but beating fast enough
to come in a close second.

Diapers?

I'll be the one
shitting my pants
but laughing at the load
of laundry that will string the three of us together
hearts fluttering with the breeze.

My poems and journal entries tend to be playful, whimsical, sometimes comical—as in the poem, "Diapers?" These writings, despite their playful ways, "remind" me that we are going to have a baby. It is in these "writerly" ways that I am able to see myself playing with the *idea* of parent: reluctantly with excitement, excitedly with reluctance, fearful yet ready, and blindly courageous. My writing also shows me, myself playing the role of father in ways I have already expressed a desire not to be: as one slightly removed, a curious visitor, a watchful, albeit enthusiastic, spectator. So I certainly make no claims that writing makes me a parent. Yet writing offers me this ongoing, tentative, healthy, fragile sense of identity negotiation.

. . .

Zinta is about to turn 10-years old. Hayden stretches toward the age of thirteen. They are both beautiful beyond description. Today, I called them "assholes," mumbling too loudly to myself as I walked away from their incessant fighting. *Fucking idiots. Did I say that out loud?* I've uncovered another other face of love, disfigured and driven through with shame: hate. I feel hatred: toward myself, my loved ones, and even strangers on the street. I've come to the realization that it's possible to love and hate my children at the same time.

Without being conscious of it, I was eager to write a fairy tale for my new family as it emerged and grew. (Busy, perhaps, writing over my own childhood and family stories with a fatter, more colourful crayon. Scared of looking in the lost and found for what I might have left there). In this story of my story, the bottom never dropped out so much as found a way of dropping in slow, steady increments making change unnoticeable. Parenting doesn't get easier or harder, it just gets different.

In my experience, a certain amount of the (lucky) charm and magic of early childhood (and parenting) eventually gives way to the plain, the ordinary, the mundane. The value of the stay-home parent is called into question when the physicality of diaper-changing, feeding, carrying and comforting begin to recede. Some research even suggests that children might be just as well off in the care of others rather than the daily marathon of the "child-parent" dance. Coffee shop conversation takes on a questioning turn: What *are* you doing still at home? Are you going to get a job? My self-worth wobbles unsteadily. My wife and partner asks the same questions. Angry and feeling defensive, my next few rolls of the dice all seem to turn up snakes. The needs of children in their middle years are, in my view, immense though often hard to identify and articulate.

Rena continues to reinvent herself daily with alarming ambition, fortitude and creativity. I'm not inclined to keep up. Our marriage feels dead in the water. I've stumbled through a couple of years of intensive experimentation with drugs: antidepressants. Anxiety has tried yet never quite managed to strangle the poems, songs, and ideas that wish to see the light of my days. I continue to work with children in schools. Lovingly. I pretend I'm functional just like everyone else. I shine; I stink. I am possessed with stupid optimism; I fill up with hope. I compose songs that shoot brilliant blue sky through the mirrored, marred surface of my existence. I don't know where they come from. I give thanks and praise.

Fifty times around the sun
Some for pain some for fun
Fifty times and still not done
Fifty times around

Fifty times around the sun
I have so much while some have none
Thy Kingdom come thy will be done
Fifty times around

Do you wonder how your life might go?
The years so fast the days so slow
So you send a prayer to heaven knows
For every time around

You watch the day turn into night
The first star tumbles into sight
You love this life with all your might
Every time around

I recently finished writing a song called "Waving Fields." The song began its life
10 years ago, as a poem written during a long road trip with Hayden and Zinta
sleeping in the back seat. I fashioned some music, just last year, to keep the lyrics
company. I could not possibly love my children more deeply without disappearing.

Children sleep The Muse it hovers
Waving fields of August pass
Sweet wind tugs the golden covers
Remember this it will not last...

I must begin writing another song right now. Or a poem, maybe, just to find out
what might happen next. (Or determine what might happen next?)

Marriages end. Families don't.
I said I would but now I won't

Someone left the door ajar
Light falls from an evening star

Sing a prayer so love might find us
Love the song that might remind us

. . .

Here's one way of writing the parenting life: place one word after
the other. Wonder over every word. Wonder which word
is the right word. Wait for the next
word to come along. Be prepared
to doubt your own words. Love them, too.
Take two words and bang them
together until something
happens. Or nothing. A spark maybe or just
an unpleasant noise.

REFERENCES

Cockburn, B. (1979). After the rain. *Dancing in the dragon's jaw* [record]. Toronto, Canada: True North Records.

Eisenberg, A., Mrukoff, H. E., & Hathaway, S. (1989). *What to expect the first year.* New York, NY: Workman Publishing.

Mitchell, J. (1982). Love. *Wild things run fast* [record]. New York, NY: Geffen.

Van Zandt, T. (1972). To live is to fly. *High, low, and in between* [Record]. Los Angeles, CA: Rhino/WEA, Tomato.

Conscious Awakening

From Impersonator to Loving Teacher

Margaret Louise Dobson

"Who are you?" For most people such a question calls for a simple, straight-forward answer that will likely include their name, address, family background, nationality, marital status, academic and/or vocational training, achievements, occupation, aspirations, beliefs, and other unique characteristics such as colour of eyes and hair, weight, and height. For me, however, things have never been quite so cut-and-dried. I have always been bothered by the niggling awareness that there was much more to my identity than can be acquired, derived, achieved, qualified, quantified, and described. I grew up with no concrete facts or supporting evidence to verify my abstract notion of a larger, deeper invisible identity other than, of course, some religious or philosophical concepts I was taught about the *soul.* Over time, like most people, I soon became accustomed to acting out the prescribed scripts of social, practical, political, and professional life to live and find meaning within the parameters of the culture and worldview into which I was born. Behind the scenes, however, the gnawing awareness that an essential component of my identity was not being adequately incorporated into the picture continued to aggravate my resolve. In truth, I often felt more like an impersonator than a real person. Eventually I became so skilled at pretence that I began to believe in the veracity of my own performance. I have always had a wonderful imagination, and I learned to play just about any role to the hilt. I knew intuitively that I was not the person I pretended to be, and yet I had no difficulty identifying with the assigned or assumed role for the sake of affected authenticity. At the best of times, I could completely lose myself in my character. Sometimes my make-believe depictions consisted of real-life personae, and at other times I took on the actual portrayals of characters on the stage. Acting the part became as easy as child's play. To me, it was all the same. The line between my construed, or storied, personality and my imagination had become so blurred that I could no longer tell where I left off and my character began. While the vague feeling that I was not the person I appeared to be persisted, overall I enjoyed being caught up in the everyday action of everyday life. In fact, I began to feel quite at home in the familiar all-the-world's-a-stage, best-case/worst-case scenarios that were being represented, and accepted by most people around me, as "reality."

Until one day. Things didn't start out well that morning. My husband had dropped me off at school during one of those nonsensical newlyweds' arguments. I was very upset by the discord. By the time I reached the door of my classroom, I found myself worked into a thick lather of funk. Stepping through the classroom door into the brightness of my students' eager anticipation, I was barely able to assume my role as their teacher, let alone feign the usual vibrancy and enthusiasm that they had become accustomed to, and enamoured with, in their pretty, young French teacher.

The daily lesson began on schedule. I was a "pro" and had no trouble automatically taking my charges through the paces of an oral French class. Part of the drill consisted of modelling and repetition, in unison, of French vocabulary, phrasing, and pronunciation. A lyrical rhythm of ebb and flow ensued as the students' voices echoed in choral response the sequences of tone and sounds that I set forth. Before long, the entire room was filled with a joyful cadence that could be likened to that of a well-tuned orchestra playing in sync with their conductor. The shining faces of my teenaged students let me know that all thirty-three of them were as aware as I that something truly extraordinary was occurring between us. Then sharply and suddenly the bell rang, and the class was over.

"I just had the best time of my life, and I wasn't even there," I exclaimed to a colleague in an effort to articulate the unusual phenomenon that had transpired in my classroom. The dramatic shift of the *before* me, an ego-centered person-in-a-funk, to the *after* me, a transcendent-self person totally alive and exuberant held a crucial lesson for me. It turned out to be a turning point from which there was no return. I became aware that the impersonator was no longer present in the teacher-student relationship that took form. I saw my *new* radiant self reflected in my students' beaming faces. Before my very eyes was the actual evidence of an identity that up until now I had only sensed as present. *If not the impersonator, then,* I asked myself, *who was the "real" teacher in the classroom that day?* That is the question that prompted my relentless personal quest for an identity that includes, but goes beyond, the socially derived and personally construed version I had almost resigned myself to accept as *"I."*

After many years of study and exploration on the subject, the discoveries and experiences of my dogged search have brought me full circle. Wondering about the possible implications that my research may have in the raising of children in general, and in teaching and learning in particular, I have come back to the figurative drawing board in the form of a doctoral program in Integrated Studies in Education at McGill University. It has taken me a while to get here—it has been a long, circuitous, and challenging road—but I have finally turned my personal experience and quest, begun in earnest on that fateful day in my classroom many years ago, into an overarching question for my doctoral work. Just as I was unforgettably transformed from an ego-centred human impersonator to a transcendent "selfless" human being in loving relationship with my students, today I ask the following question: Can the social, political, and economic program of schooling—a systematic régime of teaching and learning designed to *make* something of our "selves"—be transformed into Education (from the Latin root meaning, *educo, educare,* to lead forth *from within*) as a determined search for "self" that is not socially, politically or economically engineered, but inwardly generated?"

If we do not know who we are, how on earth can we know what we are doing? What is the purpose of education in the 21st century? Is it to continue to train future generations to uphold a worldview that is in the throes of a major transformation with a very uncertain outcome? Or, is the purpose of education to provide the conditions for the emergence of a newly conscious human identity that is no longer completely dependent on external qualifications, quantifications, and justifications for its sense of worth and meaning? Would not a self that is powerfully generated and expressed from within also generate an integral sense of purpose, belonging, and fulfillment?

In *The Human Condition* Hannah Arendt (1974) sees the identity of a person as "the source of creativity" that "springs indeed from *who* they are and remains outside the actual work process as well as independent of *what* they may achieve" (p. 211). Arendt states that the purpose of her book is to propose to a generation of "job holders" (a generation also characterized by Arendt as "unthinking") to "think what we are doing" (p. 5). She says that when people get together as *who* they are and not *what* they are, an "in-between" opens between them. Arendt maintains that only love is fully receptive to who somebody is. "Love by reason of its passion, destroys the in-between which relates us to, and separates us from, others" (p. 242). Arendt further asserts, "Love by its very nature is unworldly, and therefore is the most powerful of anti-political forces" (p. 242). Arendt's insight into the human condition of plurality points the way to the kind of thinking that is not only required, but that has already begun to redirect and reshape our attitudes towards each other and our views towards our planet and the universe. The interdependence and interconnectedness of the plural reality in which we live are no longer mere theories; the global climate and economic crises are proven matters of fact we are now required to face as a global unit.

The before person that entered her classroom that memorable day, many years ago, would not only have been unable to teach her class properly, but she could have done harm to her students had she not been willing to let go of her preoccupation with herself in order to do her job. In a similar way, in retrospect, it seems to me that ego-centred, separate human identities will not serve us well in the 21st century as we step together, interdependently, into the bright, uncertain future of the global village. My personal experience of a shift in identity from impersonator to real teacher, as I have attempted to describe it, may seem insignificant at face value; nevertheless, the change in identity, because it was recognized and consciously articulated—"*I* just had the best time of my life, and *I* wasn't even there"—could hold possible significance for educators. The awareness of the two *I*s, as articulated, may contain at least two important clues to the essential nature of the shift in consciousness: (a) the letting go of a self-centred, self-preoccupied *I*, and (b) the giving in to a loving *I* in relationship with others (especially others for whom one holds a sacred responsibility, such as in the teacher-student relationship).

How a question of identity may translate into a doctoral dissertation, and possibly into a transformed approach to education remains to be seen. Since *real* is not a concept and only concepts "about" reality can be taught, I am left with a dilemma. The last thing I want to see in education is a new and improved course or methodology for teaching *who I am* even if such an approach were to get past school officials and parents' committees. In all probability, a modern technique for teaching *authentic identity*, or some other facsimile, would not only be rejected outright by the powers that be, the results of such an unlikelihood would be disastrous at worst, or more of the same, at least.

The only hope for education, and consequently for the future of humankind, as I see it, will be for parents and teachers to become self aware through their own self-reflective living practice. There are strong indicators that such conscious awakening is well underway in many areas of human endeavour, but I see it as especially crucial for teachers to do the necessary inner work. Through the living example of their mentors, children and students will have the opportunity to grow up knowing the fullness of who they are, and no longer be reduced in their thinking to what they have been conditioned to become. Once again I quote Hannah Arendt (1974):

> Only where things can be seen by many in a variety of aspects without changing their identity, so that those who are gathered around them know that they see sameness in utter diversity, can worldly reality truly and reliably appear. (p. 57)

I envision a world that is not artificially contrived or conceptually derived, but beautifully created by the loving thoughts, words, and actions of a people who know who they are. In such a loving space of "in-between" (Arendt, 1974, p. 242), I am fully confident that the healing of current rifts between people and nations can occur, diversity can flourish, and originality can bear the unprecedented. This is the world I have always imagined being possible, but now I see that what I once only sensed to be true behind the scenes can become a practical, down-to-earth reality by reason of awakened and awakening human hearts and minds. It is after all a question of identity.

REFERENCE

Arendt, H. (1974). *The human condition*. Chicago, IL: University of Chicago Press.

Minding What Matters

Relationship as Teacher

Avraham Cohen & Heesoon Bai

Working as a collective and among a growing network of kinship, we have found varying degrees of resonance with the writing and lives of others.
—Erika Hasebe-Ludt, Cynthia Chambers, & Carl Leggo,
Life Writing and Literary Métissage

The Primacy of Relationship

M ost cultural and mythological narratives speak of individual leaders, inspirational heroes, and teachers: for example, the Canadian prime minister, the American president, Roméo Dallaire, Wayne Gretzky, the Pope, the Dalai Lama, Mother Teresa, and the Buddha. One obvious commonality is that these names all refer to one person. They are mythic giants for humanity, and their achievements stand like colossal monuments. Some of these figures seem so super-human that they stand apart from the rest of humanity, and no one even dares to imagine that they could be like them. Such individuals very often seem to become objects of worship. Are they really singular? Do they stand alone? Is worshipping them a sustainable and redemptive process? Ernest Becker (1973/1997), winner of the Pulitzer Prize in 1974 for his book *The Denial of Death*, makes a point about parataxic distortion[1] in relation to heroes:

> The mana-personality may try to work up a gleam in the eye or a special mystification of painted signs on his forehead, a costume, and a way of holding himself, but he is still *Homo sapiens*, standard vintage, practically indistinguishable from others unless one is especially interested in him. The mana of the mana-personality is in the eyes of the beholder; the fascination is in the one who experiences it. (p. 128)

Becker is underlining the reality of the inner world, and the immense capacity and propensity of human beings to construct a symbolic world and be convinced of the "objective truth" of this construction. Building on Becker here, we wish to point out that behind each of these colossal figures stand generations of humanity, history, traditions, cultural aspirations, and geographic factors: dimensions many are prone to forget as they slip inexorably into the cul-de-sac of parataxic distortion. Consider the present-day dalai lama, His Holiness the 14th Dalai Lama, Jetsun Jamphel Ngawang Lobsang Yeshe Tenzin Gyatso. The whole nation of Tibet and its karmic tradition of dalai lama re-incarnation is invested in nurturing and educating this one person. Fully knowing the vast network of interdependence and interpenetration, as understood by Buddhist philosophy, the Dalai Lama himself does not seem to be deluded and "puffed up" about his singular heroism. (Of course, our view could be evidence of our own parataxic distortions.) However, his deep humility presumably is born of the foundational Buddhist understanding of interdependence and interpenetration of the phenomenal world.

Each human being, however ordinary and limited, is—all the same—a product of a vast network and lineage of interdependence and interpenetration of people, culture, history, and geography. Each individual is the current endpoint of every ancestor who preceded them. Even more viscerally, humans are pack animals whose survival depends on close teamwork of bonding and support. This suggests that human existence, let alone flourishing, is not possible without the collective effort of well-bonded individuals caring for and nurturing each other in all dimensions of beingness: physical, social, energetic, volitional, emotional, intellectual, and spiritual. The pervasive anxiety and insecurity that characterize the existential-psychological states of being for contemporary humanity speak precisely to what is often missing: lack of adequate and sufficient collective caring and nurturing. This, in turn, highlights the core of what is missing: strongly bonded relationships and networks of relationships that support both individual and collective optimal growth and sustenance. Unfortunately, what occurs is the outcome that is represented by many human beings who are psychologically and emotionally wounded to a greater or lesser extent as a result of the insufficiency of early relationships that did not and could not provide the loving, caring, and nurturing that was needed. Evidence for this is all too painfully obvious on the streets of cities where there are increasing numbers of homeless people. This lack also shows up in classrooms, counselling offices, and in our homes. Everywhere, and most centrally in both the individual and collective psyche, existential-psychological insecurity—that is the outcome of the lacunae of validation, love, care, modelling, and experience of deep relationship—is evident.

Today, with the ever-increasing complexity that affects human lives, it seems to take far more than a village to raise a child. And yet in many instances children are being raised by a single parent and often without the support of extended families. It is possible to purchase various kinds of social and commercial services, but that certainly is not the same as strongly bonded, caring personal relationships that provide support and guidance and that can facilitate, cultivate, and nurture human growth and development. We propose that the next and crucial step to a more perspicacious understanding of humanity is to give up what is, in our view, the outdated as well as unsustainable notion of single individuals as leaders. Without falling into another illusion of collectivity that negates individuality (Ogilvy, 1992), we need to embrace the primacy of intersubjectivity. We are individuals within the context of relationships. Without the *other* we would exist as a singularity. This latter is a fictitious construction that, depending on your perspective, either is not possible and/or seriously obstructs human interrelatedness that is vital to human flourishing. Yet, the logic of apparent impossibility notwithstanding, it seems that many are trapped in a vision of themselves as singular individuals. Barry Magid (2002/2005)—a psychiatrist, psychoanalyst, and Zen Buddhist teacher—describes the human existential situation of isolation and alienation in graphic terms:

> We try to put up a shield between ourselves and life, thinking to protect ourselves from suffering. And these shields do work in their way, and perhaps at vulnerable times in our lives, we've felt we couldn't live without them. But ultimately they turn from being walls that protect to walls that imprison. One day we wake up and realize that we've crawled into a glass bottle to hide and now we don't know how to get out. (p. 45)

Notions of leadership in any sphere, including education, parenting, the workforce, or governance seem to lack this understanding about the primacy of relationship. We wonder if what leaders as singular persons attempt to provide—security, wisdom, guidance, facilitation, and role-modelling—is in actuality exemplifying the opposite of what the complexity of a postmodern world requires: relationship as teacher. Mind you, the primacy of relationship has been a part of the world's many wisdom traditions, including the previously mentioned African concept (*ubuntu*) of needing a village to raise a child. One person standing up as a leader most obviously does not stand up (pun intended) well to the words of Jesus—a super icon of heroic singularity—who seemed to have had a deep insight about the fundamental reality of human intersubjectivity: "For where two or three are gathered together in my name, there am I in the midst of them" (Matthew 18:20; Schuyler, 1952). Also, as already mentioned, the core teaching of Buddhism is about our interdependence and interpenetration—as Thich Nhat Hahn (1993) renames it, *interbeing*—of all phenomena, including humanity. The historical Buddha challenged his students to find an independent self, an *I*. Buddha's students, as well as our contemporaries steeped in *New Science* and postmodern thoughts, have confirmed that what we call *I* is really a matrix of relationships and a dynamic site of interpenetration and transformation within such matrix. Indeed, it is ironic that the two major teachers who taught intersubjectivity, Christ and Buddha, have progressively over millennia been constructed into super heroes worshipped by their followers. The message of these teachers seems to have been subsumed and consumed, as Becker (1997) points out, by a collective un-consciousness that has a voracious appetite and will for attributing god-like powers to these two very human and humane beings.

The Jewish philosopher Martin Buber (1970) encapsulated this critical understanding about human intersubjectivity: "All actual life is encounter" (p. 62). Throughout his celebrated book, *I and Thou*, Buber returns again and again to the crucial importance of human encounter: The tangible realization and substantial enactment of interbeing and creative transformation can only lie in the space between individuals and their discrete subjectivity, in intersubjectivity. We understand *substantial* to mean the nature of encounter that involves a knowing of the other and being known by the other in a multiplicity of integrated dimensions (intellect, emotions, body, and spirit) with a reciprocity and simultaneity to this knowing. Buber's (1970) articulation of these dimensions and how they manifest is rich and precise:

> The basic word I-You establishes the world of relation. There are three spheres in which the world of relation arises.
>
> The first: life with nature. Here the relation vibrates in the dark and remains below language. The creatures stir across from us, but they are unable to come to us, and the You we say to them sticks to the threshold of language.
>
> The second: life with men. Here the relation is manifest and enters language. We can give and receive the You.
>
> The third: life with spiritual beings. Here the relation is wrapped in a cloud but reveals itself, it lacks but creates language. We hear no You and yet feel addressed; we answer—creating, thinking, acting; with our being we speak the basic word, unable to say You with our mouth. (pp. 56–57)

The dimensions of intellect, emotion, body, and spirit are all included in knowing possibilities. We note that Buber's invocation of language, as a dimension of encounter, is in line with the basics of Karen Meyer's (2010) pedagogy of *Living Inquiry*. She identifies the dimensions of time, place, language, and "self-other" as central factors that affect the encounter. We believe that only substantial encounters in the relational matrix have the power of transforming how and who we are. Hence, the most powerful and authentic transformative agent of teaching and leadership is not the individual teachers and leaders, but rather the relationships—the in-between spaces of meeting—that they create and the relational encounters they both represent and facilitate. We believe that the time has come for humanity to move out of the stage of the individual leader and teacher. What is now required are relationships that are multi-dimensional and a central part of what teaches, facilitates, and leads. We propose and illustrate in our dialogue below that while a person can learn and grow in relationship, which we certainly believe, a relationship based on mutual learning and growth is itself a teacher. Two-or-more individuals within a group will supply the most important learning through the nature and process of the relationship between them.

Below is a record of a multi-faceted encounter between the two authors of this chapter. Our intention with this dialogue is to illustrate our thesis of intersubjectivity being the most transformative teaching agent. We invite you, the reader, to see what shows up and what you might learn from this relational encounter on matters that matter in our lives. Here are some guideposts as to what relationship itself can teach:

1. The how and what of engagement with the other(s)
2. A sensitivity to the other and how that facilitates respect
3. The reality of connection between beings, along with the how and what of such connection
4. The innate complexity of deep communication and connection (Cohen, 2004)
5. The nature and value of expression of feeling
6. The meaning and use of feedback in relationship.

Relationship as Teacher

Heesoon Bai (HB): When I look back at the almost seven years that I have been with you, what stands out to me is just how transformative my learning and growth has been, and how all this took place within the matrix of intense and rich relationship that you and I built and continue to build between and around ourselves. The relationship we have built is the alchemical cauldron that transformed the everyday materials—our experience of tension, conflict, confusion, and despair—as well as joy and excitement about our experience, our personal insights, and our growth. At times, more often than not at the beginning of our relationship, our relationship cauldron was not big enough or strong enough to handle the heat of all the crude matters of life we were cooking. We had some rough moments; moments when I thought, either the pot was going to explode (what a mess!) or fizzle, turn cold, and nothing will come out of it (what a sad disappointment that would have been). However, each time we persisted in shedding light on our own personal Shadow,[2] the cauldron was strengthened and enlarged. As the pot became larger and stronger through the process, the more base and subtle material it could handle.

Avraham Cohen (AC): I believe that the alchemical process is deeply influenced by the attitude of the alchemist(s). What I have learned is that my attitude is not exactly the—lovely, kind, compassionate, especially the "nice"—one that I always imagined to be central. I see that we are involved in multiple ways. We are the alchemists, the raw material, and the container. At times, it turns out, my contribution has emerged from my dark side. I have poked holes in the container, further fouled a brew that was already foul, and had attitudes and feelings that can only be described as less than constructive. I recall an incident in earlier times when we first started to co-author papers. I was the first author, or so I thought. After I gave you my initial draft I received the document back from you, filled with revision and changes. I was shocked. I couldn't recognize my work. I quickly returned the paper telling you that I had only made one change. You were shocked to find out that the one change was the removal of my name from the paper. This turned out to be my way of cranking up the temperature, stirring the ingredients, and pushing out the walls of the container. I felt that you did not understand what I was doing and did not appreciate me or my efforts. I was determined to make a strong impact on you, and to let you know that I was not going to be a pushover, and that I had some important things to say. It turned out that I was in the process of learning more about my personal psychological structure than I ever imagined possible.

HB: I can say exactly the same. I have learned an immense amount about myself during our relationship, which bespeaks its intensity and richness: how my identity is put together, where the cracks and fault lines in my personality are, where my knife of competency can either heal or kill. I really saw all my Shadow materials spilling out, at times uncontrollably and seemingly interminably. The co-authorship incident you mention above turned me inside out, too. I was shocked by your reaction, which precipitated the usual chain of flight/fright/freeze response, which, in my case, usually starts with the freeze and ends up as a fight response! I witnessed again and again what my reactive pattern is: shock and aggression. And I kept defending this particular reactivity pattern by justifying its necessity and legitimacy—I can and did argue until the light went on in my understanding that this pattern had been role-modelled for me in my family, and that I was trained to respond to challenges first by freezing (shock) and then by fighting (aggression). This whole process of witnessing and gaining understanding took place in our personal cauldron that was becoming increasingly hotter.

AC: The jet fuel of you and me was very hot; at times hotter than I thought I could bear, but bear it I have, and so have you. I am reminded of many presentations we did together, both at conferences, and in the mindfulness workshops that we developed. In these arenas the outcome of our heat emerged. I was struck from the outset by the fact that we received at least as much feedback about how we related to each other as we did about the content of our presentations. This further strengthened my growing conviction about the idea of relationship as teacher. I believe that our audiences could see that we were not two individuals coordinating but one unit of relationship that was working very hard on what mattered to us both individually and collectively, and on our collaborative contribution. My sense from these occasions was that people were seeing something unfamiliar to which they were drawn (or perhaps repelled in some cases), and they wanted to learn more.

HB: What was fantastic for me is that all that I theorized and wrote about the Buddhist philosophy of *interbeing* (Hahn, 1993) or interdependence finally became very real for me, sometimes very painfully real, and, at times I felt I had hit a concrete wall! And these moments of awareness—that I was challenged to live what I wrote about—were both fulfilling and humbling experiences as I could plainly see my shortcomings, blind spots, incongruencies, and even duplicities. I could not just dismiss them with the usual platitude of "nobody is perfect" or "we all break down now and then." They were too persistent and systemic, and at times too ugly, for me to just respond with a sheepish grin. I thought your re-working of Parker Palmer's (1998) line, "We teach who we are" (p. 1) to "We teach who we are not, and that's the problem" was just priceless! I am not an exception to the problem you are identifying here. I came to see increasingly that so many educators, my colleagues included, are mired in this problem, which collectively has a huge personal impact on all those we teach, guide, lead, and try to support. Indeed, *teaching* here often happens not explicitly and intentionally but implicitly and without the alleged intention. It's most unlikely that an educator or parent explicitly and intentionally says that they will "screw up" a student or a kid. My father did not mean to teach me to go into anger and rage when confronted with frustrating and painful challenges, but that's the patterned behaviour that I watched time and again as I was growing up, and in the absence of other, better coping responses to challenges, that pattern subtly imprinted itself in my unconscious and made itself available to me in those unguarded moments when I was bereft of any better defence mechanisms. None of this understanding would have come to the surface so compellingly if our formidable relationship cauldron was not there, ready to receive, hold, process, and feed what's cooked back to us (which sometimes caused chokes and hiccups) in order to nourish our growth. Hence my growing understanding and conviction that relationship is the teacher.

AC: I am very appreciative of your openness about your own life and your willingness to share these vulnerable personal experiences. It is great to be able to have this dialogue about your insights about yourself. I firmly believe that this openness, yours and mine, is directly related to the capacity building of our relationship and its extension into the network of other relationships we are building together. We had this idea that we could build a relationship that could teach us deeply, and we put our faith and trust into, and worked very hard to create, such relationship. We are now seeing more and more, in concrete terms, how such relationship works.

For my own part of learning through our relationship work, confronting your anger gave me the opportunity to revisit my own fears about being on the receiving end of anger, and also my own experience that was really about my fear of the damage I could perpetrate with my own anger. I remember well the exact moment in a Gestalt therapy session many decades ago where I realized that I feared that I might murder someone in a moment of anger and realized within seconds that I didn't have to, that I had choice and that I could choose to feel my anger and not act in ways that would damage others while I was trying to get rid of my excruciating feeling. As Janet Dallett (1991) so wisely put it:

> I saw, too, that my willingness to crucify myself on dark impulses and emotions distinguishes me from the criminal, who merely acts on them. (p. 11)

And:

> I want it to be clear that emotion is not what is sacrificed, but rather the acting out of godlike power. It is crucial not to repress or deny emotion, but to endure it until it changes in its own way. (p. 120)

It takes a strong psychic cauldron to hold and cook powerful emotions. When two or more people come together and create a communal cauldron, the transformative power of the brew increases exponentially. The well-known idea that the whole is more than the sum of its parts applies here. The relationship of two or more teaches far more than what each person can teach by themselves.

Coda

The braids of the métissage stories in *Life Writing and Literary Métissage as an Ethos for Our Time* (Hasebe-Ludt, et al., 2009) tightly correspond to our idea of relationship as teacher.[3] Our individual histories and stories weave into one tapestry along with the lingering strands of all those with whom we are also connected. We are "Sojourners Sojourning" (p. 97); "All Our Tangled Relations" (p. 127) continue to further tangle, disentangle, and re-entangle. We are learning from our increasingly blended and nourishing stories, and in that sense our "Stories Take Care of Us" (p. 151). We have encountered some "Dangerous Strokes" (p. 175), and from these encounters we have learned the most. And finally the sum total that is still being totalled is our growing capacity for "Opening to the World" (p. 203). So much said here and so much more in the gaps between. For now we will wrap up our dialogue about relationship as teacher.

What has become evident to both of us through this process of writing is that it is not easy to convey these living experiences in textual form, and that it is important to do so. A major challenge has been to convey the feeling or tone of each of us individually and both of us collectively. Of course, we don't know if our thesis that relationship itself is the teacher/leader is evident to our readers or not. What we have learned through the process of writing this paper is that everything we do, including this writing, leads to a deepening process between us. The major theme that has emerged is that there is no end point to this exploration and that the aliveness of the process between us is in an ongoing process of development. By writing this paper we hope to encourage you, our readers, to explore the possibilities of relationship in your own lives, both personally and professionally.

ENDNOTES

1 The tendency to conflate inner reality with what is external in the world, and, in particular with what is believed about a person.

2 This is a concept from Jungian psychology that refers to all that is out of conscious awareness of a person.

3 All quotations in this paragraph are headings from *Life Writing and Literary Métissage as an Ethos for Our Times*.

REFERENCES

Becker, E. (1997). *The denial of death*. New York, NY: Free Press Paperbacks. (Original work published 1973)

Buber, M. (1970). *I and thou* (W. Kaufmann, Trans.). New York, NY: Charles Scribner's Sons.

Cohen, A. (2004, Winter). Multi-dimensional Communication Construction in the moment. *Insights: News for Clinical Counsellors, 15*(3), 12–13, 31–32.

Dallett, J. (1991). *Saturday's child: Encounters with the dark gods.* Toronto, Canada: Inner City.

Davey, H. E. (2007). *The Japanese way of the artist.* Berkeley, CA: Stone Bridge.

Hahn, T. N. (1993). *Interbeing.* Berkeley, CA: Parallax.

Hasebe-Ludt, E., Chambers, C. M., & Leggo, C. (2009). *Life writing and literary métissage as an ethos for our times.* New York, NY: Peter Lang.

Magid, B. (2005). *Ordinary mind: Exploring the common ground of Zen and psychoanalysis.* Boston, MA: Wisdom. (Original work published 2002)

Meyer, K. (2010). Living inquiry: Me, myself, and other. *JCT: Journal of Curriculum Theorizing, 26*(1), 85–96. Retrieved from http://journal.jctonline.org/index.php/jct/article/view/150/64

Ogilvy, J. (1992). Beyond individualism and collectivism. In J. Ogilvy (Ed.), *Revisioning philosophy* (pp. 217–233). Albany, NY: State University of New York Press.

Palmer, P. (1998). *The courage to teach: Exploring the inner landscape of a teacher's life.* San Francisco, CA: John Wiley & Sons.

Schuyler, E. (Ed.). (1952). *Holy Bible: English.* New York, NY: Oxford University.

Teacher Burnout

Recovery From a Toxic Condition

Heidi Clark

Fatigue, feeling as if my body is grinding to a halt, has been a constant companion of mine. Energy dripping away like a leaky faucet, seeping elsewhere, my body is an empty husk. During the past six months, I have experienced a lack of vitality. It has manifested itself like a cancerous growth, inhibiting my physical and emotional well-being. Piercing headaches limit the amount that I can read. Removed from normal social events and spending less time at work, chronic illness breeds isolation. Fatigue is leaden. Difficulty breathing limits physical activity, a never ending spiral, leading downwards.

I understand myself and others through stories. Therefore, I will share a narrative of my life to invite others to understand my experience of teacher burnout. It isn't addressed in teacher education programs and it isn't part of polite discussion around staff room tables. While experiencing teacher burnout, I was also pursuing a master of education degree in a cohort program focussed on urban education. The focus was on critical thinking and our role in the world. I do a lot of writing…the convergence of ill health and the need to be self-reflective in my coursework compelled me to be still. I began to listen to my intuition. I confronted a part of my being which I have ignored and left unacknowledged for my entire life: Who am I as a spiritual being? I began an inner journey and explored how the practice of spirituality can enhance my well-being.

As a teacher, I endeavour to integrate spirituality into the classroom, to connect with my students at a deep level, and help them discover who they are and what their passions are. In the classroom, I develop a caring community where each is respected and free to have a voice. We express feelings and care about one another. We share our love and appreciation for one another, daily. We demonstrate and share love in a classroom community. We laugh. We play with language. I teach children, not curriculum. I provide opportunities for my students to tell their stories and make sense of them.

I value creativity and encourage it in my classroom. Whatever project my students undertake, I model for them. It is important for me as an educator to create a classroom environment which helps children foster a connection to their spirit. The arts have been the path. Creative expression through drama, painting, writing, and reading all connect me to the entire universe. For example, I become more me in my classroom when I engage with my students and partake in impromptu reader's theatre. Acting out *Knuffle Bunny* is a joyful raucous event. Dancing to the Barenaked Ladies song, "7 8 9," is bliss. I see and sense the profound engagement of my students.

One day after leading my students in a guided meditation, I asked them if they'd be interested in showing what they "saw" on paper. The class was enthused by the suggestion. I pulled out oil pastels, cartridge paper and we had a flurry of artwork. We spent the next hour drawing. These 5-year-olds had remarkable focus. A sense of calm filled the classroom. I was amazed by the concentration and level of engagement of my pupils, not to mention the visual beauty of their creations. I was delighted to see the students blossom in creative expression.

My teaching is richer when I listen to my intuition. I become inspired by picture books, poetry, and art, as well as nature and science. When I look, really, really look and observe nature I accept the mystery of life. I am in awe and wonder of a dragonfly, its iridescent body and gossamer wings. When I feel, know, or have an inkling of an idea, I am now learning to trust that intuition. I will put aside the lesson I had planned and go with the flow of the creative energy.

During the month of April, National Poetry month, I focussed on teaching my class "Jabberwocky" by Lewis Carroll. We revelled in the silliness of the poem, acting out scenes in readers' theatre where the whole class dramatized the poem.

We discussed nonsense words and figured out their meaning by using context. We discussed adjectives. Kids loved snippets from "Jabberwocky" so much that we infused them in our day. If something wonderful was happening, someone might say, "Oh frabjous day! Callooh! Callay!" In free play the boys were often heard declaring, "One two! One two! And through and through the vorpal blade went snicker-snack!"

We had numerous oral discussions about a Jabberwock. We debated what it would look like. We came to the conclusion that since it is a creature from the imagination, it would look different to each person who imagined it. In pairs we discussed the attributes of our Jabberwocks. We finally illustrated our visions and created a class display. It was stupendous! I enjoy playing with words and share my own poetry with my students.

Splatter

Rain drop

plop

Rain drop

plop

Thunder cloud

BOOM

Lightening

Zoom

Zoom

Zoom

KABOOM!

Teachers need to take care of themselves. I have noticed in the past 2 years the marked increase in illness among staff members. It is telling: we give, and give, and give, and then our bodies and spirits break. Our lives are like being in an airplane with turbulence when the oxygen masks drop down. We need to save ourselves before others. I need to learn how to better attend to my own fire.

I've learned that our gifts can become toxic. My overriding passion and dedication to my profession which has been acknowledged by a national teaching award also led me to neglect myself in the service of others, especially my students. I've learned that consuming ourselves with our jobs is a disservice to self. I am more than my profession. I need to attend to my spiritual and creative well-being. My students and colleagues deserve no less, and even more importantly, I deserve no less.

Haunting Children

Lisa Nucich

Colin

Small, frail, sweet pipsqueak.

Squinting, peering, straining to see the chalkboards.

Finally, borrowed old, too big school glasses perched on the tip of his tiny nose.

Alive. Aware. Engaged.

Same clothes, rattered, tattered, soiled, and torn—day, after day.

Give this child some food.

All I want is to take him home. Feed him a roast-beef dinner, mounds of whipped potatoes, rivers of gravy, creamy butter on a loaf of fresh fluffy bread.

Put on a pound or twenty.

Let him sleep, uninterrupted, dead to the world. In clean cool fresh sheets, nestled in a marshmallow bed.

Take him shopping. Shoes, with laces, that won't fall off. Dry with no gaping shredded holes. Jeans that aren't half a foot too short, flooding up to his ears. A shirt that is crisp, washed, and new—picked out by him, just for him.

All of his own choosing.

Embrace him in a sincere bear hug.
One his absent mother never bothered to impart.

Wrap him in safety.

Resilient.

Here one day, gone the next...

Joey

Vibrant, cohesive, positive classroom.

Happy, healthy, active class.

Lonely child, different child.

Satellite child at the age of six.

Recess:

"Why are you pegging baby birds out of their nest with rocks?"

"Because it's fun to watch them fall."

Vibrant, cohesive, positive classroom.

Happy, healthy, active class pet hamster.

Lonely child, different child.

Being raised by his 16-year-old sister.

End of Lunch:

Broken, still, furry hamster.

Blood trickling from mouth hamster.

Wrung neck.

One life less on this planet.

Lonely child, different child.

A Curriculum for Miracles

Jackie Seidel

Miracle: From the Latin *mīrāculum*: object of wonder. *Mīrāculum* from *mīrārī*, to wonder at. From *mīrus*, wonderful. From smeiros [(s) mei–PIE–proto-indo-european] "to smile, to be astonished." Also Sanskrit: smerah "smiling." Also Old Church Slavic: Smejo–to laugh.

I began teaching in 1991 when I was 24-years old. I remember thinking that I might enjoy it enough to do it for a few years and save money for what I really wanted. Perhaps a master's degree in English. Perhaps I'd write.

Then, the miracles started to happen. I was overwhelmed by the intelligence and creativity of children and by what happened when we came together around shared ideas, readings, art, thoughts, life struggles, and joys. From children, from being with them in schools in both friendship and fellowship, from walking the road of life together for one-or-sometimes-two years, I learned to live life more graciously, more deeply, more slowly, more compassionately. With more breath. I learned to expect miracles and to create space for them to happen. I learned that life itself is a miracle and that we are miracles, each of us.

. . .

BREATH

. . .

We began the third grade in mathematics by meditating on the meaning of the number one. We sat together, thought, talked for a long while, and wrote many notes together. The conversation deepened. The children got excited. Their ideas grew and bounced from one to the other.

> *There is only one universe*, said a child.
> *There is only one earth*, responded another.
> *There is only one me.*
> *And there is only one of each human person ever in the one universe.*
> *One is unique!* arrived a final comment. *Everything that is alive only happens one time ever!*

The children started to laugh. In this moment of thoughtful expansiveness a palpable ripple of delight flowed through our classroom as we experienced our mind's ability to have such thoughts.

. . .

BREATH

. . .

Recently, genetics confirmed that the common maternal ancestor of all modern human beings lived approximately 200,000 years ago (Parry, 2010). One mitochondrial mother. One common human ancestor whose miraculous survival lives on in each of us. One unique wondrous human line of life.

The skin. The flesh. The earth. One well of water. One breath. Billions of years. We are the stuff of stars. Cosmic miraculous life. We are iron and calcium and oxygen. We are the rocks and the water and the wind. Breathing the breath of plants. What if such a miracle was the ground of our curriculum? Would we be inspired to perpetual reverence and awe for life, for one another, for our home?

As a teacher, I began to wonder how to hold on to such thoughts while terrorized by the stress of narrow curriculum goals, or by those who deny the mysteries and miracles of life by seeking to quantify and know all things, or by those who seek to control teachers' minds and words with this or that method, or by those who seek to separate children into winners and losers, more and less, champions and failures, strong and weak. Deficits.

A "Curriculum for Miracles" is not a deficit curriculum. It is broad and wide and deep, holding the whole of life generously without crowding. Only in such a possibility do the deepest sorrow and suffering have a place, to be experienced alongside the greatest joy and transcendent, radiant peace. We know not one without the other.

Exhale. Inhale. The outside is in and the inside is out. The Western dualistic, individualistic mind dissolves into the miracle of life's flow.

. . .

BREATH

. . .

Sorrow.

This word appeared in the midst of reading a story together in our fourth-grade classroom. In the midst of a *grand conversation*. Many of the children were learning English and we stopped to talk about what *sorrow* means. They gave examples. Jasmina raised her hand and spoke softly: *My mom has that. She cries all day.*

Something broke. The heart stopped for a moment. How could the tongue speak these names? Bosnia. Srebrenica. Genocide. Far-away places now so close, in the very skin and breath in *our* classroom. Again, it seemed so often, we were talking about war. It wasn't in the plans for that day. Then Samir was crying, too. His family also from Srebrenica. Their parents walked with such grief their bodies seem bowed to the ground. Other children nodded. The names of their stories sounded like Iraq, Afghanistan, Cambodia, Vietnam, Tibet, Somalia, Canada...

From such moments—many of them over many years—something was born and grew in me as a teacher. An invocation. A desire. An intention towards creating a curriculum of passion, creativity, happiness, spontaneity. Community. Love. Freedom. The movement of bodies and minds not stifled by hard desks and narrow ideas and rigid purposes. Laughter. Crying together. Memories and experiences cultivated, shared.

A sudden knowledge arrived one day, soaring into the classroom on some imperceptible updraft, freeing me from burdens I didn't know I carried. I knew with certainty (as much as there is any such thing) that all I could do as a teacher—nay, all I needed to do—was to prepare a joyous, creative day for children. Children who come as they are. Each of us a miracle of our ancestors' survival, whoever they were, wherever they lived. Here we are together today and *that is all.*

No matter the suffering they experienced in their day-to-day lives, empty cupboards, trauma and anguish, perhaps no one to love them enough, they could come to school each morning, each good new miraculous morning on this planet and have a wonder-filled day. A day in which their own unique potential and wholeness was fulfilled. A day of light and surprises and learning and enjoying one another. They could come to school and experience a Curriculum for Miracles. As a teacher, this I could do. It is enough.

. . .

BREATH

. . .

When I began this writing, I did not know this story now falling from my fingers.

Isaac, beloved nephew (son, brother, cousin, grandchild, great-grandchild), just turned 12-years old, loving, full-of-life, died early this summer. Our family had gathered for a rare time of togetherness to celebrate our grandmother's (mother, great-grandmother) birthday. A shocking, life-shattering, impossible accident interrupted and superseded the curriculum we had planned for ourselves.

This.
Sudden.
Absence.

The soft, soft body. The gentle, gentle breath.

Tender hearts break open in surprise. Rivers of tears. Salt of the earth. These cycles. Life.

Isaac was a miracle. A miracle in the middle of enjoying his creative, wondrous life. A miracle in the midst of reading books and working on his own projects. In the middle of making a *Fantastic Mr. Fox* claymation film. This was his important work in the world. Work that mattered.

A Curriculum of Miracles is a curriculum of the middle. Unfolding in the midst of things. In the midst of life and death. In the midst of joy and sorrow. In the midst of creation and destruction. It expands, always big enough, to hold the breath of wonder and the breath of anguish.

Many experiences as a teacher taught me that children's lives matter now and if there is any truth in the world, this is the one I learned to hold near to my heart: *our fragile human lives are not in the future.* A Curriculum for Miracles knows that life always unfolds from here and now, from this moment lived well with generosity and goodness. It does not waste children's time and it understands that each moment is important for its own time. This curriculum has no time to make children feel bad about themselves, about who they are, about their capacities as human beings. It only has time for having love, for being creative, for full and whole days of living life.

. . .

BREATH

. . .

Four years ago, I was working on a project with a class of third grade students about the United Nations' *Conventions on the Rights of the Child*. We closely studied the history and the wording of the Rights. One day I asked them to write about the Right that meant the most to them. Their responses were overwhelmingly the same: *You have the right to be alive*. During this time, as part of my PhD dissertation-writing, I attempted to understand what it meant to be teaching in a time of ecological crisis, I studied the Chernobyl nuclear accident. I realized through this research that the future, in which all children have *the right to be alive*, in which all future children are born, will forever be a nuclear time. This was the most difficult knowledge I had ever carried.

As I watched the children in that class playing, learning, and engaging in conversations, I recalled the stories of teachers and children who survived the Chernobyl accident. An unnamed child said:

> The sparrows disappeared from our town in the first year after the accident. They were lying around everywhere—in the yards, on the asphalt. They'd be raked up and taken away in the containers with the leaves. They didn't let people burn the leaves that year, because they were radioactive, so they buried the leaves. The sparrows came back two years later. We were so happy, we were calling to each other: "I saw a sparrow yesterday! They're back." The May bugs also disappeared, and they haven't come back. Maybe they'll come back in a hundred years or a thousand. *That's what our teacher says. I won't see them* [emphasis added]. (Alexievich, 2005, p. 218)

Lyudmila Dmitrievna Polenkaya, a teacher who survived Chernobyl and was evacuated from the Zone, described her experience as "the opening of an abyss" (Alexievich, 2005). Joanna Macy (2000) relates an experience where she met a school superintendent who carried a Geiger counter in his car so he could tell children where not to play. She met a school principal who had papered his office with pictures of a forest, because they would not be allowed back into the nearby forest in his or even his grandchildren's lifetimes.

I thought of those teachers and children who faced this abyss. How could these teachers face their students after this? What did they believe they were now preparing children for? What teacher voice is possible in a post-Chernobyl world? I imagined being this teacher, telling children such a thing, that they would not see the May bugs ever again. But then I thought of how this is happening today, and I *am* this teacher.

We studied animals together; the children asked about extinctions; they worried about polar bears and coyotes. They rescued spiders. We caught a wasp that had gotten into the school and put it in a container. We examined its hairy legs and body under the microscope; we wondered at its miraculous eyes and wings. Some children were afraid of it. We had a conversation about keeping it to study—*it would die*—or about letting it go—*it would live.* "Let it live," they said, "let it live." *You have a right to be alive.* The children did not want life to die. Although they were still very young people, they were aware of the collapse of life systems that support the existence of living creatures on the planet. They were aware of the impermanence of life. They were aware of the miracle of life. It was right there in our classroom, in the midst of it all.

. . .

BREATH

. . .

A Curriculum for Miracles walks gently on this earth. It leaves footprints of love, compassion, and forgiveness everywhere. It breathes the oxygen of life, photosynthetic miraculous gift. Its blood hums with iron and air from the rocks. It bathes and drinks from the one well from which all life flows.

A Curriculum for Miracles laughs at small ideas such as preparing, "children to be future workers in the global economy," at measuring "children to one-size-fits-all." It knows such thoughts are ridiculous and hilarious; it leaves them behind. It knows that life is wondrous and takes up *life itself* as its topic. It knows that each life is but a brief flash. Unique. Alive now. Days, months, years. Immeasurable and impossible, yet here it is. Here we are together. There is no other place or time except this place and this time.

. . .

BREATH

. . .

It is from those children who were always outside the boundaries of the discourses of "normal" competition and success that I learned the most. I grew weary of arguments for and against "integration" and "differentiation." There is no argument. There is only yes and yes-and-yes. Yes to diversity. Yes to the fragile bodies and everyone being together. Yes to the infinite interconnected miracles of life on this planet.

We were sitting in a cluster together on the floor where our fourth-grade class gathered to share our ideas, thoughts, and work. We were sharing stories we had written; Marie put up her hand and grinned. She rose up awkwardly; her friends carefully made room for her to stand. Her Down syndrome health-related challenges were causing difficulty with her joints and balance. A thyroid imbalance left her listless, breathless, and feeling irritated with the world. She picked her way between the bodies of her friends sitting on the floor, swaying back and forth as she transferred weight from foot to foot; her upper body leaned forward with her hands outstretched in front, holding the book she had made. With her back to me, I could see Marie's diaper above the waistband of her twisted and not-quite-pulled-up sweatpants.

Sudden and unbidden tears prickled my eyes. This intimate, vulnerable moment. A 10-year-old's incontinence and twenty-five other 10-year olds' acceptance of this as a possibility for being human.

Marie smiled at us and read her story aloud. It was a collection of shapes and some stick figures drawn with her favourite bright, scented markers. Mostly pink. Some letters she was learning were printed around the pages. Her voice was gruff, and she spoke with few words, excitedly pointing to places on her pages. She shared her book, five whole pages, and then finished, stood proudly at attention. Waiting for a response. Expectant. Her friends burst into noisy and genuine applause. Marie was overwhelmed; her face flooded with radiant joy.

Throughout my days and years of teaching, these miraculous wondrous moments have been too many to count. These moments offered lessons in being human, in finding humility in an institution that often has too little of it; these moments offered lessons in our deep and seemingly endless capacity for genuine love and care for one another, despite and across great differences in language, culture, religion, intellectual, and physical capacity. Pedagogically I learned again and again that consciously creating a classroom that was a good and right place for Marie, with enough space and time for a child like her to participate wholly and fully each day, all day, in everything we did together, was a classroom that was good for all children and also for their teacher.

Children like Marie brought me to a deep realization of the frailty of the human condition and the importance of radical diversity to all of our survival. They taught me to reject visions of education that did not include all children completely with rich purpose and full human experience. A Curriculum for Miracles is ecological, bursting forth from the understanding that the more diverse an environment is, the more creative and emergent its possibilities.

. . .

BREATH

. . .

A Curriculum for Miracles breathes with a soft breath, and a fierce breath. Aware of the spark of life that flows everywhere at once and through all earth time. It knows that life is this fragile *inhale* and *exhale* that encircles the planet. It knows this breath is wondrous. It faces ecological crisis with courage and heart. It knows that the sanctity and reality of death is always with us, yet it also holds the spark of emergent life in its hands. It understands that schools as institutions habitually deny the imminent reality of death by casting life always into the future, and thus, it knows about time, and that breath is always *now*, and now again. A Curriculum of Miracles is one that breathes the present, holds itself intentionally close to the relational cycles of life (living and dying). It is awake to the profound, the mystical, and the sensual. It responds to suffering of all kinds and cries out against injustice because it knows that each life *is* a life. Incarnations of breath flesh bone blood spirit.

A Curriculum for Miracles understands that life can be opened from this place called a *classroom* or *school*, or it can be closed. Life can be seen as wondrous or as dull. It can creatively overflow with joy, justice, peace and love, or it can serve the future, the literal, the "non-miraculous." A Curriculum for Miracles knows that the latter are a path to the forever death called *extinction*, the end of miracles forever. Thus, a Curriculum for Miracles is a curriculum that knows that life itself is an Object of Wonder. Fragile. Unique. Interconnected. Just once.

A Curriculum for Miracles smiles and cries, and dances and laughs. It is astonished. In the midst of it all. This is the curriculum that teaching has taught me.

REFERENCES

Alexievich, S. (2005). *Voices from Chernobyl: The oral history of a nuclear disaster* (K. Gessen, Trans.). London, England: Dalkey Archive Press.

Macy, J. (2000). *Widening circles: A memoir.* Gabriola Island, Canada: New Society Publishers.

Parry, W. (2010). Age confirmed for "Eve," mother of all humans. *Live Science.* Retrieved from http://www.livescience.com

Social Work

Vulnerable Beings, Political Worlds

I want to take the small things and make them into patterns, into part of the larger flow of history.
—Rita Moir, *The Windshift Line: A Father and Daughter's Story*

We are most interested in the generation of energy for radical vision, action, and new ways of being. If humans are going to survive on this planet, we need new connections to each other and to the natural world. Changing political and economic relationships is part of the larger project of reconstituting and revitalizing all of our relationships.
—Amish Morrell & Mary Ann O'Connor, Introduction,
Expanding the Boundaries of Transformative Learning:
Essays on Theory and Praxis

I n the fourth strand, life writers exemplify how the personal is always integrally connected to local and global contexts, including political, social, racial, historical, economic, and postcolonial contexts. Like Miller (2005), life writers know that writing is "a place where the personal and the academic, the private and the public, the individual and the institutional, are always inextricably interwoven" (p. 31). Therefore, life writers write the stories of their lives in order to connect with others. Above all, they seek to enter lived experiences with an imaginative openness to the people and socio-political-historical-economic dynamics at work and play in shaping identities and living experiences. They seek to make a story in collaborative dialogue with others, always aware that every story is one of many stories, one of many versions of many stories. Like Miller, life writers promote writing that moves out from the stories of "individual life into the history, the culture, and the lives of the institutions that surround us all" (p. 25). Above all, life writers embrace Ingram's (2003) wisdom:

> If one isn't at least partially sad in witnessing this world, then one is not paying attention. What if we just let our hearts break over and over? Why not get used to living with a broken heart? In empathy with others we experience a vast range of human feelings. Their suffering is our suffering; their joy, ours. The degree to which we allow empathy with sorrow is the exact degree to which we encompass joy. (pp. 41–42)

Life writers know it is never easy to write about our lives, especially in the academy, especially with truthfulness about experiences of love, fear, hope, failure, joy, and frustration. A different academic culture is needed, a culture that supports life writing that is marked by an understanding of how writing about personal experiences is not self-absorbed solipsism, prattling confession, or salacious revelation. We need to write personally because we live personally, and our personal living is always braided with our other ways of living: professional, academic, administrative, social, and political. Palmer (2004) notes that "instead of telling our vulnerable stories, we seek safety in abstractions, speaking to each other about our opinions, ideas, and beliefs rather than about our lives" (p. 123). Life writers tell their stories creatively and critically. Like Griffin (1995) they know that "the self does not exist in isolation" (p. 50). Instead, "to know the self is to enter a social process" (p. 51). Life writers acknowledge Brueggemann's (2001) notion of "prophetic imagination" which is "the last way left in which to challenge and conflict the dominant reality" (p. 40). For Brueggemann, "the evocation of an alternative reality consists at least in part in the battle for language and the legitimization of a new rhetoric" (p. 18). Life writing is about composing the themes and threads that hold our complex, tangled lives with textual and intertextual integrity. Life writers question and challenge the stories we tell in order to remain open to new stories. Miller (2005) reminds us that "sustaining a self and sustaining a culture are ceaseless activities. Both projects are always under construction and always under repair" (p. 49).

Like Pelias (2004), life writers "want a scholarship that fosters connections, opens spaces for dialogue, heals" (p. 2). Like Pelias, they "write from the heart" (p. 2). Life writers unite creative and critical questioning by living with incisive social analysis, comtemplative practice, and political commitment. In our life writing we testify to what has passed as well as what might be. Life writing energizes and enthuses us with courage for narrating and interpreting experiences so we can live together with generative, transformative hope in the midst of the tangled, messy mysteries that compose our lives.

REFERENCES

Brueggemann, W. (2001). *The prophetic imagination.* Minneapolis, MN: Fortress Press.

Griffin, S. (1995). *The eros of everyday life: Essays on ecology, gender and society.* New York, NY: Doubleday.

Ingram, C. (2003). *Passionate presence: Experiencing the seven qualities of awakened awareness.* New York, NY: Gotham Books.

Miller, R. E. (2005). *Writing at the end of the world.* Pittsburgh, PA: University of Pittsburgh Press.

Moir, R. (2005). *The windshift line: A father and daughter's story.* Vancouver, Canada: Greystone Books.

Morrell, A., & O'Connor, M. A. (2002). Introduction. In E. V. O'Sullivan, A. Morrell, & M. A. O'Connor (Eds.), *Expanding the boundaries of transformative learning: Essays on theory and praxis* (pp. xv-xx). New York, NY: Palgrave.

Palmer, P. J. (2004). *A hidden wholeness: The journey toward an undivided life.* San Francisco, CA: Jossey-Bass.

Pelias, R. J. (2004). *A methodology of the heart: Evoking academic & daily life.* Walnut Creek, CA: AltaMira Press.

Finding Canada
in the American Midwest

Life Writing as Public Discourse

Anita Sinner

A n epiphany on the conference circuit this spring: I am beginning to forget where and what and who and why, all the sessions and presentations, even countries have blurred together over time. I am living in a sort of transience, suspended between everyday life in home places of Canada, and opting to partake in the rituals of the academy, landing this time in the United States, in the city of Minneapolis. I have no good answer for my willingness to transport my body across the continent for a matter of days to engage in forms of what often amounts to making the professional strange before moving on to the next stop. I wonder sometimes if as academics we are perhaps vaudevillian spirits, never content to be still, seduced by life on the road, searching for our next stage, dreaming of attentive audiences but seldom finding the joy we anticipate in our intellectual revelations, despite our efforts.

I unpack my suitcase and practise my latest song and dance, only to feel that niggling schism running through my veins, the conflicting embodiment as a life writer entering the layered spaces of conferences that are often wrought with contentions, discontinuities, and ever-present question marks. Perhaps it is in these moments that life writing as a way of being in the world becomes a space in-between, and on this occasion, emerges as a form of public discourse, moving from the realm of an academic conference to a particular public event that is shifting the understood American landscape, the property auction. Through the method of creative nonfiction, this story serves as both a commentary on social practice and as an exemplar of doing arts research grounded in situated knowledges. In this way, the potential for life writing opens debate about academic responsibility and the vitality of public discourse.

For me, life writing is a way to live authentically and without exception, a conviction to practise with passion, to listen and not necessarily speak when entering the world openly, trustingly, and some may say naively, values sometimes contrary to the promotive environment of the academic conference. My interest has always been the individual's life journey, and often these are the kinds of stories, responsively shared with genuine interest and sincerity that come from chance meetings. How we perceive our experience of the world is for me the most fascinating form of inquiry, and some of the most profound insights about education have come in relation to attending conferences, but not necessarily through academic papers. Instead, knowledge may be collected in fragments of conversations beyond presentations, in unexpected encounters with people of all walks of life who offer their wisdom through story, entrusting with faith that we learn together. As academics we can easily become removed from everyday moments, and as time passes, I find it becomes harder to see beyond this sometimes isolating, insular world, to observe and absorb what is immediately before us as we move through the world: Stories wanting to be heard, to be told, to be shared.

Confessions of a Conferencer

So onto Minneapolis. On any journey to a new landscape I am as always excited by the possibilities. But saturated with one form of knowledge, I wander rather than sit any longer, and my wandering take me to another wing of the great expanse that is this conference hall where I discover a property auction is about to be underway. Given this historic moment in America of mass economic collapse resulting in uncountable foreclosures, this event draws my attention and my curiosity. What is this really all about?

With the irony of a Canadian interloper, I politely find my way into this auction despite the requirement for advanced registration to attend. I do not have the required $5,000 deposit to obtain a bidding card, nor am I able to qualify for the available on-site financing where with only 5% down any given property can be mine. After all, it is important to have a full house. The ballroom is quickly at capacity and nervous energies surge in the playful flashing of bidding cards as anticipation rises, and the chattering voices echo against sterile walls and institutional floors. The centre stage stands high over the crowd with dual super screens, dual pedestals, dual sound speakers, even dual "Attention!" signs. Stevie Wonder's (1973) "Higher Ground" loops with grossly oversaturated photographs of properties, mostly new homes in idyllic scenes that remain visible for no more than three seconds by my count, interspersed with the euphoria of winning bidders at other such auctions. So much rich green grass and true blue skies! These are indeed dream homes. But the song seems like an odd choice. Higher ground? As in, a moral higher ground at a property auction?

There is no natural light, and when the doors close I feel myself locked into a prison of my choice, as Lessing (1986) describes, where hypnotic forces surround "reason" and "sanity" before the auction even begins, moving the audience toward something far more "primitive," perhaps an instinct of power. Consider the words of that iconic song, and invocations of the higher spirit, setting the stage for an act in an unfolding tragedy. Yet it seems to me the people here today are not dripping with excess; instead, there is averageness evident in jeans and fleeces and runners. We all know to obediently take our seat on these orderly red chairs tied together, organized in very precise straight lines with little room between bodies. We are placed within the understood zone of comfort. We are strangers too close to one another, close enough to hear whispers two rows ahead and behind.

Yet there is one exception, a lone late arrival, a very important person as the auction staff makes quite a display of bringing a posh chair, seating him nearby and repeated asking with an inviting smile, "Is there anything we can do for you? Anything at all? Coffee? Tea?" Hands are shaken. He appears to be in his sixties, a distinguished looking southern gentleman, reminiscent of photographs from the 1930s, his pants extend up high, held in place with suspenders. His tall frame is only interrupted by noticeable girth, which in certain circumstances may still suggest the demarcation of wealth. His thick rimmed black glasses seem tell-tale of being out of sync with those around him. His son, that is, I assume his son as he calls him so, seems rather a caricature of another era, with slicked back hair and a crushed nose, wrapped in a Miami Vice leisure suit. He does not get a chair, but makes eye contact with the crowd, aware he is being observed, actively chewing gum between words on his cell phone, a curled lip, brokering a deal of some sort, or so it is meant to seem.

The preamble runs now to over thirty minutes. Stevie Wonder still loops, along with more songs, and I catch the words to "Superstition" along the way. The photographs continue to loop too. I must look away. I feel surges of anxiety woven with elements of fear in the audience. I turn away. Along the periphery of this ballroom I notice another grouping in the shadows. Mostly middle-aged men, some accompanied by their wives who grant compassionate glances to their desperate yet steely faces, etched with grimness, for the weight of the world has befallen them. These are faces hoping for a reprieve, if not an outright release. I feel they are possibly the once owners of some of these properties, here to witness all they worked for slip away in seconds. I turn to the glossy sales brochure, evidence of how we "do" a Great Depression today, flipping through pages and pages of loss. Finally some activity at the stage, the auctioneer in his bowtie and black tuxedo rouses murmurs from the audience, but just as quickly disappears. The media has arrived. Television cameras are recording the event.

I ask my neighbour, "What do you think about all this?"

"Well, maybe we can help those people today."

Perhaps I have misunderstood. Perhaps this tragedy is only in my perception. Could this auction of property be a form of social support?

Men in tuxedos with the shiniest shoes are moving among the crowd, rovers who seek out specific individuals, glad-handing like all slick salesmen.

"No, no I'm only here for my wife!" exclaims one of the easy marks. He is encouraged to buy, buy, buy in an extraordinarily public way that has embarrassed him. Having drawn the attention of the audience he quickly bows out.

Fading to black, the loops end as a final image appears on both screens: The auctioneer and a buyer, high-fiving the buyer's remarkable savvy, he wins! I get the message. I do not want to be a loser. There is relief among the crowd, just as patience has turned to endurance, and like so many others, I am squirming in my seat. I cannot bear it any longer. With a sing-song spake of speed, the auctioneer advises this is a good time to preview the catalogue and everyone does. Every photo a sunny day. Every photo a dream of happiness. Every photo a seduction of the mind. Every photo a promise to elevate you in the world, if you buy-in.

"Just another 10 minutes folks." The speaker evaporates into the black. Though I no longer want to be here, I do not have the courage to leave.

"You just have to relax," says a husband to his wife.

"I just don't want to miss our opportunity" she defends, taking up her calculator, reworking the numbers again, reviewing their rankings and selections.

Diet Coke is placed on the pedestals. Funny, I would have thought water, but it seems this is the drink of choice for auctioneers. Dozens of bottles are placed on the tables to the right of the stage, where last-minute changes are underway. A row of workstations are ready to process purchases. Women in business attire of plain black skirts and controlled hair organize files folders. There is much rustling of papers.

Neil Diamond bursts across the speakers and the audience in collective surprise jumps as the song "America" engulfs the senses.

"I feel good!" cries the auctioneer.

And so it begins.

"Soon to be homeowners, welcome! You have made the decision. This is THE best opportunity for the rest of your life."

Like all motivational speakers, there are promises. There is cheerleading.

"Real estate is THE American dream."

Secondary staffers take detailed photographs of the crowd, up close, operating with impunity. I have become witness and evidence in my presence here today. We are distracted by this impassioned auctioneer, who turns the language of an auction into a pseudo Sunday sermon.

New homes are first.

"Starting bid on this fine executive home…$350,000."

There is no response.

"That is still $100,000 less than valued at the peak."

The price begins to drop. The auctioneer does not like this start.

"Is this on?" He taps the microphone a second time to polite laughter.

The rovers engage their section with open arms, an invitation that is judgement, projecting animation that is not to be mistaken, as if to say, 'Well? Oh come on. This is a steal!' They work their sections hard, leaning in, coaxing those on the edge, comforting words when needed, a hand on the shoulder, but a refusal results in invisibility, and the individual is just as easily forgotten for generating nothing. There is livelier prey. The esteemed gentleman in his special seat is consulted frequently. He looks past the rovers, simply and steadfastly turning his head to indicate no, again and again.

We learn to be careful of eye contact.

The action intensifies to become a fast-paced blood-letting. They blend the rituals of baseball and football, flashing hand signals to each other, to the auctioneer, there is a code here, a language I cannot access. Signals come from behind, where I cannot see: a double chop at the waist. What does this mean? The gavel crashes. The first phase is over.

Phase 2 begins. The rovers become referees, delivering intense sharp shocks to the crowd, jolting them from their reticence with whistles ringing out every few minutes, from this side, now that, from behind and beside, prolonged and sustained; the audience cowers but the bids are not going up. A referee runs up and down the section, jumping in his urgency, he comes to an unexpected stop, hands on hips, articulated elbows, his conservative chest full in judgement. We disappoint. Another takes up the cause, kneeling in a pose and proudly taking aim as he throws his arm to a direct point for there is a winner for all to see. It is too much for the weak and the first attendees begin to leave, escaping through closed doors that flood the room with bright sunlight, a contrast to a scene underway that causes a rift between inner and outer worlds.

"Please! We ask that you do not leave until all properties are sold." The command for control was tempered, "You never know, your property might come up again."

Phase 3: Little Canada. On Manitoba Lane there is a lovely cottage reminiscent of the Newfoundland seashore, so colourful and charming I want to go fishing. On Québec Street, a more western style and I wonder if I still have my Stampede hat somewhere at the back of a closet. On Ontario, I am awed by the grand red shutters of what could well be an Eastern Township chalet. Yes, take me back to Frontenac, to Mont Sugarloaf and Lake Megantic. What possessed a developer to create this housing tract in a community called Little Canada here in the Midwest, so removed from Big Canada? Is this how we are understood? As a nation mixed up in quaint stereotypic motifs? I am left to ponder what, if any, real historic links exist between Little and Big Canada.

But Little Canada is a hard sell, at least that is how it seems to me. Dulled to the whistles, rovers shift tactics to manoeuvre buyers. They charge up and down and up and down, throwing fists in the air, "Ha!" "Aw!" War cries erupting all around, howling over us, they circle round like wolves corralling a herd of caribou. Roving, shouting, cracking the air with commanding voices, clapping hands together like gun-shots, these referees transform again into hunters, nay soldiers, the auction a battle and Little Canada, a mock War of 1812. Heads drop with fear of being attacked, or unwittingly signalling a bid.

Black suits are drawing closer, overseeing me, and I sense my furious note taking has come under surveillance. Has my secret infiltration with a Canadian perspective somehow been detected? Or simply, was my purpose clearly not to bid? I quickly close my little black book and attend to the auctioneer. I am innocent of wrong-doing, but my presence as an "emancipated spectator," "challenging the opposition between viewing [the auction] and acting [in this case with the mighty pen]," becomes a point of agitation in this spectacle (Rancière, 2009, p. 13). I am under suspicion just the same. My actions have been noticed. Will my notebook be confiscated? I do not know. I do not want to risk it.

"Sold!"

Buyers are separated, pulled out of the crowd and ushered to the waiting women, to be processed before they change their minds. The auctioneer breaks the action for a fireside chat with a backdrop of staff applause for the winners during their walk of glory to sign on the dotted line.

"The original price was $475,000. It sold at $295,000."

It was a good time to reassure the crowd because more and more take leave, including the esteemed gentleman, and I join the stream exiting, slipping out as nondescriptly as I entered, with a great sigh of relief to see again the brightness of the day beyond the darkness of the ballroom. I slip back to the conference and wonder about this remarkable experience not on the agenda of my program. How do I begin to sort through my swirling ideas and observations?

What do I make of this place where everyone is genuinely polite and friendly? I feel welcome here in the Midwest. I feel safe. Looking back, it was not until the last day I saw a sign in a bank window requesting customers leave their firearms at the door, thank you. But I am glad this conference gave me the opportunity to experience that moment in time, and much like the Stevie Wonder lyrics, I know more now than I knew then. But to what end?

Does Anyone Want Little Canada?

Although Lessing (1986) notes, "writers comment on the human condition, talk about it continually" (p. 15), what value is there in rendering this event as a creative nonfiction of life writing? What did I choose to see in those moments? Are my perceptions laced with a borderland discourse, as New (1998) describes, that accentuates the social and cultural practices *we* hold about *them*? Can I ignore the symbolism of place-names and the psycho-social dimensions that were performed that day? If I do, how do I reconcile my conviction as a life writer let alone researcher? At the same time, how do I ensure my life writing does not become just another form of morbid voyeurism, laden with the banality of too much everydayness?

Extending Benjamin's (1985) proclamation that the "storytelling that thrives for a long time in the milieu of work…is itself an artisan form of communication," I question if academic conferences as conduits for life writing can become valued sites of artful inquiry, where research as a lived experience can fester until a space opens for storytelling (p. 91). Academic conferences are practised places, as Watson (2008) states:

> A conference is a place at which the personal and the institutional converge within the surreal, giving rise to a heightened sense of conscious awareness, of self and agency …a microcosm and a strange situation both of which might have the tendency to magnify these effects. (p. 78)

As a researcher, my response to the auction was rooted in reflexive practice, a cornerstone of my identity within the academy routinely performed at conferences through sources such as direct quotes, observations, and descriptive accounts. Watson too offers an account of conference life writing but Watson is far less controversial, writing about an academic conference in Canada.

My purpose is in part to propose that we deliberately attend to how we might embrace seemingly forgotten dimensions as public intellectuals when we finally step beyond the protected campuses so often removed from the societies we serve. Academic conferences provide the ideal opportunity to cross-over and engage in what Hasebe-Ludt, Chambers and Leggo (2009) identify as complicated conversations. Through storying we have the potential to renew the tried discourses of our conferences, perhaps even finding methods to return to making a difference through acts of disclosure, resistance, and representation by writing, as Eakin (2004) states, with a commitment to telling "a 'deeper' truth which is more than mere factual accuracy but a kind of fidelity to what *is*" (p. 104). Perhaps such life writing at the intersection of academic and public discourses can serve as pedagogic encounters, where "...stories become an ethos for our times, as they expose our interdependence and interrelatedness with all of the beings of the cosmos, and the necessity of compassion and generosity in sustaining those relationships" (Hasebe-Ludt, Chambers & Leggo, 2009, p. 130).

Am I misguided? Perhaps.

Or perhaps as a life writer, I have to just keep on writin'.

REFERENCES

Benjamin, W. (1985). *Illuminations: Essays and reflections.* New York, NY: Schocken.

Eakin, P. (2004). *The ethics of life writing.* Ithaca, NY: Cornell University Press.

Hasebe-Ludt, E., Chambers, C., & Leggo, C. (2009). *Life writing and literary metissage as an ethos for our times.* New York, NY: Peter Lang.

Lessing, D. (1986). *Prisons we choose to live inside.* Concord, Ontario: Anansi.

New, W. (1998). *Borderlands: How we talk about Canada.* Vancouver, Canada: UBC Press.

Rancière, J. (2009). *The emancipated spectator.* New York, NY: Verso.

Watson, C. (2008). *Reflexive research and the (re)turn to the baroque: Or, how I learned to stop worrying and love the university.* Rotterdam, The Netherlands: Sense Publishers.

Wonder, S. (1973). Higher ground. *Innervisions* [record]. New York, NY: Tamla.

Eavesdropping as Seductive Conversation

Pat Palulis

The most seductive conversation is the conversation overheard. Eavesdropping, a one-way transgression of the boundary between private and public, is a time-honored tradition of the art gallery event. This project takes this transgressive social act and ritually enacts it within the public space of the gallery.
—Paul Lewis, Marc Tsurumaki, & David J. Lewis,
Pamphlet Architecture 21

E avesdropping is, sometimes, the only way to get what Pinar (2004) calls a "complicated conversation" to happen. Lewis, Tsurumaki and Lewis (1998) work at "exacerbating the spatial conditions of eavesdropping" evoking the "moment of complicit interaction" (p. 20). As I often travel alone, I find myself easily seduced into eavesdropping on conversations nearby. Sometimes I'm stilled and silent.

Sometimes I break and enter.

Crossing the Strait of Georgia
        on a ferry from Vancouver to Victoria an overheard conversation at a nearby table in the cafeteria becomes a subversive anecdote for my presentation at a

curriculum and pedagogy conference in Victoria. A young man has just returned from a teaching post in Korea. He is telling his companion that it was difficult to have a conversation with the Korean teachers because they didn't speak English very well. I am thinking that all of Korea should have been learning English in preparation for his arrival. Startled because this could have been me during my experience teaching in Japan. The arrogance of English in the global conversation. I interrupt the conversation and request permission to share his story. My story now homegrown with his as a temporal/spatial juxtaposition.

In the Nation's Capital

at a bus stop, at the corner of Laurier and Cumberland, waiting for the number #5 bus: a man, a white man, an Anglophone, comments on our governor-general, a woman, a black woman, a Francophone—from over there and/as he points toward Québec—as the last disparaging comment. His words incite an unruly conversation in a graduate class on democracy and education. A student in my class confronts my shocked state and queries my surprise and I am confronted with my naiveté in complicated contexts. Gregory's (2004) colonial present speaks as White Male Anglophone Meets Black Female Francophone. I wanted to follow him as he changed buses on Bank Street. But I didn't. I watched silently as he boarded the connecting bus. Enraged. So I packaged his words and brought them to class with me and then deposited them in temporary storage for intermittent release. Words hurt. Words perform.

In Tampere in Finland

at a curriculum conference, an affinity for northern topographies draws me into a conversation. Eavesdropping, I interrupt a conversation and I am on my way to Lapland with two Finnish professors and a group of South African musicians; a conference takes on deeper resonances as we leave it behind. As we dwell in the wake of complicated conversation about international curriculum, we "re-visit" the provocations. We arrive at a ski lodge in Lapland interrupting a herd of reindeer roaming about the lodge. The reindeer leave their droppings as signs of having been there. I leave these inscriptions as signs of having been there and I seek returns. We tread on boardwalks across fragile landscapes through tall towering pines. In the company of fine people, in an exquisite habitat, there is a sense of homeliness here. I don't want to leave. We pack a lunch for the return trip and my South African companions tell me that they are accustomed to picnics because during apartheid they were not allowed in restaurants. The stories were multiplicities of outrageous conditions. I hear the courage of hope and forgiveness. Those conversations have settled into my bones. Interrupting my complacencies.

And finally...

In a small cluttered office on the Fourth Floor of Lamoureux Pavillon
...as I open my inbox: I have mail...

> The inky way has its own law—to create and to break. Leaving it returns—*Aller/Retour*—slowly imploding with the sign, with its share of meaning and death. (Trinh, 2011, p. 108)

In the virtual world, one occasionally bumps into a transgressive encounter—intercepts a two-way conversation in the context of email—as it slips past the gate-keepers and swerves as a diffraction into your mailbox. You have a chance to exacerbate the spatial conditions—turn it into an event—an installation in the life-writing gallery—and to respond responsibly to the event *slowly imploding with the sign.* You find yourself eavesdropping on a conversation about your "self." Startled by the uncanny appearance of your proper name. Here you struggle with the sign *with its share of meaning and death* as you find yourself under erasure. "At-work" with the ruins of exposed erasure, with dialogical debris, with the arrogance of a knowing academia, I am stunned, shocked, and outraged. Electrified. Singed. Rendered. Mute. An attempt is being made to remove me from a doctoral committee. I thought that being on doctoral committees was part of my role in academia. Listen to a highly wired wireless connection. SomeONE has requested advice. The reader is invited to eavesdrop on fragmented excerpts of messaging:

Dear _____,

I am writing to you for advice....May I ask you to comment as soon as possible on the suitability of these members for _____'s committee.

Undisclosed author(ity)

The response arrives. I am one of three committee members under surveillance. Listen to the sentencing of my proper name:

I find no substantive connection between her research interests and the proposed thesis topic. Undisclosed author(ity)

Reading is eavesdropping too. Readings alert me to be attentive to conversations. Reading subversively in architectural texts, I find myself at-work relocating words and reconstructing messages. Tracking their new releases, I relocate Lewis,

Tsurumaki and Lewis (2008) working within the space of what they term opportunistic architecture. One-way transgressions become opportunistic tendencies. Of course, I am working with "arche-texture" engaging with opportunistic text deconstruction in sly spatialities. A trio of architects invokes the active agency of an opportunistic tactic, inverting "dubious moral implications" toward "an open, generative, and creative approach to work" seeking "opportunistic overlaps between form, space, program, material, and budget" to tease "design invention" out of the richness of possibilities latent within "restrictions and limits" (Lewis, Tsurumaki & Lewis, 2008, p. 6). One becomes vigilant waiting and watching for the opportune moment. Then *CRACK*...a faultline is exposed.

Drawn to the generative possibilities of the intertext of architecture, curriculum and pedagogy, I confess once again to an addiction for architectural pamphlets from Princeton Architectural Press. This is how I first encountered this trio of curious architects who are reading (with) Foucault:

> Curiosity is a new vice.... Curiosity, futility. The word, however, pleases me. To me it suggests something altogether different: it evokes "concern"; it evokes the care one takes for what exists and could exist; a readiness to find strange and singular what surrounds us; a certain relentlessness to break up our familiarities and to regard otherwise the same things; a fervour to grasp what is happening and what passes; a casualness in regard to the traditional hierarchies of the important and essential. (Foucault as cited in Lewis, Tsurumaki, & Lewis, 2008, p. 8)

Drawing from the provocations of limitation, this trio works at "re-visioning" generative possibilities from the cultural, economical and political conscriptions that constrain us. The trio draws our attention to the role of curiosity in provoking "a charged relationship" between the project at hand and broader discursive fields (p. 8). Working the intertext, I draw from Bhabha (2007) and his conception of global doubt: "'Doubt' is a hermeneutic of truths: it is a social practice that consists in self-inquiry, critical intelligence, ethical-political deliberation, and social interlocution" (p. 15). In my sedentary status at-home in the nation's capital, curiosity and doubt must be put to work as a social practice in conversations in corridors and random events, at bus stops, on ferries, in email. Eavesdropping becomes an opportunistic interruption. In eventual sites. I borrow a play on words from Marcus Doel (1999): S(ed)uction. I am seduced into gaming with words.

Reading about my "self" in the email, I find that my "I" is a specialist in the area of English Studies/Language Arts/Literacies. I am reading that "her" publications relate to curriculum theory, writing, and pedagogy. No mention of spatiality. My "I" becomes a "her" as a third person gendered marker for disposal. At the moment of this pronominal transference, I contemplate my future as a radical feminist. As a "specialist" in "literacies" I am diagnosed as illiterate and unable to read my suitability. Perhaps it is because I am not suited-up. "Suit-ability" not substantive. I have buried my "self" alive in the titles of my writings and dwell suspended in the space between the title and the reader. Has the reader read beyond and in-between? Having found myself contained and constrained within my titled limitations, I search for a way to smuggle out some words. Perhaps I am becoming a radical feminist cyborg.

> Feminist cyborg stories have the task of recoding communication and intelligence to subvert command and control. (Haraway, 1991, p. 175)

Partial cyborg, I am at-work, recoding sets of partial connections. "Re-constructing" my "self" as a cyborg—part fiction, part reality—attempting to "subvert control and command" with BackTalk. Marla Morris (2009) contends that "the scholar who can no longer write has lost the battle against mother" (p. 228). Recalling resisting countering the institution as intrusive mother, a writing life takes on momentum…

Returning repeatedly to the authors introduced in Derek Gregory's Human Geography Class at the University of British Columbia, I poach from Nigel Thrift (2008) as he points me "in the direction of fugitive work in the social sciences and humanities which can read the little, the messy and the jerry-rigged as a part of politics and not just incidental to it" (p. 197). In this paper, I have been working with *little* words, *messy* text, and *jerry-rigged* games, as a part of the narrative of academe and *not just incidental to it*. Grateful for this invitation to participate in a compository of learning lives, my transformations are always a charged relationship. Marla Morris (2009) encourages us to let Gramsci be our guide: "We can smuggle out our dissenting counter-cultural thoughts through writing" (p. 217). I begin the word running: I, find, no,…each punctuated pause another chance to take a risk. I want to stage a redux as performative response. I poach the space of the *interstitial* from Cixous and Calle-Gruber (1997) from the entry to rootprints of memory and life writing.

Words on the run: I, find, no,. . . . .
. . . .
. . . . .SUBstantive,. . . . .
. . . . .connection,
. . . . .between. . . . .

I, find, no…these are very *little* words punctuated with pauses. Multisyllabic words can be *messy*. What does substantive mean? A word is in danger of losing its declaration of certainty as I find multiple connections and affinities within the in-between. Perhaps the imperial "I" got lost in the in-between. Stalled. Tangled up in the wirings of (dis)connection. The singularity of the "I" has disposed with the heterogeneity of contextual topographies. As the words are smuggled out of the message, a writer hitches a ride...

Language is (the) only medium that gives the time at once stopped and mobile to inscribe the interstitial.

(Cixous & Calle-Gruber, 1997, p. 80)

The arrogance of the academic "I" requesting the knowledge to be delivered undercover. The arrogance of the response, as psychoanalytic exposure of the habit of saying more than you know. The theorists of the graduate student writing life come alive on the tenure track—not just one epistemology but multiplicities to take you in hand. When I arrive at the threshold of the officiating door to seek an explanation, I am confronted with those "language games" that I play. Prefaced that this should not be construed as condescending. The "not-ness" of the "not" already designating a habitat for the signification of *condescension*. I begin my descent: Air Canada Flight 1107. A plane lands in Winnipeg. I am going to the MOSAIC Conference (Freud after Derrida) at the University of Manitoba to hear keynote speaker, Sam Weber, present his paper entitled: The singular heterogeneity of the "I." I am here for just this one presentation. I return to re-readings of *Just Gaming* with Jean-François Lyotard and Jean-Loup Thébaud (1985) and find myself consuming their words: "gaming in fine company." How does one learn to live with the arrogance of academia? The unrelenting surveillance? I am returned through writing to engage in *exacerbating the spatial conditions of eavesdropping* evoking the *moment of complicit interaction...*consuming and responding. I retreat to my library of books tracking words and silences looking for close readings with Julian Wolfreys (2000):

> To read "read" necessarily dictates the necessity of being open to receiving numerous significations, a complex web of possible meanings, a skein of traces and inscriptions within the single—and singular—word. In order to be able to begin reading what it means to read, one must open oneself to the idea that what is read is only a momentary recognition. It is perhaps a fleeting response to a certain pulse or rhythm. In order to stabilize that act of reading, one must perform the reading with a degree of violence, even while, and as a corollary of such violence, what is read is never wholly read. Something remains, something is left behind, something is missed altogether, something other is still yet to be read. (p. vii)

The violence of installing meaning—*a momentary recognition*—in response to *a certain pulse or rhythm*—political significations perhaps decided in advance. After repeated requests for clarity, another request is issued: a request for names to replace me, 4–5 names from each of two sources. It could take 8–10 names to replace me following my disposal. My decapitation is pending. A possibility of ten names for consideration. Are we now entering a *jerry-rigged* game? I am a fugitive from clarity. I meet one of the players of the *jerry-rigged* game outside a supermarket. We recognize each other. I take the risk of exposing my rage. I am told but it's over now. It's better now. I reply that it's only just beginning. Just gaming in the intertext. I wrench a string of words out of contextual holdings. Listen to Paul Miller (2007) as punctuated spatiality:

> Current. Electricity. Movement. Textuality. (p. 182)

Perhaps there is a case for movement and textuality in a high-stakes game. Perhaps I am back in the game now dealing a double hand. I am suddenly reconnected, plugged in to an electrical shock. The punctuated "stop" only adds to the suspense. How is it possible to separate movement from textuality? Someone has not been reading the French poststructuralists. Theoretical traces arrive to escort me back to the games table. Cixous insists: "I have a passion for stops. But for there to be a stop, there must be a current, a coursing of the text" (as cited in Cixous and Calle-Gruber, 1997, p. 64). Reading further, I find another affinity with Cixous: "my texts recycle themselves, but I don't think they repent" (p. 64).

Working in a bilingual university, one of my favourite French words is *mainmise* [handheld]. I was about to admit defeat and wanted to withdraw following the onslaught of demands for clarity and at the moment of the request for names. The repeated assault of the insult was becoming too agonistic. But I was reminded by the student's supervisor that it would be a betrayal to the student if I withdrew from the committee. It would be a betrayal to the student's supervisor. It would be a betrayal to the work of my mentors at the University of British Columbia. It would be a betrayal to my self. The institution as intrusive mother is a *cauchemar* [Pinar's "nightmare" takes on new resonances in French]. Just re-reading the email exchange, I am dangerously close to getting caught up once again into that *current disorder* and I struggle to work at *recoding communication* and *subverting command and control.*

As I work at rage *unwoven* I return to draw on Miller's *uncanny.* It is uncanny to work in a bilingual university that so often refuses the French poststructuralist conceptions of textuality and movement. Some of us are missing each other in the *interstitial* spaces of Cixous and Calle-Gruber. I struggle to hold on to a lifeline with my own graduate student experiences. It is a fragile tenuous lifeline but one that sustains possibilities for survival. The agonistic stance is broken only with the exquisite work that students create, with richly complicated conversations with colleagues, with coded door messages screaming silent signals to passers-by. However difficult it can become, I have learned that I must respond. Words must be smuggled out and put to work. Just gaming with Lyotard and

Thébaud (1985), I find Weber in the Afterword: he draws from Nietzsche's conception of ambivalence. Listen: "Nietzsche's conceptions lead us to ask whether it is not rather ambivalence—in other words, a certain *tension* between unity and disunity—that characterizes all games as such" (p. 113). The game becomes the seduction; the desire is to stay in the game. In my outrage, I sometimes forget that struggle is a necessary form of communication between one game and another. With Lewis, Tsurumaki and Lewis (2008), I must dwell "in the messy tension that exists in the middle of the playing field, being, as it were, caught up in the game" (p. 11). S(ed)uction redux...

Postscript: I have mail: Sendspace has sent me a file, a dissertation text. It is winter in the nation's capital. The skaters are on the canal. Cocooned in boiled wool and goat hair socks, a llama wool scarf and alpaca wrist warmers from local artisans, I dwell with my cluttering of books, s(ed)uction into elsewhere spaces. In my temporary tenancy in the nation's capital, I slowly gather local artifacts to dwell with global collections. From art-in-the-park, a stained-glass cellist in forested shards of multiple hues has taken up residence with a small mischievous clay angel from Lapland. Three tin crows chatter silently on the window sill. My "I" circulates within a polyphony of other "I" sites at-work in an atelier of writers and readers. A polyphonic circuitry that is alive with generative possibilities. The *singular heterogeneity* of my "I" shall soon be downloading a dissertation...

REFERENCES

Bhabha, H. (2007). Ethics and aesthetics of globalism: A postcolonial perspective. In A. P. Ribeiro (Ed.), *The urgency of theory* (pp. 1–20). Manchester, England: Carcanet/Calouste Gulbenkian Foundation.

Cixous, H., & Calle-Gruber, M. (1997). *Hélène Cixous, rootprints: Memory and life writing* (E. Prenowitz, Trans.). London, England: Routledge.

Doel, M. (1999). *Poststructuralist geographies: The diabolical art of spatial science*. Lanham, MD: Rowman & Littlefield.

Gregory, D. (2004). *The colonial present: Afghanistan, Palestine, Iraq*. Mississauga, Canada: Wiley-Blackwell.

Haraway, D. (1991). *Simians, cyborgs and women: The reinvention of nature*. New York, NY: Routledge.

Lewis, P., Tsurmaki, M., & Lewis, D. J. (1998). *Pamphlet Architecture 21: Situation Normal*. New York, NY: Princeton Architectural Press.

Lewis, P., Tsurumaki, M., & Lewis, D. J. (2008). *Opportunistic architecture*. New York, NY: Princeton Architectural Press.

Lyotard, J-F., & Thébaud, J-L. (1985). *Just gaming*. Minneapolis, MN: University of Minnesota Press.

Miller, P. D. (2007). Uncanny/Unwoven. In A. P. Ribeiro (Ed.), *The urgency of theory* (pp. 168–190). Manchester, England: Carcanet/Calouste Gulbenkian Foundation.

Morris, M. (2009). *On not being able to play: Scholars, musicians and the crisis of psyche.* Rotterdam, The Netherlands: Sense Publishers.

Pinar, W. F. (2004). *What is curriculum theory?* Mahwah, NJ: Lawrence Erlbaum.

Thrift, N. (2008). *Non-representational theory: Space/politics/affect.* London, England: Routledge.

Trinh, M. T. (2011). *Elsewhere, within here: Immigration, refugeeism and the boundary event.* New York, NY: Routledge.

Weber, S. (1985). Afterword: Literature—just making it. In J-F. Lyotard & J-L. Thébaud, *Just gaming* (pp. 101–120). Minneapolis: University of Minnesota Press.

Wolfreys, J. (2000). *Readings: Acts of close reading in literary theory.* Edinburgh, Scotland: Edinburgh University Press.

Death of the Black Cat

Bruce Hunter

The grey cat peers from the night table and whines
  so unlike him, urgent, and when I rise to feed him,
the silver tabby around my ankles, I find the black cat
lying before the bedroom door on his side,
my hand goes to his ribs, the chest no longer rises,
the body is warm, the tail still supple between my fingers.
He's died in mid-stride, returning from the birds feeding
at the front window at dawn, cat television in our house,
coming back to my wife's pillow, his heart likely,
after the months of death watch, the vet warned us he won't come back
easily next time, but she'll try, there's a heart murmur
in the strange little creature with a shortened tail
that appeared at our door on a winter day 10 years ago
and after months of feeding him,
on my birthday we let him in and he never left
pleased with a warm place and food, my wife's pillow at night
on my cap or coat, sometimes even my keys. A lost cat found us
on the trail for 3,000 years to the Highland crofts

from the savannas and the fires, feeding with us and following.
The tabby and the grey watch as I stroke him
and gasp, "Oh no." My wife suddenly awake begins to sob,
and from the next room my old friend Billy,
tall and grizzened, a farmer now, goes with me,
as the sun comes up,
the black cat wrapped in a towel with a unicorn on it,
burying superstition and myth in the same grave,
I hold him in its sling, his head and the supple tail
still drooping, but his eyes don't answer me.
I lay him on the grass in a grove of black cedars
that seems always to have been waiting for this
where my wife's family buried generations of dogs,
her pet duck, and someone's pony.
A scene somewhat Faulknerian in Southern Ontario,
as I sharpen my spade with a file, Billy watches
and my wife cradles the black cat and softly wails.
We are childless, and these animals are more than children, perfect
and silent as children never should be.
I cut the sod and square the hole, bevelling the sides,
a perfect small grave, my wife later asks me about,
how did you know to do it,
and I can't explain, even the gravediggers I worked amongst
in the Niagara cemetery drove backhoes,
perhaps it's an earlier memory than my own I tell her
and I was a gardener not a gravedigger, planting never burying
work always began in hope not despair.
Billy stops me, think it's deep enough, he says, as if I've been digging
for something bigger, all my life, watching his father the Dutch gardener,
him 7 years gone now, so much behind us,
both of us still learning from him,
watching, though the Ogden boys we once were,
growing up beside the railyards,
never called it a spade, always a shovel
but all I'm sure of now is the earth between the hard metal and my hands,
carefully mounding it beside the small deep hole,
everything deserves this grace, my wife hands him to me,
and I kiss the black fellow's snout before I lower him
and she tosses in a stuffed mouse he loved,

what's good enough for the pharaohs,
is good enough for the black cat,
no tears in front of Billy, though we'd both understand.
When it's done, I tamp the earth gently,
replace the sod and for weeks afterward
everywhere in the shadows I see the black cat
waiting for him to come out.
My wife says nothing, we are past the time of children
but not the time of desire or noticing,
or the need to love something both smaller and greater than ourselves,
to pass on the lives we've lived, or the love,
whatever the reasons we choose, if we do, to have children,
seeing the joy in the lives of my friends
and their children, though they tell me
if they could do it again, they wouldn't, the words
of the blessed. To have had love, it's easy now to say,
we could have done without.
A month after we buried the black cat,
the grave's level and only an outline of gravel
where the grass is slow to grow
between the black cedars, I come home
from travelling tired and at 2:00 a.m.
my wife wakes me, I'm wheezing like a cow and my breath stops,
and we drive to Emergency,
humid air in the windows of the truck, our town quiet,
and I lay for a long time, listening
to the woman in the next bed, crying, whose transplant has failed,
to the children in pain and I'm grateful for only this.
The doctor orders x-rays and I'm wheeled through the darkened
halls, the hazy breeze lifting my gown, the automatic doors open
one after another, and this is a small town, I will see her tomorrow
at the market or Tim Hortons, I apologize to the sleepy radiologist,
for getting her up. But she laughs and lifts my arms around the x-ray,
and I hug the machine that stares into my heart.
It's nothing I tell my wife, before I drift, intravenous in my arm,
we'll be fine. Until I'm wakened by her hand on my shoulder,
the doctor shows me the outline of my heart, the fluid,
enlarged, failure the only words I hear. My father and I
longest ticking of all those damn Scots' hearts,

no uncles or grandfathers in my family.
There is the banality of evil and the ordinariness of death,
as he sends me home to wait for the tests and my own doctor,
I am not afraid, this is how it happens to most of us, one day we
go and they tell us, it's time. The details suddenly don't matter anymore.
I sit up, watching the sun rise over the house
the black cedars full of birds now as they were last winter,
thousands warming the air with their wings,
they scrabble in the eaves,
swinging down to the feeders, jays, grackles, in the trees, crows,
on the roof mourning doves.
I sleep on the couch where the black cat did,
watching the sparrows in the dogwood, and the goldfinches.
Later I go to my desk, the form the lawyer gave me years ago for a will,
but I'd scoffed, too soon,
and I find my pen, write instructions for the work
that needs to be done
notes for the book I've nearly finished, but I've no regrets.
For 12 hours I wait, unable to sleep, but not awake,
walking in the yard I've cleared of dead trees,
opening it to the sky, like the prairies of my youth,
I'm not old, only no longer young, and I'm grateful for the bushes I've planted,
Weigela and ferns, Nootka Cypress, purple-leaf Hazel and the new maples,
the green lope of the lawn towards the swans and the river.
Always I've wanted land I could die on,
though I know unlike the black cat I won't be buried here.
I'm grateful for these hours
until the doctor calls, there's been a mistake,
something about the x-ray and the intern's inexperience,
a friend he apologizes for, I had supper with him the other night.
The way it is in small towns. I thank him, later my wife is angry,
but I'm grateful for both the news,
and the rehearsal, never wasting anything in my life,
except time, knowing now that I have days, months,
or maybe years, but not forever, one day
this is how it will be
and it's a shame to waste a death or a life
and that I would have done it all again.

An Ethic of Humility

Alexandra Fidyk

Works of art are indeed always products of having been in danger, of having gone to the very end in an experience, to where man can go no further.
— Rainer Maria Rilke, *Letters of R. M. Rilke, 1982-1910*

The cure for suffering—which is the collision of consciousness with unconsciousness—is not to be submerged in unconsciousness, but to be raised to consciousness and to suffer more. The evil of suffering is cured by more suffering, by higher suffering. Do not take opium, but put salt and vinegar in the soul's wound, for when you sleep and no longer feel the suffering, you are not. And to be, that is imperative. Do not then close your eyes to the agonizing Sphinx, but look her in the face, and let her seize you in her mouth, and crunch you with her hundred thousand poisonous teeth, and swallow you. And when she has swallowed you, you will know the sweetness of the taste of suffering.

— Miguel de Unamuno,
In Carl Jung's *Visions: Notes of the Seminar Given in 1930–1934*

December 2, 2009

Driving along the winding cliff roads of Malibu, I avoid the 101 freeway. I welcome extra driving time, more lights, frequent stops just to be near the

Pacific. She roars and crashes on my left. How I miss this place: its rhythm, its briny scent, its wild force.

The call comes.

I can barely steer around the curves as I hear the diagnosis. I should pull over and stop. At the least reduce my speed. I don't, not until later as the news and what I know of the disease reaches my core. When I do stop, I don't know how I will continue driving.

So many tests, questions, queries. Things that just have not been right.

Too many tumours, surgeries, hospitalizations. Symptoms that didn't match illnesses—no nice, neat packages.

The verdict: Lyme disease with co-infections of *Bartonella* and *Mycolplasma pneumoniae*. Chronic, neurological degeneration.

A death sentence.

The laundry list of symptoms—chronic pain, fatigue, vertigo, memory loss, confusion, brain fog, irritability—located. An explanation for getting lost when driving to campus; forgetting dates, events, and conversations; losing track of thought and speech in the middle of them; acting in ways that are unfamiliar even to me. A connection to my dream (six months earlier) of being diagnosed with Alzheimer's and waking in sheer panic with the immediate conviction to demand extensive medical testing.

I get to my hotel in Ventura and sit. Speechless.

The sun just out my window. The sea: I can hear it and smell it and am so grateful for this. I am consumed by a different kind of whirling now—not vertigo—but the unravelling of a life.

My life.

December 4, 2009

Another verdict. At the heart of the symptoms and cause for immediate action is an inflamed brain: swollen, burning up, pushing against a skull that will not give way; a vital organ in crisis. This after other organs, bones, tissue have surrendered.

The results of the MRI: generalized brain atrophy.

My brain is dying.

I spend a day frozen in my room. Not sure who to call, what to ask or say. Finding the faint old remnants of wanting to use my will to push back against present circumstances. This is one time that I must surrender. This is not a time to fight. This is not a choice. This is a time to accept the actual state of affairs.

I call a friend to help me find my way through the Collective Agreement and prepare a letter with recent reports to request a medical leave.

December 9, 2009

On the eve of departure, I attend a talk by James Hillman on *active imagination*. He is addressing *The Red Book*, the recordings of Jung's own psychological descent. I like being here, in this beautiful hall, with a hushed reverence for this man and for the spirit of the work that he is about to address. Hillman begins: 1914, Jung's way of being in the world has collapsed. It is a key time as it parallels WWI.

I get comfortable with pen and notebook, poised for the correspondences that are about to flow. I am suddenly aware, however, that there is no inner activation, no arousal. Usually, I am filled with rapid-fire connections, phrases spring to mind, relevant readings ring out, images and ideas for new writing pop, pop, pop. Nothing happens. There is no corresponding outpouring. I am simply sitting and hearing. I look around—the effect seems to be taking hold of others—there are nods; smiles; expressions of comprehension, agreement, and interest. Yet for me, there is nothing, only a new kind of silence and growing stillness, not the kind that I have studied, written of, practised and welcomed for years. This silence scares me for it comes when all sources of insight have been closed or blocked. I only hear and what I hear dissolves. With a sudden great panic, I take notes. I record the words that I can catch. Yet I miss many. It is a failed effort to hang on to the world as I have known it. But really they are just words, moving through me, taking hold of nothing and falling away. It is a feeble attempt to preserve on the page what I fear losing. It is not about the words, the night or Hillman's talk. I fear that I am losing myself.

> Hillman says that soul making is a *"disintegrative method"* of depth; it refers to the mythologems of Hades.
>
> Hades, the God of depths, the God of invisibles, the God of the hidden wealth or riches of the Earth.
>
> Heraclitus was the first to bring together *"psyche," "logos,"* and *"bathun"* (depth): *"You could not find the ends of the soul though you travelled every way, so deep is its logos"* (Hillman, 1979, p. 25). To enter the descent of illness and loss, one is obliged to turn to Heraclitus. He suggests that true equals deep, a viewpoint of soul, which sounds akin to *"understand."* To arrive at a basic understanding, we must look from below, from beneath; we must go into its darkness.

Monday, December 16, 2009

Specialists seen in Canada and the United States. Extensive protocols and treatments, approximately two hours each morning. I am too weak to begin treatment immediately. Too much risk of collapse or a Herxsheimer effect.

We address the brain first: reduce inflammation, build the immune system, detoxify.

Pills, pills and more pills, 60 a day, more if I don't react with diarrhea, vertigo, nausea.

Body Rules.

Nothing goes on any more inside my head.

Nothing received from the collective mind either.

I feel vacant and hollow. I follow instructions with sticky notes everywhere. What was second nature now takes great effort and concentration.

January 10, 2010

The glutathione inhaler at bedtime brings wild, vivid, violent dreams.

I wake in full body sweat. I don't know where I am.

I can no longer read. I try each day; no improvement. I am no longer bothered that my house is not unpacked or organized since the move from California in August. The books remain in boxes because I don't recognize them. I don't recall reading any of them although they are dog-eared and well pencilled.

I rarely go up to my study now as two flights of stairs leave me winded, out of breath. I sit at the top, waiting for the spin to subside.

Descent has come quickly.

February 8, 2010

I stop trying to read. The books stay piled by my reading chair and bed. They collect dust and tissues. I submit to the inevitable. My day consists of treatments, rest, food, and sleep. I no longer am bothered by the necessity to relinquish everything. I have ceased to care, ceased to belong.

There are no calls, no visitors. The world has shrunk to the space of my kitchen, washroom, bed, and chaise. The resistance felt a few months ago is gone.

I have come undone.

February 12, 2010

No feeling. No emotion. No desire. No energy. No thoughts. No anticipation. No plans.

Time has slowed.

Life passes me by.

What remains: Waiting. Wait without wanting.

Spend hours each day in the clinic. Rigorous IV protocols have started. So many rotating medications. A calendar taped to the kitchen cupboard tracks start-and-stop dates of pills, antibiotics, and treatments, along with the life cycles of those who have invaded me—living, breeding, dying—my body as host is their captive.

Fatigued. Exhausted. Spent.

> He came repeatedly to my home.
> At first he came only at night,
> quietly, and without detection.
> With time, he grew fearless
> and came by light.
>
> At first he stole only little things
> not readily missed.
> Slowly, and persistently,
> he took more and more
> until everything was gone.

July 10, 2010

> I woke
> stripped to the bone.

July 14, 2010

I woke this morning engulfed by darkness. Swallowed by black. It has been at my door for years. But for the last few months, it has found its way in, seeping through crevices, cracks around windows, spaces between walls: it has entered my home and so it has entered me. Today though, there is no separation.

> I am it.
> I am Black.
> Black, Black, Black.
> I never knew there was Blacker than Black.

July 17, 2010

The aggressive course of antibiotics has been successful in wearing down the *Spirochete*, although it is a cruel irony to regain cognitive function and to lose everything that I once believed in. Somehow, as my mind has slowly returned, something else has invaded. Not a gradual taking over, as these past months have been, but a violent stripping. Philosophies, theories, laws, stories, practice, experience taken. The entire frame of my intellectual construct fleshed out with years of living.

Taken.

Only one law remains.
Gravity.
And I have become leaden with Black.

Today concludes my medical leave. A long list calls as entrance into the world of academe.

July 18, 2010

I awake from sleep with a distinct sense of being buried up to my chest in the Earth.
No other elements exist here.
No air, no fire, no water.
No movement.
I am simultaneously both pushed down and pulled from under.

July 20, 2010

I wake to dripping along the window edge and the doorframe of my bedroom closet. The white ceiling plaster drops off on and around my bed like paste. I get up and step onto a soggy carpet. I go downstairs. Water pours in through light sockets on the main floor; the ceiling has already come down. I push furniture back. Put out buckets. Remove shoes and clothes from closets. Spread out towels to soak up water.

Two days later a demolition crew of five has stormed in and torn apart the ceilings, insulation, drywall, carpets, and hardwood on two floors. My bedroom and living room stripped to raw plywood and beams. Other areas are in upheaval. Industrial fans and humidifiers groan and hum.
That which has held me safely has collapsed.
Again.

July 27, 2010

Black mould.
Speckled spores cover the plywood ceiling in my bedroom.

A crew is hired to treat the living virus of my most-intimate living space.
Black without;
Black within.

Cats and I make plans to head to the family farm in Saskatchewan.

July 31, 2010

I talked with S today. I described what I was experiencing but I could not make it palpable for him. He mirrored back what he heard by naming it.
I say, "No, no, no."
Frustration comes with living something and its incomprehensibility to another.

What do we know of another's life except through empathy, *em-pathos*, in-feeling? Only through an empathic sensing of the other, a capacity to feel with and to share the other's presence might we glimpse another's life—and, not by a collapse or reduction of feeling into a definition, categorization or pathology. Even to allow oneself to feel into such darkness is, for some, too much.

How does one speak of a feeling of nothingness and have it held? Witnessed? How does another get close enough to "feel-in" without fearing contamination by the very experience that asks something of us?

I try again with L. My girlfriend says, "Severe depression."
I say, "No."
"It is Black," I say again.
I've been stripped, robbed of everything. Yet it is not that I feel that things have been taken, as if I could give an account of them. Rather, it is that there is nothing to account for. Even the old view that light is always present—some-where—is a lie.

"In alchemy, the loss of light renders the soul burnt out, dried up, and picked bare, leaving only skeletal remains" (Marlan, 2005, p. 26).

"The black sun, blackness, putrefactio, mortificatio, the nigredo, poison-ing, torture, killing, decomposition, rotting, and death all form a web of interrelations that describe a terrifying, if most often provisional, eclipse of consciousness or of our conscious standpoint" (Marlan, 2005, p. 11). This blackness or nigredo is part of the initial process in alchemy and marks a descent into the unconscious. It belongs to the operation of mor-

tificatio *which, literally, means "killing" and refers to the experience of death. Jung (1953) refers to the descent into darkness as* nekyia *and uses this Greek word to designate a "journey to Hades, a descent into the land of the dead" (p. 52).*

Here is where I currently live. The land of Black. The Blackest Black receded to the borders, but I am still resident in this place. Gloria Anzaldúa (1987) wrote that "when pain, suffering and the advent of death become intolerable...Coatlicue, the Earth, opens and plunges us into its maw, devours us" (p. 46). I am reminded of the initial image of the Sphinx's "hundred thousand poisonous teeth" and Jung's advice to look her in the face and let her crunch you. Shamans, Indigenous peoples, and those who have not abandoned the ancestors and spirit world believe that when the underworld gods/goddesses call upon you, there is no escape. To understand the dark truths of such a beckoning requires a return to the Earth, a swallowing by the Sphinx, a burial in the "mud mother."

Like Hades, traditional peoples believed in a life-giving goddess of the underworld known variously as Hecate, Erishkegal, Coatlicue, Cerridwen, Oya, Kali, and other names. She has been simply called the Hag who resides in an ancient, ancestral cave awaiting the inevitable return of the ill and the haunted who seek restoration, noting "there was no escaping the calling, the caves, the mud mothers....No escape" (Bambara, as cited in Duff, 1993, p. 127). She embodies the law of ruthless necessity, the regulatory force of nature. On a personal level, her presence is experienced as fate, and the physical limits and requirements of our living is painfully evident in extremes, of both the bodily and psychological kind.

Here is my encounter with the Hag. She came to me in a dream last night. She asked why I was still struggling to remain above ground. That while part of me was still not encased in the belly of the Earth, "it" was really just an illusion. Why not lift my arms into the air and let the rest of my body sink into the Earth?

What I have sensed for some time, yet cannot say for certain, is that some time early in this descent, something signalled me north. Something called me home, back to a place of familiarity and family, and without knowing why at a deeper level, I moved. The Greeks called "being" *parousia.* Its translation is a cluster of significations comprising "homestead, at-homeness, a homecoming." It is to this ground that one must strive to come home—"a return to true self" which requires that one "enters an abyss deeper than hell itself" (Jung, 1959, p. 135)—the process and goal of authentic being.

Many years ago, too, I heard a phrase that has since stuck with me: "all sickness is home sickness" and its inversion, "all healing is coming home" (Connelly, 1993, p. xvi). I am acutely aware of the interrelatedness of this ailing body; the loss of memory, mind, and identity; Hillman's reference to Jung's collapse; my flooded home; this dream body partially buried; the presence of Hades and the Hag; and their symbolic importance to being "called home." Home, for me, literally resonates with the rich, black humus of the Saskatchewan farm. It symbolizes a life lived closely with "Nature," her rhythms, beauty, and cruelty. Life lived closely with seasons and the moon, letting one's pulse resonate with the waxing and waning of light. Life located in family, community, birth, and death. I left this place long ago, and while I always return, somewhere I lost its inherent balance.

Black humus is not just any soil. It refers to organic matter that has reached a point of stability, where it will break down no further. If conditions are maintained, it may remain essentially stable for centuries. Human, humanity, humble, humility—all find their roots in this terrain. It is into this humble terra that I surrender.

> *Life writings often speak of the gifts of such journeys. We read them before descent begins and again well after ascent. In both locations, we are safe and free from the dangers of the underworld. Writing during descent is less common. We do not often write of the hell and agony, destruction and loss that are experienced during these times. Similarly, we do not often find pleasure in reading them either. Such writing, however, is not aimed to draw attention to the "I" but to invite empathy for the human condition, to better understand the complexities involved in soul making, and to mark the difference between being simply overwhelmed and bearing witness to the extremity. As Annie Dillard (1989) advises, even in these dark times, we must: "Push it. Examine all things intensely and relentlessly....Do not leave it, do not course over it, as if it were understood, but instead follow it down until you see it in the mystery of its own specificity and strength" (p. 78). The alchemists, likewise, assure us that there is a shining even in the blackest of black and that is where light and rebirth will be found.*

Two nights later, I dream and awake suddenly. The suffering is enormous. It steals my breath; it drives a jag of pain into my chest. I think that I will die of a heart-ache. Then I remember the dream.

I am back in the Earth, where I left off—up to my arms, chest in the Earth—but I do not lift my arms into the air. Instead, I slowly and gently bring them to my sides. Quietly, I assume the *corpse pose*. There is no hesitation, no resistance. My breath becomes deeper, more pronounced. I close my eyes. Time slows. Movements slow. Breath slows. Then some kind of mucous membrane, an embryonic sac, encloses me. In this hypnopompic state of sleep to waking dream to dreaming onward, I feel my body in corpse pose sliding—a slow, steady, sloping descent. Encased in this egg-like coffin, I ride into the Underworld.

REFERENCES

Anzaldúa, G. (1987). *Borderlands/La frontera*. San Francisco, CA: Sisters/Aunt Lute Book Company.

Connelly, D. (1993). *All sickness is homesickness*. Columbia, MD: Traditional Acupuncture Institute.

Dillard, A. (1989). *The writing life*. New York, NY: Harper & Row.

Duff, K. (1993). *The alchemy of illness*. New York, NY: Bell Tower.

Hillman, J. (1979). *The dream and the underworld*. New York, NY: Harper & Row.

Jung, C. G. (1953). *Psychology and alchemy* (R. F. C. Hull, Trans.). Princeton, NJ: Princeton University Press.

Jung, C. G. (1959). *Aion: Researches into the phenomenology of the self* (R. F. C. Hull, Trans.). Princeton, NJ: Princeton University Press.

Jung, C. G. (1997). *Visions: Notes of the seminar given in 1930-1934* (Vol. 2, C. Douglas, Ed.). Princeton, NJ: Princeton University Press.

Marlan, S. (2005). *The black sun: The alchemy and art of darkness*. College Station, TX: Texas A & M.

Rilke, R. M. (1945). *Letters of R. M. Rilke, 1982-1910* (J. B. Greene & H. Norton, Trans.). New York, NY: W. W. Norton.

Fieldnotes of a Punjabi-Canadian Researcher

Hartej Gill

My parents breathe in the last of India. The house is emptied of all life and belongings. All that is left is what hangs from the ceilings, the Komagata Maru men, their blood dripping on the bare white walls. From the kotas *can be heard cries and laments. Relentless pain. Stories long forgotten or unheard in other lands will echo eternally in this village, even when it is abandoned. Stories abandoned for other stories. For rags-to-riches stories. Snow-White-Cinderella stories.*

My parents try to erase the painful past from their memory as they prepare to betray their country, their home, their HIStory, their ancestors.

Instead, they try to redeem themselves. They speak of the family they helped during the Partition. In sorrow, they wonder if the Muslim family who buried their jewels in our bara *will ever come back to find them. Did they even survive? Did they make it over the b/order? Forced out of a country we are leaving by choice. My parents pray that if they return, they will find their riches by the* Saron *tree where they left them.*

Suitcases in hand they close the door slowly and sadly with a silent prayer. We walk down the long stairway in the darkness of the late evening. As we arrive at the bottom step we see for the last time the family who sleeps there under our awning. The husband, his wife and child, who beg throughout the streets of the village by day, always return here by night. This is their home, their imposed home. The home we are leaving is the home they return to. The one they are compelled to be committed to.

We walk over them, as we have become accustomed to doing. But this time is different than all the other times that we have walked over their bodies. This time as we walk over their bodies, we are walking over all the bodies of our ancestors.

Voices. Hartej Gill, 2003

Their ashes are here in this earth. Nurturing us with a constant reminder of their resistance and their despair. The rice of this land still grows with traces of a colonizer's skin.

This time as we walk over their bodies we are pained by a sense of selfish forgetfulness and shameful regret. As we walk away we know they are watching, but if we do not look back, perhaps they may never see the treason written on our betraying bodies.

From the golden domes of Delhi, our plane flies into the silvery sky and I am home away from home always searching for my home.

T his prose was written as a way of portraying the challenging social reality of finding home in the diasporic in-between in Canada, with its multicultural policies of tolerance and tokenistic benevolence rather than genuine decolonization. At that time, I never imagined that finding home in the academy would also be a painful and colonial process, one involving constant negotiation between a predetermined institutional journey and a betrayal to one's communities. The more I search for home in society and in the academy, the more Kobayashi's (2009) words become significant: "Systemic racism is a normative aspect of Canadian ways of doing things, and deeply entrenched within university culture" (p. 61). Henry and Tator (2009) further elaborate that "the Tenure process is seen as one of the most powerful examples of institutionalized racism, where-by individuals are punished or rewarded based on the adherence to obsolete rules and standards designed to ensure conformity to Whiteness and maleness" (p. 30). In my experience, these unwritten yet well-known rules are entrenched in every layer of the institution and mobilize in multiply compounded, very complex, and interlocking ways. For example, the unstated standards of the individual focussed counting game of "proper" publications not only homogenizes one's identity but also erases or at least minimizes the importance of community responsibility, relationality, integrity, and activism. This work increases in merit the more one can demonstrate engagement with the global, often at the cost of disengagement with the local. In some cases, the ethics of transferability even become secondary to the institutional requirements of "international impact." Any questioning of this colonial and patriarchal system results in utter and complete silence—room-fulls of some of the brightest individuals in the world have nothing to say—or fear saying something. This neutrality also renders the one who resists conformity—not out of disrespect for institutional norms, but rather out of an ethical responsibility to change "HIStory"—as an outsider, someone to regard with suspicion, someone who seems to be trying to get something for nothing. The nothingness being the work of community "service," activism, and decolonization: all things that aren't considered meritorious yet live deeply in the soul of the colonial body, of the diasporic body. *Publish or perish* is the motto that has been drilled into my head over my last 3 years in the academy. How does an immigrant, an anti-colonial feminist, social-justice activist, decolonizing scholar find home in such a place?

Although socially constructed hegemonic norms make "finding home" in the academy (as in society) an elusive process, and doubly so for a member of the diaspora, fortunately I have experienced moments of "being there." These inviting and embodied spaces have opened up during disruptive teaching/learning moments on social justice, or in dialogue with a passionate student, community or faculty member working in the area of decolonization, or when reading an anti-colonial-focussed dissertation or while engaging in activist research. These have all been transformative moments when the apolitical and the ahistorical in the academy have been vigorously questioned or challenged.

My recent project in schools in the lower mainland of British Columbia where I have been teaching, learning, and researching with South Asian educators and youth has been one of the most fulfilling experiences of "being at home." This project, albeit untraditional in terms of many academic norms, emerged when two very committed and passionate educators and I came together in a university class that I was teaching. Our activist interests converged into a decolonizing activism-research initiative the day they recounted the story of how their school had an unwritten rule that did not allow boys of "Indo-Canadian" background to walk together in the hallways of their school because of the fear of their gangster activity. If even one Caucasian boy was part of this group the boys were not "broken up"; however, if the group was made up solely of "Indo Canadians" they were asked to separate.... Hearing this story was so emotionally, cognitively, and spiritually moving that I am certain my ancestors were there with me during the intense stillness of this profound life-altering moment. I was immediately propelled and compelled to advocacy work with these educators in their school, which eventually became the educational activism and research context. In my experience, as is the case in this study, educational activism and decolonizing research do not begin with institutional requirements or goals of research, but rather co-emerge or are co-created relationally from a sense of ethical responsibility or as a result of passionate activism/advocacy. Our elders, in the Punjabi culture, also believe that at moments when our unique journeys come together inexplicably, it is a sign that our ancestors are close by, collectively encouraging us in meaningful and spiritual ways. The educators and I, guided by the knowledge and wisdom of our ancestors, began our work with this group of South Asian students out of a deep concern and responsibility for "our" community's youth.

At the time of this project, the involvement of Indo-Canadian youth in gang-related activities had received extensive coverage in local and national mainstream media leading to the organization of both federal-and-provincial government task forces, as well as RCMP-initiated community programs. In 2005, RCMP in the Lower Mainland, British Columbia reported that "more than 80 Indo-Canadian gangsters or their associates [had] been slain in the past decade" (Mason, 2005, p. A9). Former federal health minister, Ujjal Dosanjh, described Indo-Canadian violence as a "debilitating problem where you can see young men dropping like flies" (Bolan, 2005, p. B5). Increasingly, Canadian and Indo-Canadian media have also focussed attention on South-Asian girls with reports of gang-related involvement including prostitution and drug-running (Ashk, 2006; CBC News, 2006). The coordinator of the Surrey RCMP program, aimed at encouraging Indo-Canadian girls to make alternative choices, claimed that many of these girls were motivated by money and the desire to lure Indo-Canadian gangsters away from their Caucasian girlfriends (CBC News, 2006). With respect to South-Asian boys, the popular press has attributed the problem of gang violence to thrill-seeking, idleness, and "having things handed to them" (Bolan, 2006, p. B7). Other reports placed the responsibility on both Indo-Canadian parents and the Indo-Canadian community for a "lack" of supportive mentorship and an inability "to teach these young men their own potential…[or] the benefits of respecting the world around them" (Sidhu, 2005 p. 45).

It was within this context that the educators and I connected to work together as scholars and practitioners in order to bring theory and practice together in meaningful anti-colonial and decolonizing praxis. Deconstructing the racist media discourses above was significant work and has been discussed extensively elsewhere. Below, I highlight some unexpected and invaluable learnings that emerged throughout the project directly related to the fortunate opportunity of working as an insider/outsider in "my" community.

The first time I arrived at the "research site" to meet the educators involved, I walked into a room where several South-Asian youth from Grades 11 and 12 had stayed after school, on their own time, just to see me. They confessed that they "…had never seen an Indian professor before."

Working with the South-Asian youth and educators I learned how I had come to normalize many colonialist institutional absences. In fact when one of the boys of this project came to meet me for the first time, he kept looking around for the "university researcher." When I identified myself, he said, "Oh, I thought you would be white; everyone from the university is always white.…"

Although I have spoken extensively about representation and the importance of role models for systemically marginalized groups, it was not until this moment of contact between the "researcher and researched" in this particular educational institution that I fully "innerstood" the authentic meaning of these scholarly notions. Being an insider, although I recognize my dialectical locations as both an insider and an outsider, the words and actions of these students were troubling to me since for the first time I felt the impact of continuing colonialist institutional absences on future generations of members of a community that I knew well. At the same time, as an outsider, I realized how much I had normalized the impact of these absences within the academy, especially with regard to research praxis. Going into my own community, supposedly as an insider, it never occurred to me that most of these students or educators would never have met an Indo-Canadian professor or researcher, especially not a woman. This was shocking for someone who works in the area of social-justice education and deals with these issues theoretically on a daily basis. Was I/will I really be aware of what it meant/will mean to do decolonizing/decolonial work with a community who continues to embody and live the legacy of colonialism? I am grateful to the community of this project for helping me realize through their formal and informal roles as participant-researchers/pedagogues, the potential of participatory research as decolonizing and decolonial pedagogy, simultaneously involving shared teachings/learnings/advocacy, as well as decolonial praxis.

On another occasion, I was working with a young South-Asian girl who had identified herself as *Punjabi*. She began telling me her story in English, as I expected of these youth, many of whom were born in Canada. It was only when she switched codes—and began to refer to patriarchal experiences that she assumed, and correctly so, that we shared in common—and said: "*izat bara karke se...*like you know, it was about family honour...." that again I was shocked at my own colonization in what was meant to be a decolonizing/decolonial activism and research process. My inability at that moment to reciprocate the code-switching further made me realize my own "cognitive colonialism" (Battiste, 2000) and the colonial nature of decolonizing activism and research for colonized peoples and colonized participants/researchers. The impact of decolonizing work for activist-researchers embodying the legacy of colonialism has been given very little attention in research. This is perhaps due to the limited representation of these peoples in the academy. Recognizing educators and youth participants as formal and informal activists and researchers and reflecting on my own indigeneity and colonization as I participate in future projects of this nature will be critical to conceptions of decolonizing and decolonial praxis.

Linda Tuhiwai Smith (1999) states:

> ...deconstruction is part of a much larger intent. Taking apart the story, revealing texts, and giving voice to things that are often known intuitively does not help people to improve their current conditions. It provides words, perhaps an insight that explains certain experiences—but it does not prevent someone from dying. (p. 3)

In this manner, from the perspective of Linda Tuhiwai Smith, we might question if decolonial praxis is ever possible without participatory action or if we can ever decolonize without action or activism?

> *They threatened me. The administration threatened me. They were gonna take every single person's picture that were my friends, and put it on the RCMP website, saying that these are Indo-Canadian gangsters and please be warned if you are in any vicinity of these people....How am I a gangster? How am I a part of gang violence? Who have I shit-kicked? Who have I shot? Tell me, I want to know. I want to know, too, right? Like I wanna know. Why do you guys say that I'm some kind of gangster?...I get off of school, even in elementary, at three and by 3:10 I am at the farm, by 3:15 I am doing cashier, by 9:00 I am closing the store, by 10:00 I get home and eat. Then I do homework and pass out. There was no leisure in my life....Anyway, I agreed to do this [participate in this project] because I think this is good. At least someone will hear our voice out there. And like I'm turning twenty soon, I'm going to get married and have kids, right? And I want at least my kids to have a little bit better high school than I did. Cause this is my society, too, right? I live in this society.* (Interviews, Lower Mainland South-Asian youth, 2008)

As I start working with members of "my community"—or at least one of my communities—I am learning to be mindful of Linda Tuhiwai Smith's (1999) powerful words and to prioritize my academic responsibilities of decolonial activism over academic expectations of the counting game. I'm finding the courage to "speak truth to power," to align my words with my actions and begin to challenge hegemonic and oppressive norms within educational institutions, the university and society at large. It is only there that I will continue to find a momentary sense of "home" in the diasporic in-between as well as in the academy.

ACKNOWLEDGEMENT

I would like to acknowledge the dedicated work of the two very courageous public school educators and their students whose hard work, insights, and activism have been invaluable to the work of this project.

REFERENCES

Ashk, G. K. S. (2006, June 20). NRI girls turn criminals for money, boyfriends. *The Times of India*. Retrieved from http://timesofindia.indiatimes.com/articleshow/1665053.cms

Battiste, M. (Ed.). (2000). *Reclaiming Indigenous voice and vision*. Vancouver, Canada: UBC Press.

Bolan, K. (2005, August 5). Ottawa names committee to study gang violence. *The Vancouver Sun*, B5. Retrieved from http://proquest.umi.com/pqdweb?did=878523131&Fmt=7&clientId=65345&RQT=309&VName=PQD

Bolan, K. (2006, January 7). Gangster lifestyle difficult to escape. *The Vancouver Sun*, B7. Retrieved from http://proquest.umi.com/pqdweb?did=960274951&Fmt=7&clientId=65345&RQT=309&VName=PQD

CBC News. (2006, June 13). *More girls joining South Asian gangs: RCMP*. Retrieved from http://www.cbc.ca/canada/story/2006/06/13/girlsgangs.html

Henry, F., & Tator, C. (Eds.). (2009). *Racism in the Canadian university: Demanding social justice, inclusion and equity*. Toronto, Canada: University of Toronto Press.

Kobayashi, A. (2009). Women of color in Canadian academia. In F. Henry & C. Tator (Eds.), *Racism in the Canadian university: Demanding social justice, inclusion and equity*. Toronto, Canada: University of Toronto Press.

Mason, G. (2005, November 26). B.C. minister speaks out on Indo-Canadian gangsters. *The Globe and Mail*, A9. Retrieved from http://proquest.umi.com/pqdweb?did=1056232401&Fmt=7&clientId=65345&RQT=309&VName=PQD

Sidhu, R. (2005, October 5). Fighting back against gang violence. *Mehfil Magazine*. Retrieved from http://www.mehfilmagazine.com/ebook/eMehfil_Oct05.pdf

Smith, L. T. (1999). *Decolonizing methodologies: Research and Indigenous peoples*. London, England: Zed Books.

Blood Trails

Pauline Sameshima & Yvette Dubel

*A revolutionary leadership must accordingly practice co-intentional educa-
tion.... As [teachers and students] attain this knowledge of reality through
common reflection and action, they discover themselves as its permanent
re-creators. In this way, the presence of the oppressed in the struggle for
their liberation will be what it should be: not pseudo-participation, but
committed involvement.*

— Paulo Freire, *Pedagogy of the Oppressed*

Haunted Tower
by Yvette Dubel

one love, one world
blooming ideals in a flower garden
should = no fear of poisoned decoys
skull f**k
waiting to render

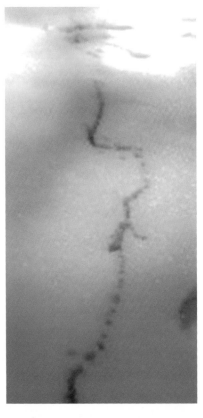

Following the Path. Yvette Dubel, 2009

pregnant wings
flightless

Warning: Keep away
from gardens
in alabaster towers
their basement bellies
in screaming silence
conceal bloody pulps
and would be's
ripped from the womb

time after time
blood trails and smudged prints

are not the only evidence of robbery
our abortions are rebranded

Selective Birthing™
sanctioned by Alabaster Towers Inc.

Clipped crimson buds
poorly cloned
and implanted
into suitably branded uteruses
birthed by less suspecting
blind ethereal extremities

who regurgitate
life sustaining
afterbirth

into shark-infested waters

Yvette: I am recovering.
I have given thought to what this "game" is. I became interested in philosophy at 14 or so. I wrestled with the paradoxes one was expected to live with and never question. Behind the principal's back, I heard teachers refer to her as "the warden" and jokingly refer to their work as "guard duty." They also understood what this was—*this was life*—if this was all there was for them, then was it good enough for us? Perhaps it was at that moment of questioning that my

relationships with teachers changed and I now had the potential for something close to learning to happen. Still, the paradox was that even that revelation only served to take me further down a path I deeply resented.

I had a modest litany of civic activities as a core part of my survival strategy, vital to help offset my low school attendance and mediocre grades in Advance Placement classes. I understood that there was a scoring system and the basics of how it worked; by 15, I thought I had the game all figured out. I was playing to win "my game," not "theirs."

No adult I questioned could deny the similarities between school and prison, although without a doubt, school was a kinder and gentler variety and definitely preferred. The game worked for me until I realized that prison was not the only alternative. My epiphany was that schooling is the business of human-capital development for the state.

Today there are many inspiring social entrepreneurs. Instead of being herded, there are those who service and manage innovative businesses to create new avenues, and to carve paths where none existed before. How could school prepare me for that? This was not how the game was played.

The game is the training ground where we go through a series of slightly modified versions of processes to teach us what we should know. My question was, "How can someone who doesn't know me make a decision about what I need to know and by default dictate how I invest my time/attention?" *Follow these steps and you will get an "education cake" with "your name here."* Extracurricular activities and civic-engagement clubs were the icing to ensure evidence that the process had delivered the universally understood result that is celebrated as "a success." The most pronounced problem is for those who don't believe in their own value, for those who can't see that gift waiting to reveal itself in the very stuff previously tossed into the furiously guarded corner rubbish pile.

History can become nothing more than the stories we tell ourselves to justify who we are and so although my schooling stories are among a heap of recollections, I had until the moment of—*oh, my hand is in the fire and that is why my flesh is burning*—more attention

Conscious Creation. Yvette Dubel, 1994

fixed on those hurtful recollections which were treasured and placed upon their pedestal with deliberateness that did not require consent. Education is part of the mythology of civilization. When I look at how it has been used I can't help but wonder how a better way could actually work.

> *I assume that amid all uncertainties there is one permanent frame of reference: namely, the organic connection between education and personal experience....The belief that all genuine education comes about through experience does not mean that all experiences are genuinely or equally educative....Some experiences are mis-educative.*
>
> (John Dewey, 1938/2009, pp. 25–26)

Pauline: I didn't notice.

Parker Palmer (1998) says, "As I teach, I project the condition of my soul onto my students, my subject, and our way of being together" (p. 1). As a student, I didn't see any relational connection between my teachers and myself. I wasn't as observant as Yvette. I didn't notice "a game" being played. I went to school. I did what I was told. I didn't even wonder where the nuns went at recess and lunch if they weren't on supervision duty. Not until I was stung.

In the apartheid 70s, Chinese children were not admitted to public schools in Johannesburg, South Africa, so I attended a private-school convent. The elementary school was on one side and the high school was on the other side, next to the church along the always congested narrow, concave street. The layout of my elementary-school building was not unlike a prison. The classrooms flanked a brickwalled, concrete courtyard where we played or lined up single file in our classes to say morning prayers.

I smile when my eldest daughter tells me that the architect of her high school usually designs prisons.

My burning-hands recollection was literally just that. I was stung by a bee.

Recess was taken in a grass playing field adjacent to the classroom/courtyard building. It was a blistering, dry day. I went to the outdoor tap that protruded from a thin, rude, brass pipe that stood on the outskirts of the fenced-in playground. I put my hand under the spout and turned the water on. I didn't realize a bee had climbed into the mouth of the tap. As the bee tumbled out with the water, it fell on my finger and stung me.

One of the supervising nuns took me across the street to the cloister. Sister Maria, notorious for dispensing ice and adhesive bandages, was on her break there. My finger was burning and swelling up. What I really needed was antihistamine, but I didn't know that. All I could feel was the throbbing in my finger and in my brain. I was in the nuns' private living quarters.

I noticed the terracotta-tiled floor as our quick footsteps clattered along the long, open hallway; the airy, cooling breeze; and the very stark, white walls accented by something like purple bougainvillea blooming in the arched alcoves. I remember feeling special. I had been invited into the "inner" circle! I was no longer just a student. I was in the nuns' home! Even more surprising was when I saw Sister Maria. She was hurrying down the long hallway towards us, her habit in her hand!

The schoolchildren always made up stories about how sisters were bald under their habits. Not true! Sister Maria had short brown, tousled hair. I felt embarrassed; her head was visible. She didn't even bat an eye, as if she were completely comfortable walking around naked. I awoke to the humanity of my teachers.

> *It is not enough to insist upon the necessity of experience, nor even of activity in experience. Everything depends upon the quality of the experience which is had. There is an immediate aspect of agreeableness or disagreeableness, and there is its influence upon later experiences.*
>
> (John Dewey, 1938/2009, p. 27)

Habit Hair. Pauline Sameshima, 2004

Yvette: I carry others' flames.

Looking back at my learning experiences, there is so much I feel that needs to be given voice because I speak not just for myself but for others along the way that has given me their story hoping I would carry them up out of the valley. *The villagers entrusted their most precious to be carried a little bit further up the road, up the mountain, understanding that I would do so for all of us.* I carry collective scars with me and into my art. When I am handed these luminaries, I am at once embraced and excluded.

I think about the "otherness" described by W. E. B. Du Bois in *Souls of Black Folk* (1903/1996) when I talk with Pauline about race, place, and learning. We are "outsiders" because we carry collective histories of our people in our blood. Biological experiences are powerful. Like Du Bois, I believe we can transcend our situations by embracing intellectualism and understanding our circumstances.

> *[The public intellectual is] an individual endowed with a faculty for representing, embodying, articulating a message, a view, an attitude, philosophy, or opinion to, as well as for, a public.…The intellectual does so on the basis of universal principles: that all human beings are entitled to expect decent standards of behavior concerning freedom and justice from worldly powers or nations and that deliberate or inadvertent violations of these standards need to be testified and fought against courageously.*
>
> (Edward Said, 1994, pp. 11–12)

Pauline: Taunted.

Growing up in South Africa during apartheid was not difficult because I didn't know any other way of being. I did not even know the word *apartheid* until I learned it in Canada in my Grade 8 Social Studies class. Racism was the cruel blond neighbour who called me names, threw stones at me, and chanted "ching chong Chinaman" songs. That's what I knew of Africaners.

Apartheid stems from the term "apartness" in Afrikaans. After the Afrikaner Nationalists took power in 1948, apartheid was law. The Population Registration Act of 1950 segregated racial categories into White, Bantu (black African), or Coloured (mixed race). A fourth category, designated "Asians" (Indians and Pakistanis), was added later. East Asians did not belong to any of the four designated groups. Chinese-South Africans were always "grey" and were classified as "Other Asian" and thus "non-white," while Japanese, Taiwanese, and Korean-South Africans were named "honorary whites" with the same privileges as whites because of South Africa's diplomatic and economic relations. In the 1980s Chinese-South Africans were exempted from some of the other non-white discriminatory laws (Canaves, 2008). The Group Areas Act of 1950 and the Land Acts of 1954 and 1955, designated different areas for where non-whites could live or do business. There were race-specific job categories and separate public facilities and educational standards (Robinson, 1999). My mother had to go door-to-door to every house on our street to collect signatures consenting to our joining the neighbourhood. In 2008, a high court in South Africa concluded that Chinese-South Africans were officially classified as "black." Chinese-South Africans were thus able to benefit from the affirmative-action policies aimed at apartheid reparations (see Canaves, 2008).

Being unclassified has an indelible effect on one's understanding of belonging and identity. People often ask if I've been back home. I feel puzzled. Although I left South Africa when I was 12, my maternal extended family still lives there, and I feel my roots there, but South Africa was never home for me. No, I have not been back.

I would ask a single question: Can we find any reason that does not ulti-mately come down to the belief that democratic social arrangements promote a better quality of human experience, one which is more widely accessible and enjoyed, than do non-democratic and anti-democratic forms of social life?

(John Dewey, 1938/1997, p. 34)

Yvette: Taunted for different reasons.

I suppose my story is more like those that I have heard Oprah Winfrey mention—being called "white girl" or "Oreo." Being accused of "acting white" or "talking white" was cause enough to provoke threats of violence at school. I hated that walk through the commons area that I had to take upon entering school because that was one of the prime opportunities for someone to get a participatory audience. The person who was willing to walk with me and carry on a conversation, as we pretended not to hear threats or feel things that might be thrown in our direction, qualified as a friend. There weren't many of them.

I spoke English without the expected southern accent in "black dialect" unless I wanted to because I had to learn to fit in. There were people around me who likewise spoke properly but among family, communications were more relaxed. My family was not wealthy, not especially intellectual, though we did have college graduates, including my younger brother who received his degree in education and literature. In my family, the assumption that ignorance and low income were synonymous was not accepted as normal. Neither was the idea that not having a degree meant one was uncultured.

How is my story like and unlike the stories of others who are struggling to make sense of themselves to retrieve their suppressed selves, to act ethically?

Laurel Richardson, 2005, p. 966

Pauline: Questioning my life.

Like Yvette, the way I spoke affected me. I lost my South-African accent in one year so I could fit in with my peer group, to blend in. Despite being in educational institutions for as long as I can remember, I am still torn. Degrees and certificates are not the measure of people. My father had a fourth-grade formal education and yet has always been one of the most inventive, clever, and research-minded individuals I know. Promoting college-for-all does not guarantee success or happiness. How do I raise my children with this dilemma between what I do and what I want to promote?

These questions around mothering and teaching rose to the fore again particularly after reading the book *Push* (Sapphire, 1997), which was made into the movie *Precious* (Daniels, 2009). The book was brutally revealing to me and made my head swirl. I questioned my own stance as a mother, as a teacher, and as a minority. The book unfolds the story of Claireece "Precious" Jones, an illiterate, obese, 16-year old with a dysfunctional and abusive home life. As a mother of three daughters, I often wonder if my husband and I are making the right choices in raising our children. Is there a right way? As a teacher of pre-service educators, am I preparing them for their futures in the best way? Can I find the best way for each student at the right time and place? The life-changing teacher in *Push* was portrayed as a teacher who cared. Can I teach pre-service teachers to care about teaching pedagogy, to think mindfully about the how and why of teaching? As a minority, how do I conceive of power that is not visible to me? This is not to say that I am powerless or that I am being mistreated in any way. I am referring to a way of being that is developed from collective experiences and family histories. How are these questions addressed in institutionalized spaces? I've asked before: What are we doing now that will be good for our children? What are we teaching and how are we teaching? I believe that telling our stories re-envisions communities through pedagogies of safety, hope, love, and liberation (Sameshima, 2009), but is that enough?

> *The principle of continuity of experience means that every experience*
> *both takes up something from those which have gone before and modifies*
> *in some way the quality of those which come after.*
>
> (John Dewey, 1938/1997, p. 35)

Yvette: Pushing ideals.

I grew up around people who read, visited museums, participated in bettering the community, and so on, so I did not exemplify the ignorance, promiscuity, and apathy that is often painted of black females from the wrong side of the tracks. In *Push*, I saw the kind of classism that was taught to me and speaks to the diversity within even low-income communities. I was taught that we were not like such-and-such next door or down the street despite what others would have had me believe.

Push represents an amalgamation of the worst and saddest stories of people I have been acquainted with, black or otherwise. I did not identify with the main character's response to life, but I see the value in helping people gain insight into the processes and experiences by which some are educated into interacting with the world within specific mental models. Take x and y, mix with a, filter with tests: a, b, and c; then simmer on and off for 13 years and get an educated individual...if only it worked that efficiently.

A story like *Push* helps to explain why different people respond differently to exposure to violence, violations of trust, spiritual deprivation, not to be confused with *religious*, and so on, to define their reality in the face of adversity.

I had schoolmates and neighbours like Precious,

Surviving the South. Yvette Dubel, 2004

so I did not need to rehash the memories of hearing fighting down the hall or upstairs in the apartment above us, the girl that got pregnant by her mother's boyfriend, or even the neighbour who with her boyfriend had held a young girl captive and raped her repeatedly right next door to us. In that place, people laughed about and told over-and-over such stories of domestic violence. Girls like Precious, and these kinds of stories about black girls, find eager audiences because the storyline is easy to understand. Precious represents and reinforces the stereotype of what it means to be poor, black and female, and stories such as this perpetuate this stereotype across generations. I resent the shadow that type of attention casts on black women. Precious is a contemporary construction of Celie from Walker's (1982) *The Color Purple*. I want more criticism of books that hyper-sexualize black women as available victims, and potentially misguide a generation of females. As black women, we have the power and freedom to explore, rather than assume, who we are.

My personal history does not define me as a victim. Rather the unhappiness and frustration were signposts that I was moving in the wrong direction. Most important is the relationships I develop with myself and others.

We conclude with our creed:

> *Read and write yourself into freedom!*
> *Read and write to assert your identity as human!*
> *Read and write yourself into history!*
>
> (Teresa Perry, 2003, p. 19)

REFERENCES

Canaves, S. (2008, June). In South Africa, Chinese is the New Black. *China Realtime Report, The Wall Street Journal.* Retrieved from http://blogs.wsj.com/chinarealtime/2008/06/19/in-south-africa-chinese-is-the-new-black/

Daniels, L. (Director/Producer). (2009). *Precious* [Motion picture]. USA: Lee Daniels Entertainment.

Dewey, J. (1938/1997). *Experience & education.* New York, NY: Touchstone.

Du Bois, W. E. B. (1903/1996). *The souls of black folk* (reprint). New York, NY: Penguin Books.

Freire, P. (1970/2009). *Pedagogy of the oppressed* (reprint). New York, NY: Continuum.

Palmer, P. J. (1998). *The courage to teach: Exploring the inner landscape of a teacher's life.* San Francisco, CA: Jossey-Bass.

Perry, T. (2003). Up from the parched earth: Toward a theory of African American achievement. In T. Perry, C. Steele, & A. Hilliard III (Eds.), *Young, gifted and Black: Promoting high achievement among African-American students* (pp. 1–108). Boston, MA: Beacon Press.

Richardson, L., & St. Pierre, E. (2005). Writing: A method of inquiry. In N. K. Denzin & Y. S. Lincoln (Eds.), *Handbook of qualitative research* (3rd ed.) (pp. 959–978). Thousand Oaks, CA: Sage.

Robinson, A. J. R. (1999). Apartheid. In Africana: *The encyclopedia of the African and African-American experience.* Retrieved from http://www.africanaencyclopedia.com/apartheid/apartheid.html

Sameshima, P. (2009). Cartographic storytelling for a changing world: The pedagogical praxis of home in school. *Northwest Passage: Journal of Educational Practices, 1*(7), 18–26.

Said, E. (1994). *Representations of the intellectual.* New York, NY: Vintage Books.

Sapphire/R. Lofton. (1996). *Push.* New York, NY: Vintage Books.

Walker, A. (1982). *The color purple.* New York, NY: Harcourt.

Each Moment, a Child of Duration

Lynn Fels

To become witness is to be exposed, vulnerable, to have something at stake.
—Julie Salverson, *Witnessing Subjects*

A sleek, brown-haired head surfaces next to me, a young boy, water slipping off his shoulders. Around us, laughter resounds as children of the island swing on a rope and drop. Splash into the water hole! They cheer each other on, their cries like birds rising from the jungle.

"Hello," he says. His accent betrays his foreignness, or rather it is I who am foreign.

I respond with a startled, *Alo!* My attempt to give my greeting a Parisian flare is laughable. Portuguese holds its own place in the world.

This moment, a child of duration accompanies me now, as I listen to the rain on the roof of my parents' cottage in Québec, countries away from this child's surfacing, writing through the questioning that has risen like morning mist rising from the lake's surface. Here, autumn threatens; the air has a bite in its touch. There, at the river's edge in Brazil, the brutal heat of early spring weighs heavily, a late-afternoon downburst pockmarking the water's surface.

A boy appears beside me, and I am called to attention. It is a *stop* (Appelbaum, 1995), *a moment of risk, a moment of opportunity*. He grins, his smile encased in braces, and I smile in recognition. Here is a child who is loved, whose parents have ambitions. "My mother says I must learn to speak...."

The rest I cannot understand, my listening inadequate, his pronunciation untranslatable. I fail him in his efforts to communicate. But I attend this encounter born within the space of *natality* (Arendt, 1958): he sees me, and is curious. *Will I see him?*

> A stop reminds us of our vulnerability; in the presence of others, we are startled to see ourselves anew. A stop is a moment of possible recognition, of reinvention, a reminder of what has been lost, an offering of what possibilities we might consider, if we reconsider our habits of engagement. A stop is an offering that attends our receiving.

. . .

In the Toronto General Hospital in 1983, a mother could return home or choose to remain for a few days so that her stitches, if any, might heal, or the newborn, if jaundiced, could receive the prescribed hours under a sunlamp. I opt for institutional care, my baby secure in the clear plastic bassinet that separates us. A waiting period, one might say, in which both child and mother adjust to each other's presence under the watchful eyes of the maternity nurse. That I might be afraid to return home, to take full responsibility for this new being, is never alluded to by the nurse attending, but I recognize my own apprehension.

On the second morning after her birth, my daughter is taken away for an injection, "just a mere prick on the foot," I am assured, and, although I am invited, I decline the opportunity to accompany her. I do not want her to equate me with acts of pain. This is the ignorance of new parenthood; we deceive ourselves that the enemy of our children is Other. On her return in the arms of the nurse, she looks about her, as if seeking me, her eyes dark with new knowledge. The myth that infants grow into who they are to become is dispelled. I realize I am in the presence of one who already knows and is waiting for my next betrayal.

Hannah Arendt (1958) asks educators if they love children enough so as to invite them into the world's renewal, not as they imagine it should be, but as it may become through their actions and presence in the world. It is the invitation of children's presence, if we are willing to attend, that offers the opportunity to reimagine ourselves. As Gordon (2001) suggests:

> Natality stands for those moments in our lives when we take responsibility for ourselves in relation to others. In this way, natality initiates an active relation to the world. It signifies those moments in our lives (and there are many) in which we attempt to answer the question that Arendt argues is at the basis of all action and that is posed to every newcomer to the world: "Who are you?" (p. 21)

This is not a question that one innocently confronts, for it asks us to consider our own complicity and resistance. The question of natality demands that we ask of ourselves, Who am I in this moment of encounter? How shall I now engage?

· · ·

We are travelling to Brazil, the five of us: my husband, my son and his girlfriend, with my daughter joining us from Toronto. I am to present at a conference in Belem, a city at the mouth of the Amazon River. Our plan is to spend 4 days in the Pantanal, a "feathered" African safari in a Brazilian savannah plain. We are to stay at a working ranch situated where cows roam. This breed, imported from India, is the only bovine species capable of surviving the extremities of rain and drought that the Pantanal seasonally presents.

In Rio de Janeiro, the walls of buildings are performed in text; graffiti and murals exploit the unguarded canvases of the city. All along Copacabana Beach, vendors weave their way, between supine bodies, call out to offer sarongs, hats, beaded necklaces. Tourists ignore them; they are intent on perfecting a tan or snapping photos of women's bottoms brazenly swaying in the bright light. I feel underexposed in my sensible swimsuit. Here, in the restless ocean, swimming lengths is impossible: instead we brace our bodies to receive the waves, and, pulses quickening, dive through towering walls of water. In an instant, I am released into turbulence, deposited rudely on the top of my head, rebounding to my left shoulder, the water drains away, and dazed, disorientated, I struggle to my feet.

This, then, is my introduction to Brazil, a country of messages—on walls, in waves, in the fevered sun—that warn me against my own ignorance.

En route to the ranch with our hired guide, luggage crammed into a white Volkswagen van; we are disoriented. Each turn in the red dust road offers a visual surprise, the landscape unfamiliar, difficult to decipher. We are glad of our guide's presence. He translates what we fail to see. We stop frequently, to take photographs, purchase bottled water, or attend to the many gates that prevent the cattle from roaming. Four hours into our journey, the van stops yet again. We wait for the dust to settle before opening the van doors. This waiting is a ritual with each stop we encounter. Our guide points to a nest high up in a tree where a stork tends to her young brood. We crane our necks, squinting in the light. It is noon hour, and the sun is cruel. Sweat-stained shirts cling to our backs. A bottle of water is shared. Above us, the stork—her right wing extended, white against blue—shades her three chicks from the glare of the sun. It is a tender moment.

Tenderness and patience, as the sun weighs upon us, becomes our mantra, as we seek relief from our everyday lives; we reach out, my husband and I, to embrace our son and daughter, the girlfriend watching, just a step outside the shadows of our joined bodies. How do I understand my presence in this land of toucans, emus, caimans, and piranhas? What has called us present to this moment?

. . .

My son disappears in the orthodontist's chair, so young and yet already we are correcting his smile, putting him through a series of painful procedures—teeth extracted, jaw cracked open—so that he may be presentable. His new smile will bear the mark of his parents' ambitions. In the waiting room, I thumb through worn copies of *Chatelaine* and *MacLean's*. I was surrounded by girls in private-school uniforms and boys hunched over handheld video games, waiting their turn in the chair. Mothers glance at each other, speculatively, time taken off work—the monthly orthodontist run, hockey, gymnastics, parent-teacher interviews—these rites of passage prepare our children for a world that we have created. We are apprehensive but confident in our strategies. They will be ready, perfect smiles in place. That is our intention.

In the evening, I set aside my writing, and with my husband, paddle the canoe on the lake. Evening approaches, water darkening to black gold as the mountain's shadow falls across the width of the lake. An object bobs, and we angle the canoe to approach it.

"Look, a frog! What's it doing in the middle of the lake?"

"Swimming."

"I can see that but where?" The frog bobs in the waves, too far from shore.

"Should we rescue it, bring it across?" My husband laughs and with a single stroke of his paddle turns us away from what seems to me to be a struggling creature.

"It's a frog. It'll find its own way."

I think of its pending journey and the as-yet unknown dangers: a quick surfacing fish, a boat's propeller, a heron stalking in the weeds. Will it safely arrive? Two days later, my husband disturbs a garter snake in the midst of engulfing a frog. He shouts and the snake, releasing the frog, slithers across the sand into a crevice in the stonewall.

"Is the frog okay?" We bend to see, only to be startled as the frog attempts a lop-sided jump. My husband scoops it up with a bailing can from the canoe, and places it in the lake. The frog turns belly up, and so is retrieved, and placed on the shore. My husband tends to it; he pours water to wash away the sand caught in the wound: two puncture marks. He places a piece of driftwood over the frog. We watch it burrow into the sand. The next morning there is no sign of the frog. We see no corpse, nor sign of struggle, nor footsteps in the sand.

In our engagement with others, what calls us to intercept, to engage, to turn away? An offer of care is an act born of complicity: who is caring for whom? In a fleeting moment of encounter, what possibilities do we create? What opportunities are lost? Who might you have become had I been present and awake?

After experiencing Brazil's feathered multitudes, I am attentive to what is absent in the forest that I have known since childhood. Each morning there is no chatter of birdsong. I seek the kingfisher as my husband and I paddle in our canoe, and am rewarded twice. We spot a blue heron; its neck elongates then folds back into itself; its intended prey eludes the sharp thrust of beak. A second heron; shoulders the blue sky, then lands in a dead tree, camouflaged against grey-blue bark. Two hummingbirds joust at the birdfeeder: whir of wings, as they jockey for access. Loons sound peals of laughter. Last year there were seven loons on the lake; my husband frantically zoomed his camera lens, as I commandeered the canoe; our chase was futile. (Brazilian birds are far more accommodating, flitting within easy proximity of the camera with satisfying frequency.) This year, only three loons return.

. . .

On our kitchen wall in my parents' cottage is a painting by my brother, done when he was eighteen, the summer he had announced he was going to art school.

"What is it?" I ask, cocking my head. On a canvas of black paint, he had painted five yellow blotches of circles joined by a single red line.

"It's the song of that bird we hear every morning. Listen." He whistles the familiar tune.

"Oh," I nod uncertainly, not seeing the visual connection. Waking early this morning, I note the absence of song. Thirty years later, the woods are ominously silent.

"Où sont les oiseaux?" I ask our next-door neighbour.

"Ils sont disparus." She tells me that she spotted two blue jays on her porch railing *"au fin de juillet,"* but it seems the species that sang my brother's painting has vanished. I whistle the yellow notes he painted. They sound sad and true.

Resilience is a word that surfaces as our time in Brazil unfolds. I learn how to move through the liquid heat, leisurely, limbs abandoning their habitual quickness of engagement. I learn to breathe one breath at a time. I relinquish my expectations, not only for what is, but also for whom I once thought I should be. I do not know if this is a position of wisdom, or a failing.

. . .

"Annie's Song" by John Denver plays on the radio next to my bed in the hospital, the first music I hear on the morning of my daughter's birth. I sing this song to her as she nurses at my breast, then on occasion through her years as a toddler into her becoming a young adult. She, like her brother, sported braces. Twenty-two years after her birth, as we drive along the highway to transport her and her belongings to medical school, I sing the song silently under my breath. "You fill up my senses...." Her father and I have been greedy for her continued presence at home, encouraging her to study locally, but now—travelling with her in a rented vehicle, with precious few belongings in the trunk, a computer, a couple of suitcases, a Raggedy Ann doll, her boyfriend's gift of selected songs playing on the car's CD player—we must give her to the world. All children leave home, and yet when the day comes, we are startled, reluctant to release them beyond our reach. *So soon?* What we had failed to understand is that she had begun her journey, taking leave of us on the day of her birth, the cutting of the umbilical cord, her cry announcing her presence.

Like the edge of a stork's extended white wing against blue sky, we tend to our young so that they might journey to horizons that beckon beyond us. We straighten their teeth; we interrupt their play; we prepare them for a world shaped by our expectations, our actions, our ambitions, and our hopes. But all these— our ambitions, our aspirations, our desires—are finite. A child's arrival in our midst is an offering to us to participate in the world's renewal. We unwittingly limit who this child might become: through our insecurity, our fear, our greed, our inability to trust, our "not-yet readiness" to release what is not ours to claim.

As educators, we cannot know what has not yet been imagined; our challenge is to be willing to be surprised, to engage anew: To receive a child in our midst, and accept that child's presence as a benediction. To learn to forgive ourselves for who we have failed to become in the presence of a child is the gift that we in turn may offer. *Take this and do it in remembrance of me....Not as I have done but as....*and here our stumbling prayer takes flight, for if we have been true in our learning, if we have truly opened our hearts, then perhaps that which we truly desire—what has not yet been imagined by us—will come into being, realized into presence by our children, and our children's children as they engage in the world's renewal.

. . .

I am, I suspect, an odd figure arriving at this place of play on the edge of the Amazon River. I ask permission through gestured hand calligraphy to join the swimmers who greet me with surprise, then wave me in. I am received with curiosity, as yet not translated. I wade waist-deep into the mud-brown water. A child surfaces next to me, his face open to my presence, to what I have to offer, even as I recognize the lack of what I bring. It is a moment that arrests me, that calls me to attention. I smile, recognizing what is possible and what is not yet possible in this moment between us, I acknowledge his presence, "*Obrigada*." (Thank you.)

ACKNOWLEDGEMENT

I would like to acknowledge writer Jana Milloy for her concept of "each moment, a child of duration" in which she speaks to the temporal "aliveness" of a moment's experience in her work on the phenomenon of writing. In our performance work, such moments haunt us, call us to attention; moments are "time-spaces" of possibility, of enduring loss, of opportunity missed, of "time-arching" relevance. Such moments are seedlings to new understandings, and in such a way, our noticing them makes present their fertility (see Milloy, 2007).

REFERENCES

Appelbaum, D. (1995). *The stop*. Albany: State University of New York Press.

Arendt, H. (1958). *The human condition*. Chicago, IL: University of Chicago Press.

Denver, J. (1974). Annie's song. On *Back home again* [record]. New York, NY: RCA.

Gordon, M. (2001). Hannah Arendt on authority: Conservatism in education reconsidered. In M. Gordon (Ed.), *Hannah Arendt and education: Renewing our common world* (pp. 11–36). Boulder, CO: Westview.

Milloy, J. (2007). *Persuasions of the wild: Writing a moment, a phenomenology* (Unpublished doctoral dissertation). Simon Fraser University, Burnaby, Canada.

Salverson, J. (2006). Witnessing subjects: A fool's help. In. J. Cohen Cruz & M. Schutzman (Eds.), *A Boal companion: Dialogues on theatre and cultural politics* (pp. 146–158). London, England: Routledge.

Floodgates

Susan Braley

Thank goodness for valves
those tireless traffic guards
of the heart; they close
and open, open and
close, patient, no matter
the weight of the surge.

No matter that, between
the ebb of one class
and the flood of the next,
you remain,
you who love Plato, to say
he tells me get rid of it,
what do you think?

No matter that, in week five,
you trace the office maze
with your guide dog
not once but twice,
can't leave 'til I say goodbye.

No matter that, after you bait
and seethe all term—
wait for bridle and bit to drop—
you, wordless, offer your hand.

No matter that, after
a winter of women's studies,
you uncover the arm
once scalded from shoulder to fist.

No matter that, at midnight,
you tweet to admit
the library does have stuff
on your topic, and you've
decided to read it all.

No matter that, when
you've been absent so often
(the woman from the hospital says),
you've wandered the campus,
stopped taking your meds.

No matter that, after you carry
Sartre and Camus from clinic
to clinic, you die in your sleep,
the cure is too much for you.

Thank goodness for valves,
who, like the weary prophet,
hold off the blood-red sea.

Vampires and Oil Spills

Patti Fraser

A thousand stories have come into the world in this place in the 10 years since the Summer Visions Film Institute for Youth came into being. Located in Templeton Secondary in Vancouver's Eastside, the institute was founded in response to the need of many of the local youth who had no work and no place to go in the hot summer months. For the past ten summers of my life, I have walked five city blocks from my home to Templeton Secondary's media studio. In the mornings of early summer even the Eastside of Vancouver is green with summer hope. Open and waiting.

I had come to think of my work at the Film Institute as that of a midwife: preparing a place for that which will come to be, challenging the young filmmakers to be patient, helping to ensure that the environment where they worked could support all of the new voices that arrived each summer.

With the exception of the Institute's fundraisers and administrators, the other colleagues at the Film Institute are youth themselves. They come here to work every summer, most of them from this neighbourhood, once participants in the program themselves. They now work as youth instructors, media producers, and mentors in a program of media production that offers 85% of its participants full scholarships to attend. We try to make it possible for everyone to come. Every summer, 150 youth come through these doors, and 30 films will be produced. Over the years, we have received national recognition for the work we have done in the Institute. Every summer I'm asked to come back, to come back to help in the act of listening, and refining the stories or treatments for their films. As we work together, a community of practice forms, and the ones that take the risk to show up begin to have a place to be that is safe for the summer.

Our unspoken ethic is that no one is turned away. On only one occasion was someone asked to leave. It is a difficult place to be. The world in all its complexity shows up with no screening program, no exclusion. The only requirement is a desire to tell a story and to produce a film in collaboration with others.

Every year, challenging the initial offer of the stories, we try to not make it easy to replicate some plot from the current season's blockbuster. Every year we seek to find ways to open up the possibilities to return through their stories to their right to play, to be seen, to express their unique inquiry into the condition of their lives, to create something new, to listen for what is trying to speak through them to us.

Every year, as a way of hearing what is in the room, we brainstorm story ideas. Every year, preoccupations unique to each summer emerge, such as reversals in time, the nature of dream and reality, and suicide, to name a few.

This year it was all about oil spills and vampires.

July 5

In the airless cavern of the studio, the door opens with a hint of sunlit air and closes as another blurry-eyed, feeling-out-of-place, young person enters for the first time.

With every opening and closing of the door, there's a rising sense of claustrophobia and the pressing feeling, stronger this year, that I'm sacrificing too much of my life to be here.

Here, in the overheated, getting-hotter-every-summer, noisy chaos, I'm losing too much of my time instead of spending it in an imagined garden, in the cool waters of an imagined lake, looking at quiet star-filled nights, imagining myself so far away from the airless chaos of the studio.

July 6

"Please come back."

"We can't do this without you."

This year's administration's lament sounds like every other year's administration's lament.

I give in.

But in the midst of all the striving and in the passing of time I'm becoming unrecognizable; known only to the few returning young media producers from "the old days."

Now even they are young adults, who used to be scruffy kids from around the block; these familiars seem distant, preoccupied with finding a place and an identity for themselves in the world as young people. We aren't sharing the same sense of endeavour we had in the years before.

Every beginning can feel somewhat like this.

But this year, something has changed. And with it a larger feeling of unease.

July 7

We start by welcoming a circle of 60 strangers and, after screening some films that were made in the past programs, we start the difficult work of coming up with a treatment or story idea.

"I wanna make a film about a guy who finds his girlfriend cheating on him, he kills her...

how about a robot girlfriend who gets dumped in a dumpster by the guy's real girlfriend....I wanna make a film about zombies...where everyone dies...

There's vampires and, it's the end of the world and we are the only people left...a giant release of some kind of virus that can't be stopped."

Thousands of stories....I've heard the beginning of thousands of stories in this way.
I talk about the falseness and boredom of the medium shot.
A forgery of balance.
Not close enough or far away.
"Our lives...the lives we live. It's not like that."
This year, irked and impatient with the ideas
I *want* to *tell* them something instead of just listening.
I want to tell them.
"By this time, by the time you are sitting here in front of me,
I know you have already learned to climb the fence.
You know exactly what spot on Hastings Street is not watched at night.

You can already slip over it and make your own way into Playland."
I want to tell them.
We are here because we want some place for you to be in summertime
safe.
A place to be
away from the street
away from your sleeping friends
in basement rooms
while the last summer sparrows
unseen
make nests under the stairs just outside the door
in a place that is still summer young with summer hope.
Away from your tiny apocalypses.
Someplace safe
from *these stories*
you keep pitching over and over again.

July 8

Feeling like the most responsible one in the room I'm still asking *them* to wait…
wait for the story with a hope that it's not a "done deal."

Not already foreclosed and mortgaged off.

But this year, for the first time, I can't tell if anyone is listening or tuned to their
entirely own preoccupations and their own emergencies.

I keep pitching them the idea

that *creating* stories that come from ourselves—and what we know or what we wish
to be or understand or imagine—can be antidotes to confusion and bewilderment.

They can help us to find a home, I say, for a while, out of the wilderness.

But I'm not so sure any more. This year seems different.

July 12

It is hotter this year than ever. There have been weather warnings about heat
stroke. We have to adjust the production schedule, try to figure out locations
where the heat isn't at its worst, a difficult task in a place surrounded by highways
and large urban transportation corridors, where we need to take buses or walk

to locations carrying all the gear. The scripts aren't ready. This year, there is an atmosphere of *persistent* unexamined violence to the stories.

I'm getting nowhere with my attempts to ask them through the stories, *what is it*, what is it that you want to *tell* us. What is the trouble?

What *is* it?

"...I wanna make a film about a super anti-hero with powers who comes into the high school and offs the principal...what about a film about someone who commits suicide in front of her friends...about a business man who steps into a square on the sidewalk and a sniper shoots him dead."

This year it's you.
...You...are the trouble.
And your stories.
The stories you want to recreate again and again are making me sick.
I always thought you were the ones we were supposed to keep safe.
But you have already left this place called "safe"; you live somewhere else.
Where are you?

And where is that which can't be colonized, taken over,
by the empire of worst nightmares?
Ever.
In the past, these preoccupations existed, but this year it's *me*—I'm getting infected by the epidemic, can't see/feel out/a way to see/show a subtle path of reconsideration, a deepening, a reversal in the fortunes and the form of the characters—

I'm trying not to foreclose on them.
Where are the possibilities for the other outcomes?
Why aren't you listening?
Where are you going?

July 16

A mother, no longer a mother, called this morning.
She left a message
The mother, now child poor,
told us of an overdose of something that found you in Playland.
This year
The story has taken us all away.
It's true.

We could not keep you safe.

July 17

Now you are my small apocalypse.
Now
this is a story about a place that has lost its light,
about a wilderness of the worst imaginings,
of anger at the contemptible permission we have given our young
especially those who don't live in safe houses
who aren't taken on holidays to other places
where, in its stead, we have allowed the worst imaginings of strangers to
entertain them—we have *let* them,
all of us let them,
sit in front-row seats
where they watch stories told by strangers
about degradation and despair,
of violence and the loss of human dignity.
These are *their* bedtime stories.

July 18

To keep you safe.
That is why I came here in the first place.
You are my last summertime hope now gone.

July 19

Now what do we do?
How do we think through with the rest of your long-lost crew
the end of your movie?
When only the image of you as an adolescent vampire remains
holding in his hand a message.
While reports from the Gulf keep telling us the spill
keeps spilling and cannot be contained.
I can't keep it together any more, can't find the way.
We are making each other cry.
Now a hand or two,
Now a touch.

July 20

I'm giving up being the most responsible one in the room.
Together your crew decides to play rewind, to go back,
we begin the painful look
at what is really there,
what has been shot,
what remains of the image of vampire you.
We start again.
Start to make a story again
with what is left.

August 2

They knew what to do
with this image of you.
Vampire,
you become our bright hope.
In vampire time in the dark airless studio in the absence of light
you are a shadow of light on the screen
and something is *realized* together.

In the passion of a loss, an unexpected event
of mutual understanding is experienced.
And *conscientia* between,
knowing with, we con/spire,
breathe with, breathe together new stories about vampire you.
And they see you,
the onliness of you, as something now terribly valuable,
and in the passion of their seeing they determine through the story and the film
they do not want
you to suffer
the insult of oblivion.
Despite the desire of many for this to be not so.
A fellowship of story makers/film makers
the young strangers who are no longer strangers
in the immediacy of grief,
your film crew/your story makers
won't let you suffer
the insult of

oblivion.
They want you to be seen and heard,
to be here as a passion in their hearts.
The bad bedtime stories can't do *this*.
They can't replace this passion.
Because this passion has never been experienced before.
It is new.
It is born new.
And this story, the new one about vampire you, can't be hijacked, can't be turned
into the bad bedtime story because
it looks and feels like where it comes from—it is the result of the labour of their
experience.
Born from the passion of not wanting you to suffer
the insult of oblivion.
I, as the story mentor, am thinking anew today.
I'm thinking like a homeopath,
thinking about what's contained in this medicine,
where the smallest degree of poison can become the greatest of remedies.

August 31

My summertime hope is tougher now and it no longer expects green pastures
and cool lakes to swim in.

Vampires and blood sucking corpses, killers, girlchild porn stars, can *be seen*, as
the work of light and shadow.

Measuring the degree of poison becomes my work now.

With the great hope you will come close enough to hold out your tongues for the
light in our hands

because you may know better than us

just what will be the right amount of poison to protect some or maybe all of your
own unique selves from

the epidemic in Playland.

Today it's the re/imagining of vampires, killings, and all
here in the
play of light and shadow
in the safety of the studio
within its four airless walls.

Next year,
I will come back again.
But not carrying an *idea* of safety with me.
I will seek out the worst stories possible
and with you make an archive
of play in light and shadow.
In the hope that these tough ones will keep coming
looking for medicine.
So we can seek together our remedies
recreating, if you insist, the worst nightmares,
under my protest
and with whatever help I can give.
Seeking to see in one another a common and not so common world.
And above all else
to not suffer the insult of oblivion.

If we're lucky
you'll keep coming back,
safe
for now,
with the bright light and the bright hope that only comes when we create something anew.

Postscript: I have come to think of wisdom, not as a form of knowledge which we can possess, but in the ways that the philosopher Bugbee (1999) understands:

> Wisdom may be better conceived as giving us the strength and courage to be equal to our situation than as knowledge giving us command of it. To the extent that human well-being and capacity for acting well ultimately turn upon understanding. (p. 65)

REFERENCES

Bugbee, H. (1999). *The inward morning: A philosophical exploration in journal form.* Athens: University of Georgia Press.

Curtis, K. (1999). *Our sense of the real: Aesthetic experience and Arendtian politics.* Ithaca, NY: Cornell University Press.

Towards a Definition
of Pornography

Bruce Hunter

One. Young men and women with degrees in English literature, living in fashionably seedy districts, writing poetry in sexually inclusive language about rape, murder, and wife-beating, all of which happens to other people.

Two. In urban clubrooms, churches, and universities, anyone engaged in politically correct discourse on pornography, violence, or Nicaragua. This is the True Story, the poem that *can* be written.

Three. My mother with a knife. This is where the definition gets personal. I am 17-years old. She steps between my sister and my alcoholic father. That night I leave home. One year later she does. Something Margaret Atwood knows nothing about.

Four. In divorce court: the judge, two lawyers, all of them male. My mother gets one dollar a year and social assistance. My father buys a new house.

Five. My teenaged brothers in jail. For minor offences, none of them malicious. On the other side of the thick plexiglas window, their faces bruised. The elevator in the police station stopped between floors. A telephone book applied to the abdomen, the ribs. Tonight is Friday. Monday morning there will be no visible damage before the judge.

Six. The police visit. My mother looking for my brothers. It is 4 a.m. This happens often. My sisters are stopped for identification checks. This too happens often. This is what they do to the lower classes in your country.

Tonight somewhere in the suburbs you are talking about us. Some of you are writing poems, taking donations, or making a film. You feel okay about this.

My mother now goes to your churches. She has forgiven you. I have not.

Hard to Place

Tasha Hubbard

A hard place.
Hardly a place.
Hard to place.

I was a "hard-to-place" child, a Cree baby given up for adoption, part of
Saskatchewan Social Services' "Adopt Indian and Métis" program. A pilot
project from the late 1960s and early 1970s, the AIM program (yes, I'm aware of
the irony of that particular acronym) strove to find homes that would welcome
an Indigenous child with open arms. Photos of children were put in the newspapers to entice potential adoptive parents.

I was fortunate. My adoptive parents, at the age of twenty-two and twenty-
three, were thrilled to have a baby, and were even interested in my Cree culture.
My new home, a farm in southern Saskatchewan, was far from any Cree community. The only other Cree people lived a half a mile away, but they were also
part of the child welfare system. Although my adoptive family did their best to

foster my sense of Indigenous identity, their Euro-Canadian backgrounds didn't prepare them to teach a child about what it means to be Cree.

Isn't that one of our first-learning exercises? To learn about the self? For me, learning about myself seemed almost impossible when it felt as though my "self" was hidden away, part of a closed file in a social worker's office.

I saw the same films and television shows that everyone else did, the westerns featuring faceless warriors on horseback, or the caricatures of Indigenous peoples in *Peter Pan* and other Disney films. In well-meaning gestures, my adoptive family gave me Indian dolls that just seemed exotic to me. My fair complexion made me feel like I didn't measure up somehow to these little glorious brown-skinned babies, clad in leather and fur.

When I look back, I remember the times that I did connect to myself; it was always about the land: the pasture behind our house, the lonely butte a few miles south of my grandparents' homestead, or the dips and swells of the Qu'Appelle Valley when we drove through on our way to visit family. It was in these places that I would feel a slight shiver, a visceral reaction, a sense of knowing that I belonged here, that this territory was my home.

When I turned 15-years old, my adoptive mother suggested I start looking for my parents. I wrote letters to Indian Affairs and Social Services asking for my information, with no luck. "Policy is policy" and the reply said that no information was to be provided to me until I turned 18. My adoptive father stepped in with a suggestion: hire an Indian lawyer he knew from high school.

It took the lawyer a week: my birth parents, both Treaty First Nations, were found. I spoke to my birth mother on the phone on my 16th birthday, and met her 3 days after that. She was a writer and a teacher and had been a political activist in her youth. I found out that, through her work, she interacted with the family of those other Cree children who grew up beside me. She and their birth mother had shared the fact they had children somewhere out there, and wondered where we were and how we were doing.

I met my birth father 3 weeks later. The lawyer we hired was a good friend of his, as my birth father was a lawyer too. As a result, he travelled a lot and stopped in where I worked on his way home from some meeting. That night, we began a conversation that has continued for 22 years.

I learned from both my birth parents about my family history, about the Treaties, the Indian Act and residential school, and the hard times for Indian people in Saskatchewan. I knew some of this already, as I had seen the evidence of those hard times on childhood trips to the city, when I pressed my nose against the window of our family station wagon, furtively searching for my birth family, wondering, "Maybe that woman is my mother, maybe that kid is my sister."

Now I knew who my other family was: a web of kinship that includes my birth parents, my ten siblings, my kokums and mosoms and aunties and uncles and so many cousins I have never yet figured out how many there are. I still didn't feel like I had learned who I was yet.

What of myself was from my upbringing, and what was from my blood?

I had spent my childhood years with an identity that included a vague sense of "Indian" and being adopted. I had been a "farm kid" and after we left the farm and began moving to follow my adoptive father's career path, I became the "new kid." Then, when we moved to a northern Saskatchewan city after I turned 15, my identity choices had become even more complex, as I quickly realized the racism was much more pronounced compared to other places I'd lived in. The week we moved there, the lead story in the newspaper told how boys from my high school beat up a First Nations man and left him for dead. For the first time, I felt fear about being "an Indian." My survival strategy? Pass for "white," which was relatively easy: I didn't say anything about it and no one asked me any questions. But after I met my birth family, everything changed. I no longer wanted to pass; I wanted to honour where I came from. So I started talking to people about my new family developments, and I watched the numbers of my friends shrink. I heard later that one girl's parents were horrified that they had let me, "an Indian," in their home. But I never regretted my choice to be open about who I was, even if I didn't understand exactly what that meant.

First of all, once I met my birth family, it took years to overcome the insecurity of feeling that I wasn't wanted, and I still struggle with feelings of abandonment. During those years, I had thoughts like *You didn't keep me as a baby, why would you want me now?* that would permeate my visits with my birth family. Eventually, I came to realize that these thoughts were keeping me from myself. Our minds work to protect us, and I was building my defences so I didn't get hurt. The problem was, those defences didn't just work one way…they also prevented me from reaching out and truly connecting to my birth family.

Finally, in my twenties, I needed a place to stay for a few months. For the first time, my adoptive parents were not there for me. An exercise in "tough love," a push out of the nest, whatever it was, it meant I was on my own. My birth dad reached out to me and offered me a home. For the first time, I lived with my birth family. I watched my little sisters and brothers go through their daily routine, I laughed at their crazy jokes, and I slept and dreamt in the same space as them.

The next significant turning point was a career choice: instead of working on an international development project, I chose to work on a film about my people's history, CBC's mini-series *Big Bear*. My job was to find 400 First Nations people to portray Cree people from the 1870s and 80s. I travelled to many communities, meeting people, and shaking hands. Because I "put myself out there," people responded by taking me in. I was told "you belong"; those words became magic to me.

"You belong" gave me courage to truly identify with my family, my community, and my nation. I learned that I was part of a *circle of interconnectivity* that distance and time could not break. Those times I felt that sense of connection as a child that the land was speaking to me. Our Cree teachings tell us that connectivity begins with the land, and I know now what my spirit knew then.

I am not saying my struggles are finished. I still find myself "in-between" my adoptive upbringing and my Cree blood, but I have accepted my position, and consider it a strength in my work and in my sense of self. I have moved back temporarily to the place where I lived as a child, and it is in this small farming community where I find myself reconnecting to the land after years of living in the city. I wander the hills that sustained me as a child. I know that my journey is not over. The lessons are still coming. What I do know is this: I am not hard to place. I have learned that I have a place in this world.

A Social Study
of the Double Helix

Denise Schellhase

As the summer winds down and I mentally prepare for the upcoming school year, I find myself reflecting upon my chosen profession and wonder how my own learning journey might inform my daily interactions with my Canadian history students. My mind is immediately drawn to one of the first graduate-level courses which I took, a course on literacy, in which my professor asked us to reflect upon three of our most educational experiences. She asked us to journal about them, elaborating on the events, the actors involved, and our feelings at the time, etc. She wanted us to re-create the experiences to the best of our ability, to excavate them from the realm of memory, to dust them off, and to re-encounter them as adults, as graduate students about to embark upon a whole new educational journey. It took some time to "oil the gears" and get going, but once I did, I wrote pages. While I was writing, I remember wondering what relevance my musings had to my work as a secondary high-school teacher. After all, they were unique to *my* life and, at the time, each one of them had prompted a very personal inner transformation. Furthermore, none of these educational experiences had actually occurred in a school.

One of my most educational moments occurred while I was attending elementary school in a rural suburb of Vancouver. One day, on the school bus ride home, a bunch of us were engaged in our usual banter about what we would do on the weekend. Somehow, the conversation turned to food and cooking and my friends started discussing the "exotic" meals which they would often have at my house. I didn't really think of the food which we ate as exotic but was happy to indulge my friends and bask in the limelight for a moment. I then began to explain that my dad was from Germany and my mom was from Pakistan and that was why our meals were so different from theirs. At this point in the conversation, something suddenly went amiss. I looked at my friends' puzzled expressions and wondered what I had said that was so perplexing to them. There was a split second of silence before one of my friends blurted out: "You mean you're a 'Paki'?!" I was truly awestruck, and in the moment between my reaction and my verbal response, many images of what I understood a "Paki" to be flew through my mind.

The first image which appeared was the familiar scene which we passed on the school bus almost daily was that of the East-Indian workers crouched in the fields harvesting vegetables. As children, we would often peer through the bus windows wondering where they went to the bathroom. We were always fascinated by the sight of what seemed like an entire family sitting amidst the rows of potatoes sharing a meal. *No, I certainly was not a "Paki."* The distance between my family and the families of those East-Indian fieldworkers seemed enormous to me at the time, and I recoiled in shame at the thought that my friends might possibly associate me with *them*.

I honestly can't remember how I responded to my friends' shocked expressions and almost accusatory questioning. Like many children, however, I just wanted to make everything all right. Being cast as exotic was okay as long as it worked in my favour. Now, however, I felt as though my whole world had come crashing down on me; I fumbled to pick up the pieces. I think that I must have muttered something about not being a "Paki," since my dad was German and my mom, though from Pakistan originally, wasn't really a "true" Pakistani. While things might have been awkward between me and my friends for a couple of minutes, our conversation quickly jumped to another topic. I was only too relieved to have the attention deflected away from my ethnic heritage.

This incident was pivotal in my life. After that point, my attitude towards my family, friends, and the fieldworkers whom I passed every day changed. As a child, I couldn't quite put my finger on it, but I felt as though something in my world had shifted, ever so slightly. As an adult, I now reflect upon this moment and realize that it was one of the first times in my life that I had encountered *difference*. Not only did I start to see myself as different from my friends, but I started wondering whether I really did share some sort of kinship with those fieldworkers whom I so desperately wanted to disassociate myself from. It was also the first time that I was confronted with my own identity and had to make choices, not only about who I was but who I wanted to be seen as. I suddenly had to position myself relative to a peer group which I had hitherto blended into so seamlessly.

Re-visiting my writing about all three of my most educational experiences, I see two important implications for my practice as a secondary high-school teacher. First of all, I am reminded of how crucial our educative experiences outside of the classroom are to our identity formation. Secondly, I realize that classrooms, such as the one created by my aforementioned professor, can be critical spaces for situating the personal within the larger social realm.

Identity and the Double Helix

One of the ways in which I have come to understand my own identity formation is through the metaphor of the *double helix*, the essential building block of life. In high-school biology class, I remember fashioning a DNA model out of construction paper and tape. It resembled a spiral with two sides which twisted into each other and were held together by "rungs," or base-pairs. The outer strands of the DNA "ladder" act as a backbone for structure, while the composite rungs which link both strands together are the key elements in determining what "life" will look like. Changes to the connecting rungs will alter the genetic makeup of a human being. For me, the left-hand side of the DNA ladder is my past; it includes the three educational experiences which I wrote about for my graduate class. The right-hand strand is my present. Both strands are objective realities which occupy a very specific time, place, and space. The base structures linking these two ribbons, however, are subjective and comprised of memories. Memory is the parts of my past which I choose to acknowledge in my present existence; memory is the stories which I tell myself "in order to live" life, an idea which Joan Didion (2006) used in the title of a recent collection of essays. Memory is the connecting thread between my past and present reality. My present helps create my memory of the past by conjuring up images, smells, and scents which validate the way in which I interpret my life at present. These memories also help me to understand present relationships. The entire double helix is my identity, but it has been carefully assembled. Though my past and present realities might be fixed, it is my remembering in the space *in-between* the two which ultimately determines who I have chosen to be and where I will be spiralling towards in the future.

Ted Aoki (1993/2005) has written about the place in-between as a place of tension and negotiation, and for me, this concept has a powerful role to play in my metaphor of the double helix. For, the section in between my past and my present is not only filled with memories but is also the site of new knowledge making. It is the place where my past and present selves merge to understand and encounter the world in a meaningful way.

Identity Writ Large

The students who sit in front of me each and every day have identities which reflect *their* individual experiences of the world to date, and as an educator I need to be reminded of this constantly. If asked, my students, too, would be able to recount the "aha" moments in their lives. They would be able to share the small epiphanies which re-ordered their experiences in a new way, causing them to look at life differently from that point onwards. How often do I welcome these experiences into our learning environment? How often do I open up a space for individual identities and stories to engage with the Canadian history curriculum which I have so carefully crafted? How do the sites of "new-knowledge making" look in my classroom. To what extent do they embrace my students' past and present realities?

My individuality encounters that of my students on a daily basis, but the relationship is complicated by the presence of a standardized curriculum, which I am expected to deliver within a specified time period. This, I would say, has been and still is my greatest challenge. However, my job as an educator requires that I find a way to embrace the personal while bringing it into conversation with the collective. In this case, we are forging a common identity, fashioned within the cellular confines of the classroom community. We are the collective self, and we reveal our identity through our shared experiences. Using my DNA metaphor once again, the first strand of the double helix represents our collective past, the other, our present reality. The base pairs in-between are the various meanings, memories, knowledges which we create, first individually and then as a group; they are the result of individual pasts manifesting themselves separately and then moving together to create a collective history. Our collective identity twists into itself, revealing individual stories but continues to spiral upward and outward beyond the individual and into the realm of Pinar's (2004) "collective witnessing." Ultimately, it is our shared sense of being which will prompt us into social action, rejuvenating and replicating healthy "cells" within human life.

Within the classroom, my students' interaction with texts, participation in discussions, contribution to the ordering of our space, causes new growth *in-between*. The elements essential to the self—the base pairs which hold the DNA sugar strands together—are always in flux and sometimes mutate as they arrange themselves in new patterns, shifting and turning with every new encounter, every new meaning which they incorporate into their being. As mentioned earlier, the place in-between the strands of the double helix is ultimately responsible for the form that the structure will take; they determine the future course of the entire organism. Keeping this in mind, then, building a classroom environment which honours the sanctity of this regenerative process is integral to my work as a teacher.

Conclusion

The late educator Haim Ginott (1972) said that the goal of education should be to help our students to become human. I sometimes forget that teaching is a way of being—that my person and the 32 students before me are involved in a complex, constructive relationship—not unlike that which is going on continually within in our individual cells. Our whole self is part of the educational experience, and what we bring to the classroom as well as the way in which it is validated and then incorporated into the creation of new knowledges is essential to growth, empowerment, and initiative. Too often, the educative moment lies in the shadow of the greater educational enterprise: the preparation of an efficient body of capable workers. The price for this way of thinking is high, resulting in a classroom devoid of body and devoid of life, which is why I have come to favour the metaphor of the double helix. The latter is the biological essence of life itself. It welcomes the textures, emotions, and smells of our everyday experiences and acknowledges the relational nature of our humanity.

I would argue that just as individual identities are carefully integrated into a collective memory so, too, must our individual classroom experiences become part of an over-arching frame of reference, one which both informs and is informed by *pedagogy-as-lived*. From here, I can begin to ask questions: Where are there gaps, and why? How accurate is our collective memory and why have some elements of our past been discarded? To what extent is there a sense of discord within individual components, and if there is, what devices can I employ to reconcile disparate parts? What is valued and what is not valued and why? These are some of the urgent questions which can direct the exploration of individual experiences and stories as part of a network of collective identities.

REFERENCES

Aoki, T. T. (1993/2005). Legitimating lived curriculum: Toward a curricular landscape of multiplicity. In W. F. Pinar & R. L. Irwin (Eds.), *Curriculum in a new key: The collected works of Ted T. Aoki* (pp. 199–215). Mahwah, NJ: Lawrence Erlbaum.

Didion, J. (2006). *We tell ourselves stories in order to live: Collected nonfiction.* New York, NY: Everyman's Library, Alfred A. Knopf.

Ginott, H. (1972). *Teacher and child.* New York, NY: Macmillan.

Pinar, W. F. (2004). *What is curriculum theory?* Mahwah, NJ: Lawrence Erlbaum.

A Métis Manifesto

Vicki Kelly

Braid One

Other people's stories are as varied as the landscapes and the languages of the world; and the storytelling traditions to which they belong tell the different truths of religion and science, of history and the arts. They tell people where they came from, and why they are here; how to live, and sometimes how to die.
—J. Edward Chamberlin, *If This Is Your Land, Where Are Your Stories?*

Indigenous peoples throughout Canada and the world have sustained their unique worldviews and associated knowledge systems for millennia, even while undergoing major social upheavals and transformations. Many of the core values, beliefs, and practices associated with those worldviews have survived and are beginning to be recognized as having an adaptive integrity that is as valid for today's generation as it was for generations past. The depth of Indigenous knowledge, rooted in the long inhabitation of a particular place, offers lessons as we all search for more satisfying and sustainable ways to live on this planet.

Indigenous epistemologies acknowledge the individual journey of lifelong learning as a pathway, a sacred way of moving toward completeness, fully achieving one's potential. Through our journey toward wholeness we are "gifting" our essence to the multitude of individual essences, which make up our world. This profound reciprocal sense that "*we* are all related, we are *all* related, we are all *related*" is central to Indigenous ways of knowing, being and participating in the world. In this process we are at once poised between an *environmental* ecology and a *spiritual* ecology (Cajete, 1994). Together they create an integrated whole, our one world.

We embrace and enact a *pedagogy of place* within landscapes of the natural surroundings, family and community, and the affective foundations of a life lived in a respectful reciprocal relationship with the world. In this relationship we are interwoven with our own ecologies and the places we are "indigenous" to. These complex ecologies involve the four elements of earth, water, air, and fire; our relatives the plants and animals; our sisters and brothers around the world; as well as the Manitous that co-inhabit these places with us. They fashion and form unique natural patterns that ultimately become our patterns. Our own understanding of our indigeneity in relation to our place and our interconnectedness with our environmental ecology leaves a qualitative signature deep within our physical, emotional, intellectual, spiritual identities.

We also embrace and enact a subtle *pedagogy of the imagination* through our participation in the spiritual ecological foundations of our lives in art, myth, and vision (Cajete, 1994). Those stories, artistic images, and emerging visions that accompany us on our journey create psychological landscapes, soul spaces, and unique ecologies where we dwell. These are the ecologies that nourish our *learning spirits*.

The implicit goals of Indigenous education are: *finding face* (identity), *finding heart* (passion) and *finding foundation* (vocation); this is the destination to which the various pathways of Indigenous pedagogy lead; we are endeavouring to "look to the mountain" (Cajete, 1994). This journey toward wholeness and the good life follows the ancient pathway or sacred way that meanders through or transverses our environmental and spiritual ecologies.

Braid Two

The truth about stories is that that's all we are. "You can't understand the world without telling a story," the Anishinabe writer Gerald Visenor tells us. "There isn't a center to the world but a story."
—Thomas King, *The Truth About Stories*

Through métissage and life writing I explore the honouring of my Métis self. I tell of the story of finding my way between: two creation stories, two worldviews, two ways of seeing and interpreting the patterns, and the qualitative signatures of the fluctuating alchemy of the world. My story speaks of learning two languages, two ways of passing on wisdom: one by listening, one by reading. It tells of being schooled by two profound literacies, of reading two books of life. It describes how standing in two worlds has led to *two-eyed seeing*: seeing with the one eye with the integrity of that eye, of not compromising the intimacy of my Indigenous eye, but also seeing with the exacting science of my Western eye. I need both eyes in order to focus and see deeply. The two eyes seeing complement each other precisely because they don't blend and blur each other's reality.

Being Métis is about: hearing with one ear laid upon the heart; listening within to the resonating and resounding voice of the Creator, Gitchie Manitou; paying attention to the songs and voices of the ancestors ringing though my "in-turned" ear. The other ear is turned outward, to other sounds and voices, the cacophony of the modern world. I have heard ancient and modern languages of the heart. I do not ask for translation but know truth spoken in two languages; for the Métis have always been the translators; the voyageurs between the worlds, the coureurs des bois, the runners of the world's woods. My métissage is a story about coming to understand that two-eyed seeing is but a pathway to *many-eyed seeing*.

The Elders say: You need to know where you are from, to know the land. You need to know the language, the family, the people, quite simply the ecology that has shaped your knowing, being, and doing. You need to know the place you are indigenous to, the ecology to which you are truly endogenous. By finding our place, we find our identity. It is an aesthetic task, one of knowing by being, blending, and bending, an act of weaving the storied braids of our Métis selves. The mixed-bloods, the "half-breeds," have now become the "wayfinders." We, the Métis, stand in both worlds; we can navigate in both. We can find our way, by day and night, on the waterways and the seas by remembering, ever mindful of where we have come from and faithfully calling up our visions of the future, like islands out of the sea. Wade Davis (2009) says that for the Indigenous peoples of the Pacific:

The entire science of wayfinding is based on dead reckoning. You only know where you are by knowing precisely where you have been and how you got to where you are. One's position at any one time is determined solely on the basis of distance traveled and direction traveled since leaving the last known point. "You don't look up at the stars and know where you are…you need to know where you have come from by memorizing from where you sailed." (p. 60)

We hold the point of where we set sail from simultaneously in our imaginations while also holding the image or vision of where we are going. Honouring our Métis selves through métissage allows us to become "wayfinders." By remembering where we set sail from, where we began our journeys, the exact ecologies of our storied landscapes, we *find face*, our identity.

In life writing through métissage we dwell there, in those overlapping places and spaces. We orient and align ourselves through reflection and contemplation until there arises in us, like a vision, the future's possibilities in our imaginations. The Métis revolutionary and visionary Louis Riel said that it would be the artists who would awaken as if from a deep sleep and call up the vision of the future like an island out of the ocean of possibility. Being Métis with the capacity of two-eyed seeing enables us to waken and read the signs, the patterns of our times with diverse kinds of knowing, being, and doing.

Braid Three

We are a Métis civilization. What we are today has been inspired as much by four centuries of life with indigenous civilizations as by four centuries of immigration. Today we are the outcome of that experience. As have the Métis people…this influencing, this shaping is deep within us.
—John Ralston Saul, *A Fair Country: Telling Truths About Canada*

As Métis we can learn to see and honour the biocultural diversity of the various ecologies around the world. We understand the profound reciprocal relationship between our earth's *biosphere* and our earth's *ethnosphere*. We realize the vanishing of the "terra-lingua" of our storied ecologies and the possible ramifications for our environmental and spiritual ecologies. We come to recognize that the environmental ecologies of our earth have created spiritual ecologies, unique responses in our cultures and languages. They are the "elegant sufficiency," the complimentary and necessary human cultural responses to their unique environmental ecologies. It is Davis (2009) who charges us:

Together the myriad of cultures makes up an intellectual and spiritual web of life that envelops our planet and is every bit as important to the well being of the planet as the biological web of life that we know as the biosphere. You might think of this social web of life as the *"ethnosphere,"* a term perhaps best defined as the sum total of all thoughts and intuitions, myths and beliefs, ideas and inspirations brought into being by the human imagination since the dawn of consciousness. The ethnosphere is humanity's greatest legacy. It is the product of our dreams, embodiment of our hopes, the symbol of all we are and all that we, as a wildly inquisitive and astonishing adaptive species, have created. And just as the biosphere, the biological matrix of life, is being severely eroded by the destruction of habitat and the resultant loss of plant and animal species, so too is the ethnosphere, only at a far greater rate. No biologist, for example, would suggest that 50 percent of all species are moribund. Yet this, the most apocalyptic scenario in the realm of biological diversity, scarcely approaches what we know to be the most optimistic scenario in the realm of cultural diversity. (pp. 2–3)

How do we honour the urgency of future sustainability? It is by writing, by spinning the living webs of words, and by weaving the threads of our stories that we create the patterns of our existence, our unique Métis sash, our métissage. By weaving the multi-coloured threads of various identities and ways of knowing and being, and by braiding the strands of overlapping stories—we are also weaving the landscapes, the "story-scapes," of our time. Our Métis selves weave the métissages of our times into the very fabric of our earth's ethnosphere.

I have come to see that the practice of life writing—through re-membering, re-imaging and re-storying—creates a *living métissage* that reveals the "mixed and mixing" of identities. It awakens and enables us to *find face*, a countenance reflected in the patterns of the water. It is as the Elders have said: we see simultaneously our own faces and the faces of the ancestors mirrored back to us from the water's surface. We *find heart* by listening to the inner murmurings of the mysterious languages of our Métis selves. We *find foundation* by engaging in a pedagogy of place in an emerging environmental ecology of being. We nurture our spiritual ecology by cultivating the pedagogy of the imagination through personal mythology, artistic practice, and spiritual vision. By acknowledging our Métis selves, and co-creating a Métis civilization, we are weaving the threads of our mixed identities; we are creating a living, multi-coloured, multi-dimensional métissage.

REFERENCES

Cajete, G. (1994). *Look to the mountain: An ecology of Indigenous education.* Skyland, NC: Kivaki Press.

Chamberlin, J. E. (2003). *If this is your land, where are your stories? Finding common ground.* Toronto, Canada: Vintage.

Davis, W. (2009). *The wayfinders: Why ancient wisdom matters in the modern world.* Toronto, Canada: House of Anansi Press.

King, T. (2003). *The truth about stories: A Native narrative.* Toronto, Canada: House of Anansi Press.

Saul, J. R. (2009). *A fair country: Telling truths about Canada.* Toronto: Viking Canada.

A Closing and a Renewed Calling

Life Writing as Empathetic Inquiry

In the traffic of our days
may we attend to each thing
so that patterns are revealed
amidst the offerings of chance.

All things want to be heard,
so let us listen to what they say.
In the end we will hear what we are:
the orchard or the road leading past.
—Rainer Maria Rilke, *A Year With Rilke*

Returning to the call we put out into the world with this collection, and the responses it elicited, we once again considered the title of this text, one that called for wisdom and empathy as notions intimately connected with life-writing work. At times we felt burdened and awed by the intricacy and intimacy of the task of braiding this métissage of stories and poems and essays; but in the act of crafting the braids it was the texts themselves that sustained us with their compelling responses to our call, their vibrant fibres and textures, and their vital appeals for empathy as an integral part of educational inquiry, curriculum, and pedagogy. Writers in this collection, in their individual and collective voices, took up this call with the kind of "habitation of a brave heart and a radiant intellect" attributed to Joan Didion (Leonard, 2006, p. xxiii).

Thinking about how such courageous and cogent texts can become meaningful reading and viewing in a variety of classrooms and educational contexts, we feel hopeful. We trust that these texts, and the dialogues they may generate, will move us towards the "massive change" (Mau, 2004) this world needs to survive. One important way is for teachers and students to rethink and reenact education as an empathetic endeavour as well as an intellectual one. We are confident that these life writings will inspire others to write their own stories into the commons of our curriculum and our social networks, for the common good. As Joan Didion (2006) reminds us in the title of her essay collection, "we tell ourselves stories in order to live." Coming back to Thomas King's (2003) profession that "the truth about stories is that that's all we are" (p. 3), we feel affirmed that the heart-and-mind matters these stories invite us to discuss, debate, and wonder about, are indeed truthful and worth telling over and over again, so that we may get better at living well together. Even though there is no definitive knowing of the effects of such writing and telling—leaving the writers vulnerable in the wake of their writing—with these pieces, new testimonies to life are released into the world. These stories constitute a brave and radiant witnessing, one that brings forward our individual and collective memories, our thinking together about "how to live in relation to the past" (Simon, Eppert, Clement, & Beres, 2002, p. 288). This life-writing project thus became "an act of study" (Simon, et al., 2002) and an activist stance. Through memory work, and witnessing as a pedagogical act, life writing radiates from the heart into an "embodied wisdom" (Pryer, 2011).

With this book, we also returned to Deleuze and Parnet's (1987) wisdom about writing, one that has been at the heart of our work: "Writing does not have its end in itself, precisely because life is not something personal. Or rather, the aim of writing is to carry life to the state of a non-personal power" (p. 50). We believe that through these Deleuzian and Aokian "conjunctive spaces," this challenge has become less daunting. The wisdom that life writing is not personal has become a stronger reality in the tensioned lifeworlds of teaching (Aoki, 1986/1991/2005) and in curriculum as a "new key" (Pinar & Irwin, 2005). As editors, this "re-newed" and "re-storied" space of calling, and "in-dwelling" with writerly companions, gave us the gift of deep attention and inspiriting energy needed to move with the writing, to "make a home for ourselves not just on paper but in the wider world" (Chambers, as cited in Pryer, 2011, p. 16). Through life writing, "home" becomes a space of responsibility to more than one location, to multiple places on our planet (Radakrishnan, as cited in Tang, 2003, p. 30). As editors, we take heart in the possibility that this book, a métissage of stories and identities, can create such a home. In our previous collection on life writing and literary métissage, we sent out our life stories into the world. With this new book, we send out more stories from more locations by more authors. In each story, like the precious jewels in Indra's net, are reflected all the other stories, in an infinite process of reflection (Loy, as cited in Jardine, Friesen, & Clifford, 2003). This braiding of stories also invokes, as Jardine et al. remind us, an "ontological claim that things are their interdependencies with all things" (p. 43). In this vein, each of the present stories must be understood as being unique only in the midst of all their relations. In that lies the power of this collective work that is at once both personal and non-personal, that is at once both located in particular places and in the topography of our transnational commons.

This collection of predominantly Canadian voices responds to the four challenges Chambers (1999) identified as facing Canadian curriculum theory: to write from this place; to write in a language of our own; to create new interpretive tools for this place and this language; and to map out a topography for Canadian curriculum studies. The writers in this book take up these challenges in their unique way, from their specific location, and through their own beautiful voices, they become part of a new "landed" collective wisdom. We hope that this collection will contribute to reshaping the topographies of Canadian curriculum theory and praxis by offering a worldly métissage, one that is—indigenous/Indigenous, ecological, interpretive, personal, political, historical, artful, articulate, and literary, and therefore—more empathetic and heart-wise.

REFERENCES

Aoki, T. T. (1986/1991/2005). Teaching as indwelling between two curriculum worlds. In W. F. Pinar & R. L. Irwin (Eds.), *Curriculum in a new key: The collected works of Ted T. Aoki* (pp. 159–165). Mahwah, NJ: Lawrence Erlbaum.

Chambers, C. (1999). A topography for Canadian curriculum theory. *Canadian Journal of Education, 24*(2), 137–150.

Deleuze, G., & Parnet, C. (1987). *Dialogues* (H. Tomlinson & B. Habberjam, Trans.). New York, NY: Columbia University Press. (Original work published 1977)

Didion, J. (2006). *We tell ourselves stories in order to live: Collected nonfiction*. New York, NY: Alfred A. Knopf.

Jardine, D., Friesen, S., & Clifford, P. (2003). "Behind every jewel are three thousand sweating horses": Meditations on the ontology of mathematics and mathematics education. In E. Hasebe-Ludt, & W. Hurren (Eds.), *Curriculum intertext: Place/language/pedagogy* (pp. 39–49). New York, NY: Peter Lang.

Leonard, J. (2006). Introduction. In J. Didion, *We tell ourselves stories in order to live: Collected nonfiction* (pp. ix-xxiii). New York, NY: Alfred A. Knopf.

Macy, J., & Barrows, A. (Eds. & Trans.). (2009). *A year with Rilke: Daily readings from the best of Rainer Maria Rilke.* New York, NY: HarperCollins.

Mau, B., with Leonard, J., & The Institute Without Boundaries. (2004). *Massive change.* London, England: Phaidon Press.

King, T. (2003). *The truth about stories: A Native narrative.* Toronto, Canada: House of Anansi Press.

Pinar, W. F., & Irwin, R. L. (Eds.). (2005). *Curriculum in a new key: The collected works of Ted T. Aoki.* Mahwah, NJ: Lawrence Erlbaum.

Pryer, A. (2011). *Embodied wisdom: Meditations on memoir and education.* Charlotte, NC: Information Age Publishing.

Simon, R., Eppert, C., Clement, M., & Beres, L. (2002). Witness as study: The difficult inheritance of testimony. *The Review of Education/Pedagogy/Cultural Studies, 22*(4), 285–322.

Tang, S. Y. (2003). Generative interplay of/in language(s) and culture(s) midst curriculum spaces. In E. Hasebe-Ludt & W. Hurren (Eds.), *Curriculum intertext: Place/language/pedagogy* (pp. 23–32). New York, NY: Peter Lang.

Contributors

CHRISTY AUDET teaches high school in a small rural community in southern Alberta, Canada. She has undergraduate degrees in English and education and a master's degree in education, all from the University of Lethbridge.

HEESOON BAI is an associate professor in philosophy of education at Simon Fraser University. She applies Eastern thought to education in her research and writing. She is a recipient of Simon Fraser University's Excellence in Teaching Award, publishes widely, and presents regularly at academic conferences.

SUSAN BRALEY lives in Victoria, Canada, where she writes full time: her fiction and poetry have appeared in *The Harpweaver, Madwoman in the Academy, Canadian Woman Studies, Island Writer,* and *Arc Poetry Magazine.* Her poem "Traces" won the Readers' Choice Award in the 2010 Arc Poem of the Year Contest. Prior to her writing career, she taught literature, writing, and women's studies at Fanshawe College and the University of Western Ontario.

CYNTHIA CHAMBERS is Professor of Education at the University of Lethbridge. She teaches and researches in curriculum and Indigenous studies, language and literacy, and life writing. Her essays, memoir, and stories are published in edited collections and various periodicals. She collaborates with Indigenous communities on literacies of place, human relations, and the material world.

HEIDI CLARK has an MEd degree from the University of British Columbia. She has spent the bulk of her career teaching and advocating for kindergarten students, in a Vancouver inner-city classroom. Clark has taught French immersion and ESL, and worked at the district level as an early-literacy mentor. In 2009, she received the *Canadian Family 2009 Great Teacher Award*.

AVRAHAM COHEN, PHD, RCC, CCC, conducts a private practice in counselling and teaches in the Master in Counselling Program at City University of Seattle, in Vancouver, Canada. He publishes widely and presents regularly at educational and counselling conferences.

MARGARET LOUISE DOBSON is a PhD student in the Faculty of Education at McGill University. She taught high-school French and English in Ontario, English literature to adults in Québec, and held leadership roles with the English Montréal School Board.

YVETTE DUBEL'S work has emerged from more than twenty years of community advocacy and public research in arts practice. As a consultant, member, or part of the board of directors for community organizations, she has worked to increase awareness of birth freedom, interventions for community violence, human trafficking and slavery, and homelessness. Her publishing credits range from thoughts on race and self-reflection in alternative education to feminist fiction and prose.

DANIELA ELZA has a doctorate in philosophy of education from Simon Fraser University. Her interests lie in the gaps, rubs, and bridges between poetry, language, and philosophy. Elza's work has appeared in over fifty literary and peer-reviewed publications. Her ebook *The Book of It: Meditations* was published in 2011, and her poetry book *The Weight of Dew* was published in 2012.

LYNN FELS is an associate professor in arts education at Simon Fraser University. Her research focuses on arts education, curriculum, and performative inquiry. She co-authored *Exploring Curriculum: Performative Inquiry, Role Drama and Learning* in 2008 and was Academic Editor of *Educational Insights* for several years.

ALEXANDRA FIDYK is an assistant professor in the Department of Secondary Education, University of Alberta, where she teaches curriculum, pedagogy, and research courses. She is also an adjunct faculty member at Pacifica Graduate

Institute in California. Her work intersects the fields of process philosophy, education, poetic inquiry, depth psychology, and Buddhist thought. She is a certified Jungian psychotherapist, trained in Family Systems Constellation and Body Psychodynamics.

LEAH FOWLER is an associate professor in the Faculty of Education at the University of Lethbridge where she teaches pre-service teachers and graduate students, researches in the fields of curriculum studies and narrative inquiry, and publishes on difficulty in teaching and Canadian literature. Her book, *A Curriculum of Difficulty: Narrative Research in Education and the Practice of Teaching*, was published in 2006.

PATTI FRASER is an interdisciplinary (theatre, film, digital video, television, and radio) writer, artist, and educator whose community-engaged projects span twenty years. She was a founding member of the nationally recognized Summer Visions Film Institute for Youth.

VERONICA GAYLIE is an associate professor in the Faculty of Education at the University of British Columbia (Okanagan), and a poet, teacher, and interdisciplinary scholar. Her books *The Learning Garden: Ecology, Teaching and Transformation* and *Roots and Research in Urban School Gardens* were published in 2009 and 2011 respectively. She has conducted funded research on the role of eco-poetry in urban schools. Her poetry appears in literary journals.

HARTEJ GILL is an assistant professor in the Faculty of Education at the University of British Columbia. Her research interests are social justice, leadership, and research as a way to bridge the gap between theory, practice, and social activism. She is a former school teacher and vice-principal.

ERIKA HASEBE-LUDT is an associate professor in the Faculty of Education at the University of Lethbridge. She teaches, researches, and publishes in the areas of literacy, teacher education, and curriculum studies. Her books include: *Curriculum Intertext: Place/Language/Pedagogy* (co-editor, 2003), and *Life Writing and Literary Métissage as an Ethos for Our Times* (co-author, 2009).

HALI HEAVY SHIELD is a literacy educator with the Kainai Board of Education in southern Alberta. She has a master of education from the University of Lethbridge. She researches family literacy, children's literature, and life writing as narrative inquiry.

TASHA HENRY is a teacher, mother, and scholar who lives on two islands: Tobago in the West Indies and Vancouver Island in Canada. She has a master's in education from York University.

TASHA HUBBARD is a lecturer in the University of Manitoba's Native Studies Department. She is a documentary filmmaker who also works in drama, experimental documentary, and new media. Her solo writing and directing project *Two Worlds Colliding* won a Gemini and a Golden Sheaf in 2005. Hubbard's academic work focuses on Indigenous representation of the buffalo, Indigenous critical theory, and transformation through art.

BRUCE HUNTER taught English and liberal studies at Seneca College. His 7th book, *Two O'clock Creek—Poems New and Selected*, was published in 2010. His novel, *In the Bear's House*, won the 2009 Canadian Rockies Prize at the Banff Mountain Book Festival.

WANDA HURREN is Associate Dean in the Faculty of Education at the University of Victoria. She is a member of Crossgrains Photographic Society, one of the few remaining darkroom societies in North America. She authored *Line Dancing: An Atlas of Geography Curriculum and Poetic Possibilities* and co-edited *Curriculum Intertext: Place/Language/Pedagogy*.

NANÉ ARIADNE JORDAN has a PhD in education from the University of British Columbia. She has degrees in photography/visual arts (University of Ottawa) and women's spirituality (New College of California). Her practice integrates writing, art making, and scholarship with women's health—including lay midwifery—mothering, ecological living, and cultivating spirit.

VICKI KELLY is an assistant professor in the Faculty of Education at Simon Fraser University. Her scholarship focuses on: Indigenous knowledges, pedagogies, and science; ecological knowledge; and Indigenous language and culture revitalization. Her research topics also include holistic learning practices, integration of the arts in education, art therapy, and transformative education. She works primarily with métissage, narrative portraiture, and arts-based methodologies.

CHRISTI KRAMER is a doctoral candidate in education at the University of British Columbia. She researches poetry and reconciliation, while working with children exiled by war.

PHONG KUOCH is a high-school English teacher with the Surrey School District. He has a BA (English) and an MA (Education) from Simon Fraser University.

where he is a PhD candidate. He was a school associate and a faculty associate at SFU, and a lecturer at the University of British Columbia and SFU.

MARGUERITE LEAHY teaches Kindergarten and Grade 1 at John Henderson Elementary School in Vancouver, Canada. She taught both elementary and high school in Kenya for several years. She has an MEd from the University of British Columbia.

CARL LEGGO is a poet and Professor of Education at the University of British Columbia. His books include: *Come-by-Chance*; *Lifewriting and Literary Métissage as an Ethos for Our Times* (co-authored); *Being With A/r/tography* (co-edited); *Creative Expression, Creative Education* (co-edited); and *Poetic Inquiry: Vibrant Voices in the Social Sciences* (co-edited).

CANDACE LEWKO is an instructor at Lethbridge College, Canada, where she teaches in an ESL literacy program (Youth in Transition), and works with immigrant and refugee youth. She also teaches courses in culture studies and English composition. Lewko has an MEd from the University of Lethbridge. Through life writing, she researches her live(d) experiences in teaching.

REBECCA LUCE-KAPLER is Associate Dean of Graduate Studies and Research in the Faculty of Education, Queen's University. Her research focusses on the integral role of literary practices, particularly writing, in the development of human consciousness and identity. She has researched senior-aged women reading and writing literary memoirs. She published a collection of poetry, *The Gardens Where She Dreams*, in 2003.

G. SCOTT MACLEOD is a painter and photographer whose work has been exhibited internationally. He has had a many-faceted career in the arts, including documentary filmmaking and animation. His work reflects social, political, and historical themes, and a love of history and storytelling. MacLeod has a BFA and is a candidate for a master in art education, both from Concordia University.

LISA NICOLE NUCICH has taught in the Vancouver School District for 15 years. Her teaching and research focus on the importance of embodying respect, and learning kindness, empathy, and compassion from animals. She has an MEd from the University of British Columbia.

PAT PALULIS is an associate professor in the Faculty of Education at the University of Ottawa. Her teaching and research interests tarry within the interstices of language, literacy, culture, and spatiality, drawing from poststructural and postcolonial discourse. She has taught in England, Japan, Libya, and Canada.

JANET PLETZ is an early-childhood teacher in Calgary, Canada. In her doctoral studies in education at the University of British Columbia, she researches early-childhood multiliteracies in school settings, relational aspects of identity, and agency.

GARY WILLIAM RASBERRY is an artist, educator, and parent. With a grant from the Ontario Arts Council, he was artist-in-residence at the Yarker Family School outside Kingston, Canada, and recorded a children's album called *What's the Big Idea?!?* He teaches songwriting and recording; he also writes and performs solo and with the acoustic trio, *Fireweed*.

PAULINE SAMESHIMA's work centres on curriculum design, arts and technology integration, collaborative and creative scholarship, eco-responsive pedagogies, and innovative forms of knowledge production and acknowledgement. Her publications include: *Seeing Red: A Pedagogy of Parallax*; *Poetic Inquiry: Vibrant Voices in the Social Sciences* (co-editor); and *Climbing the Ladder With Gabriel: Poetic Inquiry of a Methamphetamine Addict in Recovery* (co-author); and a website.

DENISE SCHELLHASE teaches high-school history in Québec. She has degrees from the University of British Columbia and Simon Fraser University, and she is pursuing a master in education at McGill University. She researches identity, history, and memory; citizenship education; and classroom discussion for critical understanding.

ANNE SCHOLEFIELD was a classroom teacher in three British Columbia school districts and abroad; she has worked in adult and teacher education at two universities on the west coast of Canada. She resides in Vancouver; her preoccupations are life's pedagogical intersections, in and out of the classroom.

DANIEL G. SCOTT is Director of the School of Child and Youth Care at the University of Victoria. He researches the spiritual lives of children and youth, drawing on their peak experiences from childhood, and the articulation of these in adolescent diaries. In addition to his academic publications, Scott has written plays, fiction, and poetry.

JACKIE SEIDEL is an assistant professor in the Faculty of Education at the University of Calgary where she teaches both undergraduate and graduate courses. She researches contemplative forms of pedagogy, curriculum studies, teacher education, literary studies, and what it means to live an ethical life in classrooms.

PRISCILLA SETTEE is an associate professor in the Department of Native Studies at the University of Saskatchewan, and she is a member of the Cumberland House Cree Nation in northern Saskatchewan. She has been a board member for the Canadian Centre for Policy Alternatives and received a Global Citizen's award. Her book, *The Strength of Women: Âhkamêyimowak*, was published in 2011.

AHAVA SHIRA is a poet, storyteller, and photographer. She has a PhD in education from the University of British Columbia. Her book of poetry, *Womb: Weaving of My Being*, was published in 2000. She is the founder of the Centre for Loving Inquiry on Butterstone Farm, Salt Spring Island, where she teaches creative and contemplative practices.

SHEILA SIMPKINS taught in China, Turkey, and northern Iraq. She has a PhD in education from the University of Victoria. She researches how the practice of métissage fosters empathy for self and other in post-conflict situations, such as Kurdistan.

ANITA SINNER is an assistant professor in the Department of Art Education, Faculty of Fine Arts, at Concordia University. Her research areas are: arts research in curriculum studies, social and cultural issues in education, and interdisciplinary qualitative approaches.

CELESTE SNOWBER is an associate professor in the Faculty of Education at Simon Fraser University. She is a dancer, writer, and educator who performs site-specific work in connection to the natural world. Her publications include numerous essays and poetry, and the books *Embodied Prayer* (reprinted several times since originally published in 1995) and *Landscapes in Aesthetic Education* (co-authored and published in 2009).

TERESA STRONG-WILSON is an associate professor in the Faculty of Education, McGill University, and Research Fellow in the Institute for the Public Life of Arts and Ideas. Her research interests include literacies, narrative, memory, teacher learning, social justice, and Indigenous education. Her book, *Bringing Memory Forward: Storied Remembrance with Teachers in Social Justice Education*, was published in 2008.

LYNN THOMAS is a professeure agrégée at the Université de Sherbrooke in Québec. She is a member of the Institut de Recherche en Pratiques Éducatives and associated with the Chaire de Recherche sur L'Apprentissage de la Lecture et de L'Écriture Chez le Jeune Enfant. She teaches and researches professional identity development, literacy in second languages, bilingualism, and purposeful teacher education practices.

SEAN WIEBE is an assistant professor in the Faculty of Education at the University of Prince Edward Island. His published essays and poetry—in the areas of the arts, teacher education, and curriculum studies—appear in various journals and edited collections.

ROCHELLE YAMAGISHI was a school counsellor and taught post-secondary courses in Alberta. She has a PhD in education from the University of Alberta. Third-generation Japanese Canadian, she curated the Galt Museum exhibit "Nikkei Tapestry: The Story of Japanese Canadians in Southern Alberta" in 2003. Her books include *Nikkei Journey* (2005) and *Japanese Canadian Journey* (2010).

Index

tensioned textured spaces, 107
tensioned worlds, 79
text-image interface, xxiii
texts, xxi–xxvii, 1–2, 28, 49, 87, 100, 181, 187–88, 199, 201, 295–97, 299, 321, 335, 360, 370
Thébaud, J.-P., 298, 300
Third Space, The, 104, 175–77
Thought of the Heart and the Soul of the World, The, 141
Three Steps on the Ladder of Writing, xxvi
threshold, 136
Thrift, Nigel, 297
thrownness, 25
Tobago, 136–37
Todd, S., xxiv
Tonglen meditation practice, 85
Tootoosis, John B., 167
Toronto, Canada, 98–99, 101, 334–35
Toward a Poor Curriculum, 43
transformation, 24, 72, 104, 117, 166, 175–76, 254, 260, 297, 357, 363
Treace, Bonnie Myotai, 141
Trinh, T. M., 295
truth, xxi, xxiii, xxv, 31, 208, 230, 292
    different, 363
    doubt, 296
    emotional, 2
    as fidelity, 292
    objective, 258
    power and, 322
    about stories, 365, 370
    telling, xxi, 207
Tsurumaki, Marc, 293, 296, 300

-U-

ubuntu, 259
Ukrainian, 76–79
Ulukhaktok, Northwest Territories, Canada, 188–189
Unamuno, Miguel de, 306
uncanny, 299
unfixing, 197
United Nations Permanent Forum, 171
U'wa Indians, 171

-V-

Vancouver, British Columbia, 99, 107–8, 110–14, 185, 293, 342, 357
Vancouver Island, Canada, 139
Van Zandt, T., 241
Vertical Mosaic, The, 167
Victoria, British Columbia, 35
Vipassana, 26, 29
Visions, 306
voice, 40–41, 156, 204, 321
    autobiographical, 209
    Canadian, 371
    layered voices of, 181
    performance, 67
    teacher, 277

-W-

wabi sabi, 73
Walker, A., 331
Walker, D.F., 201–2
waqt, xiii–xiv
Ware, K., xiv
Washinawatak, Ingrid, 171
Watson, C., 291–92
Way of Love, The, 145
weaving, 100
Weber, S., 300
Whalen, L., 26
When the Bluebird Sings at Lemonade Springs, 60
Who Do You Think You Are?, 60
Wilkie-Stubbs, C., 41
Wilson, Teresa, 37–38
Windshift Line, The, 281
Winfrey, Oprah, 329
Winter Vault, The, 111
Witnessing Subjects, 333
Wolfrey, Julian, 298
Woolf, Virginia, 36
World Council of Indigenous Nations, 168
writing, xx
    heartful poetic, 201
    mothers and, 60
    parenting and, 247

OMPLICATED

A BOOK SERIES OF CURRICULUM STUDIES

Reframing the curricular challenge educators face after a decade of school deform, the books published in Peter Lang's Complicated Conversation Series testify to the ethical demands of our time, our place, our profession. What does it mean for us to teach now, in an era structured by political polarization, economic destabilization, and the prospect of climate catastrophe? Each of the books in the Complicated Conversation Series provides provocative paths, theoretical and practical, to a very different future. In this resounding series of scholarly and pedagogical interventions into the nightmare that is the present, we hear once again the sound of silence breaking, supporting us to rearticulate our pedagogical convictions in this time of terrorism, reframing curriculum as committed to the complicated conversation that is intercultural communication, self-understanding, and global justice.

The series editor is

Dr. William F. Pinar
Department of Curriculum Studies
2125 Main Mall
Faculty of Education
University of British Columbia
Vancouver, British Columbia V6T 1Z4
CANADA

To order other books in this series, please contact our Customer Service Department:

(800) 770-LANG (within the U.S.)
(212) 647-7706 (outside the U.S.)
(212) 647-7707 FAX

Or browse online by series:

www.peterlang.com

A Heart of Wisdom

CYNTHIA M. CHAMBERS is Professor of Education at the University of Lethbridge. She teaches and researches in curriculum and Indigenous studies, language and literacy, and life writing. Her essays, memoir, and stories are published in edited collections and various periodicals. As well as researching life writing, she collaborates with Indigenous communities on literacies of place, human relations, and the material world. Dr. Chambers is also a co-author of *Life Writing and Literary Métissage as an Ethos for Our Times* (2009).

ERIKA HASEBE-LUDT is an associate professor in the Faculty of Education at the University of Lethbridge. She teaches, researches, and publishes in the areas of literacy, teacher education, and curriculum studies. Her books include: *Curriculum Intertext: Place/Language/Pedagogy* (co-editor, 2003), and *Life Writing and Literary Métissage as an Ethos for Our Times* (co-author, 2009).

CARL LEGGO is a poet and Professor of Education at the University of British Columbia. His books include: *Come-by-Chance; Lifewriting and Literary Métissage as an Ethos for Our Times* (co-authored); *Being With A/r/tography* (co-edited); *Creative Expression, Creative Education* (co-edited); and *Poetic Inquiry: Vibrant Voices in the Social Sciences* (co-edited).

ANITA SINNER is an assistant professor in the Department of Art Education, Faculty of Fine Arts, at Concordia University. Her research areas are: arts research in curriculum studies, social and cultural issues in education, and interdisciplinary qualitative approaches.